*The Varieties of
Women's Experiences*

UNIVERSITY PRESS OF FLORIDA
Florida A&M University, Tallahassee
Florida Atlantic University, Boca Raton
Florida Gulf Coast University, Ft. Myers
Florida International University, Miami
Florida State University, Tallahassee
New College of Florida, Sarasota
University of Central Florida, Orlando
University of Florida, Gainesville
University of North Florida, Jacksonville
University of South Florida, Tampa
University of West Florida, Pensacola

The Varieties of Women's Experiences

Portraits of Southern Women in the Post–Civil War Century

Edited by
LARRY EUGENE RIVERS
& CANTER BROWN JR.

University Press of Florida

Gainesville · Tallahassee · Tampa · Boca Raton · Pensacola
Orlando · Miami · Jacksonville · Ft. Myers · Sarasota

Copyright 2009 by Larry Eugene Rivers and Canter Brown Jr.

Printed in the United States of America

All rights reserved
First cloth printing, 2009
First paperback printing, 2010

Library of Congress Cataloging-in-Publication Data
The varieties of women's experiences: portraits of Southern women
in the post-Civil War century/edited by Larry Eugene Rivers
and Canter Brown Jr.
p. cm.
Includes index.
ISBN 978-0-8130-3412-6 (alk. paper)
ISBN 978-0-8130-3681-6 (pbk.)
1. Women—Southern States—History. 2. Southern States—History—1865–1951. 3. Southern States—History—1951–.
I. Rivers, Larry E., 1950–. II. Brown, Canter.
HQ1438.S63V37 2010
305.40975'090349–dc22   2009020366

The University Press of Florida is the scholarly publishing agency for the State University System of Florida, comprising Florida A&M University, Florida Atlantic University, Florida Gulf Coast University, Florida International University, Florida State University, New College of Florida, University of Central Florida, University of Florida, University of North Florida, University of South Florida, and University of West Florida.

University Press of Florida
15 Northwest 15th Street
Gainesville, FL 32611-2079
http://www.upf.com

With appreciation to all the strong women who taught us and whose influences continue to direct the courses of our lives and work

Contents

List of Illustrations ix
Preface xi

1. Catharine Campbell Hart, 1823–1897
The Uncertainties of Life as a Widow 1
Canter Brown Jr.

2. Ellen Call Long, 1825–1905
A Thorough Lady 25
Tracy J. Revels

3. Victoria Seward Varn Brandon Sherrill, 1843–1926
Community Builder 42
James M. Denham

4. Mary E. C. Day Smith, 1851–1903
Northern-Born Mission Worker
in the Post–Civil War South 64
Daria Willis

5. Mary Barr Munroe, 1852–1922
South Florida's Pioneer Zealot 85
Arva Moore Parks

6. María Valdés de Gutsens, 1860–1941
The Soul of Key West's Mercedes Hospital 104
Consuelo E. Stebbins

7. Louise Cecilia Fleming, 1862–1899
Medical Missionary 122
Larry Eugene Rivers

8. Adella Hunt Logan, 1863–1915
Educator, Woman's Suffrage Leader,
and Confidant of Booker T. Washington   151
TERRANCE D. SMITH & SALLY J. ZEPEDA

9. Florence Johnson Hunt, 1866–1953
Days of Labor of an African American Woman   171
FRED R. VAN HARTESVELDT

10. Selena Sloan Butler, 1872–1964
Atlanta Club Leader, Reformer, Educator   192
DAVID H. JACKSON JR.

11. Gertrude Dzialynski Corbet, 1874–1931
"Miss Dynamite," A Jewish Woman in Public Life
in the Progressive-Era South   215
CANTER BROWN JR.

12. Eartha Mary Magdalene White, 1876–1974
The Gentle Community Activist   236
CAROLYN WILLIAMS

13. Elizabeth Benton Moore, 1878–1932
Education and Community Activism at
Georgia's Dorchester Academy   263
DAWN J. HERD-CLARK

14. Jerenia Valentine Dial Reid, 1879–1962
Woman's Work by a Pioneer
of African American Nursing   287
ESTHER SPENCER

Contributors   311

Index   315

Illustrations

1. Catharine Campbell Hart, c. 1870s 1
2. Most Kissimmee residents traveled the Kissimmee River on the cargo and passenger vessel *Roseada* 13
3. Ellen Call Long, c. 1880s 25
4. The Grove, Tallahassee, Florida, c. 1874, with Ellen Call Long seated at center 29
5. Victoria Brandon, c. 1880s 42
6. Polk County's Holly Bowen Hill and her children at their double-pen log cabin 47
7. Mary E. C. Day Smith, c. 1902 64
8. Tallahassee's rebuilt Lincoln Academy, 1876 73
9. Mary Barr Munroe, c. 1890 85
10. Coconut Grove's first tourists, 1887 91
11. María Valdés de Gutsens, c. 1934 104
12. Key West's Casa del Pobre, Mercedes, with María Valdés de Gutsens likely standing in doorway 110
13. Louise Cecilia Fleming, c. 1890s 122
14. Harriet Beecher Stowe and family at her Mandarin home, c. 1870s 132
15. Adella Hunt Logan, c. 1902 151
16. Margaret Murray Washington, c. 1920s 159
17. Florence Johnson Hunt, c. 1910s 171
18. Henry Alexander Hunt and Florence Johnson Hunt, c. 1930s 175
19. Selena Sloan Butler, c. 1902 192

20. The Yonge Street Parent-Teacher Association, c. 1919   207

21. Gertrude Dzialynski, c. 1914   215

22. Fort Meade, Florida, school class, 1885, with Gertrude Dzialynski   217

23. Eartha M. White and Clara White, c. 1910s   236

24. Eartha M. White as a member of the Oriental American Opera Company, 1892   242

25. Elizabeth Benton Moore, c. 1927   263

26. Dorchester Academy schoolchildren, c. 1927   275

27. Jerenia Valentine Dial Reed, c. 1920s   287

28. Wake Robin Golf Club members, c. 1940   305

Preface

In 2003 eminent historian Anne Firor Scott sparked the idea that evolved into this collection of essays through words she penned in the introduction to *"Lives Full of Struggle and Triumph": Southern Women, Their Institutions, and Their Communities*, a work edited by Bruce L. Clayton and John A. Salmond and published by the University Press of Florida. Scott eloquently reflected on the romanticizing of women's lives and experiences and the misunderstandings and misrepresentations that our society and, for that matter, historians have perpetrated about women collectively and individually, misrepresentations that especially have touched southern women. "Myths have tended to fill the vacuum left because hardly anyone paid attention to women's history, to the varieties of women's experiences, or to change over time," she wrote. She added, "It was as if the world were composed only of men, or at least as if only men made history."[1]

Professor Scott's words reached us at a time when we served on the faculty of Florida A&M University. Having authored and coauthored a number of works that dealt with aspects of Florida and southern history and also having taught these subjects on the university level, we already possessed a keen awareness of the relative scarcity of available women's history. Since a good deal of our research had dealt with the African American experience, we particularly felt the lack of attention to minority women but knew well that the problem extended to virtually every classification of southern women that could be described. The possible exception, we believed, concerned the plantation mistress, the type of affluent woman whose surviving personal or family papers permitted relatively easy examination of her life and who had offered a focus for any number of respected studies.[2]

Also in 2003, our University of North Florida colleague Daniel Schafer impressed us with an intriguing study, one that not only supported the case for inclusion of black women as plantation mistresses but also—and perhaps more importantly—illustrated vividly the point that difficulty in locating source materials about women should not be used as an excuse to justify not pursuing them. His book *Anna Madgigine Jai Kingsley: African Princess, Florida*

Slave, Plantation Slaveowner combined the fruits of hard labor and creative approaches to research—including world travel and interviews of West African *griots*—to produce a life study that many historians would have considered impossible to write.[3]

In these circumstances we began to pursue the thought of a work aiming to contribute meaningfully to our collective understanding of southern women's history. The paucity of helpful information on individual lives and experiences of women who did not occupy the top tier of either society or renown, whether black or white, seemed to us to offer a significant gap we could fill. We had attempted in our earlier work to remain sensitive to the history of those who had existed below the top levels of society or success. This had meant for us those whom Frank L. Owsley called "Plain Folk," their counterparts within the African American community, and certainly not least those held in slavery. We believed, as did Dan Schafer, that the curtain of history could be drawn back upon the lives of those whose legacies deserved our attention but who did not leave substantial archival collections and memoirs. Our experience told us that such history could be dug from the cellars of the historical record. We believed this to be the case as well for southern women generally.[4]

We knew that we were not alone in desiring to relate the lives and experiences of individual southern women who lived below that top tier. Kriste Lindenmeyer had made that her goal in 2000, with publication of *Extraordinary Lives: Women in American History*. Of the collection of essays presented in that volume, Lindenmeyer noted, "This book is unique in that it focuses on the lives of ordinary women." She continued, "The varied experiences of such women help to create a more complete picture of the past by revealing the influence general historical trends have had on the lives of 'ordinary' individuals." Lindenmeyer then made what we considered a succinct point. "But ordinary does not mean lesser; nor does it denote class, race, ethnicity, or age," she wrote. "The individual women's stories that are told in the following pages show that even people who are not featured in mainstream history texts led lives that deserve the attention of those interested in understanding the past." We particularly agreed with the manner in which Lindenmeyer characterized the third part of her four-part work. She named it "The Late Nineteenth and Early Twentieth Centuries: Inventing the New Woman." Joan Marie Johnson, among others, thereafter touched upon the same theme of "new women" in her 2004 volume *Southern Ladies, New Women: Race, Region, and Clubwomen in South Carolina, 1890–1930*.[5]

Others among the colleagues with whom we had worked shared our concern over the continuing insufficiency of available material on what Lindenmeyer called ordinary women, as well as our conclusions that women involved themselves far more broadly than often is credited in activities within the public sphere, repeatedly accomplished results for which others have received credit, and reflected far more diversity than generally is recognized. These colleagues early on included Tracy J. Revels of Wofford College, James M. Denham of Florida Southern College, Carolyn Williams of the University of North Florida, and David H. Jackson Jr. of Florida A&M University. Two outstanding Florida A&M University graduate students, Daria Willis and Esther Spencer, meanwhile were evidencing in their research and writing a similar sensitivity to and level of interest in the lives of women.

In time our circle of common interest and collegial friendship expanded. Allison DeFoor, a longtime supporter of Florida historical research and a writer himself, encouraged us to contact the renowned South Florida historian Arva Moore Parks, who had already been recognized by induction into the Florida Women's Hall of Fame. The excellent scholarly publications of the University of Central Florida's Consuelo E. Stebbins came to our attention during the same period. In 2006, when we relocated to Fort Valley State University (FVSU), we were delighted to find other highly qualified scholars eager to join with us. At FVSU were Fred R. van Hartesveldt, Dawn J. Herd-Clark, and Terrance D. Smith. Dr. Smith, in turn, introduced us to his friend and mentor, the University of Georgia's Sally J. Zepeda. Our company completed, we set out jointly to produce what follows.

The establishment of parameters for our collaborative effort came easily. First, "change over time" concerned us. To grasp the dynamics of change required, in our estimation, a study that spanned generations. We concurred with Lindenmeyer's belief that the late nineteenth and early twentieth centuries had spawned "the new woman," although we envisioned the pertinent period for the South as commencing about the time of the Civil War's end and extending toward the modern civil rights era. Accordingly, our contributors selected subjects whose lives offered windows to the post–Civil War century by identifying women born as early as 1823 and as late as 1879. Their deaths ranged from 1897 to 1974.

We were not aiming, in our selection of subjects, to identify "typical" southern women. Rather, our goal was to highlight what Anya Jabour has called "the myth of the southern lady" by examining the possibilities of women's lives at times and in places where common perception had formerly placed and confined almost all women to home, wifely duties, and motherhood. We were not aiming either to explore famous women achievers. We were guided instead by a desire to highlight lives lived in relative obscurity, producing evidence that women who defied the stereotypes of the times proliferated at most every hand but, unfortunately, received little credit for their actions. Where our subjects did enjoy some level of renown, we have focused on those portions of their lives that illustrate the types of complications that often touched the southern woman's experience.[6]

In addition to the works already mentioned, we would note a debt of gratitude to similar studies that have offered us models for how to present a collection of essays such as this one in an effective manner. The Mississippi Women's History Project's *Mississippi Women: Their Histories, Their Lives* offers an excellent example. Published in 2003, it combined rich depth and content in a manner that facilitated meaningful understanding.[7] It also provided insight into the general experience of women in a discrete region and environment, just as we hoped to do.

Although the contributors to *Mississippi Women* limited their study to a particular state, they clearly believed that they were offering broadly applicable insights. This book follows the same approach. These essays focus principally on Florida and Georgia, but their reach extends throughout most of the southern United States and beyond to the District of Columbia, New York, New Jersey, and Scotland. The geographical diversity parallels a diversity of social and ethnic backgrounds. Beyond women who were black, white, or of mixed race, we chronicle, for instance, a Jewish woman and one who today would be described as a Latina but who in her day would have proudly borne the title Cuban. We want to stress that southern women simply cannot be grouped into tight categories and that appreciation of diversity holds an important key to understanding southern women.

As editors, we thank our authors who have contributed so excellently to this collection, as well as Meredith Morris-Babb, the staff of the University Press of Florida, and our talented copy editor, Kirsteen E. Anderson. For inspiration, assistance, and encouragement, please let us add thanks to Erroll B. Davis Jr., chancellor, University System of Georgia; and Susan Herbst, executive vice chancellor and chief academic officer, University System of Georgia; as well as to Darlene Clark-Hine, Michigan State University and Northwestern University; Aubrey M. Perry, Florida A&M University; Donnie D. Bellamy, Fort Valley State University; and Juanita Bellamy, Fort Valley, Georgia; Jane G. Landers and Dennis C. Dickerson, Vanderbilt University; Rosalyn Howard, University of Central Florida; Susan D. Greenbaum, University of South Florida; Susan R. Parker, St. Augustine Historical Society; Maxine D. Jones, Florida State University; Mark K. Bauman and Rachel B. Heimovics, *Southern Jewish History*; Leland Hawes, *Tampa Tribune;* George B. Howell III and Mary Elizabeth

Howell, Tampa; Melody Carter, Vickie Oldham, Lisa Scipio, Shonda Lewis, and Brigitte Hall, Fort Valley State University; Anza Bast, Osceola County Historical Society, Kissimmee; Tom Hambright, Monroe County, Florida, Public Library; the late Dena E. Snodgrass, past president, Florida Historical Society and Jacksonville Historical Society; and the late Samuel Proctor, University of Florida. Special words of thanks also go to Phyllis Rivers Mosley, Harriet Rivers Chapman, Patricia Rivers King, Wanda Moon Brown, and Gwendolyn Brown. Above all, we thank our partners and inspirations, Betty Jean Hubbard Rivers and Barbara Gray Brown.

Notes

1. Anne Firor Scott, introduction to *"Lives Full of Struggle and Triumph": Southern Women, Their Institutions, and Their Communities,* ed. Bruce L. Clayton and John A. Salmond (Gainesville, Fla., 2003), 1. See also Anne Firor Scott, *The Southern Lady: From Pedestal to Politics, 1830–1930* (Chicago, 1970); Anastasia Sims, "Anne Firor Scott: Writing Southern Women into Southern History," in *Reading Southern History: Essays on Interpreters and Interpretations,* ed. Glenn Feldman (Tuscaloosa, 2001), 233–46.

2. See, for instance, Catherine Clinton, *The Plantation Mistress: Woman's World in the Old South* (New York, 1982); Elizabeth Fox-Genovese, *Within the Plantation Household: Black and White Women of the Old South* (Chapel Hill, 1988); John Hammond Moore, ed., *A Plantation Mistress on the Eve of the Civil War: The Diary of Keziah Goodwyn Hopkins Brevard, 1860–1861* (Columbia, S.C., 1996); Melanie Pavich-Lindsay, ed., *Anna: The Letters of a St. Simons Island Plantation Mistress, 1817–1859* (Athens, Ga., 2002); Anya Jabour, *Scarlett's Sisters: Young Women in the Old South* (Chapel Hill, 2007); Margaret Ripley Wolfe, *Daughters of Canaan: A Saga of Southern Women* (Lexington, Ky., 1995).

3. Daniel L. Schafer, *Anna Madgigine Jai Kingsley: African Princess, Florida Slave, Plantation Slaveowner* (Gainesville, Fla., 2003).

4. Frank L. Owsley, *Plain Folk in the Old South* (Baton Rouge, 1949); Canter Brown Jr., *Florida's Peace River Frontier* (Orlando, 1991); Larry Eugene Rivers, *Slavery in Florida: Territorial Days to Emancipation* (Gainesville, Fla., 2000); James M. Denham and Canter Brown Jr., eds., *Cracker Times and Pioneer Lives: The Florida Reminiscences of George Gillett Keen and Sarah Pamela Williams* (Columbia, S.C., 2000); Larry Eugene Rivers and Canter Brown Jr., *Laborers in the Vineyard of the Lord: The Beginnings of the AME Church in Florida, 1865–1895* (Gainesville, Fla., 2001); Canter Brown Jr. and Larry Eugene Rivers, *For a Great and Grand Purpose: The Beginnings of the AMEZ Church in Florida, 1864–1905* (Gainesville, Fla., 2004); Canter Brown Jr. and Barbara Gray Brown, *Family Records of the African American Pioneers of Tampa and Hillsborough County* (Tampa, 2003).

5. Kriste Lindenmeyer, ed., *Extraordinary Lives: Women in American History* (Wilmington, Del., 2000), xvii, 133; Joan Marie Johnson, *Southern Ladies, New Women: Race, Region, and Clubwomen in South Carolina, 1890–1930* (Gainesville, Fla., 2004).

6. Jabour, *Scarlett's Sisters*, 1.

7. Martha H. Swain, Elizabeth Anne Payne, and Marjorie Julian Spruill, eds., *Mississippi Women: Their Histories, Their Lives* (Athens, 2003).

*The Varieties of
Women's Experiences*

CHAPTER I

Catharine Campbell Hart
1823–1897

The Uncertainties of Life as a Widow

CANTER BROWN JR.

CATHARINE SMITH CAMPBELL HART was widowed on March 18, 1874, when her husband, Florida Governor Ossian Bingley Hart, died suddenly at their Jacksonville home. At that moment twenty-three and one-half years remained to her life. Those years, marked with triumph and tragedy, were to prove exhilarating and terribly challenging to Kate, as her family and friends knew her. Along the way life forced her to grapple with its challenges, and she was not alone in doing so. The struggles of Hart's widowhood remind us vividly of the challenges faced by many, if not most, widows during a time before widespread availability of government and private pension payments and Social Security checks. This was a world within which opportunities for women came highly restricted. In the era of Hart's widowhood, for example, less than

Figure 1. Catharine Campbell Hart, c. 1870s.
(Collection of the author; courtesy of Timmy Sorrow.)

20 percent of the nation's labor force were women—called "working women" in the parlance of that earlier era. Those working women amounted to only 10 percent of all women. As one historian has noted, "Most Americans, male and female, still believed that Providence had created 'spheres' of human endeavor, and that home and family marked the 'undisputed sphere of woman.'" Sadly, as Hart discovered, a woman could not count on a home or family always being there, nor could most women—even women of prominence—count on life to protect them from a slide toward poverty and want.[1]

Catharine Smith Campbell's origins little bespoke her life's course. She was born September 7, 1823, in Newark, New Jersey, the daughter of Abner Campbell and Deborah Conger Campbell. Her father described the Campbells as "plain Mechanicks—having experienced considerable of the upps & downs of life." Still, Abner had achieved prosperity based upon a paint, glass, and framing business. Kate came as their sixth child, with five more to join the family by sister Charlotte's birth in September 1835. Mostly, Deborah raised the children. Abner meanwhile regretted that his business kept him from greater involvement with their lives. "When I look back over my own history as the Father of such a Family who have been brought into the world through my instrumentality," he recorded, "it fills me with pain & grief that I have done no more in counciling and endeavoring to lead them in their tender years in the way of life."[2]

The financial and other demands of such a family imposed constraints upon Abner and Deborah Campbell. It limited them, for instance, in the schooling they could provide for their children, especially the girls. Kate received a basic education in Newark schools that, nonetheless, stopped short of the opportunities provided to young ladies by a "finishing school." Still, her younger sister Emma F. R. Campbell, born in 1830, would go on to pen popular hymns, poetry, and inspirational works for young people. With sister Charlotte she would help to pioneer the kindergarten movement in New Jersey and otherwise contribute by teaching. In time, Kate would aid her sisters in that work.[3]

While family life nourished Kate, Newark's climate undermined her health. In the winter of 1841 Abner and Deborah dispatched her to sojourn with an uncle, Obadiah Conger, who lived at the relatively primitive Florida port town of Jacksonville. There she met Ossian Bingley Hart, the twenty-year-old son of town founder Isaiah Hart, who was preparing in his father's office to become an attorney. After Kate's return to Newark, friendship blossomed into love. The couple wed in her parents' home on October 3, 1843, with the minister of the First Presbyterian Church performing the rites. "I think him very pleasant but I should not fancy him for myself," Kate's sister Abby H. Smith recorded. She continued, "I hope he will make her a good husband. I think he has a mild disposition altho he is all ambition to get rich." Abby added, "He knows nothing of religion, hardly one persuasion from another. I wish he did."[4]

The next quarter century saw Kate's life turned topsy-turvy as weather, Indian troubles, disease, urban vices, community disintegration, and civil war took turns challenging the Harts. They commenced the cycle at Fort Pierce, an isolated former military post at Indian River on Florida's lower Atlantic coast. The Harts built a frontier homestead there, only to see it destroyed by an 1846 hurricane. Meanwhile, when Ossian traveled over many months to Jacksonville and Tallahassee to serve in the 1845 legislature, Kate found herself left with responsibility for their nascent farm and citrus grove. Washed out at Fort Pierce by the hurricane, the Harts then attempted to recoup their fortunes at Key West, soon to become the state's largest and most cosmopolitan town despite a population that reached only about three thousand by 1860. Ossian practiced law, dabbled in Whig politics, supported the local temperance movement, prosecuted for the state, and otherwise reveled in the town's atmosphere, while Presbyterian Kate reacted strongly to the "vice and immorality and licentiousness" that she witnessed. "I do not like the place so well as some others I have seen, neither is the society so pleasant as it might be, but it is of but little consequence to me for I have plenty to do at home and care little for society," she asserted in 1847. "There are a few ladies who have sought my acquaintance and are very pleasant good people," Kate added, "the ballance are a class I do not want to have anything to do with."[5]

As for her home duties, Kate provided a description for Charlotte ("Lottie") in 1851. "How do you think I find time to write as often as I do, and not neglect any of my domestic affairs or my husband?" she first asked. Hart continued,

> I have my house to attend to, true I have a woman and a boy now but I have been doing my own work for a month past. I have all my sweeping and dusting to do and all the sewing for myself and husband. Last week I made three pair of drawers besides my usual amount of mending, and a great part of my time is taken up with visiting and receiving visits. It is done much more here at the south than you have any idea of. Many ladies here have nothing else to do, and unless they are running about from house to house there time hangs heavy on their hands, poor creatures. I do not envy them.[6]

The stress of what she perceived as Key West vice and the solitude compelled by her rejection of it caused Kate physical ailments, as stress would continue to do at various future times. "I have had several attacks of ulcerated sore throat since I have been here," she noted as early as 1847, "and the last which was about a month ago and very severe, more so than any I have had before." She added, "It commenced feeling sore about 2 Oclock in the afternoon and at sundown when Ossian came home from his office he found me with a very hot fever and my throat in a high state of inflammation. It was very painful that night and the next and then formed into ulcers about the size of a shilling first on one gland and then on the other." She concluded, "I was sick about a week before they healed." Four years later, she offered a similar refrain. "You know that I have been in very bad health much of the time for the past year, some time confined to my bed," she wrote to Lottie, "and was obliged to leave the island for a short time and try traveling in the woods." She concluded, "I returned some what better, but was soon down again."[7]

A yellow fever outbreak, followed by Indian war in 1855, served as prelude to the Harts' next move. The conflict had brought a degree of prosperity to the village of Tampa, where the army's Fort Brooke was located. Ossian's political mentor, Judge Joseph Lancaster, lived and practiced law there as well. When Lancaster died in late 1856, Ossian moved to pick up his lucrative legal practice on the expanding southwest Florida frontier. Once at Tampa, Kate found release from the stresses of Key West life and thrived accordingly. As she exulted in 1860, "My health is good, very much improved indeed." She added, "I am very much attached to Tampa, like it better as time advances. I never before in all my married life felt so well content and happy in my house as I do now. I feel the force of that beautiful poetry every day of my life." She had such positive feelings despite Tampa's flirtation with vigilante violence, political turmoil, and yellow fever in the aftermath of the Indian war's conclusion. Of great importance to Kate's happiness, a widowed Key West friend—Louisa Brown Porter—moved to Tampa, and her presence afforded Kate sisterly ties. Childless like most of her sisters, Kate virtually adopted Louisa's daughters, Anna Hayden Porter, born in 1846, and Mary Brown Porter, born in 1851. Eventually, the Porters would live within the Hart household. Beginning in October 1861 Ossian's orphaned niece, Mary Ellen Hart, similarly joined the family.[8]

Whatever emotional bonds tied her to the Porter girls, Kate found her "baby" in a child born at Tampa in 1863. Flora A. Henderson's father, John A. Henderson, was a former Confederate officer who served as regional Confederate tax collector. Flora's mother Mary Turman Henderson died in November 1864 when the child was only one year of age. Unable to raise his daughter himself, Henderson asked the Harts to care for Flora. They did so willingly, with Kate embracing the infant as her own. Emma Campbell, referring to a potential visit by Kate to New Jersey in 1866, put the matter into words. "She will bring her baby, I suppose," Emma declared. "She thinks it a wonderful child."[9]

Hart's willingness to touch the lives of these four girls proved no obstacle to her relationship with her husband. The tests the couple faced drew them together in a manner that endured until Ossian's death, even though, it is true, his more easygoing ways sometimes butted against Kate's staunch Presbyterian morality. Fort Pierce neighbors had viewed them early in their marriage as "a happy, devoted pair." Four years later she would write, "Ossian is still the same kind affectionate devoted husband he was the first week we were married." After seventeen years together—that is, in 1860—she had not changed her mind. "As his goodness corresponds with his size [Ossian had gained weight]," she related to Lottie, "we can overlook the latter in admiration of the former." Ossian reciprocated. "I hope that wisdom will come with age," he commented to her in 1863. He added, "One thing I know, my love for my dear wife waxes warmer all the time, and the happiness with which her unparaleled love and devotion blesses me becomes greater every year, and it is all because she is there to bless me."[10]

Civil War–era events and circumstances tested their bond severely. Ossian's father died in late 1861, requiring that Ossian spend considerable time during the conflict's early years at and near Jacksonville, administering Isaiah's affairs as well as his own inheritance and that of Mary Ellen Hart. The estate—consisting primarily of slaves, a plantation called Paradise, and scores of Jacksonville lots and properties—lacked cash resources. As Unionists, the couple meanwhile increasingly felt the opprobrium of many of their neighbors, and the ordeal of war took its toll. In January 1865, as the conflict neared its conclusion, Kate expressed her despair to family members. "I do so long to see you all once again; and to mingle with you all, as in days past, but *when* will that day come again," she expressed, "when will this unnatural war be over, when will peace and prosperity bless our distressed country again?" Kate continued, "This the fourth year has dawned upon us; and still the two sections of the country stand in antagonism toward each other. Sometimes I am led to think God has forsaken us, and intends to let us destroy each other; wickedness of all kinds prevails, on the right hand and on the left."[11]

During 1866 Kate's dream of seeing her family members again came to realization, although not before the Harts had relocated to Jacksonville, where family properties and prospects for community growth offered the possibility of future security and even prosperity. The chance for a New Jersey visit arose out of Ossian's service as a delegate to the Southern Loyalists Convention held that summer at Philadelphia. A highlight of the sojourn was Kate's reunion with her ailing mother, who subsequently passed away in May 1867. (Abner Campbell had preceded his wife in death on April 8, 1859.) The loss of her mother struck Kate a hard blow. She called her reaction "our great bereavement" and months afterward attempted to express the depth of her feelings to Lottie: "God in his great mercy and in answer to my prayers, supports and sustains me to do my duty to the love[d] ones around me, though my heart is heavily pressed with grief, and mind burthened with the loss of our Sainted Mother," she wrote. "I go from room to room, and from one duty to another, but one thought is ever present with me: Ma has left me to struggle alone," Kate continued. "I have no mother now," she added, "but for Ossian's dear sake who is all love and kindness; and who feels all the grief I suffer in sympathy, I try to be resigned and do my duty here, that we may meet her here after; I am so glad I was able to go home last summer and did not put it off till this summer, had I have done so, how much harder would have been the blow."[12]

Kate's bereavement seems to have pushed a simmering family problem to the surface, one that would come back to haunt her in future years. It appears that Kate never felt the close ties of affection to Ossian's niece Mary Ellen Hart that she held for the Porter girls and certainly for Flora Henderson. During the summer of 1867 the Harts sent Mary to school at the Providence Conference Institute in Rhode Island. A Jacksonville friend's sister, Connecticut-based teacher and poet Jane Gay Fuller, had made the arrangements. Kate seemingly chaperoned Mary on the journey, but thereafter the young woman rarely returned to Jacksonville. Instead, she often opted to spend vacation time with Lottie and Emma, who by then had established themselves at Morristown, New Jersey.[13]

As Mary pressed her independence from Kate, post–Civil War life for the Harts began to take on more comfortable aspects. Although required to borrow heavily against real property assets that could not yet be sold, Ossian and Kate began to live more comfortably as Jacksonville emerged from "a most melancholy sight" into the state's bustling center for business and banking. The physical evidence of that newfound prosperity came for the Harts in the form of a beautiful new home. Erected in a suburb known as LaVilla, the large, two-story structure sat in the middle of a city block. The Harts soon bordered their property with citrus trees. Landscaping nearer the home featured roses, Kate's favorite flower. The project took several years to complete, and the home could not be occupied until late 1871 or early 1872. Kate busied herself with the details. "Our house is not done yet," she explained in December 1871. "The sashes & blinds are on their way from N[ew] York and there is considerable work still to be done. We hope to have it finished by spring."[14]

Having so large a home relative to their previous residences, Kate in 1872 began boarding visitors during the winter tourist season, which proved a good thing for her. The income helped to ease chronic cash shortages, and the guests eased the loneliness that Kate experienced during Ossian's increasingly frequent absences to attend to political and professional chores. Having labored as an attorney in Florida for the Bureau of Freedmen, Refugees, and Abandoned Lands (Freedmen's Bureau), Ossian had emerged in 1867 with the beginning of Congressional Reconstruction (sometimes called Military Reconstruction) as Florida's chief voter registrar. That year he hosted the founding of Florida's Republican Party in his Jacksonville law office. Early the next year Hart's contributions proved crucial to rewriting the state constitution. The new Republican governor then appointed him to the three-member state supreme court. In 1870 the legislature elected Ossian to the U.S. Senate, but the Senate refused to seat him in favor of a northern-born incumbent. By then the state's Republicans had split into warring camps, a split that found its apparent cure in 1872 with Hart's selection as the Republican candidate for governor. He achieved election in November by a comfortable margin and quickly established, beginning in January 1873, the foundations of a successful first term as the state's chief executive officer.[15]

Kate delighted in her husband's accomplishments. "We have been very kindly received by both parties; have had over 60 calls, very different from the opening administration of Gov [Harrison] Reed [in 1868]," she informed family members from Tallahassee in mid-February 1873. "Ossian had no trouble in getting his Cabinet officers confirmed, and now has one of the strongest best working set of Officers in the US—all get along smoothly and pleasantly." She added, "Many good bills have been passed and become laws at his suggestion, and will be a benefit to Florida we hope."[16]

Not long after Kate penned those words, her plans for the foreseeable future began to change unexpectedly. She had believed that she and Flora would remain in the state capital with her husband throughout his tenure, particularly if the legislature appropriated funds "for the rent or purchase of a house for the Gov." When budget concerns forestalled the appropriation, she instead returned to their Jacksonville home. The relocation caused her little concern, but the state of Ossian's health did. On the campaign trail in the fall of 1872 he had taken ill, and the problems persisted. "Ossians heath is still feeble, has a bad cough and his business duties now during the session of the Legislature are so onerous and imperative that he cannot take time to recover," she recorded in February 1873. Three months later she lamented, "Ossian is still very far from well, in fact we have not been able to return to the Capitol on account of his health." In these circumstances the couple traveled to New Jersey for the summer, remaining at Morristown with Emma and Lottie Campbell until the governor's health began to improve in November. The 1874 legislative session, while again proving a success for him, nonetheless taxed Hart nearly beyond his ability to manage. Once the session concluded, he returned to Jacksonville and died there suddenly on March 18, 1874.[17]

Just as suddenly Kate found herself a widow, grieving desperately for a lost husband and anxious about the future. To the good, she enjoyed the presence of close family and personal friends, although her closest friend, Louisa Brown Porter, had passed away in 1873. Louisa's daughter Anna taught school in Jacksonville, however, and her other daughter Mary—married in 1873 and now Mrs. Alexander G. Bigelow—remained even closer to her surrogate mother. Additionally, the former wife of Ossian's brother Oscar Hart had established strong ties with Kate since the Harts had moved to Jacksonville. The friendship of Virginia "Jennie" Crews Hart, soon to be Mrs. George M. Wells, would outlast Kate's lifetime. And, of course, there was Flora, now age eleven, who remained with Kate despite her father, John A. Henderson's, remarriage, move to Tallahassee, and climb in state politics to the state senate and leadership of the Florida Democratic Party. Kate also drew strength from her own family. From the estates of her parents and grandparents she enjoyed an income of approximately $100 per month. Even more importantly her sisters attempted to offer their support. Particularly, Emma and Lottie buttressed Kate, encouraging her to spend summers at Morristown and aid them in maintaining their kindergarten and other educational and business activities. Kate eagerly accepted their welcomed invitation. Commencing in the summer of 1874 and each summer thereafter when possible, Kate journeyed with Flora to New Jersey for at least two months' respite from the Florida heat and other challenges.[18]

Challenges there were, and they came sooner rather than later. Although Ossian left considerable assets in real property, his debts ran high and required cash for their payment. Kate quickly attempted to sell Jacksonville lots to satisfy taxes, cover living expenses, and assuage creditors. Her efforts met with insufficient success. By late 1874 one of the major creditors, the estate of former Confederate congressman and Hart family friend John P. Sanderson, sued for payment. This action seems to have stemmed partly from anti-Hart sentiments held by the estate's administrator Edward M. L'Engle, a staunch anti-Republican Democrat. L'Engle soon threatened to foreclose on the Hart home. Kate battled back, claiming homestead rights as a widow. By July 1875 she was compelled to file a notice of insolvency. Two months later the local circuit court ruled against her in the Sanderson suit. She appealed to the state supreme court.[19]

Meanwhile, Hart strove to maximize income from running her home as a boarding house. She undertook repairs and painting to make it more attractive and tried to rent as much of it as possible. During the winter of 1875–1876 this meant leasing the entire home, an approach that she quickly reconsidered. "My house I have rented for boarding and I retain my own room, with the privilege of taking my meals here or else ware," she related in January 1877. "This is a little more to my comfort than the bargain I made last winter." Kate added, "I get $150. per month. The law suit is still in progress, moves on very slowly and we cannot see as yet how it will terminate." The next year she reflected on the vicissitudes of dependence upon the boarding of guests. "I ran my house myself the past winter and have had a family of 15 since the first of Nov. until Thursday of the past week," she recorded on June 2, 1878. She continued,

> But I am sorry to say I have done nothing more than making a living but I have had the satisfaction of controuling my own house and using my own furniture. The business was injured by the yellow fever scare [of 1877] and hard times, and financial difficulties, which we hope will improve before another season. I think I shall try another winter, and if I do not do better I will rent again—that I can always do.[20]

High points for Kate during the years immediately following her widowhood usually related in one manner or another to Flora. As a mother she worried through her daughter's every malady. "Flora has been out of school with eye problems," she wrote in a typical comment in mid-1878. "I regret so much to have her lose so much time." Kate then proudly observed, "She has grown to be a large girl—some taller than myself." As noted earlier, Kate and Flora traveled together each summer, and the 1876 trip proved especially meaningful to them because it permitted a visit to the Centennial Exposition being held at Philadelphia. "There was so much to see, and so much that she will never have the chance to see again," she boasted to sister Abby Smith. Hart continued, "Flora and I were there three days, but we did not see the half of it. The painting interested me more than any thing else." The era of their intimate day-to-day mother-daughter relationship soon drew to a close, however. In the fall of 1879 Kate escorted sixteen-year-old Flora to finishing school at New Scotland, Connecticut. While they remained close, Flora never again would reside for any lengthy period in Kate's home.[21]

The six months or so that followed Flora's departure proved less difficult for Kate than she might have expected. For one thing, in January 1880 former President Ulysses S. Grant visited Jacksonville, prompting festivities in which Kate, as the widow of a Republican governor, almost certainly was involved. On the heels of that event her niece Katie Smith visited for three months from

New Albany, Indiana. "Kate's visit to me has been a comfort and source of great pleasure," Kate told sister Abby, the younger Kate's mother. "I missed Flora very much indeed when I first came home, and hardly knew how to go through the winter without her." Katie, a teenager, delighted in the sojourn. She found her aunt "as jolly & spry as ever." In early April Katie informed her mother, "Aunt Kate seems to enjoy my being with her ever so much & is just as good & kind as can be." The weeks were filled with picnics, visits to the state fair, steamboat rides to resort towns up the St. Johns River, and the excitement of dynamic Jacksonville with its booming tourist trade. Meanwhile, the Hart home boomed as well. "Aunt Kate has quite a house full," Katie observed in February. "They are all real pleasant people & we have jolly times." Among those who had chosen to live with Kate by that time were Alexander and Mary Porter Bigelow. So one prodigal "daughter" had returned to the fold while Kate endeavored to embrace a niece on the threshold of womanhood.[22]

These surprisingly happy months unfolded within a stressful context that soon would conclude in tragedy. The Sanderson suit had been under review by various courts. The state supreme court had sided with Kate in 1877, but a lower court had again ruled against her. This ruling had led on March 8, 1880, to an order for foreclosure on her home and certain other properties. Before Kate could appeal again to the supreme court her home burned on April 26, 1880. "We go up and take a look but only to return and realize more keenly how much of this world's goods I have lost," she recorded. At a public sale held under the previous court order in early May, Edward M. L'Engle personally took the properties. "The lots [upon which the house stood] and nine others was sold last Mon[day] just one week from the burning of the house," Kate shared with Katie on May 7. "They brought a very small price of course and L'Engle bought them in." She continued, "I offered him 1000 [dollars] for the four homestead lots if he would give me a quit claim deed, but he would not do it for less than 2000. My lawyer advises me not to give it; his title to them is not good for much." Kate then summed up the options as she saw them: "I think if I had clear title in my own name I would try and rebuild," she commented. "I must do something, and this is all I can do, and why not do it." She again appealed to the state supreme court but in early 1881 lost in a decision that upheld the foreclosure.[23]

Kate understandably struggled financially in the fire's aftermath. She apparently benefited from at least some of the proceeds of a $4,000 insurance payment, but this offered little comfort. She and Jennie Wells moved into "a little cottage back of the Windsor hotel" for several weeks while she pondered her next step. As they did, news arrived at Jacksonville that properties in Kate's mother's estate at Newark, New Jersey—upon which her monthly income depended—had also burned. When family members offered financial support, however, she rejected their generosity. "I never can let my brothers and sisters support me," she responded, "so long as I have health and strength, no never." As soon as her immediate affairs were attended to, she departed for Morristown to recuperate while working for her living with Emma and Lottie. Flora joined her there.[24]

Then, before the summer could run its course, Kate's travails deepened when Mary Ellen Hart reappeared in her life. Now a mature woman, Mary Ellen had married Thomas E. Stribling at Jacksonville on July 23, 1879. Kate did not attend the ceremony, remaining instead at Morristown. Perhaps urged on by her new husband, Mary Ellen soon demanded a payment of $8,000 from Kate, disavowing in the process an agreement that she (Mary Ellen) had reached, following her twenty-first birthday, with her guardian Ossian and with a number of guarantors. In September 1880 she filed suit on the alleged debt. Kate and the guarantors stalled proceedings that November, but on May 25, 1881, their temporary victory was overturned. Five months later the court ruled against Hart. With Kate unable to pay, Mary Ellen pursued the guarantors in litigation that stretched through the decade. Not until mid-1889 did the Florida supreme court dismiss Stribling's action.[25]

Meanwhile, Kate spent as much time in Morristown as she could. The first definite indication of a recommitment to Florida occurred in November 1881 when she and Flora journeyed together from Morristown and New York to Savannah and Jacksonville. Since Kate no longer enjoyed the comforts of a Jacksonville home, the two traveled on by rail to Tallahassee, where Flora's father, John A. Henderson, had offered a refuge. "Flora is through school and has returned home for the winter and expects to have a good time," Hart explained on Christmas Day to Katie Smith. Kate's own sentiments about the town remained mixed, however. "Tallahassee is dull however not like Jacksonville," she wrote. "It is the capitol of the State, but that is all you can say about it." She continued on a somewhat brighter note: "You might live in New Jersey ten years and you would not meet as many socially disposed people. This is the difference between the north and South. I quite enjoy getting back again."[26]

At Tallahassee friends of the widow and her deceased husband attempted to aid her search for a new direction and, in so doing, brought her back to goals that she had shared as a young bride opening a homestead at Fort Pierce. Former Governor David Walker, a Democrat, was one of those people. "Judge Walker an old friend of Ossians offered to give me ten acres if I would set it out in oranges in Sumter County," she recorded. "This is below the frost line and on the line of the new rail road south," Kate described. "This is new land and the labor of clearing it is quite an important item." Such opportunities in the peninsula appeared enticing in light of Kate's circumstances. "If I was in Jacksonville I could do more towards finding a place, but up here in the northern part of the state I cant do much except to buy wild land," she informed sister Abby. "I hoped in coming south this winter to find some way to buy a lot and build a house in Jacksonville for boarders or to rent furnished rooms," Kate added, "but property has gone up so high that I fear I cannot do so unless we can persuade [brother Charles G. Campbell of Newark] to sell the Market Street property [owned by Deborah Campbell's estate]." Kate wondered if Abby might not invest with her in citrus, revealing that her (Hart's) funds available for such a project totaled one thousand dollars. "Find out how much you could spare in cash to invest in a grove," Kate directed.[27]

The offer of assistance likely of most interest to Kate came from Charles H. Foster, who had been clerk of the Florida supreme court when Ossian had sat on the panel, had served as state treasurer in Hart's administration, and by 1882 filled the position of clerk of the U.S. District Court for the Middle District of Florida. A one-time Tallahassee mayor and native of Massachusetts, Foster recently had purchased the once-elegant sugar plantation owned by the Braden family and located along the Manatee River at today's Bradenton near Kate's old home at Tampa. On the property he had constructed a magnificent home that he called Fair Oaks, described by an area historian as a "delightful retreat for nature lovers." Kate accepted Foster's offer to come for a visit and to look around the vicinity. She traveled there, at least as far as Tampa, in company with John and Flora Henderson.[28]

The stay at the Manatee River lasted until May 1882. During those months, however much she enjoyed Fair Oaks, Hart was drawn instead, as were most area residents, to news that iron rails finally had pierced the heart of the peninsula. Henry Plant's South Florida Rail Road had extended itself by March 14 past Orlando to the cattle and timber-milling village of Kissimmee. Plans called for an extension of that line and construction of other lines in the immediate future as far as Tampa and points south. "There is a tremendous amount of money coming into South Florida these days," a Tampa newspaper blared in May.[29]

This news appears to have set Kate on her future course. Perhaps as early as her return to Jacksonville in late May she began to put her plans in motion. Another family friend, Horatio Bisbee of Jacksonville, remained a Republican member of the U.S. Congress. Likely through the congressman's influence with the Republican administration of President Chester A. Arthur, Kate by May

Figure 2. Most 1880s–1890s Kissimmee residents, likely including Catharine Hart, traveled the Kissimmee River on Captain Clay Johnson's cargo and passenger vessel *Roseada* (seen here c. 1890). (Courtesy of Osceola County Historical Society.)

1883 had achieved appointment as Kissimmee's postmistress. A month or two was required for her to make arrangements to take up the position. These included bringing Abby and brother-in-law Isaac P. Smith to the bustling village in hopes of enticing them to invest with her in a city block of property. They ultimately agreed, and during the summer Hart relocated to what Emma Campbell later described as a "shanty" on the southern half of the block that Kate and Abby had purchased together. The building had served previous owner I. M. Mabbette as a restaurant, store, and dwelling. Now, Kate operated there a post office, stationery shop, and bookstore. She lived there as well. The site later was occupied by Kissimmee's Hart Memorial Library.[30]

The Kissimmee that greeted Kate remained a frontier outpost and "cow town" in most respects. "The first bars in America established to accommodate mounted customers were built here for cowmen about 1870," historian Joe A. Akerman Jr. has written. "Cowmen simply rode up to these outside refreshment stands and ordered their poison—whether it be corn whiskey, peach spirits, rot-gut or cane skimming whiskey." One newcomer, describing the scene upon her arrival at about the same time as Kate's, noted at least some improvements to the community. "Arriving on a belated train, no porters nor conveyances were in evidence; yet from the oil street lamps the little city, now numbering about one thousand inhabitants, presented a picture of tropical beauty," she related. "From the depot a board walk led to the large and commodious hotel, 'The Tropical,' the most spacious as well as the most expansive hotel south of Jacksonville." The newcomer continued, "Board walks lined the 100 foot Broadway Street, which was beautiful in a solid turf of Bermuda grass, giving to Kissimmee the distinction of having the only grass covered street in the United States."[31]

Community institutions grew slowly in the roughhewn environment. Kissimmee managed to incorporate as a municipality just a few months before Kate arrived. The beginnings of schooling also commenced in 1883 with a three-month school term and tuition payments required. The first church had come the year before when the Baptists organized a congregation. The Methodists followed in 1884, as did the Presbyterians. The latter did so with a modest sixteen members. If Kate was not present when the Presbyterian congregation coalesced in September, she associated with it soon thereafter. The members met in the schoolhouse until their $2,400 sanctuary was completed in 1886. It stood nearby at the intersection of Church and Monument streets.[32]

Given the rough atmosphere Hart found at Kissimmee and in light of her relatively humble circumstances, she initially chafed at the conditions she faced. The stress, in turn, produced health-related problems similar to those she had endured at Key West in the late 1840s and 1850s. Kate's ire initially centered upon her house, and by September 1883 she was beseeching sister Abby to divide their jointly held property. As she explained,

> I have been down with a turn of fever very much like yours when here—and I am now very weak and nervous—can scarcely write. I expected to start for a 30 day vacation north this morning but Lizzie [Smith, Abby's daughter-in-law by marriage to her son Ed, whom Kate had employed at the post office] struck for higher wages—last night, and so I will change my plans and as the end of the quarter is so near—will give up going and try to get well here—one reason I was so anxious to go—was that I might raise some money to build a house. During the rainy season this house was wet and damp from one end to the other—and I think has something to do with my present ill health. If I build of course I do not wish to do so with the titles as they are. I want a quit claim deed to the two unimproved lots and I will give you a quit claim deed to these two with the house on. The half interest in the house and improvements is worth 350.00. I would be willing to take 300. from you, but from any one else I would not take less than 350.00. I wish you to attend to it just as soon as possible.

Kate added, "I have set out 250 pines on this lot and some of them are growing finily. I find chickens interfere very much with the successful growth of a garden—although the fence is high and close[,] they get in and destroy more than they are worth."33

If Kate—who anticipated her sixtieth birthday the day after this letter was written—believed that almost sixty-eight-year-old Abby would meekly follow her curt directions, subsequent events proved her quite wrong. Abby, seemingly put off by Kate's tone and concerned about her motivations, had her attorney, son James R. W. Smith of Louisville, Kentucky, respond. He rejected Kate's proposal and countered that his mother desired to retain the block's northern half rather than deed it to Kate. The possibility of litigation hung in the air. "It is certainly very unnecessary to speak of Arbitration or Law suit," Kate informed Abby in late December, "as I am perfectly willing and anxious to have a fair settlement." Sisterly affection unfortunately had degenerated into quibbling by mid-January 1884. Abby's announcement in May that "I am in no hurry to sell," coming at the same time as word that their sister Mary had passed away, produced a sharp response from Kissimmee. "The warrentee deed we hold from Mr. Mabbett is not worth the paper tis written on—he is bankrupt—does not own one dollars worth of property in his own name," Kate declared. "I have no desire to fight a law suit—beside I want all the money I can raise to build me a house on my own lot," she continued. "I do not want the [present] house—prefer the unimproved lots." Disheartened at the results of her own actions and attitudes, Kate began to contemplate her own death when she referred to Mary by adding, "She was always so kind and unselfish—one more gone from the home circle, a few years more, and we too will go to join the home circle above." There the matter of property division rested for the following six years.34

Her inability to resolve her differences with Abby, coupled with other events and circumstances, slowly precipitated a turn in Kate's sentiments about life in Kissimmee. For one thing, reforms that she had instituted in the post office began to receive statewide attention. Presumably, her income from her position also increased. "From a correspondent at Kissimmee, we learn that the postoffice at that place opened as a money order office on the 21st inst.," the *Tampa Sunland Tribune* first reported on July 26, 1884. "The postoffice is an excellent index of the growth of the town, and shows that the young city of the lakes is marching forward with rapid strides." The article continued, "Only eighteen months ago the office had only eighteen call boxes; it now has one hundred, with a fair prospect of a further increase in the near future. The office is managed by two ladies, Mrs. O. B. Hart and her assistant, who are both always pleasant and obliging and ready to accommodate the public." The following month the organization of the Presbyterian congregation provided Kate the comfort of a spiritual home. By 1886 she also had adopted a cause. A lifelong "tea-totaller" who abhorred alcohol consumption, Kate helped to found a Kissimmee chapter of the Women's Christian Temperance Union. On the chapter's twenty-fifth anniversary, its historian would recall that Hart thereafter "devoted her life to temperance work." By the 1890s, this included editing the WCTU column in the local *Kissimmee Valley Gazette*.[35]

Ironically, as Kate grew fonder of Kissimmee, her problems there mounted as community expectations found themselves blunted by railroad construction, bad weather, and various other acts of God and of man. This train of events had commenced in 1883 with the burning of the Tropical Hotel. A replacement sponsored by the railroad opened for business in February 1884 but not before the passage of many months during which visitors enjoyed no adequate accommodations to draw them to the place. Then, Henry Plant's crews opened Kissimmee's rail link with the Gulf of Mexico at about the time the new hotel debuted, diverting attention from Kissimmee to Tampa as the end of the line. Tampa commenced to blossom as Kissimmee endeavored to cope with the changed dynamics, a not-too-surprising outcome given that nationally circulated reports were describing Kissimmee's vicinity as "poor and barren." By that time months of drought had parched the land and frustrated farmers and citrus planters. In late 1885 and early 1886 hard freezes added to the damage. The bad publicity and the sag in local morale intensified, particularly at Christmastime 1885 when local race relations plummeted after the murder of Marshal R. A. Gibson. In the aftermath of that crime "a band of cowboys" ordered all blacks from the town or else. Most fled, at least temporarily. Eventually some good news did break the trend when, in September 1887, Kissimmee received the nod as the seat of newly created Osceola County.[36]

Despite her more positive outlook on Kissimmee life, Kate endured bad news in her personal life during this period, a circumstance that may well have prompted a visit from Flora aimed at offering comfort. Hard on the heels of the Gibson murder and the January 1886 freeze, the administration of President Grover Cleveland, a Democrat, announced Republican Hart's replacement as head of the local post office by Democrat Nathaniel C. Bryan. Almost immediately Flora, now twenty-three years old, made her way to the Hart home from the state capital, intent upon offering to Kate the support that she had received from her adoptive mother earlier in life. As the *Kissimmee Leader* announced in March, "Miss Flora Henderson, daughter of Col. Henderson, of Tallahassee, Fla., has been visiting Mrs. C. S. Hart the past week." The length of Flora's 1886 stay at Kissimmee cannot be determined, but its importance for Kate at this time and place should not be underestimated.³⁷

The comforts of Flora's love and an improved attitude enabled Hart for a time to support herself despite the loss of income from her position at the post office. She operated the bookstore and stationery shop and added school supplies to her inventory. Eventually, she managed to buy additional property near the Presbyterian church. On one of the newly purchased lots she erected what she described as "a small cottage." She described the adjacent lot, upon which she intended to build a new home at some future date, as "the vacant lot or parcel of ground adjoining the [Presbyterian] Church property—about 70 feet front on Church Street and running back to the depth as now separated by a fence from a lot on which I have erected [my new rental home]." Meanwhile, she continued to live and work in the original house that she had resented so deeply at mid-decade. "There are too many discomforts about this one," Lottie would declare. "We don't think she ought to live so, and the carpenters say it will not pay to fix it up."³⁸

The stresses of everyday life for the aging woman and the dampness and lack of comfort in her home took their toll on Kate. Her health declined as the decade of the 1880s closed, and she entertained thoughts of moving from Kissimmee. Her health issues intensified before she could relocate, however. This caused grave concerns, and Emma and Lottie hastened to her bedside. On February 1, 1890, Kate executed a last will and testament. In it, she bequeathed her newly purchased lots to the Presbyterian Church and, to Flora, "my fine solid silver chocolate spoons." She honored Ossian's memory as well, directing the payment of "not less than five hundred dollars and so much more as my said Executors may deem best" to "erect a good fence enclosing my lot in the cemetery in the City of Jacksonville Florida—and also erect a neat monument over the grave of my husband Ossian B. Hart." Almost everything else, to the extent that anything remained, she willed to Emma and Lottie.³⁹

Fairly quickly thereafter, Kate began to recover. By March she felt well enough to set out on a difficult journey down the Atlantic coast to Fort Pierce. She traveled with Emma in hopes of reviving her claim to ownership of the old Hart homestead of 1843. Regarding that property, Lottie recorded, "She wants to sell it if she can get a good price, so as to have money to put up a comfortable house here for herself." The results of the trip remain unknown, but it cheered Kate nonetheless when Emma decided to buy herself a Kissimmee home. Before long the three sisters made their way together to Morristown, where Hart spent the summer recuperating and otherwise reviving her spirits. During Kate's stay there, and perhaps as a result of her recent illness, sister Abby consented to a division of their jointly held Kissimmee property mostly along the lines Kate earlier had dictated. Kate took the northern half of the city block. On one of the two lots she put up another small cottage. It would command a mere eight dollars per month in rent.⁴⁰

If Hart's decision to remain in Kissimmee hinged upon the town's prospects, her hopes came crashing down in the early 1890s. Using unknown resources she did manage to build a new and more comfortable home on the lot next to the Presbyterian church. By the time she could occupy it, though, a series of disasters began disturbing the local scene. A freeze in January 1891 preceded by only nine months the burning of city hall and destruction of all municipal records. Four months later a second freeze wreaked havoc on local citrus trees such as the ones that Kate had nurtured. In May 1893 the local economic malaise compounded itself when the financial underpinnings of the town's principal bank collapsed amid tax fraud scandals. This happened just as the economic depression known as the Panic of 1893 gripped the nation. Quite understandably, Kate, now approaching seventy, relapsed into health problems or, as sister Emma described them, "stones in her stomach." Kate's ability to work with Emma and Lottie diminished, and she now made jellies when she could to supplement her income. As late as October, while Hart rested at Morristown, the economic doldrums persisted in Osceola County. "There is no more encouraging news from Kissimmee," Lottie reported. "Em's house is still unrented also Kate's Cottage." She added, "K. is afraid to return on account of yellow fever, however she thinks she will venture about November 1st."⁴¹

Economic times proved no more hospitable at Kissimmee for Kate in the mid-1890s than they had earlier in the decade. On September 25, 1894, a brutal storm lashed the community. "The hurricane . . . did considerable damage to the orange and vegetable crops and caused the destruction of much property of all kinds," a commentator observed. "Great damage was done to houses and railroads by the unprecedented downpours of rain besides what was done by the wind." A freeze followed in December and, two months later, the "Great Freeze" of 1895. A man living nearby explained the impact. "It is well to look things squarely in the face," he wrote. "It is at best a serious disaster, to many it means ruin; to all it means a time of care, anxiety and doubt as to the future." Historian Alma Hetherington noted that the freeze "influenced many families to pack up and leave the Kissimmee area." By summer the town's population stood only slightly higher than it had when Kate arrived in 1883.⁴²

The highlight of these twilight years for Hart involved a major turning point in Flora Henderson's life. In May 1896 she was married at Tallahassee to George E. Waldo of New York City, whom she apparently had met years before when they both attended school in and near New Scotland, Connecticut. "Mr. Waldo is a lawyer of note in his city," advised press reports of the ceremony, "prominent in political circles, a member of the legislature of his state, and a clever polished gentleman." Waldo would go on to election in 1904 as a Republican member of the U.S. House of Representatives and would serve two terms there as a close ally of President Theodore Roosevelt. Flora, thirty-three when she married, was considered "a general favorite in social circles at the [state] capital, possessed of many charming and dignified traits of character." The fact that she chose "a quiet marriage" at "the palatial new residence of Col. Jno. A. Henderson" suggests that the bride adjusted her nuptial plans in light of Kate's continuing infirmities.[43]

The likelihood that Flora did so is borne out by the fact that Kate survived the wedding by less than eighteen months. She "died suddenly" at Morristown on October 9, 1897. The local newspaper reported, "She had not been well for several days, but her illness was not considered serious." A few days earlier Kate had penned a letter to Mary Bigelow at Jacksonville, announcing "her early return to Florida" and her intention "to complete the story of her life which she was writing." That endeavor went unfilled except to the extent that surviving manuscript pages may have contributed to Emma's brief 1901 publication *Biographical Sketch of Honorable Ossian B. Hart, Late Governor of Florida, 1873*. "Mrs. Hart is well remembered by the older people of the city," the *Jacksonville Florida Times-Union and Citizen* proclaimed at the time of Kate's death, "and was known as a woman of strong religious tendencies, being a member [at one time] of the Ocean Street Presbyterian Church, a devout Christian, kind and loving in disposition, and a woman whose good works will ever be remembered." At Kissimmee, many residents reportedly reacted with shock to the news. "The Presbyterian Church here," a letter noted, "will sadly miss Mrs. Hart, as she was a very earnest worker in church matters." The *Morristown Jerseyman* added, "She made many friends, who with her bereaved brother and sisters, mourn her loss." Catharine Hart is buried in Jacksonville's Evergreen Cemetery next to her husband, Ossian B. Hart.[44]

Although at times accustomed to the finer things in life, Catharine Hart died without wealth. Her home went to the Kissimmee Presbyterian Church for a manse and, having given the adjoining lot and cottage to the congregation, she also managed, in Emma's words, "[to] give them a little income." Emma observed, "They appreciate the gift very truly." Other than that, little remained following decades of a widowhood during which, for her like many other widows, challenges came fast, hard, and often unexpectedly. "There is another cottage which is rented for 8.00 a mo[nth]," Emma noted of the paucity of assets at hand. "[This] is the only income we have to settle bills & pay expenses." A strong sense of morality, coupled with fierce determination despite human frailty, had left Catharine Smith Campbell Hart little in the way of worldly goods. She had, however, earned the respect and affection of many. Her life had proved a testament to her fortitude and courage. In that, her life reflected the stories of countless others.[45]

Notes

I appreciate the kind generosity and assistance of Timmy Sorrow of New Albany, Indiana, a descendant of Catharine Hart's family, who shared letters from and about Catharine as well as her photograph. Her collection will be cited as Sorrow Collection. I thank also the late Dena E. Snodgrass of Jacksonville, who encouraged my interest in the Harts and preserved a collection of Catharine's letters to her sisters Charlotte Campbell and Emma F. R. Campbell. Miss Snodgrass's collection is at the P. K. Yonge Library of Florida History, University of Florida, Gainesville, and will be cited as Snodgrass Collection. I additionally recognize my continuing debt of gratitude to the late Samuel Proctor for his mentorship, friendship, and understanding. Additionally, let me acknowledge David J. Coles, then of the Florida Archives and now at Longwood University, Farmville, Virginia, for his always generous assistance and support. Please note that Catharine Hart and others sometimes spelled her first name Catherine. The former spelling is utilized throughout this essay.

1. Canter Brown Jr., *Ossian Bingley Hart, Florida's Loyalist Reconstruction Governor* (Baton Rouge, 1997), 294, 302; Donald E. Sutherland, *The Expansion of Everyday Life: 1860–1876* (New York, 1989), 62. The principal sources presently available on Kate Hart's life are Brown, *Ossian Bingley Hart*; and Emma F. R. Campbell, *Biographical Sketch of Honorable Ossian B. Hart, Late Governor of Florida, 1873* (New York, 1901); Canter Brown Jr., ed., "'Very Hard to Bear': Florida's First Lady Catharine Hart Travels the Southern Judicial Circuit in 1852," *Sunland Tribune: The Journal of the Tampa Historical Society* 22 (November 1996): 87–91; idem, "'Very Much Attached to Tampa': The Civil War–era Letters of Catharine Campbell Hart, 1860, 1865," *Sunland Tribune: The Journal of the Tampa Historical Society* 23 (November 1997): 63–69. Florida's other first ladies have received scant attention from biographers with the exception of Rachel Jackson, wife of Andrew Jackson. Only two other than Jackson have received book-length coverage, while a similar number have enjoyed recognition through biographical essays. See, for instance, Queena Pollack, *Peggy Eaton, Democracy's Mistress* (New York, 1931); Linda D. Vance, *May Mann Jennings, Florida's Genteel Activist* (Gainesville, 1985); Frank L. Snyder, "Nancy Hynes DuVal: Florida's First Lady, 1822–1834," *Florida Historical Quarterly* 72 (July 1993): 19–34; John T. Foster and Sarah Whitmer Foster, "Chloe Merrick Reed: Freedom's First Lady," *Florida Historical Quarterly* 71 (January 1993): 279–99; idem, *Beechers, Stowes, and Yankee Strangers: The Transforma-

tion of Florida (Gainesville, 1999). Of the minority of Florida's governors who have received book-length biographical treatment, information on their wives may be found in, among others, Herbert J. Doherty, *Richard Keith Call, Southern Unionist* (Gainesville, 1961); Samuel Proctor, *Napoleon Bonaparte Broward, Florida's Fighting Democrat* (Gainesville, 1950); Wayne Flynt, *Cracker Messiah: Governor Sidney J. Catts of Florida* (Baton Rouge, 1977); Martin A. Dyckman, *Floridian of His Century: The Courage of Governor LeRoy Collins* (Gainesville, 2006); Edmund F. Kallina Jr., *Claude Kirk and the Politics of Confrontation* (Gainesville, 1993); S. V. Date, *Quiet Passion: A Biography of Senator Bob Graham* (New York, 2004).

2. Maxine Crowell Leonard, *The Conger Family in America* (Janesville, Ill., 1972), 712; Abner D. Campbell to Ossian B. Hart, June 30, 1843, Snodgrass Collection; Abner Campbell to Isaac P. Smith, September 8, 1839, Sorrow Collection.

3. *Morristown* (N.J.) *Jerseyman*, August 24, 1875, March 28, 1879, January 26, 1912, and February 28, 1919; Julia Keese Colles, *Authors and Writers Associated with Morristown, With a Chapter on Historic Morristown* (Morristown, N.J., 1895), 79–81.

4. Brown, *Ossian Bingley Hart*, 43–48; Abby H. Smith to Isaac P. Smith, September 25, 1843, Sorrow Collection.

5. Brown, *Ossian Bingley Hart*, 38–98; Catharine S. Hart to "My dear Parents," August 29, 1847, and Kate Hart to Lottie Campbell, April 21, 1851, Snodgrass Collection.

6. Hart to Campbell, April 21, 1851.

7. Hart to "My dear Parents," August 29, 1847; Hart to Campbell, April 21, 1851.

8. Brown, *Ossian Bingley Hart*, 98–123; idem, "Very Much Attached to Tampa," 64–65; Timmy Sorrow to the author, September 11, 2007 (in possession of the author); *Jacksonville Florida Times-Union and Citizen*, October 14, 1897; *Jacksonville Florida Times-Union*, May 18, 1913; Mary-Louise Howard, *Old City Cemetery, Union Street, Jacksonville, Florida* (Jacksonville, 1993), 12, 106.

9. Brown, *Ossian Bingley Hart*, 150; Emma Campbell to Abby H. Smith, April 27, 1866, Sorrow Collection.

10. *Stuart* (Fla.) *News*, January 9, 1964; Brown, "Very Much Attached to Tampa," 67; Dena E. Snodgrass, "My Dear Wife," *Papers of the Jacksonville Historical Society* 5 (1969): 47–50; Brown, *Ossian Bingley Hart*, 50.

11. Brown, *Ossian Bingley Hart*, 107–52; idem, "Very Much Attached to Tampa," 68. As to Florida women generally during the Civil War, see Tracy J. Revels, *Grander in Her Daughters: Florida's Women during the Civil War* (Columbia, S.C., 2004).

12. Brown, *Ossian Bingley Hart*, 179–83; Leonard, *Conger Family*, 712; *Jacksonville Florida Union*, June 22, 1867; Kate Hart to Lottie Campbell, July 3, 1867, Snodgrass Collection.

13. Various receipts, petitions, and accountings, 1867–1871, in Mary E. Hart file; Duval County, Florida, guardianship records, Duval County Courthouse, Jacksonville (available on microfilm at Florida State Archives, Tallahassee); Mrs. W. J. Arnold, *The Poets and Poetry of Minnesota* (Chicago, 1864), 281–83; D. H. Greene, *History of the Town of East Greenwich and Adjacent Territory, from 1677 to 1877* (Providence, R.I.,

1877), 218–24; 1870 U.S. Decennial Census, Kent County, Rhode Island (population schedule); Kate Hart to Abby H. Smith, February 17, 1873, Sorrow Collection.

14. *Jacksonville Tri-Weekly Florida Sun*, January 29, 1876; Brown, *Ossian Bingley Hart*, 224–27; Kate Hart to Abby H. Smith, December 28, 1870, April 17, 1872, and January 22, 1877, Sorrow Collection. On Jacksonville's post–Civil War development, see Richard A. Martin, *The City Makers* (Jacksonville, 1972).

15. Brown, *Ossian Bingley Hart*, 190–281. The principal sources on Florida during the Reconstruction era may be found in William Watson Davis, *The Civil War and Reconstruction in Florida* (New York, 1913; reprint ed., Gainesville, Fla., 1964); Jerrell H. Shofner, *Nor Is It Over Yet: Florida in the Era of Reconstruction, 1865–1877* (Gainesville, Fla., 1974); Canter Brown Jr., *Florida's Black Public Officials, 1867–1924* (Tuscaloosa, 1998). On the Florida supreme court during Ossian B. Hart's tenure as an associate justice, see Walter W. Manley II, Canter Brown Jr., and Eric W. Rise, *The Supreme Court of Florida and Its Predecessor Courts, 1821–1917* (Gainesville, 1997), 211–70.

16. Hart to Smith, February 17, 1873, Sorrow Collection.

17. Ibid., February 17 and May 4, 1873; Brown, *Ossian Bingley Hart*, 269–96.

18. Lucy Ames Edwards, *Grave Markers of Duval County, 1808–1916* (Jacksonville, 1955), 12; 1870 U.S. Decennial Census, Duval County, Florida (population schedule); *Jacksonville Tri-Weekly Florida Union*, March 1, 1873, and December 22, 1874; *Jacksonville Florida Times-Union*, March 21, 1911, and May 18, 1913; Brown, *Ossian Bingley Hart*, 89, 227; Jennie Wells to "My dear afflicted friends," October 7, 1897, Snodgrass Collection; Hart to Smith, February 17, 1873, and Emma Campbell to Abby H. Smith, April 6, 1898, Sorrow Collection; *Tallahassee Weekly Floridian*, May 21, 1872.

19. Various filings, documents, notices, and receipts, 1874–1875, in Isaiah Hart, Ossian B. Hart, and John P. Sanderson files, Duval County Probate Records, and Mary E. Hart file, Duval County Guardianship Records; Index to Record, *Hart's Executrix &c. v. Sanderson's Admns.*, Supreme Court case file 0519, Records of the Supreme Court of Florida, Florida State Archives.

20. Various filings and receipts for repairs, Ossian B. Hart probate records; Kate Hart to Abby H. Smith, January 22, 1877, and June 2, 1878, Sorrow Collection.

21. Hart to Smith, January 22, 1877, June 2, 1878, and April 12, 1880; Kate Smith to Abby H. Smith, February 1, 1880, Sorrow Collection; Brown, *Ossian Bingley Hart*, 301.

22. *Tallahassee Weekly Floridian*, January 13, 1880; Kate Smith to Abby Smith, February 1, 24, March 23, April 1, 12, 19, 1880; Hart to Smith, April 12, 1880, Sorrow Collection.

23. *Catherine S. Hart, as Executrix and in Her Own Right, Appellant v. Sanderson's Administrators, Appellees*, 16 Florida Reports, 264; Index to Record, *Hart's Executrix &c. v. Sanderson's Admns.*; *Tampa Sunland Tribune*, May 6, 1880; receipt from *Florida Union*, May 4, 1880, John P. Sanderson probate records; Kate Hart to Katie Smith, May 7, 1880, Sorrow Collection; *Catherine S. Hart, as Executrix and In Her Own Right, Appellant v. Sanderson's Administrators, Appellees*, 18 Florida Reports, 103.

24. *Tampa Sunland Tribune*, May 6, 1880; Hart to K. Smith, May 7, 1880; 1880 U.S. Decennial Census, Morris County, New Jersey (population schedule).

25. Duval County, Florida, Marriage Records, Book 5, p. 41, Duval County Courthouse, Jacksonville (available on microfilm at Florida State Archives); *Thomas E. Stribling et Ux., Appellants v. Catherine S. Hart, Executrix, et als., Appellees*, 20 *Florida Reports*, 235; *Catharine Hart, Executrix of the Last Will of Ossian B. Hart, Deceased, Abel S. Baldwin, Paran Moody, Calvin L. Robinson, William P. Marvin, Administrator De Bonis Non of the Estate of H. H. Hoeg, Deceased, and Ozias Buddington, Appellants v. Thomas E. Stribling and His Wife, Mary E. Stribling, Appellees*, 21 *Florida Reports*, 136; *Catherine S. Hart, Executrix of O. B. Hart, Deceased, Napoleon B. Broward, Sheriff, Administrator of the Estate of Paran Moody, Deceased, and Abel S. Baldwin, Appellants v. Thomas E. Stribling and Mary E. Stribling, His Wife, Appellees*, 25 *Florida Reports*, 435.

26. Kate Hart to Kate Smith, December 25, 1881, Sorrow Collection.

27. Ibid.; Hart to Abby H. Smith, January 22, 1882.

28. Brown, *Ossian Bingley Hart*, 228, 272; *Jacksonville Florida Daily Times*, February 11 and May 21, 1882; *Tampa Sunland Tribune*, April 23 and May 7, 1881, February 3, 1882; Lillie B. McDuffee, *The Lures of Manatee: A True Story of South Florida's Glamorous Past* (Manatee, Fla., 1933), 246.

29. Dudley S. Johnson, "Henry Plant and Florida," *Florida Historical Quarterly* 45 (October 1966): 122; *Tampa South Florida Progress* quoted in *Tallahassee Weekly Floridian*, May 23, 1882.

30. Brown, *Ossian Bingley Hart*, 228, 258–59, 266, 275, 295; Edward C. Williamson, *Florida Politics in the Gilded Age, 1877–1893* (Gainesville, 1976), 13–14, 43–44, 56, 61, 81–82, 91, 93, 97–99, 109, 112–16, 118–19, 192; Alma Hetherington, *The River of the Long Water* (Chuluota, Fla., 1980), 17, 23–25, 27; Steve Rajtar, "Kissimmee Historical Trail" at www.geocities.com/yosemite/rapids/8428/hikeplans/kissimmee/plankissimmee.html; *Jacksonville Florida Daily Times*, May 30, 1883; Kate Hart to Abby H. Smith, September 6, 1883, and Emma Campbell to Abby H. Smith, March 24, 1890, Sorrow Collection.

31. Joe A. Akerman Jr., *Florida Cowman, A History of Florida Cattle Raising* (Kissimmee, 1976), 152; Hetherington, *River of the Long Water*, 24.

32. Hetherington, *River of the Long Water*, 24–27.

33. Hart to A. Smith, September 6, 1883.

34. James R. W. Smith to Catherine S. Hart, October 10, 1883; Abby H. Smith to Kate Hart, January 7, c. January 20, and May 19, 1884, and Kate Hart to Abby H. Smith, January 14 and May 28, 1884, Sorrow Collection.

35. *Tampa Tribune*, July 26, 1884, quoted in *Jacksonville Florida Times-Union*, August 12, 1884; *Kissimmee Valley Gazette*, January 27, 1897, and February 24, 1911.

36. *Jacksonville Florida Times-Union*, February 12, 1884, December 29, 30, 31, 1885, and January 1, 1886; Canter Brown Jr., *Florida's Peace River Frontier* (Orlando, 1991), 321; Hetherington, *River of the Long Water*, 30–31.

37. *Jacksonville Florida Times-Union*, February 7, 1886; *Kissimmee Leader* quoted in *Tallahassee Weekly Floridian*, March 18, 1886; Hetherington, *River of the Long Water*, 30.

38. 1887 Kissimmee city directory; Last will and testament of Catharine S. Hart, Osceola County Probate Records, Osceola County Courthouse, Kissimmee; Charlotte Campbell to Abby H. Smith, March 24, 1890, and Emma Campbell to Smith, April 6, 1898, Sorrow Collection.

39. Last will and testament of Catharine S. Hart.

40. Charlotte Campbell to Abby H. Smith, March 24, 1890, Charles G. Campbell to A. Smith, August 12, 1890, and Emma Campbell to A. Smith, April 6, 1898, Sorrow Collection.

41. Brown, *Florida's Peace River Frontier*, 321; idem, *In the Midst of All That Makes Life Worth Living: Polk County, Florida, to 1940* (Tallahassee, 2001), 183; Hetherington, *River of the Long Water*, 42; *Tampa Weekly Tribune*, May 16, 1893; Emma Campbell to "Dear friends at home," August 15, 1893, Charlotte Campbell to Katharine Smith Wade, October 14, 1893, Emma Campbell to Abby H. Smith, April 6, 1898, Sorrow Collection.

42. Jay Barnes, *Florida's Hurricane History* (Chapel Hill, 1998), 75; Brown, *Florida's Peace River Frontier*, 321–22; *Bartow Courier-Informant*, February 13, 1895; Hetherington, *River of the Long Water*, 45; John L. Crawford and L. B. Wombwell, comps., *Census Report of the State of Florida, for the Year 1895* (Tallahassee, 1897), 15.

43. *Tampa Morning Tribune*, May 19, 1896; *Biographical Directory of the United States Congress, 1774–1989, Bicentennial Edition* (Washington, D.C., 1989), 1993.

44. Brown, *Ossian Bingley Hart*, 301–2; *Morristown* (N.J.) *Jerseyman*, October 15, 1897; *Jacksonville Florida Times-Union and Citizen*, October 14–15, 1897; Campbell, *Biographical Sketch*.

45. Campbell to Smith, April 6, 1898.

CHAPTER 2

Ellen Call Long
1825–1905

A Thorough Lady

TRACY J. REVELS

ELLEN CALL LONG, the "first white child born in Tallahassee," loomed as a living symbol of Florida in the mid- and late nineteenth century. The daughter of a territorial governor, Ellen came of age in the political whirlwind of early statehood. Marriage, motherhood, and finally secession—from matrimonial ties and federal bonds—forced her into the role of Confederate matron. It proved a difficult adjustment; Ellen's wartime public work and private writings reflected her divided heart as the daughter of a proud Unionist and the mother of a Southern soldier. After the war she experienced a personal reconstruction, evolving in her beliefs about race and equality and linking civil rights of former slaves to her father's republican ideology. Ellen's later years shone with the gilt of New South optimism. She labored ceaselessly to promote her state and

Figure 3. Ellen Call Long, c. 1880s. (Courtesy of Florida State Archives.)

repair the damage of the Civil War without abandoning her sentimental attachment to the ideals of antebellum gentility. Personal tragedies, emotional abandonment, and financial insecurities confronted her, but she strove to put public service ahead of personal matters. A writer, thinker, and activist whose dedication to Florida never wavered, Ellen Call Long's life transcended the limitations placed on women in the nineteenth century.

Ellen came into the world the product of a proud patriot lineage. Her father, Richard Keith Call, was born in Prince George County, Virginia, in 1792. His family included a number of Revolutionary War luminaries. His uncles, all men of prestige and political power, lived in Kentucky where his widowed mother relocated during his childhood. Call received a frontier-style education at his mother's knee and in the woods and, in 1813, helped organize a company of volunteers for Andrew Jackson's campaign against the Creek Indians. Jackson admired the young man's initiative. Call quickly became one of the general's military and political protégés, living at the Hermitage as part of a large quasi-family that included Sam Houston, Andrew Jackson Donelson, and John H. Eaton. Call followed his mentor to Florida in 1818 during the First Seminole War and again when Jackson was appointed provisional governor three years later. Call grew enamored of what he saw: a new, raw land where a young man with stamina and ambition could rise rapidly to prominence.[1]

Romance, too, figured in Call's life. While residing in Nashville he had cut a figure among the local belles, although he soon settled on a beauty named Mary Kirkman. Kirkman's parents unfortunately hated Andrew Jackson and refused to consider any suitor with Jackson connections. Mary proved unwilling to marry against her parents' wishes, so Call waited. Jackson—with his usual lack of patience—played Cupid for the couple, urging Call to romantic action. Still, a wedding did not take place until Call served as a congressional delegate for territorial Florida and Mary had come of age sufficiently to defy her parents. The marriage occurred at the Hermitage on July 15, 1824. Kirkman's family proved slow to forgive; when Jackson approached Mrs. Kirkman in hopes of restoring peace, the offended mother drew a pistol on him.[2]

Although their marriage was celebrated in Tennessee, the couple found their home in Florida. In 1825 Call received appointment as receiver of public monies for the land office in Tallahassee, the newly established territorial capital. This position favored a newlywed with a child on the way, allowing Call to indulge in profitable land speculation and political jockeying. Sometime between 1825 and the early 1830s, growing prosperity enabled him to begin construction on a substantial brick house in Tallahassee. Later named The Grove, it remains a capital-city landmark, overlooking the modern, less impressive governor's mansion. Ellen Call was born on the property on September 9, 1825. Initially a disappointment to her parents, who had hoped for a boy to name after Call's great patron, Ellen would grow up very much her father's image in all things political. She also would endure further family disappointment. Between 1826 and 1834 three sisters and a brother died. Mary, her only surviving sibling, joined the family in 1835. Sources reveal little of Ellen's early years except that, like other children of the nineteenth-century frontier, she became aware of the fragility of life at a tender age. The constant loss of younger siblings impressed on her the horrors of sudden disease and death; the image of two Call children buried together in the same coffin during 1834 particularly haunted her.[3]

On the other hand Ellen also knew the pleasures of a Tallahassee girlhood. Her family prospered and had domestics to handle household chores. A rough-around-the-edges frontier village, Tallahassee brimmed with excitement for a child. Neighbors often killed wild animals just beyond The Grove's doorsteps, while Seminole Indians traded goods and taught woodcraft to local boys. Yet, life pampered Ellen. Florida First Lady Nancy DuVal, wife of Governor William Pope DuVal and known as "the mother of Tallahassee society," particularly doted on her. Ellen meanwhile heard of duels and brawls, not to mention lightning-fast courtships and unexpected weddings. Most memorable to the budding politico were sociable evenings hosted by her father and DuVal, where "frequent trips to the sideboard" resulted in laughter and noisy camaraderie. Throughout her life Ellen cherished recollections of "these republican sovereigns, in their republican detached shirt bosoms of linen." She saw them as "real monarchs for the time."[4]

At age nine Ellen went away to school at Franklin, Maryland, a reflection of the customary practice for daughters of affluent southerners to attend boarding institutions. Ellen's family hoped that her matriculation in northern climes would protect her from Florida fevers. She benefited mostly, though, from recent dramatic changes in the female educational curriculum. Spawned by a nationalistic ideology that required patriotic mothers capable of indoctrinating future sons in the glories of their new country, antebellum ladies' academies cast off dancing and stitching for, as Ellen reported, "Grammar, Geography, Dictionary, Scientific Dialogues, and French." While piety was not neglected, the new educational ideal stressed elegant language and competency in many subjects. Like any child sent away from home, Ellen endured lonesomeness despite the proximity of relatives in Baltimore. "Do come dear Mother I want to see you so much," she pleaded in an 1835 letter.[5]

Other factors compounded Ellen's loneliness at Franklin, in particular, her mother's death on February 28, 1836. The loss prompted the girl to devote herself even more than previously to her father. As she pledged in her response to her father's letter about her mother's passing, "I will do anything to make you happy." She added, "I shall hereafter try to obey you in everything." Fortunately, the rift between Call and the Kirkmans had finally been mended, and responsibility for Ellen's upbringing shifted to her maternal grandmother, who sent her to a series of schools and collected her for long visits with the family in Nashville and New Orleans. Ellen's promise to care for her father did not bring her home to Tallahassee until 1843, when Call was serving his second term as territorial governor. He had by then switched his political allegiance to the Whigs, and the teenaged Ellen found herself surrounded by debates and political discussion. She absorbed it all, and throughout her life remained her father's most eloquent defender.[6]

Ellen's return to The Grove at seventeen also marked her debut as a socialite. Southern women typically experienced their greatest freedom during their brief period as belles, those few years between their introduction into adult society and marriage. As the daughter of the territorial governor, Ellen ranked first among her peers, virtually the first lady of Florida. She attended the balls, May parties, theater performances, and patriotic picnics that characterized the capital's "gay life." The wealthy planter class that dominated politics considered such frivolities and diversions essential to maintaining their status. Ellen later recounted these events in a published novel, *Florida Breezes,* demonstrating her remembered fondness for them.[7]

Ellen soon closed her brief period as a belle by choosing a husband at the age of eighteen. A Tennessee native, Medicus A. Long appeared as a promising young attorney who enjoyed partnership benefits with Richard Keith Call's cousin George Walker. That Long was more than a decade older than his bride and also a Democrat offered ill omens for the future. Nonetheless, the couple married at The Grove on June 20, 1844. The newly founded Long family grew in 1846 with the arrival of Richard Call, followed by Hugh in 1848, Mary Louisa in 1849, and Ellen Douglas in 1851. Mindful of his daughter's needs and perhaps still smarting from defeat in his 1845 bid to become Florida's first state governor, Call retired to his Orchard Pond plantation, located in pastoral solitude not far from Tallahassee. He then gave The Grove to Ellen. A final child, Eleanora "Nonie" Kirkman, came to the Longs in 1854.[8]

The early years of her marriage saw Ellen devoted to intensive mothering and housekeeping while her husband worked at building a name and reputation for himself in the Florida Senate. Significantly, he sponsored the 1857 bill that established a "seminary west of the Suwannee," the predecessor institution of Florida State University. In a letter written to son Richard while he attended

Figure 4. The Grove, Tallahassee, Florida, c. 1874, with Ellen Call Long seated at center. (Courtesy of Florida State Archives.)

boarding school in Elmira, New York, Ellen followed the nineteenth-century code of true womanhood by promoting her husband's sphere while downplaying her own. "My time is principally devoted to my children and their care and instruction, only allowing so much time to society as duty seems to require," she noted. "Your father is now a member of the State Senate and as a politician stands well. As a lawyer he is eminent in the state, remarkable for the clearness, energy, and promptness with which he prosecutes his profession."[9]

Like her own mother Ellen knew the pain of burying small children, a fate that her father considered "only the common lot of humanity." Hugh did not survive infancy, and in 1853 Ellen Douglas died. Mary Louisa succumbed at eight, leaving only Richard and Nonie. Following Ellen Douglas's death, a close friend advised Ellen to take care to love her children only with a "chastened affection" and not allow her maternal love to "degenerate into idolatry," implying that God had taken the child to save the mother's soul. Ellen responded to her losses with natural grief but also with resoluteness, as if the deaths of her children solidified the inner strength that soon became her hallmark.[10]

Other aspects of life naturally offered happier circumstances. For instance, Ellen's household often was enlivened by her sister, Mary, who returned to Tallahassee in 1853 after attending schools in Nashville and New Orleans and who divided her time between The Grove and Orchard Pond. Quiet and refined, she shared her elder sister's cosmopolitan traits and love of travel. Not as civic-minded, however, Mary preferred aesthetic and domestic pursuits to keeping up with political debates. The attractive young woman married Tallahassee lawyer Theodore Washington Brevard in 1859. The couple made their home first on the Orchard Grove plantation and, later, in a house near The Grove. Theodore W. Brevard would go on to fame as a Confederate brigadier general, and Mary would present him with eight children, some of whom were born in their aunt's home.[11]

Mary's presence was a highlight of Tallahassee life for Ellen, but issues of major consequence eventually undermined that contribution to her happiness. In the late 1850s the peace of The Grove was broken by Medicus Long's political views. Political sensitivities had begun to mount by the mid-1850s. Soon, Long's beliefs clashed with those held by his father-in-law, who had switched to the American (or Know-Nothing) Party. Call believed that the Know-Nothings held more tightly to Jacksonian ideals than did the Democrats. In 1855, the one-time governor's son-in-law opposed him in public debate. Ellen—who remained supremely loyal to her father through her life—characteristically would have sided with her father in such a family dispute. Additionally, ill health plagued Long, and he often struggled with respiratory ailments. Long eventually dealt with mounting household and personal problems by departing. In 1859 he moved to San Antonio, Texas, ostensibly to "improve his health and professional prospects." He established there a lucrative practice, became an ardent secessionist, and eventually served as a Confederate judge. His political career continued after the peace, and for a period his son joined him in his legal practice. Long never returned to Tallahassee. He died in Austin on September 21, 1885.[12]

Whatever true motivation lay behind the couple's separation, a divorce—rare and socially unacceptable—was not a viable option. Under law and practice of the time, Ellen likely would have lost custody of her children. Instead, she accepted the lot of an abandoned woman, left to raise the couple's offspring alone. While her prosperous father could meet her financial needs, one can only speculate as to how emotionally painful the loss of her husband might have been to Ellen. Undoubtedly, she experienced some social embarrassment and gave awkward responses to tactless questions. Possibly, however, she preferred her new independence and freedom from potential marital disputes. Whatever her feelings about the loss, Ellen refused to go into self-imposed retirement. The most interesting part of her life was just beginning.[13]

Politics and questions of rights and governance provided the background for Ellen's emergence as an independent individual. By the late 1850s Florida swirled in the turmoil that produced the Southern independence movement. The aging Richard Keith Call took a Jacksonian stance that all secession talk was insanity. Ellen concurred. When Florida delegates adopted a secession ordinance, Call's furious reaction included a dire prediction that the delegates "had opened the gates of Hell, from which shall flow forth the curses of the damned which shall sink you to perdition." Ellen meanwhile questioned the sincerity of Southern female devotion, noting that local women so eager to buckle the swords on their "scessh gallants" husbands would be less enthusiastic about doing the honor for their sons. One of her Northern friends sympathized with the family's uncomfortable position. That person assured the "Countess of Tallahassee" that her father's name would "endure as one who tried to stem the tide of a fanatical and ill-judged revolution," while his daughter need not fear having her head shaved should she journey to Philadelphia for a visit.[14]

The war, when it came, soon touched Ellen's life directly. Her son Richard enlisted in the Confederate army and served as a courier for General William Miller. As the mother of a soldier and the premier dame of Tallahassee, Ellen attempted, whatever her private sentiments, to live up to the image of the stoic Confederate matron. She plunged into activities associated with supporting the cause, including organizing a Ladies Aid Society headquartered in the capitol building. A dutiful fund-raiser, she received frequent wartime accolades even though she remained a Unionist who resented her state's actions. Other factors, however, soon forced her away from such issues and toward more practical ones. The loss of her father on September 12, 1862, left her brokenhearted but with little time to mourn. She had inherited his plantation and its sixty-six slaves.[15]

Yet the dynamics of civil war did not escape Ellen's consideration. Unlike others who questioned their faith, accusing God of abandoning the South as the war went badly, Ellen blamed the Southern people who "sold their birthright for a mess of pottage." Her disappointment and disapproval could not always disappear behind a mask of socially acceptable Confederate patriotism. As an example, William Stockton—a Quincy resident who was entertained at The Grove on his way to assume military duties—observed Ellen's "occasional bitterness." Still, Long remained outwardly a loyal Southerner, opening her home to wounded soldiers and continuing the endless task of supplying provisions. She took apparent pride in Southern victories. Ellen particularly hailed Florida cavalry Captain John J. Dickison's August 1864 skirmish—which her son witnessed—as a milestone because of the behavior of Gainesville's women, whom her son claimed returned fire on the Yankees. "Our enemies will find it difficult," she exuded, "to subdue a people with such women among them."[16]

Southern loss nonetheless remained the war's most probable outcome in her view, with the peace holding few promises of anything better. "Well, I believe the war is over," Ellen confided to her diary on April 23, 1865, "our suffering may have not yet begun however." A realist, Ellen had predicted this result ever since the halcyon days of secession, never accepting the last-minute hopes that "the Yankees" might be defeated. She felt that refusal to accept Lee's surrender could only lead to a guerrilla war, a great tragedy because women and children "can not bush whack." Ellen witnessed Union Brigadier General Edward M. McCook's entry into Tallahassee and sarcastically noted the warm reception some of the best families offered to their erstwhile enemy. As dearly as she loved the Union, Long secretly confessed that she found no pleasure in Confederate defeat. "The humility of the south, her utterly crushed condition," she recorded, "makes my heart ache."[17]

Long's premonition of what peace would entail grew to realization before her eyes, although in time she handled the changed circumstances well. "To be a conquered people is a new and novel experience," she observed, "and we have daily both amusing and mortifying incidents in our unadaptedness to the change." The behavior of former slaves who, once meek and subservient, now refused to doff their hats when meeting her on the streets exasperated her. Like many Southerners she began romanticizing the past and justifying slavery, opining that freed slaves "would be the sufferers, for there is not one in a hundred that knows how to make a living and many must starve and die for the need of the fostering care of their masters." But her problems soon extended beyond negative attitudes toward freedmen as she found herself financially strapped at a time when both her children needed funds for education and travel. Richard wanted to go to Texas, while Nonie was of age to begin attending boarding school. Given the circumstances, Ellen turned to the most reliable and accessible method for raising funds. She rented portions of her large home to boarders. A traditional option for widows, the practice of turning one's home into a hotel was common throughout the country and became the hallmark of Southern elite women who had large homes and pride but little in the way of ready cash. Ellen also mortgaged one hundred acres of land subject to a note that would not be redeemed until 1888.[18]

Moreover, Ellen's children repeatedly turned to her for support in the postwar years. Nonie became a popular belle, and many have presumed her to have been the inspiration for Maurice Thompson's 1881 novel *A Tallahassee Girl*. Richard, who returned home in 1870, failed at managing his mother's property.

He retreated to Texas to study law with his father. Despite negative portents for the future, he met on a visit to Tallahassee and soon married Cora Gamble, the daughter of a prominent family. The relocation to Texas made Cora unhappy, and she returned in 1874 to reside at The Grove. Richard, who shared his father's propensity for poor health, was reluctantly coached home to begin what turned out to be an undistinguished law practice.[19]

These complications aside, at a time of life when many women would have settled into a comfortable domestic existence as a doting grandmother, Ellen became even more active and involved in public affairs. This afforded her the opportunity for the third act of her life. She grasped it by adopting a constant theme of promoting her state and restoring the South to "its accustomed place in national life."[20]

One of Ellen's most visible roles during that third act involved serving as Florida's goodwill ambassador at national celebrations. She believed enthusiastic participation in these fairs and exhibits would heal some of the wounds of the war while simultaneously promoting the state and women's initiatives. Confident to the point of arrogance, Ellen often tried to browbeat her unreconstructed Floridian sisters into following her course. "Fifteen years bitter struggle has crushed nearly every speck of patriotism from the Southern breast," one of her correspondents informed her, indicating that assistance would not be forthcoming because it "will be hard to bury the past."[21]

Ellen—for all her private pain and wounded Southern honor—stood more than ready to pick up the shovel and rebuild. In 1874, using her connections with childhood friends in northern academies plus early successes with fund-raising, Ellen secured the position of corresponding secretary for the state of Florida for the Centennial Exposition. Despite its prestige, the position proved a thankless one. It required Ellen to be "a thorough lady" while dealing with vendors and collecting examples of state artistry for display. She struggled against a decided lack of public enthusiasm for the project. "Public-spirited" women often reacted to her entreaties with polite but infuriating refusals. The most frequent form of fund-raiser was the "Ladies Tea." Women repeatedly begged off of such events, however, citing other responsibilities such as church activities. Even women in Unionist areas—women who, in theory, should have been more excited by a Centennial Exposition—remained apathetic. The people of the southernmost city of Key West, then Florida's largest municipality, could not "arouse themselves to that height of ardor which is a necessary premise to satisfactory success," a local historian opined. Although many of Ellen's contacts agreed that something "must be done," few were willing to do it. Small successes did reward Long's efforts in the relatively prosperous and forward-looking cities of Jacksonville and St. Augustine, where residents perhaps recognized the Centennial Exhibition's importance for the promotion of internal development and tourism. Eventually, even Key West rallied and managed to raise $155 from a Centennial ball. After long months of work, Ellen attended the opening of the gala, where she "assumed command of the troops" in Florida's contributions to the women's pavilions.[22]

Leadership of this sort naturally brought Long to public attention. Florida's governors of the postwar period, for instance, came to know Ellen both by reputation and as a neighbor. They quickly recognized that, in her, they had found the ideal personification of the old Florida and the new. As historian Margaret Chapman commented, Ellen "seemed to be on good terms with them, whether native Southerners or carpetbaggers, whether Democrats or Republicans."[23]

Ellen accordingly continued to receive appointments to represent the state at national events. In 1884 she served as a delegate to the Cotton Centennial and Industrial Exposition at New Orleans, where she befriended suffrage activist Julia Ward Howe. She thrilled even more at her commission to represent Florida's interests at the Paris Universal Exposition in 1889. There, ironically, she complained that she missed her children. Yet, she wrangled a meeting with the Marquis de Lafayette's grandson, requesting that he donate family furnishings to decorate the Lafayette Room in the Hermitage. In 1892, Ellen also lent her abilities to the directorate charged with raising $100,000 for a Florida exhibit at the World's Columbian Exhibition, a major event scheduled for Chicago the following year. The seasoned campaigner undoubtedly found herself chagrined when the directorate failed to gain public support for the project. Ultimately, only a facsimile of St. Augustine's Spanish fortress Fort Marion and an unsightly hodgepodge of produce stood for Florida at the famous "White City."[24]

Long's friendship with Julia Ward Howe raises questions about Ellen's stance on suffrage and other feminist aspirations. Her actions demonstrated feminine competence in public affairs, and letters exchanged with Howe show that Howe urged Ellen to become involved in establishing women's exchanges in Florida. A number of suffrage tracts and circulars that predate the Howe friendship are preserved in the Call family papers, although Ellen never made a public comment on women's rights. She appears to have believed that she already had all the political rights she needed.[25]

Ellen never limited herself to traditional feminine hobbies and service activities. She shared many of her late father's scientific interests, including a desire to develop new agricultural products for Florida. Just as Call had endeavored to create "Florida hemp" out of bear grass, Ellen experimented with silkworms.

To further the project, she converted cottages and the basement of The Grove into greenhouses. Assisted by friends and her grandchild Reinette, the innovator refined enough silk for the construction of a large American flag. This she ceremoniously presented to Governor Edward A. Perry, a former Confederate general, at his 1885 inauguration. To encourage the fledging industry, Ellen wrote an illustrated monograph entitled *Silk Farming in Florida,* published in 1883. While the silk industry never blossomed in the Sunshine State, Ellen's expertise received wide acknowledgment.[26]

Long also shared with her father an intense interest in forestry. She served as secretary for the National Forestry Association in 1887, and in 1889 she pointed out the connection between periodic forest fires and the success of longleaf pine seedlings. While acknowledging that laws preventing burning were necessary for the protection of barns and fences, Ellen warned her readers that the "total abolition of forest fire in the South would mean the annihilation of her grand lumbering pineries." As a later botanist noted, her theory was received with "incredulity or indifference" because it seemed to refute common sense. She had however based her insights on careful observation of and a familiarity with pine habitats. Today, periodic burning is recognized as a necessary forestry practice.[27]

Ellen's creative interests ranged widely. Publishing stories, sketches, and monographs offered a way for respectable nineteenth-century women to earn money and a modest amount of acclaim. Long became one of a cadre of women writers who created a new image of Florida in the postwar years. The most famous of these celebrity authors was Harriet Beecher Stowe, who had taken up residence at Mandarin on the St. Johns River. Other female writers of travel books and Florida fiction included Abbie M. Brooks, Margaret Deland, and Sarah Stuart Robbins. Collectively, these women imaged Florida as a "female frontier," an exotic and seductive land free of the stiff propriety and entrenched gender roles of the Puritan North.[28]

Long joined this company in 1882 with her novel *Florida Breezes, or, Florida, New and Old,* a barely fictionalized account of life in Tallahassee before and during the Civil War. Like many other women, she adopted a male voice, assuming the persona of a character named Harry Barclay, a Bostonian advised to seek refuge in Florida due to poor health. The rambling novel presents more a slice of life than a story and reflects the social customs and mores of Florida's frontier society. Ellen claimed that "except the medium of narration, the characters are all veritable people and events—real matters of fact." But in striving for accuracy, she often demonstrated a lack of tact. In the words of historian Herbert J. Doherty, *Florida Breezes* dared "to treat the intrigues, animosities, and conflicts within this social circle as well as its glittering social activities." Too many Tallahasseans saw themselves in the characters, often in an unflattering light.[29]

Long stirred her Tallahassee friends in other ways as well. Also in 1882 she became embroiled in public controversy by refusing to accept a nomination from one-time Republican governor Harrison Reed to replace William G. Stewart, a black man, as Tallahassee's postmaster. Though the position would have benefited her financially, Ellen already had promised her support to Stewart. Her stance provoked ire among the white population. Ellen defended her decision with an argument that reflected her father's tutelage: "It is a conviction of mine that when a negro proves himself worthy morally and capable intellectually of the rewards of citizenship by the practice of honesty, & soberness and discretion, he is entitled to enter the list for competitive places of preferment," she expressed. "This doctrine was taught by the Republican pioneers in Florida." With remarkable boldness for such an intolerant era, Ellen responded to the charge that she had been seen in public with two blacks. "I must assure you," she informed her most prominent critic, "(painful as it must be for you to accept it) that I should not hesitate one moment to accompany two, three or a dozen negroes . . . to call on the President of the United States, the Queen of England, or even if you will the King of the Cannibal Isles." Her remarks demonstrated remarkable personal growth from a callow slave owner who once privately had dismissed the pain experienced by slave spouses separated by sale. And she made clear that she would risk her social status in Tallahassee to apply a longstanding principle in a new way.[30]

The combination of an indiscreet novel and progressive political opinions proved, perhaps inevitably, lethal to Ellen's financial ambitions. Local residents and their friends destroyed most of the copies of *Florida Breezes*. She made little money from the novel which, for all its faults, remains an important contribution to regional literature. Despite being a prolific and moderately talented writer, Ellen repeatedly met with rejection and frustration. Harrison Reed published a number of her articles during the mid-1870s in *The Semi-Tropical*, a magazine stuffed with Florida promotional literature and dedicated to "dispersing the gloom of the lost cause." Ellen's work met with warm praise but little remuneration, and *The Semi-Tropical* expired after a brief run. Her father's memoirs, which she had compiled and edited, were turned down for publication in 1870. Houghton, Mifflin and Company rejected her manuscript on the history of Florida in 1892. Various legislators solicited a Florida history for schoolchildren from her pen, but no solon or other sponsor came forward to finance it. Ellen had hoped for the kind of literary success that would have elevated her from genteel poverty, but both fame and fortune eluded her.[31]

Though many of her fellow Tallahasseans bristled at her journalistic efforts and her increasingly positive attitude toward African Americans, Ellen remained one of Florida's most famous women, a celebrity mostly because of her family connections and links to the past. In recognition of that fact, she received a nomination to serve as vice-regent for Florida on the Mount Vernon Ladies Association, a nod that she declined due to commitments to the Centennial celebration. In 1892 and as the guest of honor, she attended the Hermitage Ball, a glittering affair organized by railroad magnate Henry Flagler at his spectacular Hotel Ponce de Leon in St. Augustine. The event raised money for the restoration of Andrew Jackson's plantation, which Ellen had visited as a child.[32]

Ellen also continued her reign as a popular society hostess. The Grove frequently witnessed dances and weddings. Columns in the *Tallahassee Weekly Floridian* chronicled balls given "by the young gentlemen of Tallahassee, complimentary to visiting young ladies" and games of lawn tennis, in which the winner "was awarded the first prize, a beautiful silver nut bowl." A bride recalled her reception at The Grove, where the walls of the main hall were covered from floor to ceiling in roses. Such lavish hospitality reminded weary Southerners of bygone days, even as—in such novelties as women's sports—the region celebrated new technology, innovation, and freedom.[33]

Hospitality came at a steep price, as did the constant travel that Ellen enjoyed. Her son had proved to be an inefficient manager and generally a disappointment. His shortcomings left her with little choice but to begin whittling away at her inheritance to cover current expenses. In 1887 she sold the southern portion of her property to the Tallahassee Land and Improvement Company. Then as now, the proposed development of lovely, unspoiled acreage spawned public outrage, and many letters called for the land to be preserved as a public park. As usually has occurred in Florida, the developers prevailed. For Ellen, such sales could serve only as stopgap measures, however, especially given that the family was becoming ever more dependent on its matriarch. Nonie had married Edwin K. Hollinger, but his death in 1891 brought her home with two young sons. Richard soon moved his family to another house on the property. Dogged by debt, Ellen in 1899 proposed to sell The Grove to the state, writing Governor William D. Bloxham to suggest that the old home be purchased for the state's executive mansion. Her timing was unfortunate, as the governor was embroiled in controversy over relocation of the capital. Though Ellen continued her quest until just before her death, hoping that the state would preserve the historic property intact, the government proved unresponsive.[34]

Unwilling to sell the house outright, Ellen began the mournful task of stripping it of valuable artifacts, sacrificing heirlooms to keep the family from penury. Marble fireplaces, oil paintings, and even the inscribed limestone tablets taken from the garrison at St. Marks, a Spanish position near the Gulf of Mexico south of Tallahassee, were sold. In 1901, Ellen parted with letters written by Andrew Jackson to Richard Keith Call, selling them to an autograph collector. All the while she remained determined that, if The Grove could not be rescued for the state, it should go to Nonie. However, Ellen's granddaughter Reinette, Richard's daughter, coveted the property. In 1897, Reinette married Charles Hunt, a New York businessman. Six years later Hunt offered to help Ellen avoid a court-ordered foreclosure. Believing Hunt was assisting her in getting a necessary loan, Long executed a transaction that gave him title to The Grove. Hunt then passed the property to his wife. Ellen considered herself swindled, and the bitter business deal poisoned her final year of life, especially when it appeared that Richard had colluded with his daughter in the matter.[35]

Ellen Call Long died at The Grove on December 17, 1905, at the age of eighty. A final photograph, taken on her front porch, reveals a somewhat stout woman in a wheelchair, wrapped in a long dress and an afghan. The face shows signs of sorrow but also something of the flinty determination that defined her character.[36] The *Tallahassee Weekly True Democrat* described her funeral as one "of the most beautiful and impressive ceremonials that has ever occurred in Tallahassee." An impressive guard of honorary pallbearers—including former Governor Bloxham and incumbent Governor Napoleon Bonaparte Broward, plus the Florida comptroller and chief justice—escorted her to the grave. She rests beside her father in a small cemetery close to the house, in the center of all that she had loved.[37]

Notes

1. Herbert J. Doherty Jr., *Richard Keith Call: Southern Unionist* (Gainesville, 1961), 1–21. On Richard Keith Call, his family, and his descendants, see also LeRoy Collins, *Forerunners Courageous: Stories of Frontier Florida* (Tallahassee, 1971), 151–212.

2. Doherty, *Richard Keith Call*, 14–34.

3. Ibid., 41–43, 46, 66; Jane Aurell Menton, *The Grove: A Florida Home through Seven Generations* (Tallahassee, 1998), 17–18; Doherty, *Richard Keith Call*, 51. The deceased Call children were Mary Rachel, Laura Randall, Mary Jane, unnamed twin girls, and Richard. An important study of the dangers of childbirth and the high infant mor-

tality rates of the South is Sally McMillen's *Motherhood in the Old South: Pregnancy, Childbirth, and Infant Rearing* (Baton Rouge, 1990).

4. Frank L. Snyder, "Nancy Hynes DuVal: Florida's First Lady, 1822–1834," *Florida Historical Quarterly* 72 (July 1993): 27–33; Ellen Call Long, "Social Life among Slaveholders of Tallahassee in the Early Thirties," *Jacksonville Florida Times-Union and Citizen*, March 6, 1898. On Tallahassee's most famous duel, see James M. Denham, "The Read-Alston Duel and Politics in Territorial Florida," *Florida Historical Quarterly* 68 (April 1990): 427–47. Regarding elite society of early Leon and Jefferson counties see Anya Jabour, "'The Privations & Hardships of a New Country': Southern Women and Southern Hospitality on the Florida Frontier," *Florida Historical Quarterly* 75 (Winter 1997): 259–75. On antebellum Florida violence, see James M. Denham, *A Rogue's Paradise: Crime and Punishment in Antebellum Florida, 1821–1861* (Tuscaloosa, 1997).

5. Doherty, *Richard Keith Call*, 93; Ellen Call to Mary Kirkman Call, July 18 and August 24, 1835, Call and Brevard Family Papers, Florida State Archives, Tallahassee (hereafter, Call Papers). See also Catherine Clinton, *The Plantation Mistress: Woman's World in the Old South* (New York: Pantheon Books, 1982), 123–38; Anna Jabour, *Scarlett's Sisters: Young Women in the Old South* (Chapel Hill, 2007).

6. Richard Keith Call to Barbara Kirkman, February 28, 1836, Call Papers; Menton, *Grove*, 23–28.

7. Bertram H. Groene, *Ante-Bellum Tallahassee* (Tallahassee, 1971), 143–55.

8. Doherty, *Richard Keith Call*, 135–38; Menton, *Grove*, 26–27, 29–31.

9. Menton, *Grove*, 30–31; Groene, *Ante-Bellum Tallahassee*, 134; Ellen Call Long to Richard Call Long, August 16, 1853, Call Papers. The roles and expectations of nineteenth-century middle- and upper-class women are memorably explored in Barbara Welter's "The Cult of True Womanhood: 1820–1860," *American Quarterly* 17 (Summer 1966): 151–74.

10. Richard Keith Call to Ellen Call Long, August 23, 1853, and H. Douglas to Ellen Call Long, August 31, 1853, Call Papers; Menton, *Grove*, 31.

11. Menton, *Grove*, 31–32.

12. H. Douglas to Ellen Call Long, April 18, 1857, Call Papers; Menton, *Grove*, 32–33; Doherty, *Richard Keith Call*, 151; Rootsweb ftp.rootsweb.com/pub/usgenweb/tx/smith/bio/txgray/longma.txt; http://freepages.genealogy.rootsweb.ancestry.com/~tory/long/wmf.html.

13. Menton, *Grove*, 33. For a discussion of the repercussions of divorce in the antebellum South, see Clinton, *Plantation Mistress*, 80–85.

14. Ellen Call Long, *Florida Breezes, or, Florida, New and Old* (Jacksonville, 1882; reprint with introduction and index by Margaret Louise Chapman, Gainesville, 1962), 282, 306–8; E. R. Lea to Ellen Call Long, January 26, 1861, Call Papers.

15. Doherty, *Richard Keith Call*, 155–61; Menton, *Grove*, 33–36.

16. Doherty, *Richard Keith Call*, 138; Ellen Call Long diary, September 11, 1864, and May 10, 1865, M. Crawford to Ellen Call Long, March 7, 1864, George Crawford to Ellen Call Long, March 8, 1864, all in Call Papers; William Stockton to Julia Stockton,

July 30, 1861, in Herman Ulmer Jr., ed., "The Correspondence of Will and Ju Stockton, 1845–1869," transcribed by Herman Ulmer, State Library of Florida, Tallahassee. For a more extensive exploration of Ellen Call Long's wartime work and writings, see Tracy J. Revels, *Grander in Her Daughters: Florida's Women during the Civil War* (Columbia, S.C., 2004).

17. Ellen Call Long diary, April 16, 21, 23, and May 10, 21, 1865, Call Papers.

18. Long, *Florida Breezes*, 381; Ellen Call Long diary, May 23, June 27, 1865, Mortgage Note, Ellen Call Long to Alfred P. Nourse and Hiram W. Brooks, September 13, 1869, Call Papers; Menton, *Grove*, 38–39.

19. Menton, *Grove*, 38–39.

20. Margaret Louise Chapman in Long, *Florida Breezes*, xiii.

21. Ibid.; Ida Wood to Ellen Call Long, April 8, 1872, Call Papers.

22. Alice C. Ewing to Ellen Call Long, March 1, 1874, E. F. Hovey to Ellen Call Long, November 9, 1874, A. Martin to Ellen Call Long, November 19, 1874, J. F. Bernand to Ellen Call Long, November 23, 1874, M. L. Girardeau to Ellen Call Long, December 20, 1874, Alexander Fullerton to T. Gardiner Littell, March 13, 1875, Rebecca White to Ellen Call Long, April 14, 1875, Joseph B. Browne to Ellen Call Long, December 1, 1874, Emma Westcott to Ellen Call Long, February 3, 1876, Anne Randall to Ellen Call Long, February 21, 1876, T. Gardiner Littell to Ellen Call Long, May 18, 1876, Call Papers; Chapman in Long, *Florida Breezes*, xiv.

23. Chapman in Long, *Florida Breezes*, xiv.

24. Menton, *Grove*, 38–39; William D. Bloxham to Ellen Call Long, November 11, 1884, Edward D. Perry to Julia Ward Howe, February 9, 1885, J. L. Gaskins to William B. Franklin, c. 1889, Ellen Call Long to T. T. Wright, November 20, 1889, Ellen Call Long to Edmond de Lafayette, November 21, 1889, Call Papers; Stephen Kerber, "Florida and the World's Columbian Exposition of 1893," *Florida Historical Quarterly* 66 (July 1987): 31, 33, 41; Julia Ward Howe, *Reminiscences, 1819–1899* (Boston, 1899; reprint ed., New York, 1969), 394–99.

25. Julia Ward Howe to Ellen Call Long, January 3 and August 27, 1885, May 24, 1889, Citizens Suffrage Circulars, 1873, 1874, Call Papers.

26. Richard Keith Call to George Bancroft, November 10, 1845, Call Papers; Doherty, *Richard Keith Call*, 137; Menton, *Grove*, 39; Chapman in *Florida Breezes*, xi–xvii.

27. William W. Corcoran to Ellen Call Long, March 1, 1887, T. L. Lamont to Ellen Call Long, November 14, 1887, V. C. Haven to Ellen Call Long, June 20, 1886, Call Papers; E. F. Andrews, "Agency of Fire in Propagation of Longleaf Pines," *Botanical Gazette* 64 (December 1917): 497; Harold H. Biswell, *Prescribed Burning in California Wildlands Vegetation Management* (Berkeley, Calif., 1989), 82.

28. Susan A. Eacker, "Gender in Paradise: Harriet Beecher Stowe and Postbellum Prose on Florida," *Journal of Southern History* 64 (August 1998): 497–503.

29. Ibid., 498–99; Chapman in Long, *Florida Breezes*, v; Herbert J. Doherty Jr.,

"Writing in Florida History on the Period 1821–1860," *Florida Historical Quarterly* 37 (October 1958): 161.

30. A. Hopkins to Ellen Call Long, April 18, 1882, Ellen Call Long to A. Hopkins, April 21, 1882, Call Papers; *Jacksonville Florida Daily Times*, February 11, 1882; Chapman in Long, *Florida Breezes*, xxi. On William G. Stewart, see Larry Eugene Rivers and Canter Brown Jr., *Workers in the Vineyard of the Lord: The Beginnings of the AME Church in Florida, 1865–1895* (Gainesville, 2001); Canter Brown Jr., *Florida's Black Public Officials, 1867–1924* (Tuscaloosa, 1998), 4, 22, 27, 35, 46.

31. Columbus Drew to Ellen Call Long, March 11, 1870, Houghton, Mifflin and Company to Ellen Call Long, August 12, 1892, Call Papers; Richard Nelson Current, *Those Terrible Carpetbaggers: A Reinterpretation* (New York, 1988), 390; Chapman in Long, *Florida Breezes*, xxi.

32. Menton, *Grove*, 38; Thomas Graham, "Flagler's Magnificent Hotel Ponce de Leon" *Florida Historical Quarterly* 54 (July 1975): 9.

33. *Tallahassee Weekly Floridian*, March 10 and August 4, 1887.

34. Menton, *Grove*, 41–43; William D. Bloxham to Ellen Call Long, March 30, 1899, Call Papers.

35. Walter R. Benjamin to Ellen Call Long, July 28 and October 10, 1900, Henry M. Flagler to Ellen Call Long, March 20, 1902, Call Papers; Menton, *Grove*, 44; Chapman in Long, *Florida Breezes*, xv–xvi.

36. Menton, *Grove*, 44.

37. *Tallahassee Weekly True Democrat*, December 22, 1905.

CHAPTER 3

Victoria Seward Varn Brandon Sherrill
1843–1926
Community Builder

JAMES M. DENHAM

FLORIDA EMERGED DURING THE TWENTIETH CENTURY as one of the nation's most dynamic states, with a 2010 population exceeding eighteen million despite a geographical base that ranks only twenty-second in size. Key to its development, as has been true in many parts of the United States, was the establishment and growth of urban areas. By the early 1900s Florida had begun to claim precedence as the most urbanized of southern states, a mark that post–World War II growth solidified and enhanced. Historians recently have begun to explore the origins of that urban orientation, whether in northeast Florida, the central peninsular region, or South Florida. Interestingly, these studies have pointed in part to the influence of African American leaders and businessmen

Figure 5. Victoria Brandon, c. 1880s. (Courtesy of Lisa Rodriguez.)

in spurring the growth of towns and cities. Less recognized, unfortunately, is the fact that, in many cases, women provided the spark that launched community development. Victoria Seward Varn Brandon Sherrill's life and legacies offer one such story and illustrate similar women's contributions elsewhere in the Sunshine State and the South.[1]

At the outset it should be noted that, whatever her contributions to community building, Victoria Sherrill walked paths already blazed by other Florida women while seeing, during her adulthood, women around her accomplishing similar goals. Ohio native Julia Tuttle, whose mythic orange blossoms lured railroad baron Henry Flagler to isolated Miami after the Great Freeze of 1895 and who launched one of the nation's great cities in the process, obviously merits recognition. She was not alone. Ivy Stranahan participated in all facets of her community's development to the point that she is justly known as "the Mother of Fort Lauderdale." Similarly, Frances Macfarlane aided the development of West Tampa, now incorporated into the city of Tampa but in the 1890s an independent municipality. As for a town of more modest proportions, Cuthbert Rockner's extraordinary efforts to organize and promote the state's one-time cattle industry center at Fort Meade remain impressive. Because—as historian Doris Weatherford noted in her study of Macfarlane—a woman's accomplishments often have been "credited solely to her husband," more such stories likely have been obscured through the passage of time, stories that should and, I hope, will be known.[2]

Victoria Sherrill preceded Tuttle, Stranahan, and Macfarlane in pioneering the way for her city, and the legacy of her efforts stands today as the city of Brandon. Neither as famous nor as large as some Florida municipalities, Brandon nonetheless is a suburban center of significance. Tracing its official history back nearly 120 years, it lies one dozen miles or so east of Tampa on U.S. Highway 60. In the year 2000 its limits, strictly construed, contained just fewer than 78,000 persons, but the vicinity claimed as many as 110,000 in eighty-nine square miles. Primarily residential rather than agricultural or industrial, Brandon boasted inhabitants with substantially higher incomes than the state median, but its Central Florida location meant that their homes averaged less-costly price tags: $173,400 versus $189,500 for the state as a whole.[3]

Brandon's present suburban sprawl contrasts starkly with the region's nature when Victoria Seward, as she was then known, first set eyes on it as a young girl. In 1854 the Tampa Bay area had yet to endure its last Indian war. Its sandy soils, not conducive for the most part to cotton, yielded instead to grass and other plant life nourished by some of the world's richest deposits of phosphate. The land, as a result, sustained enormous herds of cattle. Families used to living in cotton-belt lands found themselves faced with challenges and experiences far different than they had seen in their former Georgia, South Carolina, Alabama, and Mississippi homes. For more than a generation this land would remain isolated, save from the ravages of weather, war, and worry. Profits from post–Civil War cattle trading and the beginnings of a citrus industry afforded prosperity for many families, but before the advent of railroads in 1884, they enjoyed little opportunity to spend the Spanish gold doubloons that cattle sales brought to them. The railroads, though, eventually opened up the land for settlement and development. Their arrival also offered the key for Victoria Seward Brandon to secure her own future through community development.[4]

While the region that would encompass Brandon remained an isolated frontier, women faced significantly greater challenges than did men. As some scholars have noted, frontier women were distinguished from their more urban counterparts by the degree to which circumstances beyond their control forced them to play a greater role in raising children and civilizing their communities. A kind of wanderlust proliferated among males on the frontier, particularly in Central Florida. Whether in hunting cattle, searching for more fertile lands, or just looking for new opportunities, males often left their families for extended periods of time. Thus, women often were compelled to live and raise their families by their own resources. This situation, of course, could break down women. Yet, it also could happen that women on the frontier might adjust more easily to (and even flourish in the aftermath of) widowhood. As will be seen, Victoria profited from the example of women who were not broken down but instead thrived when relying upon their own resources.[5]

Victoria's story commenced not on the Florida frontier, however, but in Mississippi. Born January 31, 1843, she was the daughter of Zachariah and Sarah Seward. The large family, of which Victoria Martha Seward constituted the third child and third daughter, lived in or near Carrollton, Carroll County, Mississippi. North Carolina–born Zachariah farmed a modest acreage, but his passion lay in service to the church. He and Sarah had affiliated with the Carrollton Baptist Church in the mid-1830s, and one of the family's few slaves, Jim Seward, had followed them in membership by 1839. So, too, had a number of Zachariah's siblings and other relations. He preached when he could and otherwise aided the cause. Surviving congregation records do not indicate that Victoria joined in membership before the family distanced itself from the congregation in late 1851 and early 1852. The cause for this split remains unknown, although future events suggest that Zachariah chose to found his own congregation.[6]

Shortly after the Sewards departed the Carrollton Baptist Church, their stay in Mississippi came to an end. In the winter of 1854 members of the extended clan loaded their possessions in wagons and commenced an overland journey to the heart of the distant Florida peninsula. The journey required months, and upon their arrival at their destination—the abandoned military post known as Fort Fraser, located forty miles east of Tampa and twenty-five miles east of the future Brandon—they found themselves pioneers of a land just opened to settlement courtesy of the U.S. Army and Mississippian Jefferson Davis, then serving as secretary of war. In fact, even the roads the family traveled in the region mostly had resulted from the work of army engineers during or subsequent to the Second Seminole War of 1835–1842. Their new home sat directly on such a road, one that linked Fort Brooke at Tampa with a crossing of the Peace River to the east and then ran to the Kissimmee River. Because lands in the vicinity of Fort Fraser were arguably fit for cotton culture, the Sewards appear originally to have been intent, naively as it turned out, on reproducing their Mississippi lives in frontier Florida. In any event, they established themselves on the shores of a body of water still known as Seward Lake in what today is called the Lakeland Highlands area of Polk County. This spot lies south of present-day Lakeland and just southwest of the small community of Highlands City.[7]

Although Victoria's memories of childhood and adolescence at Fort Fraser have not come to light, those of several of her contemporaries allow us insight into her experiences. Isolation loomed large. "We had nothing then," Lydia Hendry Blount recalled. "It was twenty-five miles to a church from my home." She added

> Some who claim to have been pioneers and who in a measure were pioneers will tell you of the good times of those days, country dances and frolics and picnics. But we were before even that day. We ate, slept, and kept house while the men folk hunted cattle. Later when more settlers came in, we visited about. And when we went visiting, we spent the night. Every one's house was open to his neighbor and even to the stranger.[8]

Day-to-day living in this environment centered for girls around the hard work compelled by frontier farm life, even when slaves bore the most laborious of the chores. The family, for instance, grew corn, dried it, and ground it to make grits or meal for bread. Its members also roasted field corn until it was dark brown, ground the kernels, and used the result for coffee. Baked sweet potatoes constituted a staple of their diet. Lydia Hendry Blount provided additional detail: "Girls learned housework in those days," she recollected. "I remember one time my sister shot three wild turkeys, but as a usual thing we didn't hunt or fish or ride in the woods much." Blount continued, "There was always a lot to do [to] keep the house up. We swept and cooked, wove cloth, and did the thousand and one things to be done in a home where nothing came from the store."[9]

For the Sewards, when it came to religion such isolation quickly proved unacceptable. So, in their log cabin on September 3, 1854, father Zachariah and mother Sarah created their own church. As a local historian put it, "Zachariah Seward . . . gathered his family around him in his own home and organized the 'Peas Creek Baptist Church.'" Seven of the eight members of what is credited as the first regularly organized church in present-day Polk County were white members of the Seward family or one of their relations. The eighth member was the slave Jim Seward or, as church minutes listed him, "Colored Man Jim." The same minutes reflect that, at a reception of members on January 11, 1855, "Martha Victory Seward" joined the church along with her newfound friend Frances S. Varn. Both girls received baptism on the following day. Victoria was almost twelve. Frances was a few months away from fourteen. Within a short time the two girls' friendship would grow much stronger, a bond encouraged by the 1855 marriage of Victoria's sister Ellen to Frances's brother William B. Varn.[10]

Victoria and Frances may have met at what passed for school at Fort Fraser. A classroom situated a dozen miles north at Socrum was described as "a crude log cabin," and it requires little imagination to picture a similar structure at Fort Fraser. Another friend of Victoria's left recollections of his experiences there during annual school terms of perhaps three months. "I advanced rapidly in my choice branches, which were setting near the large girls and whispering to them during school hours, and walking to and from school with them morning and evening," William H. Pearce recorded. "So at the close of the school I was nearly graduated, and thought I was almost old and big enough to marry, but, by the way, I had learned to spell baker, and read and write a little, and this, mixed in with a few other things, such as falling in love and being kicked out, etc., was doing pretty well in the way of a South Florida education."[11]

Even this modest education soon found itself disrupted. The Third Seminole War arose from government policies designed to open the Tampa Bay and Peace River frontier areas to settlers such as the Sewards. It flared near Christmastime 1855, and its violence reached quickly toward Fort Brooke and Fort Fraser, although it did not touch either place directly. In spring 1856, though, a supply train journeying from Brooke to Fraser came under attack close to the future site of Brandon. Casualties resulted, but not so many as might have been expected because Jim Seward, his services hired out as a teamster, grabbed a

Figure 6. Polk County's Holly Bowen Hill and her children at their double-pen log cabin, a frontier homestead typical of what Victoria Brandon would have lived in during her Florida youth. (Courtesy of Canter Brown Jr.)

rifle and commenced an effective defense. His heroic efforts cost him the loss of an eye due to a gunshot. Nonplussed, Seward mounted a horse, charged through the attackers, and carried the terrible news to Fort Fraser. One account suggested that, literally, he yelled "Charge!" as he sped through the raiding party.[12]

By the time of Jim Seward's bravery, panic had already been gripping the frontier for months. "On Christmas Day, 1855, a courier was dispatched from Tampa, informing us, and all frontier people, that an Indian War was upon us and to care for ourselves the best we could," one area resident related. "This was a veritable clap of thunder from a clear sky," he continued. "The people were excited and quickly congregated for self-protection." The Sewards, the Varns, and other nearby families "congregated" within the ruins of Fort Fraser, where the men and older boys organized militia companies in the absence of regular army troops. Zachariah Seward joined Captain Francis M. Durrance's company, a unit headquartered at the fort.[13]

The following two and one-half years of conflict changed Victoria's life. Writing of the scene fifteen miles south of Fort Fraser at Fort Meade, Oregon Hendry Blount explained the situation as far as area children were concerned.

"Life at the fort was lots of fun," she recorded. "[I] had plenty of companions to play with and everything was exciting and new." Part of that excitement for a young woman came from interacting with young militiamen. One in particular drew Victoria's eye. Days before the war commenced, Josiah Varn—a brother of Frances's—reached age twenty. At the time, though, Victoria was a mere girl approaching thirteen. Nonetheless, interest grew between the two young people. As the war wound down, the attachment matured. Ultimately, as the war came to a close they married. The ceremony took place on July 29, 1858, when Victoria was fifteen.[14]

Although the Sewards and the Varns possessed considerable assets, including slaves, life for the young couple would have proven difficult. "The citrus, phosphate, and tourist industries were far in the future," Polk County historian Louise K. Frisbie commented. "The homesteaders were, perforce, almost entirely self-sufficient." She added, "They were small-scale farmers, skilled in hunting, fishing, and defending their homes and families from the dangers of wild animals and a few still-hostile Indians." For their part, the Varns relocated following the war to a site two miles south of Polk County's present seat of Bartow and established a farm on Six Mile Creek. Victoria and Josiah either joined his relations there or remained only a few miles to the north near Fort Fraser and Seward Lake. By 1860 the couple could boast 30 acres of improved lands, 130 acres of unimproved lands, a farm worth $1,000, $1,412 dollars of livestock, and other assets. Among those assets was a son, William, born in October 1859. A daughter, Annie, would follow in 1862, the year that Victoria turned nineteen.[15]

The year of Annie's birth brought even more profound changes to Victoria's life, ones that resulted from the Civil War. Florida seceded from the Union in January 1861, and by March 10, 1862, Josiah and his fellow militia company members had been mustered into Company E, 7th Florida Infantry. His unit, the "South Florida Bulldogs," soon marched off to faraway battlefields. The two young people never saw each other again. Josiah was declared missing and believed killed on November 25, 1863, following the Battle of Missionary Ridge outside Chattanooga, Tennessee.[16]

Now, Victoria was thrown upon her own resources. She bore full responsibility for preserving and working the family farm while caring for her children, and circumstances required her to do so during an extremely difficult period in the region's history. Her father may have provided some assistance, particularly by giving Victoria a young slave woman named Cecily. As Victoria later related to her granddaughter, she took pride when she, Cecily, and a slave couple planted a vegetable garden without help from her father, husband, or brothers.

"You know my grandmother was raised somewhat of a lady," the granddaughter reflected with only a degree of exaggeration. "She never had to do this kind of thing before." Meanwhile, Victoria's father dedicated a good bit of his time to preaching obedience and Christian charity to area bondsmen and bondswomen on behalf of the Peas Creek Baptist Church. As times grew ever more stressful, the congregation swelled and Victoria joined in the religious fervor reflected in that growth. By summer 1864, according to church minutes, "there was a great revival influence realized." Cecily had joined the body by then, after war-weary church members had collected the considerable sum of $447.70 "to send the gospel to soldiers of the army."[17]

For the Sewards, Varns, and other families of the Peas Creek Baptist Church—arguably the largest concentration of slaveholders in the region—the peace that ended the Civil War brought economic ruin as slaves obtained their freedom and isolation forestalled attempts to recover farm prosperity through crops less durable than cotton and corn. For Victoria the ruin extended to a more personal level. Already a widow, she soon lost her father as well. A Tampa newspaper noted simply, "DIED.—at his residence in Polk County, Fla., 18th of January [1868], the Rev. Zachariah G. Seward, aged fifty-one years, after a protracted and painful illness." Meanwhile, Victoria's brother, Zachariah Jr., had relocated to Tampa where he attempted to found a grocery. When that enterprise collapsed, he moved northward to Brooksville in Hernando County. Now, even the hope of her brother's support waned with distance and difficulties of travel.[18]

Faced with challenges greater than her immediate ability to deal with them, Victoria opted for a solution chosen by many of her peers. She remarried to a much older man who could offer her security and protection. John William Brandon had been born in Madison County, Alabama, on October 26, 1809. On January 20, 1857, he, his wife Martha Brown Carson, numerous children, and slaves had relocated from Mississippi to the Tampa Bay vicinity. They homesteaded twelve miles east of Tampa on the site that, decades later, would become Brandon. When Martha passed away in 1867, John decided to move on to better economic prospects than eastern Hillsborough County could afford. His new home lay at Fort Meade, a key crossing point of the Peace River then emerging as the residential and trading center of Central and South Florida's burgeoning cattle industry. John required a wife, however, to tend to his remaining minor children and to other needs. So, on September 17, 1868, he wed Victoria Seward Varn. Perhaps love played a role in the union. Economic realities certainly did.[19]

At the time of their marriage John Brandon had nearly reached his fifty-ninth birthday, while Victoria's age was only twenty-five. Still, vigor remained to John and at least five children were born to the couple. John LeRoy Brandon came on September 20, 1869, with Mark Zachariah following on November 3, 1871. Nearly two years later, on September 11, 1873, Lovic Pierce's birth added another son. His sister, Sadie Ellen, took her place on July 15, 1875, with Albert Jordan concluding the births on October 8, 1878. Given these facts, it may easily be seen that the responsibilities of motherhood did not weigh lightly on Victoria Brandon.[20]

As the family grew, the Brandons found modest prosperity at Fort Meade. By 1870 cattle owners had established a lucrative trade with Cuba, permitting several merchants to thrive in the village. It also had allowed John Brandon not only to grow corn and sugarcane for sale through those stores, but also to open his own grist mill and general store. At the same time, longtime cares of isolation eased for Victoria. Doubtlessly, this process was aided by the arrival in the community of Victoria's sister, Mary, following her marriage to Frederick N. Varn. Friend Frances S. Varn, who had wed George Washington Hendry, also lived nearby a good bit of the time.[21]

Community delights created happier times for Victoria; conditions also allowed her to witness firsthand the process of community building and the role that a woman could play in it. Cuthbert Wayne Lanier Hooker with her husband, John I. Hooker, had purchased Fort Meade's abandoned army buildings in 1854. They transformed the officers' quarters into a comfortable home and worked to make the locale attractive to others. John I. Hooker then died during the Civil War. Though her husband's cattle holdings had been immense, money was scarce and Cuthbert struggled to raise her family as best she could. The emergence of the postwar cattle industry, though, improved her prospects and those of Fort Meade. Remarried to businessman and cattleman Julius C. Rockner, Cuthbert set about with him to create a town. First, they engaged County Surveyor William B. Varn, Victoria's brother-in-law, to plat the land Cuthbert had inherited from her first husband. Varn had finished the task by January 1874, and the Rockners commenced selling lots. By the summer of 1876 talk of incorporation circulated, a step that would have made Fort Meade the first incorporated municipality in interior South Florida.[22]

At that point the couple's plans hit a snag. In 1871 a U.S. Navy representative had quietly posted nearby lands as belonging to a naval live oak reservation. John Brandon had attempted to resolve questions about the landownership as related to a tract that he had purchased from Cuthbert Rockner's father. At that time Brandon expressed to state authorities the degree of confusion that existed and the likelihood of "serious lawsuits" as the "land had changed hands several times since [it was] entered." Still, the matter remained in limbo while numerous parties discovered that they could not obtain clear title to their property. Since the matter was not settled until late 1881, the Rockner plans for incorporation sat unfulfilled while the community grew. Julius C. Rockner, meanwhile, was gunned down in an ambush near Victoria's home by an area cattleman, leaving Cuthbert again a widow. Nonetheless, she continued to press her claims until she succeeded. When the town of Fort Meade ultimately was incorporated in January 1885, the community based itself upon the survey of her land that the Rockners had commissioned in 1873. In March 1885, Cuthbert supplemented her original scheme with "Mrs. C. M. Rockners Addition to the Town of Ft. Meade," a development that added nine more city blocks to the community plan.[23]

Their inability to obtain clear title to their Fort Meade lands seems to have prompted the Brandons' relocation to John's original homestead in the vicinity of the future Brandon, a move that occurred in 1874. In addition, John's son James had remained in Hillsborough County, where his real estate acquisitions and large cattle herds made him one of the area's most significant figures. Another factor may have weighed in the decision. Local historian Paul Dinnis has speculated that one motive for the Brandons' return to the "New Hope" vicinity, as it was then called, involved their determination to establish a church. Whatever the motivations for the move, in 1878 the Brandons donated five acres for the founding of the New Hope Church, forerunner of the First Methodist Church of Brandon. This act suggests that Victoria had embraced the Methodist faith of her husband, although as time would tell, she had not abandoned her Baptist roots entirely.[24]

As the Brandons settled into their New Hope home in the late 1870s and early 1880s, the small communities of Limona, Bloomingdale, Mango, Valrico, and Seffner sprang up near the Brandon homestead. Many settlers trekked to the area from worn-out Deep South cotton farms, but perhaps the most significant influx involved well-to-do midwesterners along with others seeking a warm climate for health reasons, particularly for respiratory ailments. The Moseleys, who came to the new community of Limona from Illinois, offer an example. On June 28, 1882, a few days after she arrived, Julia Moseley informed relatives in Illinois that she had visited the New Hope Church "out in the wood" for a "fish fry." The church was a "pleasant place in spite of its uncouthfulness," she wrote condescendingly. "Nearly three hundred people were present," she continued. "It was the first entertainment of singing and recitations that a large portion of them had ever even heard or taken part in before. They came in all directions, in ox carts, in mule teams, on horseback and on foot." Moseley added, "Had one no sense of the fitness of things and not a vestige of reverence they might have remained only out of curiosity and made merry out of what they saw and heard, for it was a 'motley crew.' But their attempts at adornment were pitiful and their ignorance sad, and when one stops to realize that these wild shreds of humanity have had little better advantage than the birds and compare it with the enlightened North, your deepest sympathies are stirred."[25]

Comments such as Moseley's typified many northern women's observations of Florida's common folk, whom they sometimes disparagingly referred to as "Crackers." While Moseley's passage contains no malice toward or even contempt for her new neighbors, she felt sympathy for the children at the gathering, and this emotion compelled her to step forward to offer up a spiritual message of "of life and effort as I never dreamed of before." Such a verbal demonstration from a Yankee woman-newcomer could, at the very least, have raised the eyebrows of longtime residents. If Victoria Brandon was in the crowd, which she likely was, she probably resented Moseley's demonstration intensely.[26]

Of these new communities, the future appeared brightest for Limona. Located only a mile or two west of the Brandon homestead, it reflected the entrepreneurial compulsions of Judge J. G. Knapp of Madison, Wisconsin. Having arrived in 1876, Knapp had evidenced energy not usually associated with inhabitants of the semitropical Tampa Bay area. "Within months of his arrival, Judge Knapp began writing to midwestern newspapers about the potential to be found at Limona," explained a community historian. In a typical article published in the *Wisconsin State Journal*, he extolled Limona's quiet habitat, rich lands for homesteads, low cost for land, pine trees, citrus cultivation, bananas as a possible farm crop, healthy climate, moderate temperatures and protection from freezes, and more. "Within a year," the community history added, "he had convinced E. E. Pratt of the Elgin Watch Company to settle and develop a retirement community for Elgin's employees." The Limona Park Association resulted, bringing a level of success to Knapp's endeavors in 1878 in the form of a post office and, by 1880, a public school. "The future is bright," Knapp assured his readers the following year. By 1886 he felt sufficiently encouraged to author a book that he called *Only One Florida, Considered from Every Point of View*.[27]

As Knapp had pointed out, by the late 1870s and early 1880s the economic potential of eastern Hillsborough County was luring families of settlers; so, too, was the region's attractive climate. Investors and their agents flocked to the area to scout out likely acreage for agricultural enterprises and winter homes for affluent northerners. Still, the lack of transportation links retarded growth. An 1881 Limona report stated the matter clearly: "Where is the railroad to be located?" it asked. "Want of railroad transportation has kept this region away from the markets of the world," Knapp explained in *Only One Florida*. "Where bold pioneers settled and, in part, developed the region, capitalists have followed, a single railroad has pierced it, and its advantages are being seen and felt, and other roads are pointing towards it." Knapp's dilemma was that the "single railroad" that pierced Hillsborough County in 1883 and 1884 had bypassed Limona. Henry Plant's South Florida Railroad, which finally tied Tampa to the outside world, had opted for a route several miles to the north. In doing so, it worked to the advantage of an "Instant Florida Town" that took the name Plant City, sponsored by future Governor Henry Mitchell and others.[28]

The possibilities of community development such as that occurring at Limona did not escape John and Victoria Brandon's attention. They planted a citrus grove, and John established a blacksmith shop and gristmill that could attract the interest of settlers. As mentioned, in 1878 they helped to launch the New Hope Church. They also donated land for a school. John mirrored as well Judge Knapp's practice of mailing local news to area newspapers, using the community name of Brandon in these communiqués. "Real estate in this neighborhood is changing hands," he boasted in 1883. "Thirteen out of eighteen settlers in this immediate vicinity are new-comers within the last eighteen months." Brandon continued, "All the new-comers in this vicinity are worthy of being called neighbors. They are industrious, good citizens, and we will take some more of the same sort."[29]

When John wrote those words, he almost had reached age seventy-four and, to the detriment of his and his wife's plans, he had few years left to live. The end came for him on May 16, 1886, shortly after a disastrous freeze. He succumbed not to old age but to a hunting accident. As he died intestate, Hillsborough County Judge Charles E. Harrison appointed John's son James and Victoria as executors of his estate. By all accounts James and Victoria worked well together, although principal responsibilities for John's sizeable holdings fell to Victoria because of James's frequent absences in connection with his cattle dealings. They eventually settled the estate in 1890.[30]

Between John Brandon's death and the settlement of his estate, events and dynamics changed the circumstances that Victoria faced and opened the door to possibilities that she might not have imagined in May 1886. First, Judge Knapp died suddenly in July 1888. "In his death," the *Tampa Tribune* reported, "Florida loses a friend and worker whose place can never be filled, and particularly will he be missed in Hillsborough County and Tampa." At that time Victoria may have hoped that she could "fill" his place in community development. At Fort Meade Cuthbert Rockner's example had illustrated to her a woman's potential in the man's world of town building. Rockner, coincidentally, had managed to finalize her initiatives the year prior to John's death. Moreover, northern women living in the Tampa Bay area were beginning to take increasingly more active roles in their communities. These were sophisticated "club women" who engaged in temperance, suffrage, and a whole host of other progressive causes. On a personal level, Victoria likely looked upon many of these women with ambivalence. Indeed, their manner, behavior, and clothing at times would have revolted the conservative southerner. (One of her neighbors, New Hampshire émigré Clementine Averill, actually wore bloomers!) But this ambivalence likely could have nurtured in Victoria a determination not to be outdone in securing for her community and family the benefits of growth that she saw as inevitable. Additionally, she seems to have become determined not to allow newcomers to marginalize the original settlers. Even though she lived on the outer fringes of Tampa's growing urban community, Victoria understood the possibilities for dynamic leadership.[31]

One other factor influenced events to come. Despite the Freeze of 1886 and the resultant economic calamity, railroad construction in Central Florida continued. Large strikes of phosphate during the late 1880s facilitated this movement. Brandon benefited in 1890 when the Florida Central and Peninsula Railroad extended its tracks toward Tampa along a line that ran through the Brandon property, linking eastern Hillsborough and Polk counties directly with Tampa. The railroad built depots at Valrico (to the east of Brandon) and Limona (to the west). Residents at nearby Seffner already had erected a depot in 1884 and platted their town one year later. Expectant settlers in Brandon's neighborhood gravitated closer to the railroad tracks, worrying all the while that prosperity might whistle right by them.[32]

Victoria Brandon—with stepson James and son Mark—took the initiative to found a town. "Victoria had a surveyor, a Mr. [C. S.] Noble, lay out about forty acres of land and streets for the town and deeded the property to the county," Tampa Mayor Donald B. McKay recalled. Streets were named Noble, Victoria, and Sadie after family members. A public announcement soon followed. On May 22, 1890, the *Tampa Tribune* remarked that the "new city of Brandon is located ten miles east of Tampa on the F.C. & P.R.R." The item continued, "The site is on a beautiful, level tract of high pine land, on the south side of the railroad track, while on the north side of the track is situated the beautiful orange grove of Mrs. Victoria Brandon, which nestling between the city on the beautiful circling lake and deep hammock, on the north-east, is indeed a beautiful picture."[33]

The *Tribune* item provided further detail, lauding Brandon's potential as a commuter suburb. The journal noted that although the depot was not yet constructed, a side-track and platforms permitted receipt of freight. It added that large quantities of vegetables were being shipped every week. A number of stores and mills, including one owned by a relative of Victoria's first husband, were relocating to the town. "It is a delightful locality," the article noted, "and if proper [railroad] rates can be secured it will eventually become a popular locality for residences of parties doing business in Tampa in as much as with the present schedule the trains go into the city early in the morning and go out at night, affording an opportunity for persons to attend to a day's work and return at night." But, more than anything else, the town was a "lovely and healthy place to reside and is surrounded by a very fertile country which is dotted with large bearing orange groves and quite a number of young groves, all of which are in a most prosperous condition." The *Tribune* concluded, "We predict for the young city a bright future."[34]

With the town established Victoria undertook the task of providing leadership for its maintenance and growth. As a first step, she became its first postmistress. With her encouragement townspeople soon constructed a train depot. As one old-time resident later explained, "When the railroad [came] through there, they built a depot at Valrico and one at Limona, and the people at Brandon wanted one there, and the railroad didn't think they needed one there, so the community went to work and built their own depot and they accepted it."[35]

Settlement quickened. As it did, Victoria's large house grew in importance as a focal point for her community. As her grandson Mark Brandon remembered, it was a large house built of virgin yellow pine and containing a formal dining room, a very large kitchen, two large bedrooms downstairs, and three large bedrooms upstairs. Fireplaces served both downstairs and upstairs rooms. An attic large enough to become an apartment offered additional space. So ample was the structure that Victoria easily provided living accommodations for Brandon's public schoolteachers.[36]

The Brandon house, as it turned out, served an even larger purpose in Victoria's promotion of Brandon. Competition from nearby communities made it difficult for Brandon's possibilities to be heard above the din. Some of those communities, including Limona, enjoyed the benefit of longstanding formal organizations aimed at community development. Victoria, in contrast, was compelled to rely mostly upon herself, her relations, and her ingenuity. Faced with the challenge, her genius appeared most evidently. Recognizing that competing communities oriented themselves toward a northern or midwestern clientele by representing their lifestyle as an extension and improvement of old-home circumstances, she chose to emphasize Brandon's southern charms. While she could not employ professionals to assist her, she did benefit from the fact that a leading area newspaper, the *Tampa Journal*, employed women journalists routinely and in positions of significance. She commenced inviting them to her home along with tour groups riding out from Tampa on Sunday rail excursions. The depot, the vistas, her home, and New Hope Church then played their roles in selling the community.[37]

Perhaps an article that appeared in the *Tampa Journal* on October 2, 1890, best reflected Victoria's approach. Entitled "A Day at Brandon," it offered complimentary details of one tour group's experience visiting the new community on a rainy and gloomy Sunday. Soon after arrival at Brandon's depot, the reporter detailed, the party was escorted directly "to the Brandon home . . . where Mrs. Victoria Brandon welcomed us so hospitably that all the clouds disappeared and everything assumed a sunny brightness." It continued, "What a breakfast we had—fragrant coffee with thick sweet cream, plump young chicken fried to perfection, with rich cream gravy; fine Eggs, bread, and crisp, flakey biscuits; sweet, golden fresh country butter; oatmeal and cream; and all the other good things that only a first class Florida host can conjure to perfection." The report added,

> Too full for utterance, the party, in time, adjourned to the front piazza where rocking and other comfortable chairs abound, and, to their shame be it said, instead of going into ecstasies over the glorious scene about them . . . where every leaf, twig, and flower, every blade of grass and every spider web that festooned the fence of timber and brick piles, and even the timber and bricks themselves, shivered with the weight of sunlighted gems that sparkled and dazzled in the fresh morning air, shimmering, glinting and counting the time to the chirping of the birds and whisperings of the wind until we grew dizzy with new found absolute content—those horribly healthy people absolutely ignored the beauty about them and actually chewed cane, ate on and talked the most delightful noise until church time.[38]

The party thereupon adjourned "to New Hope Church in Limona," where the Reverend LeRoy Brandon conducted services for them. The article described happenings thereafter:

> Those of the party who were not afraid of the rain returned with Mrs. Victoria Brandon in her special conveyance to a site on the piazza of her house [in order to look at] the piles of brick and lumber scattered about, eloquent of immediate improvement, the pretty new depot and the residences—old and

new that, since the advent of the F.C. & P. road, have changed the beautiful broad acres of the old homestead to a thriving community that promises to be a most important suburban station, that will not only buy of and sell to the Tampa market, but will ship its products up and down the road.[39]

As the article suggested, Brandon's rail link enhanced newcomers' possibilities for establishing citrus groves, an innovation that the Brandons had helped to pioneer in that vicinity and an economic mainstay that Victoria maintained in the 1890s. In 1894, for example, Charles Linsley—a recent emigrant from the North—described to a cousin the thirty-five-acre citrus grove he had just purchased. In one seven-acre grove, Linsley estimated, about 250 out of 350 trees would bear fruit, with "perhaps 250 boxes of the coming crop as far as I can tell." Linsley proudly enclosed a map that he had drawn illustrating his own acreage adjacent to the Brandon groves and house. Telegraphing the new ease of transportation, he clearly depicted the Brandon railroad station on the map's northern perimeter.[40]

Brandon managed to survive its infancy and eventually to consume Limona and surrounding areas, although Victoria's dreams for its development as a commuter town for Tampa took generations to realize. Rural trumped suburban. Mostly, area people farmed, tended cattle, and raised citrus. By 1910 land costs had risen to about $15 per acre, a substantial price although much lower than in some other developing Florida locales. One account provided a glimpse of farm life there: "The typical farm consisted of a few acres of oranges which served families as a cash crop, a small plot of sugar cane which was turned into syrup and a portion for candy, and a vegetable garden for home use." The account added, "Chickens and hogs were raised, and the family usually kept at least one cow for milk. Other cash crops included peaches and grapes."[41]

Brandon's sluggish growth may have resulted from a refocusing of Victoria's energies. In the late 1890s she met Charles Clark Sherrill, formerly a prosperous farmer and civic leader in Berrien County, Michigan, who had taken on responsibilities as a Baptist "mission worker." The couple wed on October 4, 1900. Little record of their marriage has survived, although Charles and Victoria appear to have lived for a time at his Buchanan, Michigan, home. Census records hint that the Sherrills may have separated by 1910. Upon his death on June 20, 1917, it was said that he died of senility. Victoria meanwhile had returned to Brandon, apparently needing resources and assistance. "My mother is an invalid and has been for several years," LeRoy Brandon recorded at the time, "and at her age will not in all probability live very long." Her plight produced for her maintenance a Confederate pension from the state of Florida in the amount of $180 per year, a subsidy paid in recognition of her first husband, Josiah Varn's, Civil War service. Victoria Seward Varn Brandon Sherrill died at Brandon on December 4, 1926, mourned widely in her community and among her friends and relations.[42]

By the time of Victoria Sherrill's death, the Florida frontier had long passed from the environs of the Tampa Bay area. The small community that owed its existence to her insights and determination had grown to roughly one thousand persons. Hillsborough County then contained more than two hundred thousand. Thereafter, Brandon grew slowly but steadily. By the last quarter of the twentieth century it indeed had become the bedroom community for Tampa that Victoria had envisioned. As a 1998 study indicated, "Neighborhoods sprung up north and south of State Road 60, and, in the process, Brandon swallowed up such communities as Bloomingdale, Dover, Durant, Lithia, Mango, Seffner, and Valrico." It added, "The greater Brandon area included 106,000 residents, supporting over 150 churches, and more than 5,000 businesses. With such growth, people began to grumble about traffic along State Road 60 during the 1970s, and the grumbling (for good reason) continues to this day." Victoria's dreams had been realized beyond the limits of her imagination, and another of Florida's larger urban centers had found itself dealing with problems of the modern world.[43]

Notes

I thank Shelby Bender, Paul Dinnis, Elizabeth Dunham, Rodney Kite-Powell, Julia Moseley, Travis Puterbaugh, Lisa Rodriguez, Joe Spann, and Doris Weatherford for their assistance in writing this essay.

1. On the origins of urban areas in Florida, see, for example, Richard A. Martin, *The City Makers* (Jacksonville, 1972); James B. Crooks, *Jacksonville after the Fire, 1901–1919: A New South City* (Gainesville, 1991); Canter Brown Jr., *Tampa before the Civil War* (Tampa, 1999); idem, *Tampa in Civil War and Reconstruction* (Tampa, 2000); Harry A. Kersey Jr., *The Stranahans of Fort Lauderdale: A Pioneer Family of New River* (Gainesville, 2003); Raymond A. Mohl, ed., *Searching for the Sunbelt: Historical Perspectives on a Region* (Knoxville, Tenn., 1990). On African American leadership and community development, see Canter Brown Jr., *Florida's Black Public Officials, 1867–1924* (Tuscaloosa, 1998), 43–54; Patricia L. Kenney, "LaVilla, Florida, 1866–1887: Reconstruction Dreams and the Formation of a Black Community," in *The African American Heritage of Florida*, ed. David L. Colburn and Jane L. Landers (Gainesville, 1995); Marvin Dunn, *Black Miami in the Twentieth Century* (Gainesville, 1997); Canter Brown Jr. and Barbara Gray Brown, *Family Records of the African American Pioneers of Tampa and Hillsborough County* (Tampa, 2002).

2. On Julia Tuttle, see E. Lynne Wright, *More Than Petticoats: Remarkable Florida Women* (Guilford, Conn., 2001), 20–30; Edward Akin, *Flagler: Rockefeller Partner and Florida Baron* (Kent, Ohio, 1988), 160–63; idem, "The Cleveland Connection: Revelations from the John D. Rockefeller–Julia D. Tuttle Correspondence," *Tequesta: The Journal of the Historical Association of Southern Florida* 42 (1982): 57–61; Sidney Walter Martin, *Florida's Flagler* (Athens, Ga., 1949), 152–53; David Leon Chandler, *The Astonishing Life and Times of the Visionary Robber Baron Who Founded Florida* (New York, 1986), 158–72, 178–79. For Ivy Stranahan, see Harry A. Kersey, *The Stranahans of Fort Lauderdale: A Pioneer Family of New River* (Gainesville, 2003); and for Frances Macfarlane, see Doris Weatherford, *Real Women of Tampa and Hillsborough County from Prehistory to the Millennium* (Tampa, 2004), 101. On Cuthbert Rockner, see Canter Brown Jr., *Fort Meade, 1849–1900* (Tuscaloosa, 1997), 21, 42, 57, 88–89. For information regarding involvement by activist women in areas related to community building, development, and improvement, see Linda D. Vance, *May Mann Jennings: Florida's Genteel Activist* (Gainesville, 1985); Leslie Kemp Poole, "The Women of the Early Florida Audubon Society: Agents of History in the Fight to Save State Birds," *Florida Historical Quarterly* 85 (Winter 2007): 297–323; Nancy A. Hewett, *Southern Discomfort: Women's Activism in Tampa, Florida, 1880–1920s* (Chicago, 2001); idem, "Varieties of Volunteerism: Class, Ethnicity, and Women's Activism in Tampa," in *Women, Politics, and Change*, ed. Louise Tilley and Patricia Gurin (New York, 1990); Weatherford, *Real Women*; John T. Foster Jr. and Sarah Whitmer Foster, *Beechers, Stowes, and Yankee Strangers: The Transformation of Florida* (Gainesville, 1999); idem, "Chloe Merrick Reed: Freedom's First Lady," *Florida Historical Quarterly* 71 (January 1993): 279–99; Patricia Dillon, "Clubwomen and Civic Activism: Willie Lowry and Tampa's Club Movement," *Florida Historical Quarterly* 77 (Spring 1999): 429–44; Sally Vickers, "Ruth Bryan Owen: Florida's First Congresswoman and Lifetime Activist," *Florida Historical Quarterly* 77 (Spring 1999): 445–74; Maxine D. Jones, "'Without Compromise or Fear': Florida African American Female Activists," *Florida Historical Quarterly* 77 (Spring 1999): 475–502; Raymond Arsenault, Jack E. Davis, and Kari Frederickson, *Making Waves: Female Activists in Twentieth-Century Florida* (Gainesville, 2003).

3. See "Brandon, Florida" at the City-Data.com website www.city-data.com/city/Brandon-Florida.html and the Brajeshwar website www.brajeshwar.com/info/brandon_florida_realestate.html.

4. On the frontier period in Tampa Bay–area history, see Donald B. McKay, *Pioneer Florida*, 3 vols. (Tampa, 1959); James W. Covington, *The Story of Southwestern Florida*, 2 vols. (New York, 1957); and Canter Brown Jr., *Florida's Peace River Frontier* (Orlando, 1991). On Tampa Bay–area frontier women and families, see Canter Brown Jr., *Women on the Tampa Bay Frontier* (Tampa, 1997); idem, *Children on the Tampa Bay Frontier* (Tampa, 1996); Weatherford, *Real Women*; Janet Snyder Matthews, *Edge of Wilderness: A Settlement History of Manatee River and Sarasota Bay, 1528–1885* (Tulsa, Okla., 1983); James M. Denham, "Cracker Women and Their Families in Nineteenth-Cen-

tury Florida," in *Florida's Heritage of Diversity: Essays in Honor of Samuel Proctor*, ed. Mark I. Greenberg, William Warren Rogers, and Canter Brown Jr. (Tallahassee, 1997), 15–28.

5. Brown, *Women on the Tampa Bay Frontier*, 46–47.

6. Morace C. Duncan, "Brandon Family Cemetery," at ftp.rootsweb.com/pub/usgenweb/fl/hillsborough/cemetery/bran-fam.txt; 1850 U.S. Decennial Census, Carroll County, Mississippi (population schedule); "Carrollton Baptist Church Records, Carroll County, Mississippi" at www.rootsweb.com/~mscarrol/cemeteries/carrolton bapt.htm.

7. *Fort Meade Leader*, December 20, 1917; Brown, *Florida's Peace River Frontier*, 41–102; idem, *In the Midst of All That Makes Life Worth Living* (Tallahassee, 2001), 17–61; Lillian R. Carpenter, "A History of the First Methodist Church, Bartow, Florida, and Its Methodist Background" (typescript, 1944; available at Polk County Historical and Genealogical Library, Bartow, Florida; hereafter, PCHGL).

8. Wallace Stevens, "Saved by Florida Cowboys," in *Atlanta Journal Magazine*, May 31, 1931, quoted in Brown, *Women on the Tampa Bay Frontier*, 22.

9. Stevens, "Saved by Florida Cowboys."

10. Carpenter, "History," 32; "Minutes of the Baptist Church of Christ at Peas Creek in Hillsborough County, South Florida, Constituted September third 1854," 5–7 (available as photostatic copy in Minute Book 1 at PCHGL); Virginia W. Westergard and Kyle S. Van Landingham, *Parker & Blount in Florida* (Okeechobee, 1983), 345–46; *Bartow Courier-Informant*, November 23, 1904.

11. Canter Brown Jr., *Teachers and Schools on the Tampa Bay Frontier* (Tampa, 1997), 19; *Bartow Informant*, December 9, 1882.

12. James W. Covington, *The Billy Bowlegs War, 1855–1858: The Final Stand of the Seminoles against the Whites* (Chuluota, Fla., 1982), 1–45; Brown, *In the Midst*, 65.

13. Brown, *In the Midst*, 66–67; Francis M. Durrance to James E. Broome, January 13, 1856, and Jesse Carter to Francis M. Durrance, February 28, 1856, Francis M. Durrance Papers (transcripts at PCHGL).

14. Brown, *Fort Meade*, 31–32; David W. Hartman and David J. Coles, comps., *Biographical Rosters of Florida's Confederate and Union Soldiers, 1861–1865*, 6 vols. (Wilmington, N.C., 1995), 2:732.

15. Louise K. Frisbie, *Yesterday's Polk County* (Miami, 1976), 16; McKay, *Pioneer Florida*, 3:89; 1860 U.S. Decennial Census, Hillsborough County, Florida (population and agricultural schedules).

16. John E. Johns, *Florida During the Civil War* (Gainesville, 1963), 13–21; Brown, *In the Midst*, 84–98; Hartman and Coles, *Biographical Rosters*, 2:732; Victoria M. Sherrill Widow's Pension Claim (Josiah Varn), #A01983, Florida Confederate Pension Applications, Florida State Archives, Tallahassee; Lloyd Harris, "The South Florida Bulldogs," *Polk County Historical Quarterly* 20 (December 1993): 7–8.

17. 1863 Polk County, Florida, tax rolls (available on microfilm at Florida State Archives, Tallahassee); "Minutes of the Baptist Church of Christ at Peas Creek," 38–39,

43, 48; *Macon* (Ga.) *Christian Index*, April 29, 1864. Family tradition also notes that Victoria benefited immeasurably from the loyal service of a slave couple. They helped her in "plowing the fields, planting sweet potatoes, sugar cane and corn. Together they rounded up the range cows and milked them, considering themselves fortunate if the scrawny beasts yielded as much as a full pint of milk ... they managed to butcher hogs, smoke the hams and harvest sweet potatoes and corn." In exchange for their loyal service, the account continues, Victoria deeded the couple forty acres of land. Victoria related this account to her granddaughter Louise Martin Caldwell. James Scott Hanna, *The Brandon Family of Southwest Florida* (Leander, Tex., 1968), 65–66; personal interview with Louis Martin Caldwell by Paul A. Dinnis, October 13, 1979 (notes in possession of Paul A. Dinnis).

18. Brown, *Florida's Peace River Frontier*, 215–22; *Tampa Florida Peninsular*, May 11, 1867, February 8, 1868, and January 30, 1869.

19. Clara Brandon Kruger, "Brandon History" (typescript in Hillsborough County Historical Commission Collection, Tampa Bay History Center, Tampa); McKay, *Pioneer Florida*, 3:741–42; Covington, *Story of Southwestern Florida*, 1:523; Brown, *Fort Meade*, 52–61. For information on Hillsborough County during this period, see Brown, *Tampa before the Civil War*; idem, *Tampa in Civil War and Reconstruction*; John Solomon Otto, "Florida's Cattle Ranching Frontier, Hillsborough County (1860)," *Florida Historical Quarterly* 63 (July 1984): 71–83; idem, "Hillsborough County (1850): A Community in the South Florida Flatwoods," *Florida Historical Quarterly* 62 (October 1983): 180–93.

20. "Bible Record: Brandon" (transcript in Hillsborough County Historical Commission Collection).

21. Brown, *Fort Meade*, 53, 57–58, 67, 70–71, 78, 160; McKay, *Pioneer Florida*, 3:89, 741; Polk County, Florida, Marriage Records, Book A, 102; *Fort Meade Leader*, January 2, 1919.

22. Brown, *Fort Meade*, 62–66; Polk County, Florida, Deed Records, Book B, 274–79, E, 179.

23. John Brandon to David S. Walker, February 10, 1872, Internal Improvement Trust Fund General Correspondence, Record Group 593, Series 914, Box 14, Florida State Archives; Brown, *Fort Meade*, 66–97; idem, *Florida's Peace River Frontier*, 258–61; O. H. Wright, "The U.S. Navy's 'Land Grab' in Polk County," *Polk County Historical Quarterly* 24 (June 1997): 4–5; *Fort Meade Leader*, December 14, 1984; Polk County, Florida, Deed Records, Book E, 17, J, 434. On March 8, 1894, the *Tampa Tribune* noted Cuthbert Lanier Hooker Rockner's passing. It commented that Mrs. Rockner lived a "Life Pure and Lovely in All Social and Christian Characteristics."

24. Kruger, "Brandon History"; "Bible Record: Brandon"; personal interview with Paul E. Dinnis by the author, August 2, 2007 (notes in possession of the author). See also Paul E. Dinnis, *The Early Days of New Hope Church: A Presentation and Data and Observations Commemorating the Centennial of Methodist-Oriented Worship in the Community of Brandon, Florida* (Brandon, Fla., 1976), 1–11, C-3, C-6. Also for

comments on what Dinnis calls the "Alafia–Peas Creek Axis" and the development of Methodism in the Polk-Hillsborough frontier, see Dinnis, *Flickering Flames along the Alafia, 1850–1900* (Brandon, Fla., n.d.), 1–13, 18–24.

25. Julia Winifred Moseley and Betty Powers Crislip, *"Come to My Sunland": Letters of Julia Daniels Moseley from the Florida Frontier, 1882–1886* (Gainesville, 1998), 39–40, 227.

26. Moseley and Crislip, *"Come to My Sunland,"* 39–40. Similar first impressions of Crackers were expressed by Ellen and Corinna Brown, sisters who came to Florida from Portsmouth, New Hampshire, in 1835. See James M. Denham and Keith Huneycutt, eds., *Echoes from a Distant Frontier: The Brown Sisters' Correspondence from Antebellum Florida* (Columbia, S.C., 2004). For more on the observations of northern women vis-à-vis Crackers, see James M. Denham and Canter Brown Jr., *Cracker Times and Pioneer Lives: The Florida Reminiscences of George Gillett Keen and Sarah Pamela Williams* (Columbia, S.C., 2000); James M. Denham, "The Florida Cracker before the Civil War as Seen through Travelers' Accounts," *Florida Historical Quarterly* 72 (April 1994): 453–68; idem, "Cracker Women and Their Families."

27. *Limona: Gornto Lake, Lake Chapman* (Tampa, 1998), 2; *Wisconsin State Journal* quoted in *Tampa Sunland Tribune*, August 4, 1877; *Tampa Sunland Tribune*, April 23 and July 10, 1881; J. G. Knapp, *Only One Florida, Considered from Every Point of View* (Jacksonville, Fla., 1886).

28. *Tampa Sunland Tribune*, July 30, 1881; Knapp, *Only One Florida*, 8; Quintilla Geer Bruton and David E. Bailey Jr., *Plant City: Its Origins and History* (Winston-Salem, N.C., 1984), 71–77.

29. Lisa W. Rodriguez, "Brandon, Florida, 1890–1990: A Photographic Essay," *Tampa Bay History* 12 (Fall–Winter 1990): 31; *Brandon (New Hope): Buckhorn Creek* (Tampa, 1998), 2; *Bartow Informant*, April 28, 1883. See also Victoria Parsons, "Centennial Spirit," *Tampa Bay Life* (August 1990), 44; Hanna, *Brandon Family*; Kruger, "Brandon History"; McKay, *Pioneer Florida*, 3:738–40; Ed Hirshberg, "Brandon: The Pioneers," *Good Life Guide* (April–May 1984): 14–16; Mark Gale, "Gravestones Record History of Brandon," *Tampa Times*, January 31, 1980; Leland Hawes, "Brandon Grew Up as a Neighborly Place," *Tampa Tribune*, September 9, 1990; Michelle Jones, "A Two-Rutted Road, Cattle Drives, and Alligator Caves," *Tampa Tribune* (East Hillsborough Section), April 12, 1982; Ann Ahern, "He Lent His Name to Brandon," *Tampa Times*, October 7, 1974; Jennifer L. Stevenson, "Brandon Poised to Celebrate Its Beginning, Its Pioneers," *St. Petersburg Times*, February 11, 1990.

30. John Brandon probate file, #414, Hillsborough County Probate Records, Hillsborough County Courthouse, Tampa.

31. *Tampa Tribune*, July 5, 1888; Weatherford, *Real Women*, 75–139; Moseley and Crislip, *"Come to My Sunland,"* 30, 222–23.

32. Ernest L. Robinson, *History of Hillsborough County, Florida: Narrative and Biographical* (St. Augustine, 1928), 72–79.

33. McKay, *Pioneer Florida*, 3:742; *Tampa Tribune*, May 22, 1890, quoted in *Brandon (New Hope): Buckhorn Creek*, 2–3.

34. *Tampa Tribune*, May 22, 1890.

35. Dinnis, *Early Days of New Hope Church*, F-13.

36. Cynthia C. Watkins, "Mark Brandon Reminiscences about Early Days," *Brandon News*, October 21, 1982.

37. Weatherford, *Real Women*, 119–21.

38. *Tampa Journal*, October 2, 1890.

39. Ibid.

40. Charles Linsley to "Cousin Ed," February 19, 1894, in vertical file "Brandon," Tampa Bay History Center.

41. *Brandon News*, October 21, 1982; William Sherouse, *Born in the Heart: A History of the First Baptist Church* (Orlando, 1986), vii–x; McKay, *Pioneer Florida*, 3:741–42; Lisa W. Rodriguez, "The History of Brandon," *Community Connections* (August 2, 1990); Parsons, "Centennial Spirit," 44; *Brandon (New Hope): Buckhorn Creek*, 4.

42. Brandon, *Brandon Family*, 17; Edward B. Cowles, comp., *Berrien County Directory and History, Containing Historical and Descriptive Sketches of the Villages and Townships within the County, and the Names and Occupations of Persons Residing Therein* (Buchanan, Mich., 1871), 14, 378; 1880 and 1910 U.S. Decennial Censuses, Berrien County, Michigan (population schedules); 1920 U.S. Decennial Census, Hillsborough County, Florida (population schedule); Charles Clark Sherrill death certificate and LeRoy Brandon to Ernest Amos, August 1, 1917, in Victoria M. Sherrill Widow's Pension Claim.

43. *Brandon (New Hope): Buckhorn Creek*, 6.

CHAPTER 4

Mary E. C. Day Smith
1851–1903

Northern-Born Mission Worker
in the Post–Civil War South

DARIA WILLIS

> *The Negro's inspiration for poetry, music, and the fine arts, proves conclusively that there dwells within him a higher and better nature, which needs only to be developed to its fullest capacity to convince the world beyond the possibility of a successful contradiction that his standard of good morals is as elevated as that of mankind in general.*
> —Mary E. C. Day Smith

MARY E. C. DAY SMITH expressed these optimistic thoughts in 1902, based upon the hard experience of forty years as a northern-born mission worker in the post–Civil War South. While the thoughts may not surprise, that she was African American might. As the historian Joe M. Richardson has pointed out,

Figure 7. Mary E. C. Day Smith, c. 1902. (From Culp, *Twentieth Century Negro Literature*.)

the very fact that African American women joined in the education of freedmen and freedwomen flies in the face of common perception. Whether viewed as "courageous heroes or hypocrites who taught blacks with ulterior motives," these educators consistently have been remembered as white. Fortunately, the veil that has hidden the achievements of African American women has begun to lift. And, as the life and careers of Mary E. C. Day Smith will illustrate, contributions such as hers proved meaningful, long lasting, and remarkably complex. The historical record once again proves far richer than memory.[1]

Although Mary Smith would influence principally Florida's freedmen's community, her story began more than one thousand miles distant in New York City. Born about 1851 as the daughter of Anna and Peter H. Day, Mary was raised as a free black child during the antebellum period and the Civil War. At the time of her birth, New York's African American community had evolved to the point that a place of prominence seemed a natural condition amongst the city's black elite. While it cannot be conclusively determined whether Mary shared all of the comforts of being a member of the black elite, her parents' influence strongly affected her, especially Anna's. "From early childhood," Mary's friend Daniel Wallace Culp recorded, "she showed strong power of mind and inherited from her mother that force and determination of purpose which prefigure success in whatever is undertaken."[2]

The teachings of prominent male educators in the city benefited Mary too. She was described as being "well cared for" and, considering the stature of her teacher, it is no surprise that her education came highly regarded. Professor Charles L. Reason, her mentor, had been born on July 12, 1818, in New York City to Haitian refugees. He had attended the Mulberry School for Colored Children (also known as the African Free School, No. 2) alongside others who would leave their mark, including George Allen, Isaiah Degrasse, J. McCune Smith, Samuel R. Ward, Henry Highland Garnet, and George T. Downing. In the words of Carla L. Peterson, "From humble origins, these young graduates of the African Free School rose to form the core of New York's antebellum black elite." Professor Reason, who began his career as an adjunct instructor of mathematics at the New York Central College in Courtland County, eventually made his mark as a mathematician, poet, and educator. By 1850 he assisted as head of the Saturday colored normal schools but soon emerged as a principal of a black normal school. He persisted in that vocation until 1892.[3]

One dynamic concerning the evolution of New York's schools would touch significantly upon the lives of Reason and of Mary Day. As the decades progressed, the city's schools for black children slowly began to be absorbed by the Public School Society and the Board of Education. As a result, as it has been reported, "the black elite continued its efforts to improve colored schools." Black parents as well as teachers often voiced their complaints about the inadequacies of their children's school buildings. Charles B. Ray, a prominent educator and president of the Society for the Promotion of Education Among Colored Children, commented upon the dilapidated facilities to which the children were subjected. "From a comparison of the school-houses with the splendid, almost palatial edifices, with manifold comforts, conveniences and elegancies which make up the school-houses for white children in the city of New York," he wrote, "it is evident that the colored children are painfully neglected and positively degraded." Ray added, "Pent up in filthy neighborhoods, in old and dilapidated buildings, they are held down to low associations and gloomy surroundings."[4]

Significantly, many black teachers and parents, including the Days, refused to allow poor public support to degrade the quality of educational opportunity offered to students. In spite of the physical disparities of the "colored" schools, for example, Charles B. Ray concluded that "the reading and spelling [are] equal to that of any schools in the city." Mary Day's personal experience provides a case in point. Presumably, she attended one of the colored ward grammar schools in the city. Nonetheless, Mary managed to excel. She demonstrated her zeal and aptitude, as well as the quality of her instruction, by repeatedly winning "one of the Ridgeway prizes for good scholarship, which were given annually to successful contestants." These prizes were distributed by Charles Ray and Philip White (also a prominent member of the Society for the Promotion of Education Among Colored Children). They normally were given to the most outstanding scholars in the areas of writing, spelling, geography, grammar, arithmetic, and astronomy. Most prizes consisted of two silver medals and books paid for by Charles Ridgeway, a black barber.[5]

Lessons learned in such a school environment, as well as at home and in church, profoundly touched Mary at an early age. At ten the astute child, having already qualified as an excellent Bible student, was elected a teacher in her local Sunday school. "At this age she was impressed with the idea that it was her duty to go to the South to instruct her people who were just emerging from bondage," Culp recalled. Thusly, Mary committed herself to teacher training. After completion of "the common branches" in the colored ward schools, she accordingly entered Professor Reason's supplementary class for normal school training. While studying under his auspices, she learned "a high sense of the purpose of teaching and a conviction of the virtue of discipline." As a pupil in the supplementary course she took the same examinations as her white cohorts in the city. She often attended classes with up to thirty students—mostly female—and she flourished as a scholar. Mary completed the supplementary course by 1866 and graduated with Professor Reason's blessings and well wishes for her future path.[6]

A bishop of the African Methodist Episcopal (AME) Church and the man who was about to regularize the church's organization in Florida subsequently provided the means for Mary Day to realize her professional dreams. In 1866, prior to her graduation, the venerable Bishop Daniel A. Payne was laboring to bring his beloved church back to the South, with early emphasis upon South Carolina and adjacent areas. At Savannah, Georgia, in May 1866, he charged the Reverend Charles H. Pearce with responsibility for outreach to the sparsely populated, frontier Florida. Pearce set his sights on missionary efforts in the state's former plantation belt, a region known as Middle Florida that centered upon the state's capital at Tallahassee. Here, in the counties of Jackson, Gadsden, Leon, Jefferson, and Madison lived the bulk of Florida's African American population.[7]

The town and region to which Pearce headed had barely emerged from Civil War conditions; nonetheless, institutions already had begun to sprout within the African American community. Particularly, the Reverend Robert Meacham had laid the foundations for a black church in Tallahassee. Born in 1835 in nearby Gadsden County, Meacham with the cooperation of the Reverend James Page, a Baptist minister, had established what was known as Bethel AME Church on February 20, 1866. Its sanctuary lay at the corner of Virginia and Duval streets. According to one source, most of Meacham's congregation "were once members of [what would become] St. James CME who left the church because it was controlled by the white Methodist church."[8]

Schooling remained close to Meacham's heart and to those of his congregation members. Sabbath schools especially formed an integral part of church operations, while private or public schools also might meet in a sanctuary. By March 1866 a Tallahassee newspaper carried a report of rapid movement to establish such schools throughout North Florida. "We have Sabbath schools," it noted, "in Tallahassee, Monticello, Madison, Houston, and Lake City." Expectations in those first days of freedom, though, ran closer to the modest than to the grandiose. "We don't expect to make doctors, lawyers, politicians, or statesmen," a local man recorded, "but *we can learn them to read the word of God and we will do it.*"[9]

At the same time the call for teachers, whether for Sabbath schools or regular schools, was sounded at Tallahassee and, for that matter, throughout the South. Of particular interest, the calls for teachers often were directed primarily at southern teachers. As Joe Richardson pointed out, "White teachers from the North were better trained than their Negro cohorts, but they were more disliked by Florida whites." In practice, northern white teachers often met with severe hostility from southern whites, and many lasted in the region only a short while. Blacks, for their part, sometimes declined instruction by white northerners, feeling that many northern white teachers did not connect well with the ex-slaves.[10]

White southerners in the circumstances preferred to educate the freedmen by their own standards. Many southern whites realized well that the typical teacher laboring during the Reconstruction period was as much missionary as teacher. The goal was to ensure that the missionary, in a general sense, was teaching from the correct gospel. Former slaveholders and planters accordingly were urged to contribute to educational efforts. "Let every planter build a house for a church, sabbath and day school," Florida's Assistant Superintendent for Public Schools for Freedmen E. B. Duncan declared. "There's missionary work without going from home." Qualified teachers also were summoned, so long as their qualifications met certain criteria. "And when we can get a teacher to teach a day school," Duncan continued, "[we want] a nice southern young lady in your family or young gentleman, if not your son or daughter, to engage heartily in this work." Duncan concluded his summons by appealing to the religious hearts of white southerners. "If we carry it out," he insisted, "the world would admire and heaven bless us—in a word let us go at it like putting out fire."[11]

Whatever the intentions of E. B. Duncan and others, Charles H. Pearce sought to establish a different state of affairs as he departed for Florida, one that included well-trained, highly intelligent African American teachers such as Mary Day, educated in the North and dedicated to ministering to the freedmen of the South. In fact, Pearce already had enlisted Mary's support in 1866, even though she had attained only the tender age of fifteen. With her and two other women from New York City, he traveled to the Sunshine State in October. At Tallahassee Pearce displaced Meacham as pastor of Bethel AME Church and placed Mary in charge of its Sabbath school operations. She achieved early success. Within two months following her arrival, "Bishop" Pearce and "preceptress" Mary could proudly display the talents of the youngsters in their school. On December 25 and 26, 1866, the Sabbath school held an exhibition and concert in the city. According to a published advertisement, "The exercises will consist of Dialogues, Recitations and Music—Vocal and Instrumental." The ladies of the church sponsored the event, with a twenty-five-cent admission charge. In a larger sense, the exhibition offered a highly visible and easily understood image of what could be accomplished by the AME Church.[12]

Despite her age Mary Day took to her vocation in Florida effectively and with a maturity that evidenced considerable leadership skills. Meanwhile AME ranks in the state—and with them, her challenges—swelled. "Two years ago we [had] only 125 members and two local preachers in this State," Pearce reported in June 1867, "now we number about five thousand two hundred and forty-two." As the church grew, Tallahassee's Bethel AME offered its new Florida Conference a headquarters. From there Pearce and Day exercised influence in much of the settled portion of the state, she with respect to Sabbath school operations. The "bishop" evidently took pride in her accomplishments. "We have about two thousand children attending Sabbath School," he bragged in the June 1867 report, "[all] under the guardianship of the A. M. E. Church." Pearce added, "We are all looking forward to a glorious future."[13]

Mary's participation in church affairs was to prove deep and meaningful. Her thoughts about that and the reality of her experiences found their echoes in remarks she gave on the achievements of women in Florida at the twenty-fifth anniversary celebration of the South Carolina AME Conference. Entitled "Pioneer Women of East Florida," the presentation stressed women's roles in church affairs and their fundamental importance in making a better life for freedmen and their families. "Such are the characters of the women whom the Church delights to honor—the Pioneer Women of East Florida, women who withstood the toils and hardships of a rugged life, in the wilderness of our church in making a better life for freedmen and their families," she began. "From the earliest period of man's existence, woman has played an important part in the drama of life, and she has ever wielded a quiet but steady influence over all the affairs of the human race." Mary then passed on to the stories of individual women, describing them as "zealous Christian workers in the cause of Christ" who "went about doing good." She continued, "They held up the missionary's hands when they were weak. They bore the heat and burden of the day." These women had "labored faithfully and assiduously for [the church's] upbuilding," she insisted, "as well as for the welfare of their race." Having spoken so, Mary again addressed the women collectively: "The Church and School [have] ever been closely allied in this great and glorious work of progress," she observed, "and, by the combined action of the missionary and teacher, light has been slowly but surely dispensed and darkness compelled to recede." She concluded, "Our prayer is, that the blessing of God may ever attend them, that they may be encouraged to continue to do good work begun, until the Lord shall say—'Well done.'"[14]

Though she did not neglect her church obligations in doing so, at some point Mary commenced teaching in the Leon County day schools. County school records that cover the period before the mid-1870s have been lost, but Day's debut as a teacher in a regular classroom, if it did not come earlier, likely occurred in 1869 or within a year or two following the state legislature's 1869 decision to create a state public school system. If she began in 1869, she probably did so in connection with a Freedmen's Bureau school newly constructed at Tallahassee that later would bear the name Lincoln Academy. The same year Pearce became Leon's superintendent of public instruction, a fact that almost certainly assured Day of a position. The academy unfortunately burned in 1872, and not until 1876 would a suitable replacement building be erected by the county school board.[15]

The first documented record of Mary teaching in the county's various public schools can be dated to June 1875, by which time she had emerged as a veteran educator. On that occasion members of the board of public instruction visited her Tallahassee school. The men's report commented on her progress. "[On the day of our visit] there was a large attendance of pupils, and many of the friends and parents of the children," it noted. "We had not much opportunity to judge of the progress of the pupils, but from what we witnessed we are satisfied that they are laying the foundation of a good education, and making satisfactory advancement in all the elementary branches." They found much to praise about Mary's work and the lessons that she instilled in young people. Their report continued,

> Several compositions, the efforts of the pupils, were read in our hearing, which were exceedingly meritorious, the sentiment being good and the style excellent. In geography the scholars acquitted themselves admirably, showing a most intimate acquaintance with the oceans, seas, gulfs, bays, straits, rivers, mountains, and cities distributed over the globe. The children also sang, with an organ accompaniment, and with very pleasing effect. The order was good, indeed everything that came under our notice was unexceptional [meaning that no exception need be taken to it] and highly gratifying to the school officers and the friends present.

In concluding, the school board members summarized their judgment of Day as an educator. "Miss Day is one of the best teachers in the service of the board," they declared, "and her abilities are thoroughly appreciated by the school officers."[16]

Regular assignments generally came Mary's way thereafter, although the end of Reconstruction and commencement of the Redemption period in 1877 seem temporarily to have interrupted her service. In September 1875 the Republican board of public instruction assigned her to "[School] No. 6, Tallahassee," apparently the school substituting for the burned Lincoln Academy. Two years later a Democratic school board stalled her reappointment. An account of its October 6, 1877, meeting noted, "The Superintendent stated that several petitions in favor of Miss Day had come into his hands since the last meeting." Mary had to wait until the board's November meeting for a decision. At that time her abilities outweighed a desire for political cleansing of the schools by Democrats. "Ordered that the Superintendent be and is hereby authorized," the board's minutes declared, "to give to Miss Day any school that is or may hereafter be vacant in the county using his discretion." It remains unclear where Mary was placed, but she remained a potent force for African American education in the county.[17]

The year 1878 brought improvement in Mary's assignment as a teacher and her reputation as an educator in the eyes of local whites. A vacancy at Lincoln Academy, which had reopened in 1876, had been advertised early in the year after an assistant teacher had resigned. Mary and two others applied to fill the position. The Democrats now saw little to be gained in challenging Day based on her abilities. "[After careful consideration] a motion was made that Miss Day be elected to fill the vacancy," the April board minutes read, "and was carried by a unanimous vote." Moreover, while Day taught at Lincoln, she did not limit herself to one school or, perhaps as a condition of her employment, she was required to teach in two places. Specifically, records bearing a date two months following her Lincoln appointment suggest that Mary also lent her services to a rural school. Funding for this second position ran low. At the June 1, 1878, board meeting an appropriation of only $20.00 was allotted to Day for "School No. 31."[18]

An indirect glimpse at the nature of Day's daily life and routine as a teacher during the late 1870s can be discerned from guidelines established by the county school board in 1879. School hours were set according to location. Facilities within Tallahassee ran from 9:00 a.m. to 2:30 p.m., with a thirty-minute recess allowed. Rural schools operated from 9:00 a.m. to 12:00 p.m., recessed for an hour, and returned from 1:00 p.m. to 4:00 p.m. All students were required to have all textbooks, and instructors, understandably, were required to be present daily. As would be expected, books the county used addressed spelling, mathematics, geography, grammar, history, natural science, penmanship, and rhetoric and composition. At least six volumes were prescribed for spelling, with one book set aside for penmanship. Five books were chosen for natural science and arithmetic, and three books for geography. Regardless of race, Leon County students apparently learned from the same textbooks.[19]

In October 1879 the leadership of Lincoln Academy changed to Mary's benefit, as the principal's job transferred from E. F. Holloway to former school board member R. A. Shine. Four assistant teachers were elected by the board at the same time, but now Day was named as the lead assistant teacher and, thus, the senior African American teacher. While it seemingly took until 1879 for Mary to advance to a senior administrative position, her abilities had earned her a comfortable salary long before that date. She and her friend and colleague Lydia Smith stood out as two of the highest paid black women teachers in Leon County, at least judging from records for 1874 and 1875. Credentials provided one edge for them. The county paid even illiterate teachers for their services to freedmen, but the salaries of the illiterate teachers paled by comparison to those of the well-trained teachers. For example, on January 6, 1874, Mary Day and Lydia Smith each received $40, while Miss Pennie Powers received $6. Mary and Lydia, in fact, were getting paid more than some male teachers. James Smith (Lydia's husband) received a mere $20. Hours worked or else where they were worked (town or countryside) seemed to have factored in salaries as well. On February 7, 1874, Mary received $25, while Lydia earned $40. Then, on February 9, Mary collected an additional $40. On March 19, 1874, Mary was paid $38, and Lydia collected $35. Two months later both women collected $40. Finally, throughout 1875 Mary and Lydia continued to collect $40 for their services.[20]

Although the salary she received allowed Mary to live comfortably, this did not mean either that she did so or that she managed to amass any substantial savings from her earnings. A person of Day's disposition and religious commitments naturally would have been drawn to the cares of those more needy and would have shared of her resources to ease their pain and otherwise to further the work of her church. Even if she did manage to save, she did not necessarily manage to keep those savings. The decade of the 1870s brought troubled economic times that almost certainly touched Mary negatively. Specifically, she placed her funds beginning in 1869 in a Tallahassee branch of the National Freedman's Savings and Trust Company, a federally chartered institution that had just opened locally. She ranked among some 1,300 local people, most of them African American, who did so. Then, mismanagement combined with the impact of the national economic depression known as the Panic of 1873 reduced the bank to hard times. Eventually, the institution closed its doors, and those who had deposits in it found themselves unable as of 1875 to retrieve their savings.[21]

In 1880 further changes ensued for Mary that, among other things, would compel her to move from the town that had offered her a home for the past fourteen years. At age twenty-nine and as Leon County Democrats increas-

Figure 8. Tallahassee's rebuilt Lincoln Academy, 1876. (Courtesy of John G. Riley Center/TCC Archives.)

ingly curtailed expenditures for local black schools, she may well have felt that her capacity and capabilities as an educator were not being utilized to their fullest potential, or else she may have faced harder attitudes on the part of white officials and residents. Something of this nature prompted Mary on March 26, 1880, to ask "for a hearing from the Board . . . to be excluded as a teacher from the Public Instruction." Mary apparently already had accepted an offer to relocate nearly two hundred miles to the east at Jacksonville. The dynamic and growing Jacksonville, at least when compared to economically stagnant Tallahassee, possibly reminded her of her life in New York City. The city did not depend upon the plantation system as the basis of its economy and allowed the chance for entrepreneurship and other opportunities to its black residents. There she accepted a major position as principal of Duval County's Oakland School for blacks.[22]

Bishop Daniel A. Payne, it should be noted, possibly played a part in Mary's decision to relocate. He had begun to winter in Jacksonville and appears to have come to the conclusion that an organized effort by women could improve conditions there for many. If that was the case, it should not surprise that, by 1885, Mary had emerged as president of Payne's project, the Women's Missionary Society. Charlotte Forten Grimké acknowledged the difficulties that Mary encountered in leading a women's organization. "I told the president Mrs. Day," Grimké recorded, "how sincerely I could sympathize with her in her struggle to make the society a success." She added, "It will be a joyful day when we can see the women of our colored churches really and deeply interested in mission work." Subsequently, the difficulties that Mary faced—and her successes— prompted Grimké to initiate a Women's Missionary Society chapter at her own church.[23]

Jacksonville in the years that followed brought important changes to Mary's life, including an attempt to found a family. In that city she met and, on December 8, 1886, married a Colored Methodist Episcopal minister named Charles Smith. A native of the Jacksonville area, Smith had forged close relationships with other leading ministers in the region, making him a perfect choice for Mary. Details regarding the union remain few. According to the 1900 Duval County census Mary was widowed and, by then, had given birth to two children who had died. No known records indicate the births or deaths of these children or the death of her husband. Many different possibilities offer themselves, including death by natural causes or from the yellow fever epidemic that struck the city in 1888. Whatever the case may be, Charles Smith survived at least until 1894, when he attended a Jacksonville function that involved his wife.[24]

Whether accompanied by her husband or not, Mary Day Smith emerged as a fixture in the educational and religious aspects of African American life at Jacksonville. She continued work commenced earlier as secretary of the Colored Teachers Institute, along with teaching and performing duties in the AME Sunday school. Mary seems not to have stopped her work or engaged in any breaks during the late 1880s and early 1890s. As she touched Jacksonville's community, she rarely participated in purely social events. Jacksonville's black community remained in good part vibrant and filled with energy. Accordingly, countless social events took place in any given period of time. Yet, Mary's name does not appear on guest lists published in surviving newspapers, with the exception of attending a surprise party for a friend on January 6, 1894.[25]

Mary Day Smith, despite her busy schedule, found time to cast her sights beyond the Jacksonville vicinity and, in the process, helped to create Florida's first statewide organization for African American teachers. The Colored State Teachers Association (CSTA) began in July 1889, with thirty of Florida's prominent teachers meeting at the Missionary Baptist Church in Tallahassee. Smith served on the executive committee. Breaking the chains that barred women from holding leadership roles, Mary set a precedent by being the only female on the four-person committee. She remained a highly respected member of the association in the times thereafter.[26]

Through these years Mary emerged as a respected, professional educator, often in demand as a speaker at conferences and assemblies. In such forums she shared views on a wide variety of topics. As would be expected, education ranked high on the list. On June 25, 1891, for example, she read a paper to CSTA members entitled "The Chief Requisites in a Teacher," stressing good teaching. The paper also insisted upon accountability by Florida's black educators. Within months she had been elected CSTA vice president. In that role Smith assisted President Thomas DeS. Tucker, the principal of the predecessor institution to Florida A&M University.[27]

In another important presentation Mary tackled the controversial assertion of "The Moral Depravity of the Negro," thereby assuming a direct and public role in crucial public debates then surrounding the rise of Jim Crow racial discrimination. She focused on the fabrications of the white race regarding the Negro, and her words directly challenged and disproved racist assertions then current: "A closer inspection of the Negro's home life reveals him as an upright, religious character," she asserted, "and even under the most adverse circumstances of his unholy environments he was in many instances so tenacious of his preconceived standards of good morals that he defended his principles even to the extent of yielding his life." Mary offered her perspective on the truth in order to generate the uplifting of her people. In the process she articulated for the black community its duty of morality, even in adverse conditions and situations. She did not hesitate to point out the weaknesses of her fellow humans. On the other hand, she offered methods of improvement. Mary emphasized that "the essential need of the human family is charity." Instead of excluding other races, Mary included all within that statement. She made an effort to keep the community together, so that its members could work cooperatively and help one another. She concluded by expressing a wish for peace, unity, and prosperity for both whites and blacks. "Man to man united," she declared, "the whole world shall be lighted, as Eden was of old." This paper, as did others, revealed to her people her dream for the world, with emphasis on the African Americans around her.[28]

Given Smith's stature as a professional educator and the respect held for her within the AME Church, she found herself called upon as the 1890s opened to assist in efforts to transform Jacksonville's denominational high school into an institution of higher learning. Edward Waters College's elevation from Divinity High School, where Mary earlier had taught, stood out as a major advance for the community. The church's national organ *The Philadelphia Christian Recorder* exalted the new school in the summer of 1890, reflecting the importance of contributions by Smith and others. "Edward Waters College will expand the intellect, enlighten the mind, cultivate the brains, train the hands, direct the heart and purify the morals of the coming sons and daughters of Afro-Americans in Florida," it proclaimed. At the college Mary labored as the first principal of the Normal Department. In that capacity she saw to it that prospective teachers would be trained properly, just as Charles Reason had ensured the quality of her own education.[29]

Mary's first period of service at Edward Waters College lasted but a brief time, and she may have agreed to contribute only to the extent of getting the Normal Department up and running. Once that task had been completed, she returned to teaching duties in the Duval County Public Schools. Then, in the spring of 1893 she shifted her attention northward. "Mrs. M. E. C. Smith will leave at 6pm via the F. C. & P. for New York City," a local newspaper reported, "where she will remain a month, she goes on a business trip." Mary arrived in her home city on May 1. Presumably, she resided with her adopted daughter, the future Mrs. Annie Lightbourn, at 769 Herkimer Street. While there Mary became so involved with church and educational matters that she decided to remain for five months. To do so, she turned down an offer from the Duval County School Board of a position at the Oakland School.[30]

During her New York sojourn Mary, at least for a time, decided to follow in her mother's footsteps by extending her services and affection to orphaned children. Anna Day had managed the New York Colored Orphan Asylum from 1837 until well after 1849. Having raised Mary as a widow, Anna naturally spoke repeatedly of her passion for needy children. Those words seemingly came back to Mary in the summer of 1893. "Mrs. M. E. C. Smith is now matron of the colored orphan asylum on Dean street, near Troy, in Brooklyn, N.Y.," a report published at Jacksonville noted in August. "Her many friends are glad to hear of her success in securing such an important position."[31]

For reasons not entirely clear Mary's tenure at the orphan asylum proved short-lived, and she had returned to the South, to Jacksonville, and to her Florida vocation by early October. "Mrs. M. E. C. Smith will open a select school for the present at her residence in Oakland, and should occasion require will in the future move to more commodious quarters," the *Jacksonville Evening Telegram* observed on October 3. "Mrs. Smith is thoroughly known to the public, and needs no recommendation as an educator," the item continued. "Those who wish their children to receive a careful, moral, religious and intellectual training will do well to send their children to her." It added, "Particular attention will also be given to those who wish to become thorough in the rudiments of music. Terms moderate." It may have been too late in the season, however, to launch a private school, as a notice published two weeks later suggested. "Mrs. M. E. C. Smith," it observed, "is now teaching school at Winter Park." Presumably, Smith already had ventured to that community near Orlando, but she remained there for only one school term.[32]

The church's need for Mary's contributions and talents brought her back to Jacksonville in the spring of 1894, a fact that led her in a significantly new direction. As a local newspaper reported on April 16, "Mrs. Smith who has been licensed to preach by Rt. Rev. Bishop T. M. D. Ward, D.D., delivered her first sermon last night at the Zion AME Church." An onlooker commented, "Rev. Mrs. M. E. C. Smith spoke to a crowded church last night much to the satisfaction of all." Smith thus joined the struggle for women to gain major leadership roles within the church. Mary's call to the ministry paralleled the ordainment of Julia Foote as a deacon of the New York Annual Conference and Mary Frances Green as official conference missionary. A shortage of preachers in the South may have brought these women into the pulpit, but their manner of articulation and their education pushed them to the forefront of the local ministry.[33]

The launch of her ministerial career included efforts by Mary to extend her ministry to children. She accepted the position of lady superintendent of Jacksonville's Boylan Home, where she saw to it that young people received a proper education along with their everyday needs. Meanwhile, her charity work flourished. On June 4, 1894, for instance, she participated in a charity event for the Colored Orphans' and Industrial Association. Her contributions drew praise, with the state's principal daily newspaper referring to her as "a leading lady for the race." Members of Sarah's Court and the Afro-American Women's Association assisted her in activities touching the sick, elderly, homeless, orphaned, and hungry. In one example, the association led a New Year's dinner drive under Mary's leadership so that the needy could celebrate the holidays. Smith's work with the Colored Orphans' and Industrial Association and the Afro-American Women's Association lasted into the twentieth century.[34]

While Mary remained busy with charity work and aid organizations, she also maintained loyalty to her profession. Illustrating that fact, on April 12, 1895, the *Tampa Morning Tribune* commended Smith on her paper entitled "The Importance of a Trained Teacher," which she had presented to a crowded church in that city in an effort to recruit more qualified educators. Even though progress had been made toward the education of the South's black children by 1895, considerable numbers remained illiterate and unknowing of formal instruction. According to the newspaper, "The impoverished condition of many parents is not only the apparent but the real cause of this." The persistence of that problem alarmed Mary, the AME Church, and the CSTA. Mary's paper insisted that, regardless of what each person was supposed to do in life, all should receive training as a teacher. "Taking the broad assumption that everybody should be trained regardless of what is to be their life work," the *Tribune* declared, "her ideals were high and her observations in strict keeping with the standards."[35]

Still, her mission in the mid-1890s increasingly involved church affairs. Particularly, she contributed her time to the important position of AME East Florida Conference missionary. By 1896 she had completed her first year in that role, and she thereafter proudly reported her results. "She entered the work one year ago under favorable circumstances," an onlooker recorded, "and her report showed that she has done good work for the cause." Again, Mary proved herself to be an extraordinary asset in addressing the needs and the desires of her church. In the meantime—by November 1895—she also had resumed her position as president of the Sunday school at Jacksonville's Mt. Zion AME Church. In that capacity she taught lessons each Sunday morning at 9:30 a.m.[36]

As it turned out, the church needed Mary's contributions as an educator more than her missionary services. Edward Waters College had entered upon hard times during the mid-1890s, and only with the arrival in 1898 of a new principal, A. St. George Richardson, did its affairs begin to turn around. Likely at Richardson's insistence, Mary was enticed to return to her old duties as head of the school's Normal Department as well as to accept those of women's principal. The *Christian Recorder* the following year praised her performance. "Sister M. E. C. Smith, the lady principal, is an untiring worker for the school and her church," it commented, "and one of the best teachers in the state." By 1900, thanks in substantial part to her efforts, Edward Waters appeared to be standing on the brink of a period of unprecedented growth and prosperity.[37]

The normality of Mary's life and the satisfaction that she felt as she entered the twentieth century can be seen in her activities during early 1901. First and foremost, she remained in Florida to serve her church, her school, her community, and those in need. The year opened, to cite an example, with an attempt to raise funds for the Sunday school mission through an entertainment held at the Christian Aid Hall. Along with her friend Effie Dix, Mary saw her work result in a major success. She continued as well to present speeches, lectures, and formal papers on educational issues, including one entitled "The Relation of Reading to the Work of Education." In this essay she promoted literacy as being the major portion of learning for African Americans. Without doubt she continued to bear as a personal burden responsibility for ensuring that Jacksonville's residents knew how to read and write.[38]

Then came the Great Fire of 1901 that destroyed much of Jacksonville. The disaster occurred on May 7 and, before its flames could be extinguished, it had consumed churches, schools, homes, and businesses. Edward Waters College fell victim. During and after the blaze, though, Mary Smith responded to the needs of her school and her community. She gave shelter, food, and clothing, for instance, to at least fifteen people in her home for approximately one month. The town commended her for her generosity and hospitality. Old contacts fortunately aided her efforts, including Miss Morehouse of the Boylan Home and Victoria Matthews of New York City, who sponsored a clothing drive. The Afro-American Women's Club supported the outreach with donations of food, clothing, toys, and money.[39]

Interestingly, Mary did not permit the disaster to divert her from a very personal interest, the promotion of artwork created by the women of Jacksonville and of New York. In July 1901 she departed for Buffalo, New York, to further that cause but managed also to attend the annual conference of the National Association of Colored Women held in New York City. During her absence Edward Waters College reopened in an unused school building located in the Jacksonville neighborhood of LaVilla. Not until October did she return to Florida, a fact that suggests a vacation to recuperate from exhaustion.[40]

Further suggesting a need for the now fifty-one-year-old woman to rest and recuperate, Mary in August 1902 traveled to Ashville, North Carolina. There she fell and sustained serious "wounds." One report described the injuries. "The smaller bone in one of her legs was broken and the larger bone was fractured," it read. "All must know that these injuries cause her much suffering, and for a woman of her age recovery will not be so speedy." The report concluded, "It is hoped that she is being well and properly cared for." As the weeks passed, it became increasingly clear to her friends and admirers at Mt. Zion AME Church that the matter had become extremely serious. "It was not known whether or not Mrs. Smith was in need of aid, but all know that she is not rich, and to secure medical and other attention there among strangers must cost her considerable," a member observed. "Be it said to the credit of the teachers and pupils [in the Sunday school], the suggestion of their superintendent was followed up promptly with gifts of cash and subscription." The member added, "The fact cannot be too often referred to: Mrs. Smith has stood in the front rank of the educators of her race in Florida for the past thirty years or more. Her labors both in church and school have been many and arduous." The report noted further, "It is learned that she desires to come home just as soon as she is able to travel." That relocation had been effected by late October. "She . . . wishes to inform the public that she is steadily recovering from her injuries," a published card detailed, "and hopes very soon again to be at her post of duty, striving to render some service to God and her race."[41]

Bravely, Mary did resume her duties at Jacksonville in late 1902, especially those inherent in the office of president of the Afro-American Women's Club and as a teacher at the Oakland School. Yet, she remained weak. By November reports circulated that "Mrs. M. E. C. Smith . . . was on last Sunday morning taken quite suddenly and seriously ill." Early December brought the news that "[she] continues to be in feeble health, at her home on Pippin street, near Florida avenue." Ultimately—on December 19, 1903—her lifelong journey of charity, leadership, sacrifice, and love for education reached its earthly end. She died at her home on Pippin Street in Oakland, mourned by "men, women, boys and girls [all over Florida] who at some stage in their school lives have been taught by Mrs. Smith." Her funeral followed on Monday, December 21, at Mt. Zion AME Church. "The esteem in which this veteran teacher and worker in all humane causes was held by the community was fully attended to by the large concourse of people that filled the church long before the service began," a newspaper article declared. Interment followed at Mt. Olive Cemetery.[42]

Her friend Nettie E. L. Baker attempted to summarize the sentiments of those who had known Mary Day Smith, writing,

> Dear friend of mine, thou art gone forever,
>   Among the blest thou art secure,
> And the tie that naught could sever
>   Will remain forevermore.
>
> Precious to our memory clinging
>   Are thy many deeds so pure;
> All our sorrow to thee bringing,
>   But thou will speak to us no more.
>
> How I long to hear thy sweet voice
>   Speaking to me as of yore.
> O how my heart would rejoice;
>   But thou art gone forevermore.
>
> We loved her, yes, we loved her,
>   But the angels loved her more,
> And they have sweetly called her
>   To yonder shining shore.

> The gold gates were opened,
> A gentle voice said come,
> And with farewells unspoken
> She calmly entered in.[43]

Ironically and without reference to herself, Mary E. C. Day Smith may have offered her own best obituary years before her death in the words of her essay "Pioneer Women of East Florida." There, she commented, "Thus has the work of the Church and School ever been closely allied in this great and glorious work of progress, and, by the combined action of missionary and teacher, light has been slowly but surely dispensed and darkness compelled to recede." She concluded, "We will ever honor the memory of those dear women who have been instrumental in this good work."[44]

Notes

I thank Althemese Barnes, Maggie Lewis Butler, and the John G. Riley House of Tallahassee, Florida, for assistance in researching and preparing this essay. The epigraph to the essay is taken from Mary E. C. Smith, "Is the Negro as Morally Depraved as He Is Reputed to Be?" in *Twentieth Century Negro Literature; or, A Cyclopedia of Thought on the Vital Topics Relating to the American Negro*, ed. Daniel Wallace Culp (Naperville, Ill., 1902), 251. Portions of this essay previously appeared in Daria Willis Joseph, "Mary E. C. Day Smith: An Intimate Portrait of a Pioneering Black Educator and AME Minister in Post–Civil War Florida," *A.M.E. Church Review* 121 (July–September 2005): 12–20, and are used by permission.

    1. Joe M. Richardson, *Christian Reconstruction: The American Missionary Association and Southern Blacks, 1861–1890* (Athens, Ga., 1986), 163. Among excellent studies available concerning or touching upon African American mission workers in the South, see, for instance, Adam Fairclough, *A Class of Their Own: Black Teachers in the Segregated South* (Cambridge, Mass., 2007); Kathleen Berkeley, "'Colored Ladies Also Contributed': Black Women's Activities from Benevolence to Social Welfare, 1866–1896," in *The Web of Southern Social Relations: Women, Family, and Education*, ed. Walter J. Fraser, R. Frank Saunders Jr., and John L. Wakelyn (Athens, Ga., 1985), 181–203; Willard B. Gatewood Jr., "'The Remarkable Misses Rollin': Black Women in Reconstruction South Carolina," *South Carolina History Magazine* 92 (July 1991): 172–88; Tera Hunter, *To 'Joy My Freedom: Southern Black Women's Lives and Labors after the Civil War* (Cambridge, Mass., 1997); Jacqueline Jones, *Soldiers of Light and Love: Northern Teachers and Georgia Blacks, 1865–1873* (Chapel Hill, 1980). For an interesting study touching upon aspects of Mary E. C. Day's work at Jacksonville, Florida, see Shirletta J. Kinchen, "Edward Waters College, 1890–1901: The Experience of Pioneering Women Educators," *A.M.E. Church Review* 120 (July–September 2004):

30–39; a revised version appeared as Kinchen, "Edward Waters College, 1890–1901: The Experience of Pioneering Women Educators," in *Go Sound the Trumpet! Selections in Florida's African American History*, ed. David H. Jackson Jr. and Canter Brown Jr. (Tampa, 2005), 137–51 (this is the version cited henceforth).

2. Mary Day entry, Registers of Signatures of Depositors in Branches of the National Freedman's Savings and Trust Company, 1865–1874, Tallahassee, Microcopy M816, National Archives, Washington, D.C.; Culp, *Twentieth Century Negro Literature*, facing p. 246.

3. Benjamin W. Arnett, *Proceedings of the Quarto-Centennial of the African M. E. Church of South Carolina, at Charleston S. C., May 15, 26 and 27, 1889* (Charleston, S.C., 1890), 440; William J. Simmons, *Men of Mark: Eminent, Progressive and Rising* (New York, 1968), 1105; Carla L. Peterson, "Black Life in Freedom: Creating an Elite Culture," in *Slavery in New York*, ed. Ira Berlin and Leslie M. Harris (New York, 2005), 183–84; Carleton Mabee, *Black Education in New York State: From Colonial to Modern Times* (Syracuse, N.Y., 1979), 105.

4. Simmons, *Men of Mark*, 208; *Anglo-African Magazine* (July 1859), 223.

5. Simmons, *Men of Mark*, 208; *Anglo-African Magazine* (July 1859), 223; Mabee, *Black Education in New York State*, 106; Peterson, "Black Life in Freedom," 208; *New York Tribune*, July 17, 1855, and June 30, 1856; *New York Anglo-African* October 15, 1859.

6. Culp, *Twentieth Century Negro Literature*, facing p. 246; Mabee, *Black Education in New York State*, 106–7.

7. Daniel A. Payne, *History of the African Methodist Episcopal Church* (Nashville, 1891; reprint ed., New York, 1968), 3–34, 469–70; Larry Eugene Rivers and Canter Brown Jr., *Laborers in the Vineyard of the Lord: The Beginnings of the AME Church in Florida, 1865–1895* (Gainesville, 2001), 31–42; *Philadelphia Christian Recorder*, February 24 and June 9, 1866; Larry Eugene Rivers, *Slavery in Florida: Territorial Days to Emancipation* (Gainesville, 2000), 16–46. On Charles H. Pearce, see Dorothy Dodd, "'Bishop' Pearce and the Reconstruction of Leon County," *Apalachee: The Journal of the Tallahassee Historical Society* (1946): 5–12. See also Robert L. Hall, "Tallahassee's Black Churches, 1865–1885," *Florida Historical Quarterly* 58 (October 1979): 185–96.

8. Rivers and Brown, *Laborers in the Vineyard of the Lord*, 31–34; Canter Brown Jr., "'Where Are Now the Hopes I Cherished?' The Life and Times of Robert Meacham," *Florida Historical Quarterly* 69 (July 1990): 1–5; *Tallahassee Semi-Weekly Floridian*, February 20, 1866; William Guzman and Tameka Bradley Hobbs, *Landmarks and Legacies: A Guide to Tallahassee's African American Heritage, 1865–1970* (Tallahassee, 2000), 19. On James Page, see Larry E. Rivers, "Baptist Minister James Page: Alternatives for African American Leadership in Post–Civil War Florida," in *Florida's Heritage of Diversity: Essays in Honor of Samuel Proctor*, ed. Mark I. Greenberg, William W. Rogers, and Canter Brown Jr. (Tallahassee, 1997), 43–53.

9. *Tallahassee Semi-Weekly Floridian*, March 13, 1866.

10. Joe M. Richardson, *The Negro in the Reconstruction of Florida, 1865–1877* (Tallahassee, 1965), 97–111; Fairclough, *Class of Their Own*, 62–65.

11. *Tallahassee Semi-Weekly Floridian*, March 13, 1866.

12. Ibid., December 21, 1866; Rivers and Brown, *Laborers in the Vineyard of the Lord*, 39–40.

13. *Philadelphia Christian Recorder*, July 13, 1867.

14. Arnett, *Proceedings of the Quarto-Centennial*, 186.

15. Althemese Barnes and Debra Herman, *African American Education in Leon County: Emancipation through Desegregation, 1863–1968* (Tallahassee, 1997), 1–16; Larry E. Rivers and Canter Brown Jr., "A Monument to the Progress of the Race: The Intellectual and Political Origins of the Florida Agricultural and Mechanical University, 1865–1887," *Florida Historical Quarterly* 85 (Summer 2006): 4; Guzman and Hobbs, *Landmarks and Legacies*, 28; Sheryl Marie Howie, "State Politics and the Fate of African American Public Schooling in Florida, 1863–1900" (master's thesis, University of Florida, 2004), 17.

16. *Tallahassee Sentinel*, June 5, 1875.

17. Ibid., September 4, 1875, October 6, 1877, and November 8, 1877.

18. Ibid., April 6, 1878; minutes of the Leon County Board of Public Instruction, June 1, 1878, Leon County School Board, Tallahassee.

19. *Tallahassee Sentinel*, September 14, 1878, and October 2, 1879.

20. Ibid., October 2, 1879; Register of Trustees and School Property of the Leon County Board of Public Instruction, 1874–1875, Leon County School Board.

21. Guzman and Hobbs, *Landmarks and Legacies*, 5–6; *Tallahassee Semi-Weekly Floridian*, December 21, 1876.

22. Minutes of the Leon County Board of Public Instruction, March 26, 1880; *Philadelphia Christian Recorder*, October 30, 1884; *Jacksonville Evening Telegram*, October 28, 1891.

23. Brenda Stephenson, *The Journals of Charlotte Forten Grimké* (New York, 1988), 519.

24. 1900 U.S. Decennial Census, Duval County, Florida (population schedule); Duval County Marriage Records, Book 6, 519, Duval County Courthouse, Jacksonville (available at Florida State Archives, Tallahassee).

25. *Jacksonville Florida Times-Union*, June 9, 1886, and January 6, 1894.

26. Ibid., April 10, 1891.

27. Ibid., May 12 and June 26, 1891.

28. Culp, *Twentieth Century Negro Literature*, 252–53.

29. *Philadelphia Christian Recorder*, June 19, 1890.

30. Kinchen, "Edward Waters College," 139–43; *Jacksonville Evening Telegram*, April 19, May 1, and July 25, 1893.

31. Rochester (N.Y.) *North Star*, May 4, 1849; *New York Colored American*, April 29, 1837; *Jacksonville Evening Telegram*, August 3, 1893.

32. *Jacksonville Evening Telegram*, October 3 and 16, 1893; *Jacksonville Evening Times-Union*, April 16, 1894.

33. *Jacksonville Evening Times-Union*, April 16, 1894; Canter Brown Jr. and Larry Eugene Rivers, *For a Great and Grand Purpose: The Beginnings of the AMEZ Church in Florida, 1864–1905* (Gainesville, 2004), 78, 116–17.

34. *Jacksonville Evening Times-Union*, June 4, 1894.

35. *Tampa Morning Tribune*, April 12, 1895.

36. *Jacksonville Florida Times-Union*, February 23, 1896.

37. Kinchen, "Edward Waters College," 148; *Philadelphia Christian Recorder*, July 13, 1899.

38. *Jacksonville Evening Metropolis*, April 9, 11, 22, and 25, 1901.

39. Ibid., May 8, 9, 11, and 25, 1901; Kinchen, "Edward Waters College," 149.

40. *Jacksonville Evening Metropolis*, June 17, 20, and October 2, 1901.

41. Ibid., September 2, 24, and October 29, 1902.

42. Ibid., December 24, 1902, and November 7, December 10, 21, and 22, 1903.

43. Ibid., December 23, 1903.

44. Mary E. C. Day Smith, "Pioneer Women of East Florida," in Arnett, *Proceedings of the Quarto-Centennial of the African M. E. Church*, 186.

CHAPTER 5

Mary Barr Munroe
1852–1922

South Florida's Pioneer Zealot

ARVA MOORE PARKS

WHEN MARY BARR MUNROE died unexpectedly on September 8, 1922, South Florida lost a piece of its soul and the state of Florida lost one of its most forceful leaders. Tributes poured in from all over the state, newspapers recalled her many accomplishments, and speakers extolled her virtues. All agreed that she was a rare woman, a born leader of strong personality, brilliant, inspiring, dominating, fearless, and never neutral. She cared deeply about many things and once a supporter, never wavered in her zeal to persuade others to her point of view.

Mary Barr Munroe moved to South Florida with her husband, Kirk, in 1887—nine years before the birth of the city of Miami. But Mary's pioneering spirit was not defined simply by her being an early resident in a still-unexplored

Figure 9. Mary Barr Munroe, c. 1890. (Courtesy of Historical Museum of Southern Florida.)

wilderness. She also blazed trails in many other arenas. She was a leader in the early women's club movement, advocated for the Seminoles, stood up for blacks, fought for protection of birds and forests, and sought to preserve Florida history.

Mary's emergence as an individual did not come easily. The wife of Kirk Munroe, a famous author of boy's books, she carried the double burden of also being the daughter of another national personality—Amelia Barr, a popular romance novelist who became the highest paid female writer in America. Never content to remain in the shadows of two famous people, she quickly forged her own, independent identity. Although usually called "Mrs. Kirk Munroe," as the social custom of the era dictated, she was her own woman—respected for her distinct, and some said overly confrontational, personality. Nonetheless, Kirk and Mary Barr Munroe were a formidable team of equals—in startling contrast to their generation's view of marriage. They supported each other's passions and complemented each other's personalities. Often, Kirk would intercede and smooth the waters when Mary's energetic, impulsive outspokenness got her into trouble. Through it all, they enjoyed an especially close marriage and an unyielding dual commitment to making a difference.

During her thirty-seven years of Florida residence Mary, perhaps even more than Kirk, rarely missed an opportunity to speak up for the things she valued. The legendary writer and environmental activist Marjory Stoneman Douglas recalled that, of everyone she met when she arrived in South Florida during 1912, it was Mary Barr Munroe she remembered most.[1]

Mary's origins lay an ocean away from the Sunshine State. She was born on January 5, 1852, in Glasgow, Scotland. She was the first child of Amelia Huddleston, the educated daughter of a Methodist minister, and Robert Barr, a prosperous wool merchant. Shortly before Mary's birth, Robert Barr's firm went bankrupt. The family faced embarrassing financial problems and Mary's parents recognized the need for change. In late 1853, hoping to start a new life, the Barr family—now including a second daughter—immigrated to the United States. Fortunately for historians, Amelia Barr chronicled the family saga in a revealing autobiography entitled *All the Days of My Life*, published at age eighty-one. She portrayed herself as an individual who, with a rapidly expanding family, followed her husband from city to city as he sought permanent employment. By the time the Barrs settled in Galveston, Texas, in 1866, Amelia had borne eleven children and buried six. Sadly, the family tragedy was not over. During the summer of 1867 yellow fever gripped Galveston and, within a matter of weeks, Robert Barr and both Barr sons had succumbed to the disease. A pregnant, penniless widow, Amelia found herself with three young daughters to support (her last child, Andrew, born six months after his father's death, lived only five days).²

When Amelia took charge of family affairs, she did so with determination and purpose—a model that did not escape daughter Mary's attention. Despite the years of suffering and grief, the indomitable widow sold all her possessions and used the proceeds to book passage for her and her three daughters on a steamer to New York City. She fantasized that there the famous minister Henry Ward Beecher, whom she had met in Scotland seventeen years earlier, would help her find a job. After a stint as a governess, she finally summoned enough courage to write Beecher. To Amelia's surprise, Beecher offered her a writing job at his *Christian Union*. Thus, at age thirty-nine, Amelia Barr launched what she called "her new life."³

By this time, daughters Lilly and Mary were earning their own keep as governesses. After briefly living independently, they moved back into their mother's household when Amelia's financial circumstances improved with her success as a novelist. She proved a domineering, controlling mother. Still, despite her overbearing nature, the family remained close and devoted to one another. Mary and Lilly took turns caring for the youngest sister, Alice, who may have been mildly retarded. Mary sewed for the entire family and shared household chores. With her mother as her role model, Mary—who inherited her mother's determination and spirit—also set out to become a writer. She occasionally sold articles to *Harper's Young People*, a popular children's magazine edited by a dashing young outdoorsman named Kirk Munroe. Soon after their first meeting in 1880, Kirk and Mary fell in love.⁴

Mary's future husband was a most unusual young man. Born in a one-room log cabin on the Wisconsin frontier, he spent his early years there with his Harvard-educated father and Boston-society mother who served as Indian missionaries. When Kirk Munroe attained school age, the family returned to Boston, but his frontier experience continued to shape his future. A self-described indifferent scholar, at age seventeen he left school, joined a surveying party, and traveled throughout the southwestern United States, ending up in California. During this first trip, he fought Indians, or so he claimed, and met George Armstrong Custer, Wild Bill Hickok, and Kit Carson. He described these experiences in detailed letters to his parents that the Boston press published. Returning to Boston at his parents' insistence, he spent a year at Harvard's Lawrence Scientific School before joining another western surveying crew that took him to the Pacific Northwest. Drawing on his eyewitness encounters with the closing American frontier, he began writing stories for the *New York Sun*. Soon, he became a full-time *Sun* reporter.⁵

Kirk found ways to enjoy the outdoors even in New York City, and his predilection would touch Mary's life deeply in the years of her marriage. He bought a sailing canoe he named *Psyche* and engaged in various waterborne activities. He entered races, participated in regattas, and joined the New York Canoe Club, where he quickly became commodore. His dynamic personality and leadership abilities led him to create the American Canoe Association. He also became an avid bicyclist and founded the League of American Wheelman. These national organizations, and his pivotal role in their founding, afforded him his first national recognition but did not distract him from writing. In 1879, when he was only twenty-nine, he left the *Sun* to become the first editor of *Harper's Young People*, a new magazine created for boys and girls by the well-known Harper's Brothers organization. At about the same time, his sister Susan married Charles, the son of Harriet Beecher Stowe, the author of *Uncle Tom's Cabin* and by the 1860s a Florida resident. This union brought Kirk to Florida to visit Charles and Susan, who were staying with Charles's mother at her Mandarin home on the St. Johns River near Jacksonville. After his first visit, what he called his "inextinguishable wanderlust" struck again. He resigned his *Harper's* editorship in 1881 and, with his beloved *Psyche* in tow, embarked on another adventure in Florida.[6]

That adventure unexpectedly would lead Mary to a new home. In November 1881, Kirk Munroe began an incredible and often harrowing, three-and-one-half-month solo journey on *Psyche* through the unexplored Florida wilds. Beginning in the Okefenokee Swamp in North Florida, he descended the Suwannee River to the Gulf Coast and then traveled via the Gulf of Mexico to Key West. Returning to the peninsula through Punta Rassa on Florida's west coast, he ascended the Caloosahatchee River past today's Fort Myers, crossed Lake Okeechobee to the Kissimmee River, and ventured on to the St. Johns. As he journeyed, he recorded that he wrote to and received letters from "Mala," his endearing nickname for Mary. Mala notwithstanding, this trip, and another through Central Florida swamps and streams the following winter, gave his writing a new perspective. Soon, the Kirk Munroe byline became nationally known through a variety of newspapers and magazines.[7]

Kirk's "inextinguishable wanderlust" may have taken him to the Florida frontier, but his heart never left New York and his beloved Mala. When Amelia Barr realized that her daughter and Kirk wanted to marry, she opposed the union, even though she liked Mary's choice. "What chance had I," she wrote, "against a lover of such manifold attractions?" Amelia added, "If Mary was happier with a stranger, than with the mother who had cherished her for thirty-three years, well, I must [be] content to shave my own pleasure."[8]

Kirk and Mary married on September 15, 1883, in New York's Holy Communion Church. They immediately left on a three-month honeymoon canoe cruise. It took them down Florida's St. Johns and Indian rivers into Lake Worth, a body of water close to modern-day Palm Beach but then in an isolated and sparsely populated region. Within a year they purchased property in Lake Worth, planning to make their winter home there. Busy times followed, especially for Kirk. Between 1883 and 1886, under the name C. K. Munroe, he edited and published yearly editions of a Florida travelogue and almanac called *Florida Annual, Impartial and Unsectional*. His first book, *Wakulla: A Story of Adventure in Florida*, appeared in 1885 after being serialized in *Harper's Young People* the previous year.[9]

At about the time *Wakulla* appeared on bookshelves, Mary found herself preparing for relocation. In 1886, during their winter sojourn in Lake Worth, she and Kirk took a trip to Key West. By chance, they met a man named William Brickell who ran an Indian trading post on the Miami River. Curious about that vicinity's Biscayne Bay, Kirk traveled with Brickell to see the area for himself. When he arrived at Miami, he found what could barely be described as a settlement. Brickell's house and trading post dominated the river's south shore and the remains of Old Fort Dallas, the north bank. Except for a few scattered homes in the backcountry and two small outposts called Lemon City and "Cocoanut Grove," the area was unimproved and unexplored. Much impressed with this forgotten frontier, Kirk returned a month later with Mary. This time, they stayed at the half-completed Bay View House in today's Coconut Grove. This small community, just coming together, was made up of Bahamian fishermen; Charles and Isabella Peacock, proprietors of the Bay View House; and a Staten Islander named Ralph Munroe (no relation to Kirk). Ralph Munroe, who had discovered the area a decade earlier, had persuaded the English-born Peacocks to open an inn so that visitors would have a place to stay. He promised that, if they built it, he would bring in the people.[10]

Biscayne Bay and its surroundings captivated Kirk Munroe; Mary, however, was less impressed. Coconut Grove lay a long way from New York, and was a smaller and more isolated community than Lake Worth. "Oh, how I wish we were back in NY," she confided to her diary. Then, with second thoughts, she crossed out the line and added: "I did not mean it, I like Florida and L.W. in particular."[11]

Mary's reluctance to embrace Miami and Coconut Grove failed to stem Kirk's enthusiasm, and she accepted the need to adjust. Within days of their arrival, Kirk prepared to buy the only available improved tract in Coconut Grove. It belonged to George and Kitty Frow Roberts and was part of the area's first homestead. It boasted a simple, unpainted wooden cabin built from lumber salvaged from a wreck. Mary chose not to confide much to her diary about the Robertses' place except that Kirk wanted to buy it. At least for the time being, her stay ended quickly. After almost two months in Coconut Grove and the purchase of the five-acre Roberts property for $250, the Munroes returned to New York for the summer where Kirk worked busily on his next book *The Flamingo Feather*, the second with a Florida theme. Kirk and Mary returned to Coconut Grove on January 17, 1887, to take possession of their new home. Following the customary itinerary and because there were no roads to the area, they first sailed to Key West on a Mallory steamer from New York, then boarded the schooner *Newport* for the trip up the Keys to Coconut Grove. Joining them were several others who would later settle in the Grove. One was Flora McFarlane, who was a companion to Ralph Munroe's mother. At first meeting, Flora and Mary became friends. At the time no one could have imagined the impact they would have on Coconut Grove.[12]

Mary's new friendship with Flora McFarlane proved a harbinger of the warm welcome she would receive in her new home. All of the Coconut Grove community came together to help their newest and most famous residents move in. Mary's diary, in a departure from the tone of previous entries, now carried glowing descriptions of the home they named "The Scrububs." Kirk documented the genesis of this unusual name in the first pages of their guest book:

> It was a region of rugged rock, primeval forest, dense overgrowth matted with a tangle of vines and palmetto scrub. Bearing this in mind, one of its new proprietors when sallied upon dwelling in the suburbs replied: "Suburbs! It is more like a 'Scrububs.'"[13]

Mary, in the years that passed, carefully recorded their activities and the names of the many visitors at Scrububs, a home that, under her care, emerged more as a community and hospitality center than a simple residence. She included colorful descriptions of the almost daily visits from friendly Indians. She wrote of William Henry Thomson, a young black Bahamian who came to work for them and whom they treated to a birthday sail on Biscayne Bay.[14]

For the Munroes, like the rest of the Coconut Grove residents, sailing was more than a diversion. Because there were no roads, nearly everyone traveled by sailboat. In fact, Kirk wrote that, during the first ten years of their residency, he did not remember ever making a trip by land to Miami. With all the sailboats, Kirk and Ralph Munroe came up with the idea of having a sailing regatta on Washington's birthday. This first communitywide event brought the diverse

Figure 10. Coconut Grove's first tourists, 1887; Mary Barr Munroe stands on the top level with her back to the camera, while Kirk Munroe sits on the steps wearing a straw hat. (Courtesy of Historical Museum of Southern Florida.)

population together and launched the Biscayne Bay Yacht Club, South Florida's oldest continuous institution, founded by the two Munroes. Ralph named himself commodore, and Kirk named himself secretary. Mary made the first flag.[15]

The moment of Mary's arrival at Coconut Grove proved an important turning point for the region as well as for her. The early spring of 1887, as it turned out, proved unlike any other in Miami's history. In fact, Coconut Grove had so many visitors that Ralph Munroe gathered them together on Mary and Kirk's front porch and took a historic photograph to document what has been described as Miami's first tourist season. It was a rather sophisticated group, including Kirk's brother-in-law the Reverend Charles Stowe and a scattering of Europeans.[16]

From 1887 until their deaths, Mary and Kirk would call Coconut Grove home, and its attraction for and importance to them grew with the passage of time. At first they went north for the summer, but their absences became shorter as the years passed. Often, however, Mary found herself alone when Kirk took extended trips to gather more material for his novels. In 1902–1903, for instance, he traveled for almost a year when Harper's Brothers sent him around the world. Mary remained at home in Coconut Grove, taking care of business with a power of attorney to manage their affairs. As she did, she came to love the pioneer life but recalled that it was not always easy. In 1909, she wrote an essay for the *Miami Metropolis* entitled "Pioneer Women in Dade County." It was more autobiographical than she admitted. "Pioneer life, as we know, is always harder on the woman," she opined, "but one of the wonderful things about it is a woman's ever willingness to follow the man of her choice. The great loneliness of the early days," she continued, "seems always to be the thing remembered by the women." But she concluded on a positive note, adding, "Pioneer days are wonderful days, and there is one thing certain, they bring out all there is in a man and a woman."[17]

Mary's pioneer experience certainly brought out the best in her. Within days of her arrival, she befriended the village children, both black and white. She read to them, invited them to tea parties, and gave them gifts. She also helped their mothers, sharing housekeeping tips and even teaching some to read. She and Kirk also became strong supporters of the Seminoles who frequently camped on their front lawn. The Indians trusted the Munroes, giving Kirk the Indian name Okeechobee and calling Mary Okeechobee's squaw. Mary and Kirk wrote positive stories about their Indian friends for the national and local press. When movies were introduced, Mary even took on the nascent film producers, demanding they film Indians in a more positive light.[18]

Having already emerged as a community activist, in early 1891 Mary found an unexpected platform when Flora McFarlane enlisted her help to start a women's organization. They called it the Housekeepers' Club. Its purpose was "first to bring together the mothers and housekeepers of our little settlement and by spending two hours a week in companionship and study, learn to know each other and thereby help each other and add to the Sunday School building fund." Flora, like Mary, was cultured and educated, in contrast to many of the other women who lived in Coconut Grove. But both women envisioned a club with no social boundaries. This club, and the women who joined it, would help to shape their community's enduring character. Miss Flora, as local people affectionately called her, took the reins of leadership as the first president. "They elected me president," Mary wrote in her diary, "but I don't think I will say yes." Under these circumstances, Mary became secretary at the first official meeting on February 19, 1891. Besides Flora and Mary, the other original members included Isabella Peacock and three women—Mrs. C. J. Peacock, Mrs. Benjamin Newbold, and Mrs. Joseph Frow—who were all born in the Bahamas. The Housekeepers' Club grew quickly. Each week, the members gathered for needlework, listening to a reader as they sewed. Their goal was to make items to sell at a bazaar that would raise money for the Sunday school building. In 1892, Kirk convinced the Harper's organization to include an article about the club in *Harper's Bazar*.[19]

A few months after the Housekeepers' Club commenced its activities, Mary took on a second community enterprise. The idea came from Kirk, who suggested that she start a club for the young girls in the community who had been gathering at the Munroe home every Saturday afternoon. With nine charter members, all daughters of Bahamian fishermen or backwoods homesteaders, Mary created the "Pineneedles." Their first order of business was to adopt Kirk as "Father Needle." He participated in their activities and taught them a military drill that they did with brooms as weapons. The Pineneedles' broom drill became a popular entertainment at village events, including the first Housekeepers' Club bazaar held at the Munroes' boathouse.[20]

Through the Pineneedles, Mary found that the visitors she hosted could contribute to the betterment of the community. This realization came when Mrs. Thomas Carnegie, sister-in-law of Andrew, visited the Grove on her yacht and heard about the girls' club. Afterwards, Lucy Carnegie sent Mary twenty-five books from her personal library. In 1895, under Kirk and Mary's leadership, the growing Pineneedles' book collection became the nucleus of the Coconut Grove Library. With Mary's strong support and encouragement, Kirk became the library association's first president. Annually, she held a tea to benefit the library fund. In 1901, at Kirk's request, Ralph Munroe donated land and loaned money to build a permanent library building—the first in South Florida.[21]

Race naturally factored into Mary's life at Coconut Grove. Although blacks and whites lived in separate communities, as was the custom of the day, the black community—Kirk named it Kebo after a mountain in Africa—lay adjacent to their property. The Munroes had a particularly close relationship with many of the families there and built homes for several Kebo residents. They also attended church and community events with these neighbors. Kirk opened a library in Kebo's Odd Fellows Hall with books he and Mary collected. One of Mary's early causes in the Housekeepers' Club was support for their school. When Dan Anderson began working for the family in 1890, Mary often referred to him as "our Dan" and was close to his wife, Katherine, whom he brought from the Bahamas. An early interior photograph of Scrububs shows Dan's portrait hanging over the Munroes' fireplace. Today, the portrait is the proud possession of his granddaughter, Thelma Anderson Gibson, a noted Miami activist.[22]

Despite Mary's growing activism and independence, she clung to many traditional values involving home and family. Her diary reflected her constant support of her husband's activities, recording when he started each new book or when he sold it and received payment. She served as his reader and editor, sometimes even telling him she did not like what he wrote. One of her most important roles was hostess par excellence. Mrs. Florence Haden summed up Mary's influence at a Housekeepers' Club tribute given after her death. "I think of all the women I've ever known that Mrs. Munroe has entertained more people and in a way that gave great pleasure to them too, than anyone else I know."[23]

As early as the 1890s, the Munroe home had become a way stop and community center. Numerous important people visited Scrububs and signed the guest book. They included literary luminaries such as James Whitcomb Riley, author and Everglades explorer Hugh Willoughby, politicians, naturalist David Fairchild, and many artists. Henry Flagler visited the Munroes on more than one occasion, as did Julia Tuttle. James Ingraham, Flagler's chief deputy, was also a frequent visitor and became a close friend. "Here is a home," historian F. W. Decroix wrote, "where the most cultured of artists and scientists have met, here have mingled."[24]

Mary and Kirk entertained more than the rich and famous. The doors of Scrububs always stood open for visitors and, as Mary's diary attests, hardly a day went by when someone—man, woman, or child—did not drop in. Although they were childless, the Munroes had a special affinity for children, and children loved them. Patty Munroe Catlow, Ralph Munroe's daughter, recalled how children always found a warm welcome, even if they only stopped by for cookies. If they were lucky, Mary would let them hold a beautiful old China doll named Amelia that she kept in a box. Each Christmas the Munroes held a Christmas party for both the white and the black children.[25]

For the adults other treats awaited at Scrububs. Mary's "little teas" took on legendary status. A renowned cook, she gained local fame for her sponge cake. She often took her baked goods to friends, visitors, and community bazaars. Besides bringing together individuals and small groups, she and Kirk also invited a myriad of community organizations and diverse groups to meet at Scrububs if their cause benefited society. "I didn't begin to know the Grove," Marjory Stoneman Douglas wrote, "until I sat on Mrs. Munroe's front porch at a Bird Club meeting."[26]

For a time, the Housekeepers' Club remained Mary's principal vehicle for leadership but, with time and events, the situation changed. In March 1895 Mary agreed to become its president and spent most of the year that followed trying to raise money to build a clubhouse. Reelected the following year, she then abruptly resigned as president one week later. By this time her mother's personality had begun to assert itself; Mary's penchant for resignation when she did not get her way would continue for the rest of her life. This time she quit because her fellow members rejected Ralph Munroe's new wife, Jesse, whom she had proposed for membership. Some said that the ladies had hoped Ralph Munroe would marry Flora McFarlane. When he chose another, they were not happy. Mary's resignation prompted reconsideration at the next meeting, and Jesse was voted in. Mary, however, did not return until 1905 although her influence continued. "She managed all Coconut Grove with a high hand," wrote Marjory Stoneman Douglas.[27]

South Florida experienced great change in 1896 with important consequences for Coconut Grove. Henry Flagler's railroad arrived in April, linking Miami to the nation. Three months later, 344 citizens incorporated the city of Miami. South Florida's frontier days were rapidly ending. The pace of change prompted early efforts to protect the area's unique environment. Not surprisingly, Mary and Kirk Munroe took positions at the forefront of a variety of such causes. In 1900, Mary spoke out to preserve the bluff rocks on what is today's South Bayshore Drive from road widening. She must have succeeded because the bluffs remain today and are now protected by the state of Florida.[28]

Mary's greatest passion soon became apparent as she and Kirk committed themselves and their time to protecting birds. Their leadership, both singly and together, made a difference that resonates yet today. At the turn of the century, Kirk, who was writing as many as three books a year, was considered one of Florida's most famous residents and outdoorsmen. In 1902, soon after a group of Floridians formed the Florida Audubon Society, Kirk Munroe became a vice president, joining other notables including Edward Bok, Thomas Edison, and Governor William Sherman Jennings. One of the society's first efforts led it to press for the passage and enforcement of legislation against plume hunting. In this era, ladies' millinery featured a variety of bird feathers and plumes called aigrettes. Because of the demand for and high prices of feathers, plume hunters ignored the laws then on the books and prowled the vast expanse of the Florida Everglades, looking for prized egret plumes. Following a strong letter from Kirk that described the tragic situation, the activities of "the relentless plume hunter," and the impending "utter extermination" of the beautiful Everglades birds, the National Audubon Society took Munroe's suggestion and hired Guy Bradley as the first Everglades bird warden. After a plume hunter murdered Bradley in 1905, the call for enforcement intensified. While Kirk worked within the Audubon Society movement, Mary undertook an aggressive one-woman campaign against women who wore feather-adorned hats.[29]

About the time of Bradley's death, Mary rejoined the Housekeepers' Club. This occurred soon after the Florida Federation of Women's Clubs held their annual meeting in Miami during January 1905. The Housekeepers' Club entertained the federation delegates at their Coconut Grove clubhouse and, between meetings and dinner, more than one hundred women walked down the Coconut Grove trail to Scrububs to be entertained by Mary and her husband. During one of the federation sessions, Mary spoke on "Early Club Life in South Florida." At another session Housekeepers' Club member Edith Gifford, wife of the well-known forester Dr. John Gifford, convinced the federation to endorse a resolution to make a federal forest reservation of Paradise Key, a step previously taken for Pelican Island. The Key, a hammock island in the Everglades, hosted a large stand of native royal palms. Although nothing came of this resolution at the time, Paradise Key became another of Mary's passionate causes.[30]

Within one year of Mary's return to the Housekeepers' Club, she again became president. These new responsibilities, however, could not stem the tide of her activism or the flow of her energy. In addition to her Housekeepers' Club duties, she organized the Dade County Federation of Women's Clubs and became its first president. She gained some notoriety in this role by refusing to call the members "ladies." Instead, she preferred the term "women," especially when she wanted the members' undivided attention. She was also active in the state federation and became state secretary to the general federation, the national women's club organization.[31]

Back at home, she organized a group of boys into what she called "The Coconut Grove Rangers," a sort of junior Audubon Society. She was their inspiration and leader, and held most of their meetings in her home. She also organized a similar group in the black community and encouraged the Rangers' later admission of girls. As her profile grew, she became a much sought-after speaker. "Mrs. Munroe is a most resourceful woman and manages to infuse her enthusiasm and personality into making each revealing program better than the last," a *Miami Herald* reporter wrote after one of her speeches. She also busied herself writing for newspapers and magazines, first under the pseudonym Melvina Myrtle and then as Mrs. Kirk Munroe. Given her other responsibilities, Mary turned down reelection as Housekeepers' Club president in 1906 but again assumed the presidency in 1909 and 1910. She also chaired the Florida Federation of Women's Clubs' Forestry Committee and served as a board member of the Florida Audubon Society.[32]

During this period the question of Paradise Key's preservation again captured her attention. In February 1909 her good friend James Ingraham reminded her of the key's singular importance. He had revisited it during construction of Henry Flagler's Florida East Coast Railroad, which was snaking its way down the Florida Keys to Key West. Mary came up with the idea that the best way to save Paradise Key was to encourage Flagler to give it to the Florida Federation. Within a month Ingraham replied that he had talked to Flagler and that the tycoon was amenable to the proposal. When Ingraham learned that not all the land belonged to Flagler, he encouraged Mary to write to the trustees of the Internal Improvement Fund of the State to inquire whether the federation could purchase the land. Following his suggestion, Mary fired off letters to both the trustees and the governor. The tangled chain of title slowed the effort down, but Mary and Ingraham persisted.[33]

Years of frustration followed until May Mann Jennings—wife of former Governor William Sherman Jennings—became president of the Florida Federation of Women's Clubs in 1914. Mary and her friend Edith Gifford, who had proposed the earlier resolution, encouraged Jennings to make the acquisition of Paradise Key one of her highest priorities. "The women down in that part of the country are very enthusiastic over the park subject," May wrote. In December 1914, she came to Miami to see for herself what the women described. Included in the motorcade to Homestead were Mary Barr Munroe; Mrs. T. V. Moore, federation member at large; Mrs. A. Leight Monroe, president of the Miami Woman's Club; former Governor Jennings; and the Jennings' son. Upon seeing the hammock in person, May Mann Jennings concurred enthusiastically that the ecological treasure must be preserved. On the way back from Paradise Key, Mary suggested naming the new highway to the area after James Ingraham, who had been so pivotal in spearheading negotiations to this point.[34]

Despite setbacks and complicated legislative and land transactions, within two years the Florida Federation of Women's Clubs—aided by a gift of additional land by Mrs. Henry Flagler—became the only women's club in America to own a state park. When the grand opening occurred as part of the federation's twenty-second annual convention held in Miami, a motorcade of 128 cars left Miami for the dedication. Included as honored guests were Mary and Kirk Munroe and Edith Gifford, who was named the chairwoman of the federation's Royal Palm Park Committee. No one knew it at the time but Paradise Key, renamed Royal Palm State Park, would become the nucleus of the future Everglades National Park.[35]

One year before Royal Palm State Park opened, Mary launched the Coconut Grove Audubon Society. Three years later, she opened the Miami branch. The only surprising thing about this effort is that she did not do it sooner. The Coconut Grove Rangers served as bird protectors, but the Audubon Society had the prestige and influence to make things happen. On April 16, 1915, Kirk Munroe, as state honorary vice president, called a meeting at the schoolhouse to officially launch the Coconut Grove Audubon Society. By this time the Grove was home to many wealthy residents, William Matheson, William Deering, and Arthur Curtis James among them. Unlike in some other parts of the country where the wealthy lived behind closed gates, these industrial leaders and their wives participated in community affairs and were the first to give large checks to the new organization. No one was surprised when those assembled elected Mary president.[36]

For Mary, this new responsibility proved a natural fit. "Her objection to feather wearing is well known," Audubon Society chronicler Lucy Blackman asserted. "Wherever she goes she has distributed thousands of leaflets on 'The White Badges of Cruelty.'" Blackman summed up her method and its effect.

> "Whensoe'er Mrs. Munroe's keen eye saw an aigrette waving, there she followed, cornering the wearer—be it on the street, in the crowded hotel lobby, on the beach, at church or entertainment or party—there compelled her to listen to the story of cruelty and murder of which her vanity was the contributing cause. And Mrs. Munroe was eloquent and several were known to have taken off their hat and destroyed their aigrettes as a result of their encounter of Mrs. Munroe. It was not unusual for women to be reduced to tears, whether of anger or humiliation or repentance.

Mary saw to it that the Housekeepers' Club had a sign prohibiting women from wearing feathers at its events. Once, after a particularly heated altercation with a feather-wearer, the club's executive board wrote a letter of apology for their president's aggressive behavior. But despite Mary's sometimes offensive manner, Blackman wrote that her "militant power" was the most effective weapon in combating the killing of plume birds.[37]

For some years Mary had been identified with fights to save birds, the Seminoles, and the natural environment. "Conservation is such a big subject one almost wishes to call it a religion," she insisted. "And in a way it is, because to save life and the best things in life is a great and good work and brings its reward." In pursuit of her goals, Mary attended many state and national meetings, traveling alone to distant places. As chairman of the Florida Federation's Conservation Committee she was particularly pleased to be the federation's delegate to the second meeting of the National Conservation Congress held in St. Paul, Minnesota. Here, she rubbed shoulders with the giants of the fast growing national conservation movement: President Theodore Roosevelt,

President William Howard Taft, and Secretary of the Interior Gifford Pinchot. Something happened at the meeting, however, that caused Kirk to protest the way one of the male delegates treated the women. "My wife has done more for conserving natural resources in this state than all the men put together," he wrote. The Housekeepers' Club followed up with a resolution supporting Munroe's position.[38]

As the years of the mid-1910s unfolded, Mary turned a portion of her attention to writing, combining her activist zeal with her favorite cause. In 1914 she became a regular contributor to Lebarron Perrine's new publication called *The Tropic Magazine,* which focused on important local issues. Mary chose to name her column "Bird Gossip." She wrote about her favorite subjects—"Plume Bearing Birds," the Coconut Grove Audubon Society, and sometimes just a loving muse about a bird. Interestingly, she signed all these articles Mary Barr Munroe instead of Mrs. Kirk Munroe, the name she had previously used.[39]

Besides her other activities Mary took on another important cause: preserving Florida history. Although always interested in the subject, her involvement came about by accident. In 1911, after again resigning from the Housekeepers' Club, she realized that she needed to be connected to a club in order to keep her membership in the Florida Federation. So in March 1911 she started what she called "my club." Kirk suggested the name Folio Club, and within a week she had written a constitution and signed up some of the Grove's most notable residents. Her next step was to get the club admitted into the federation, which she achieved easily. Although Florida already had a historical society, within a short time the Folio Club became the second organization to collect and preserve Florida history. By 1917, she had launched chapters all over the state and, according to the *Miami Herald*, had gathered a significant collection of "unusual and verified historical facts." The article continued, "Although the club membership is not large, the work they are doing will be of great value to the future writers of our state's history and romance." The item concluded with notice that the *Jacksonville Florida Times-Union,* considered by many to be the state's principal daily newspaper, had run a glowing editorial praising the club's work.[40]

Following her customary practice, Mary combined her passion for club work with her passion for Florida history. She accepted the position of chairwoman of the Florida Federation's history committee, a committee she probably suggested. In 1921 she turned all her historical data—which included a statewide collection of pioneer histories, photographs, family letters, and memorabilia—over to Royal Palm Park, which she envisioned would become the historical center for the state.[41]

Kirk and Mary remained engaged in public affairs, but age started to limit their activities. They also faced financial difficulties. Kirk had not written a new book since 1906, so they were living on small royalties and income from magazine and newspaper articles. By 1920 they had sold off most of the land they had acquired in the early years except their beloved Scrububs. As the Florida boom of the post–World War I era heated up, they realized that, if they sold Scrububs, they would have the means to maintain their lifestyle. Another factor in their decision related to the arrival of both of Mary's sisters to join their household following Amelia Barr's death in 1919. Sadly, in April 1920 they sold Scrububs to John B. Semple of Pittsburgh for $100,000 and purchased the DeForest Christiance home on Leafy Way for $35,000. "It was a trying time," Mary recorded, "but we got through with it." On October 24 she noted, "Our last day in dear old Scrububs." Kirk shared his feelings in the guest book when he added, "Moved to Kirkland House, October 25, 1920, after 35 happy years spent therein."[42]

Life for Mary in the Munroes' new home involved little day-to-day sacrifice. Kirkland House stood out as a substantial Tudor-style residence. It had a cottage where sisters Alice and Lilly resided, making the living accommodations easier for everyone. The guest book shows that visitors continued to come— Marjory Stoneman Douglas, soon-to-be Congresswoman Ruth Bryan Owen, and artist Maxfield Parrish, to name a few. Mary continued to have her "little teas," but in May 1921 she confided to her diary, "Had my last tea. Only I knew it would be my last."[43]

Mary continued to speak at club events and celebrations but was clearly slowing down. On April 20, 1922, she wrote that she "fell and hurt myself." Despite a bandaged arm and shoulder she made her last public appearance at the Housekeepers' Club on April 28. "With a flash of her old spirit that made her a dominant figure for so long in the Housekeepers' Club," Jefferson Bell observed, "she insisted on standing to speak, and gave one of her characteristic talks, full of interesting and intimate little references to pioneer club life."[44]

Mary's decline was a matter of public concern. Throughout the summer newspapers occasionally reported on Mary's condition, usually expressing hopeful sentiments that she was getting better. Besides having broken bones, it also appears she was depressed. On September 8, 1922, after spending a happy and cheerful day lying on the sofa in Kirk's office while greeting friends, she died quietly late in the afternoon. She was buried the next day at Woodlawn Park, a fitting final resting place. She and Kirk had purchased the cemetery's first lot, and she had led the charge to make Woodlawn a bird sanctuary. Kirk recorded her passing in the Scrububs guest book:

The *gracious, loving, all presiding* spirit [of] the home—Mary Barr Munroe—passed from it, forever! on Friday Sept 8 at 4:30 o'clock, and was buried in Woodlawn at 11 o'clock am of the following day. And thus a chapter of happy life is closed. KM[45]

Kirk Munroe outlasted his wife by eight years. In 1924 he married Mabel Stearns, who made efforts to save and protect both Kirk Munroe's and Mary Barr Munroe's papers, now housed at the Library of Congress. As Kirk's physical and mental condition deteriorated, Mabel put him in a sanitarium in Orlando where he died in 1930.[46]

As a couple Kirk and Mary Barr Munroe had few rivals in Florida history. Singly, each left a special legacy. But it was Mary's unique personality that people remembered and valued most. As the *Miami Herald* put it:

> Mrs. Munroe was a real personality, a figure of dominating interest and value in the whole early history of this country's development. She has left no one who can take her place among us, who can in any degree fill that place her vibrant, energetic and highly individualized presence made.... Her familiar figure, the keen sparkle in her eyes, the vigor, the grasp, the stimulus of her excellent mind, she will be missed for a very long time.[47]

Notes

1. Marjory Stoneman Douglas, "Fine People Who Made the Grove," *Village Post* 8 (March 1964): 7.

2. Amelia Barr, *All the Days of My Life: An Autobiography* (New York, 1913), 119–285.

3. Ibid., 300–19.

4. Kirk Munroe, "Autobiography," as quoted in Irvin Leonard, *The Florida Adventures of Kirk Munroe* (Chuluota, Fla., 1975), 25.

5. Ibid., 11–15.

6. Leonard, *Florida Adventures*, 22–24.

7. Kirk Munroe, "'The Lost Psyche': Diary of a Canoe Trip, (Monday, November 28, 1881 to March 12, 1882)," as quoted in Leonard, *Florida Adventures*, 39–60.

8. Barr, *All the Days*, 374–75.

9. Leonard, *Florida Adventures*, 2–3.

10. Diary of Mary Barr Munroe, January 24, February 2, and March 4, 1886, in Papers of Kirk Munroe, 1850–1940, Manuscript Division, Library of Congress, Washington, D.C. (hereafter, Munroe Diary). On Ralph Munroe, see Arva Moore Parks, *The Forgotten Frontier: Florida Through the Lens of Ralph Middleton Munroe* (Miami, 2004).

11. Munroe Diary, March 11, 1886.

12. Dade County Deed Records, Book B, 323–24, Dade County Records Center, Miami; Munroe Diary, January 16–17, 1887.

13. "The Scrububs" guest book, 1–2, Papers of Kirk Munroe.

14. Ibid., 1–83.

15. Kirk Munroe, Ralph Middleton, and Vincent Gilpin, *The Commodore's Story* (New York, 1930), 166–69.

16. Parks, *Forgotten Frontier*, 95.

17. Mrs. Kirk Munroe, "Pioneer Women of Dade County," *Miami Metropolis*, July 3, 1909.

18. Mary Barr Munroe, "The Seminole Women of Florida," introduction by Arva Moore Parks, *Tequesta: Journal of the Historical Association of Southern Florida* 41 (1981): 23–32.

19. Gertrude M. Kent, *The Coconut Grove School in Pioneer Days, 1887–1894* (Miami, 1972), 22–23; Munroe Diary, February 13, 1891; "Housekeepers' Club Minutes," February 19, 1891, University of Miami Library Special Collections; "A Housekeepers' Club," *Harper's Bazar*, April 16, 1892, 310.

20. Munroe Diary, May 26, 1891.

21. "Coconut Grove Library Has Romantic History Dating Back to Settlement Days," *Miami Herald*, September 19, 1921.

22. "Coconut Grove Items," *Miami Daily Metropolis*, December 31, 1897. See also Arva Moore Parks, "The History of Coconut Grove, Florida, 1821–1925" (master's thesis, University of Miami, 1971).

23. Florence P. Haden, "Our Pioneers of the Housekeepers' Club," *Miami Metropolis*, March 29, 1922.

24. F. W. Decroix, *Historical, Industrial, and Commercial Data of Miami and Fort Lauderdale, Dade County, Florida: The Most Progressive and Conspicuous Section of the East Coast; Facts and Figures Relating to Miami and Fort Lauderdale and Other Growing Cities and Settlements* (St. Augustine, 1911), 304.

25. Personal interview with Patty Munroe Catlow by the author, September 16, 1982 (notes in possession of the author).

26. Douglas, "Fine People," 7.

27. Ibid.

28. "Housekeepers' Club Minutes," April 19, 1900.

29. Stuart B. McIver, *Death in the Everglades* (Gainesville, 2003), 8.

30. Mrs. Kirk Munroe, "Early Club Life in South Florida," *Miami Metropolis*, January 24, 1905; Lucy Worthington Blackman, *The Florida Federation of Women's Clubs, 1895–1937* (Jacksonville, Fla., 1939), 21.

31. Jefferson Bell, "Told Under the Palms," *Miami Herald*, Sept. 17, 1922; "The Florida Women's Club Exhibit at Biennial of General Federation," *Miami Metropolis*, June 30, 1908.

32. "All Day Meeting at Larkins by Women's Clubs," *Miami Herald*, March 3, 1918.

33. Mrs. W. S. Jennings, "Historical Sketch: Royal Palm State Park," *Homestead* (Fla.) *Enterprise*, November 23, 1916.

34. May Mann Jennings to Mrs. William Hocker, January 8, 1915, as quoted in Linda D. Vance, *May Mann Jennings, Florida's Genteel Activist* (Gainesville, 1985), 83; Jennings, "Historical Sketch: Royal Palm State Park."

35. Vance, *May Mann Jennings*, 92.

36. "Minutes," Coconut Grove Audubon Society, 1915–1922, Coconut Grove Audubon Society Records, Historical Museum of Southern Florida.

37. Ibid.; clipping, *Miami Herald*, November 1915; Lucy Worthington Blackman, *The Florida Audubon Society, 1900–1935* (privately published, n.d.), 20–21 (pamphlet on file at the Historical Museum of Southern Florida); Edith Gifford to Mrs. Commins, April 9 (no year), "Housekeepers' Club Minutes."

38. "Women's Club Talks 'Conservation' with Mrs. Kirk Munroe as Leader," *Miami Herald*, February 17, 1915; "Kirk Munroe Flays Professor Condra for Rudeness to Women Delegates," *Miami Daily Metropolis*, September 17, 1910.

39. Mary Barr Munroe, "Bird Gossip," *The Tropic Magazine* (June, July, September 1914, and January, April–July, 1915).

40. Munroe Diary, March 2–15, 1911; "Annual Report of the Folio Club, Cocoanut Grove," *Miami Herald*, January 7, 1917.

41. "Preserving Historical Data," *Homestead* (Fla.) *Enterprise*, December 15, 1921.

42. Munroe Diary, April 17, 1920. "The Scrububs" guest book, 61.

43. Ibid., May 3, 1921.

44. Jefferson Bell, "Housekeepers' Club Celebrates Pioneer Day with Most Interesting Program," *Miami Herald*, April 28, 1922.

45. "The Scrububs," guest book, 67.

46. Leonard, *Florida Adventures*, 31–32.

47. Editorial, *Miami Herald*, September 11, 1922.

CHAPTER 6

María Valdés de Gutsens
1860–1941

The Soul of Key West's Mercedes Hospital

Consuelo E. Stebbins

THE ISLAND OUTPOST OF KEY WEST, Florida, forever changed beginning on October 10, 1868, when the Ten Years War erupted in Cuba. Waves of Cuban refugees swept onto American shores, their strong social bonds enabling them to survive the hardships of unfamiliar surroundings and political strife while maintaining their sacred cultural heritage. Proud and committed to their lineage, the Key West émigrés flourished as they kept a nurturing watch over one another. In times of great incertitude, one conviction remained clear for them: they would never lose their cultural identity. No one exemplified more clearly the traits of the virtuous Cuban woman who clung to that identity than María Valdés de Gutsens, who dedicated her adult life to tending the sick and

Figure 11. María Valdés de Gutsens, c. 1934. (Courtesy of Monroe County Public Library.)

poor at Key West. Juan Pérez Rolo, a contemporary, described María as a true mother of those in need; a person who spent her life taking care of the poor during their final days.[1]

María Valdés de Gutsens earned recognition, in part, for her service as the director of Key West's Casa del Pobre (Poorhouse). Also known as the Mercedes Hospital, the facility opened in 1911 and closed in 1943. For more than thirty years, María labored as director and major fund-raiser, donating her time and efforts to the difficult task of keeping the charitable institution open in order to serve the medical needs of the poor. Few residents earned more love than did "Mamá" Valdés, who walked the island's streets daily for much of the first half of the twentieth century to solicit donations for the hospital. Anyone who needed medical attention could find it at the Casa del Pobre, thanks to the tireless dedication of María Valdés de Gutsens.

The Valdés family in many ways typified those who fled war-torn Cuba for Key West in the post-1868 era. Its members sought jobs in the island city's hundreds of cigar factories. In 1888, when the Valdés family arrived, the industry particularly needed workers as it rebounded from troubled times, including the labor strikes of 1885, a devastating fire of March 1886 that destroyed the commercial district, and an 1887 outbreak of yellow fever. Within six months after the great fire, though, an industry renaissance had begun. A number of factories reopened, and their need for workers drew an increasing number of Cubans, both returning former residents and new arrivals from Havana or Tampa. "The factories are all getting down to solid work again," a local man reported in September 1887. "By the first of October we expect to see Key West resume her air of thrift and cheerfulness—by that time we think it will be safe for the refugees to begin returning, that is, if there is no more cases of the fever."[2]

The Key West that greeted María in 1888 appeared remarkable in comparison with the rest of poor and scarcely populated Florida. "There is hardly anything in Key West to remind one of any other town in the United States," a visitor observed. "We are on a little island here, cut off from the rest of the world, both civilized and uncivilized, and absolutely dependent upon Havana, New Orleans, Tampa and New York, especially the last-named place. . . . But the great peculiarity of the place is in its population and their mode of life. There is such a congregation of American colored and white folks, Cubans, colored immigrants from Nassau and Conchs, and such an admixture of them all that it is impossible to determine where the line begins and where it ends." The visitor concluded, "The Cubans run the island to a very great extent. They not only control the cigar business, which is the leading and almost only industry here, but they seem to own a majority of the smaller shops as well."[3]

As these observations suggest, the Key West Cuban community had sunk deep roots in American soil, and its members had no hesitation about exerting their influence in politics and elsewhere. Although political circumstances would change dramatically in the years ahead, in 1888 most Cubans joined black voters in supporting Republican candidates. Both Cubans and African Americans served in public office. In fact, in 1888 Monroe County elected a black sheriff and a black county judge, both Republicans, thanks in part to Cuban votes. "Talking about enthusiasm, why the way the colored and white Republican Cubans, the colored Americans and Baham[ian]s and the American white Republicans celebrated the election of the National Republican ticket here as well as their own [local] ticket," the same visitor observed, "was enough to make old Zach Chandler turn in his grave." He continued, "They not only painted the town vermillion, but every other color. Torchlights, brass bands, Cuban dances, Chinese lanterns, barbecues, cards marked 'free trade' and attached to the caudal appendages of horses, endless exclamations in Spanish and English—these are some of the manifestations of Key West enthusiasm."[4]

Given that this enthusiasm erupted just as the era of Jim Crow laws was dawning upon Florida and the South, it suggests that a special environment existed upon the key. "Notwithstanding [some] manifestations of prejudice Key West is the freest town in the South," the visitor—an African American—related, "not even Washington excepted." He went on to add, "There is a liberal sentiment here due to the presence of foreigners, for any ex-slave-holding foreigner is better than an ex-slave-holder [from the South]. The Cubans probably have the same reason for being prejudiced as the Southern whites, but notwithstanding slavery has been only recently abolished there they are not equally so by any means. They have prejudices no doubt, but they are not so foolish as to let the bugbear of social equality frighten them into denying a man his natural rights because he happens to be colored."[5]

This is the complex and exhilarating world María entered when she, then aged twenty-eight, and her parents, Raphael and Francisca, traveled from Cuba as the 1880s drew to a close. Unfortunately, details regarding María's early life, beyond the names of her parents and the estimated date of her birth in Cuba, remain obscure. It is known that, at about the same time as the Valdés family arrived in the United States, so did a young man named Antonio Gutsens. Although Antonio was ten years younger than María, within a few years they married, on March 29, 1893. By that time Antonio had established himself in the local community; yet, he retained that fierce sense of pride in his homeland that marked Key West's Cuban community. During the War of 1895, a renewed effort aimed at freeing Cuba from Spanish control that led to the Spanish-

American War, Antonio served as a captain in the Cuban Liberating Army. When the war ended in 1898, Antonio returned to Key West. By that time he worked as a barber. It does not appear that the couple had children. Records from 1910 list María and Antonio remaining together. Living with them were boarders Carmelina Martínez, aged nine, and María Martínez, aged twenty. The young women probably were relatives of María's or Antonio's.[6]

When Antonio landed at Key West for the second time in 1898, the environment within which he and María lived had begun to deteriorate. Where an atmosphere of "good feeling" had prevailed earlier, cultural disharmony had commenced to rule the day. This shift—based originally in political dynamics related to efforts by white Democrats to overcome their Republican opposition and of white Republicans to eliminate the influence of their black counterparts—had evidenced itself as early as 1889 when Florida's governor ousted African American Judge James Dean from office ostensibly because, contrary to state law, he had married a "white" Cuban man Antonio González to a mulatto woman named Annie Maloney. The governor's act angered African Americans, but Dean's response outraged the Cuban community. "This man [Antonio González] is a Cuban, and it is a notorious fact, that stands uncontradicted in this community, that nearly nine-tenths of the Cubans here are mulattoes, and they are so treated by the Caucasians of this place; those of pure Spanish blood being the only pure whites that are unquestionably accepted as such to all intents and purposes," he asserted. Dean added, "It is also a fact that large numbers of these mulatto Cubans pass for white. In fact, they are not white." The split in the formerly powerful political alliance between Cubans and blacks grew wider when Governor Francis Fleming named Ángel de Lono as Dean's replacement, thus furnishing Monroe County with its first Hispanic judge and further angering the black community.[7]

As María and Antonio would have witnessed, racial tensions continued to heighten. Whites in 1889 obtained passage of a state law that seized control of local government and placed power in the hands of Key West's conservative white leaders. Their friends in the legislature additionally imposed a poll tax as a prerequisite for voting, a move that, within only a few years, had reduced the Cuban and African American electorates substantially. Meanwhile the island's economy struggled as competition from Tampa's Ybor City bled the local cigar industry and drew from the island many of its Cuban-born workers. By the mid-1890s the city found itself forced to yield to Jacksonville the honor of being the state's largest city. Little wonder that an observer of the local scene in 1907 would note, "This key is settled by Cubans, negroes, Conchs and Americans." He added, "Placing the population at 15,000, the proportions are about five, four, five and one. These proportions live in an agreeable state of contempt and discord."[8]

The contempt and discord touched most segments of life, and as María would have attested, this included health care. Especially needed was a hospital to attend to the medical problems of local civilians. Since 1844 Marine Hospital had been serving the community, even though its mission focused on sick or injured seaman servicing Key West and other shipping ports in the Gulf of Mexico. By the turn of the century, however, the need for a civilian hospital to attend to the local citizens, among them men injured while constructing the Florida East Coast Railroad from Miami to the island city, was apparent. Local white leaders proved unwilling, however, to spend tax dollars on a facility that would serve all members of the community and were even less inclined to construct separate facilities to serve each ethnic community. Responding to the need, Dr. John B. Maloney opened the city's first private hospital in October 1908. In 1911, he expanded his operations. The newly remodeled Louise Maloney Hospital, named after his wife, was equipped with thirty beds and an operating room. It now received funding from the county.[9]

Dr. Maloney's commendable enterprise still left most Cubans and African Americans without access to hospital care. Fortunately, the local influence and mentorship of Dr. Joseph Yates Porter, a former Marine Hospital physician who served from 1889 to 1913 as the state's public health officer, had produced at or else attracted to Key West numerous highly qualified physicians, black and white. Typically, these medical doctors treated Cuban and black patients in their homes. Accordingly, surviving accounts from the early twentieth century note events such as "Mrs. Lucy Palacios, a well known citizen, died March 17 at her residence" or "Mrs. Alice Jackson, 306 Virginia street, is critically ill [and] friends are asked to call."[10]

An attempt was made as early as 1904 to improve health care and other services for the Cuban community when a group of Cuban women—inspired by the insights and determination of Dolores Mayg, a Cuban refugee—founded a charitable organization called the Beneficencia Cubana. The society aimed to provide basic necessities for the poor, especially for Cuban émigrés. Impressed by their initiative, Antonio Díaz Carrasco—the first consul of the Republic of Cuba—pledged his financial and moral support. The Beneficencia Cubana subsequently made positive contributions to the community, but did not command the necessary resources to erect a hospital.[11]

That task was left to María V. Gutsens and others, and not until 1910 did those concerned individuals manage to make concrete progress. In December of that year María and other members of the Dolores Mayg Society—including Blanca Ferriol de Pérez, Carlotta Cenarro de Alayeto, María Manas de Betancourt, Esperanza La Fe, Felicia Rodríguez de Rueda, Caridad Rodríguez, María Escalante, Palmenia Hernández, María L. Carrasco, Leopoldina Elizarde, and Ignacia and Angelica Fernández—conceived a plan to open a charity hospital serving anyone in need, regardless of race or nationality. It would offer patients a caring environment where they would be attended by doctors who volunteered on a monthly basis. Since the hospital was a nonprofit organization, no city or county funds were pledged; funding would have to come from donations. The task of collecting these donations fell to María Gutsens.[12]

Dolores Mayg died before her dream could become a reality, but the women of the Dolores Mayg Society kept her memory alive by working tirelessly for her cause. Particularly, María Gutsens and other committee members appealed to cigar industrialist Eduardo H. Gato for the use of his private home near Division Street (now Truman Avenue) and North Beach Drive (now José Martí Drive), a structure that had been unused since Gato returned to Cuba in 1898 after the War of Independence concluded. To further their efforts, María and her associates skillfully applied public pressure through newspaper publicity, as illustrated by an article published in the *Jacksonville Florida Times-Union* in April 1911: "The ladies of the Cuban charitable society, Dolores Mayg, are hard at work upon their project to open a hospital, which it is hoped to have ready for patients by May 20," the item began. It continued,

> Negotiations are pending between the society and E. H. Gato, whereby it is thought that the old Gato residence property on Division Street and North Beach Drive may be secured for the hospital. Theodore Pérez left this week to confer with Mr. Gato regarding the matter. At a meeting of the society held on Wednesday night, a special committee was appointed to solicit funds for the establishment of the hospital. . . . They will begin a canvass of the city on Monday and any contribution, however small, will be gratefully received.[13]

Success crowned the efforts. Impressed by the activities of María and her associates, Eduardo H. Gato gave the society permission to use his home, rent-free, for five years. In a move that almost certainly assured future aid from the Gato family, the women astutely named their hospital after Gato's wife, Mercedes. They then faced the task of converting the Gato home into a two-story medical facility. A committee of five women—including María V. Gutsens, María Betancourt, Mrs. Antonio Izaguirre, Mrs. Pacho, and Mrs. Concepción

Figure 12. Key West's Casa del Pobre, Mercedes, with María Valdés de Gutsens likely standing in doorway, c. 1920s. (Courtesy of Monroe County Public Library.)

Ramírez—dedicated themselves to this task. Only Concepción Ramírez, who agreed to live at the facility in order to attend to the patients day and night, was to receive a salary.[14]

The task of raising approximately $100 per month to keep the facility operating fell to María Gutsens, an endeavor in which she enjoyed significant support. While specifics of her fund-raising methods have not come down to us, at least some details of her successes have. Eduardo Gato had agreed to provide partial support for five years, and after that period ended, his children fortunately continued to offer modest donations. Dr. Joseph N. Fogarty, a Key West physician, also supported the hospital, to the point that one leading figure among local white citizens attributed to Fogarty much of the credit for its establishment. "He contributed liberally in cash," Jefferson B. Browne asserted in 1912, "donated all the instruments and equipment for the operating room, and furnished and maintains a room."[15]

María surely beamed with pride when the Casa del Pobre, Mercedes, opened on October 10, 1911. The week prior to its inauguration, executive committee members had met at the home of Cuban Consul Carrasco to finalize the festivities for the opening. They chose the date of October 10 to commemorate the beginning of the Ten Years War (1868–1878), which started with the call to revolt, the Grito de Yara. Local officials and Cuban dignitaries were invited to participate in festivities that included speeches at the San Carlos Institute and a "monster parade." On the morning of October 10, the executive committee, including María, met the steamship *Miami* when it arrived from Havana. On board were Cuban dignitaries, 1895 War of Independence veterans, and civic leaders. A large parade that afternoon moved from the San Carlos Institute to the Mercedes Hospital for the opening ceremony. Following the ceremony the parade headed for the Key West Cemetery to place wreaths on the gravesites of Cuban soldiers who had died during the war, the victims of the destruction of the *Maine,* Dolores Mayg, and Mercedes Gato. That night a large gathering of Cubans met at the San Carlos to hear speeches made by the visiting Cuban dignitaries.[16]

Yet again María and her associates took care to ensure maximum publicity for their cause and its various successes, well understanding the press's ability to aid their search for support. Key West newspapers of the era largely have not survived, but this article regarding the dedication appeared in the state's largest circulation daily newspaper:

> Everything was in readiness for the great festivities in connection with the celebration of Yara day today and the opening of the Mercedes Hospital for the poor. The festivities began with a grand ball at the Cuban Club Monday night. At 5:00 am Tuesday morning a large delegation met Major General Loynaz del Castillo, Colonel Manuel Piedia and Commander Manuel Secades at the P&O steamship dock on the arrival of the steamer *Miami* from Havana. The distinguished visitors were escorted to San Carlos and a welcome extended by Cuban Consul Antonio Díaz Carrasco in behalf of the people of Key West after which they were taken for a drive over the city. At 1:00 pm Tuesday, the parade formed on Duval Street and marched on Division Street and then to the Mercedes Hospital near the North Beach....
>
> Upon arriving at the hospital the ceremony of the inauguration took place and the Cuban, American, and Red Cross flags were carried. After the addresses, the parade formed again and marched to the city cemetery where the graves of the Cuban martyrs and the victims of the *Maine* disaster were decorated as well as the graves of Mrs. Dolores Mayg and Mrs. Mercedes Gato, after which the parade disbanded. In the evening appropriate exercises were held at San Carlos. After which a banquet to the distinguished Cuban visitors was given at the Del Monico Restaurant. The Yara celebration commemorates the first outbreak of the Cuban revolution in 1868 on October 10.[17]

The magnificence of the hospital's opening found reflection in its initial successes. In fact, by 1913 Eduardo Gato, pleased with the dedication shown by

María and the women of the Dolores Mayg Society, formally presented the Sociedad Dolores Mayg with the title to the building and the land on which it stood. The Mercedes Hospital then boasted five rooms equipped with twenty-eight beds. Illustrating the astute awareness of María and her fellow volunteers for fund-raising possibilities, each room was named for one of the Gato family members: María Marques de Gato, María Mañas, Fernando Gato, Pedro Rueda, and Regla Sañudo.[18]

Such happy beginnings regrettably gave way to greater challenges for María as the years passed. World War I produced local prosperity as the island city contributed to the war effort, but the peace in late 1918 dealt a blow to the economy. The following year a "hurricane of terrible intensity" struck Key West, leaving a "toll of destruction in its wake." The city reeled from the "appalling" devastation. "The naval hospital roof was blown off and the institution flooded," one account observed. "The patients were rushed into the halls." The report continued, "The building is damaged many thousands of dollars." No description of damage at Mercedes Hospital has survived, but hurricane damage may have prompted the relocation of the building that year from its original site near North Beach to a location on Virginia Street where it remains today, now converted into condominiums.[19]

Whatever damage the hospital sustained in 1919, María ensured that it was repaired and the facilities otherwise improved. Raoul Alpizar y Poyo, for one, described the facility in 1926 as "large and beautiful." Acknowledging Eduardo Gato, he ascribed much credit to "the director of the hospital ... a noble, distinguished and altruistic woman called María V. Gutsens." Clearly, at some point Gutsens had assumed the directorship, although it is not known when. The institution was evidently successful in fulfilling its mission. "In Key West, there is Casa del Pobre, Mercedes, for the local poor who enter without being asked their names or where they came from," Alpizar y Poyo proclaimed. "The nurses there attend to the sick and give them all types of medical assistance in a loving way."[20]

Alpizar y Poyo's comments highlighted an important point about María. More than an administrator or a fund-raiser, she was a kind person who treated others with respect and love. Pérez Rolo described María's personal dedication in attending the poor. "Always kind, she devoted her life to charity and loved each individual who entered the hospital," he recorded. "She took care of the aging émigrés on the island, who one by one, ended their days in her loving care." He concluded, "She always had a friendly smile for them and was a true mother of the poor."[21]

Until her death in 1941 María Gutsens continued to direct Mercedes Hospital and raise funds to serve the community's poor. Despite overcoming almost-daily difficulties, she nonetheless faced criticism. One issue, María's generous policy of admitting patients who could have been cared for by relatives, stood out. Money also factored as a secondary issue. As Key West's economy declined through the 1920s, certain local residents questioned María's handling of the finances. In an action that spoke well for her, a local editor came to her defense. "The Mercedes Hospital is a sanctuary of love for those who live here, and it is for some of our residents who occupy it; but how many times have we heard critical remarks against this charitable institution?" the man asked. "It is clear that those who criticize the hospital do so without any knowledge of this Casa del Pobre because if they were familiar with the hospital they would never criticize it.... Some have even asked for a financial accounting of this institution. I wish there were an audit so that people could see how little money is donated to sustain it and those who are asking for the audit, have probably never contributed to the hospital's maintenance.... Our newspaper, *Florida*, offers its sincere debt of gratitude for those who support this noble institution."[22]

Yet, some local residents continued to criticize María's administration. In 1925, one year after the preceding editorial, the *Florida* again found itself compelled to defend her. It pointedly reminded residents that the clinic provided the poor with needed medical attention and even assisted with burials. "This newspaper has said on several occasions that the Mercedes Hospital of Key West, poor and forgotten by man, has nevertheless, continued to exemplify the most beautiful acts of piety in our town," the newspaper intoned. "The pain that is there finds relief; the afflictions there are changed into smiles of love, and these acts should inspire us and give us respect for this place of refuge." The newspaper concluded by asking, "Why do some people, and among them those who should go to the Hospital, try to degrade with their gossip and criticize Mrs. María Gutsens who directs and administers with motherly love this home for the poor?"[23]

Personal tragedy for María followed the public criticism. On February 12, 1934, Antonio Gutsens died, at the age of only sixty-two. The Havana native had lived at Key West for forty-six years, forty-one of them with María. His profession had shifted with the march of Jim Crow discrimination from barber to cigar worker. His widow, María Gutsens, and his brother, Luis Gutsens, survived him.[24]

Not long after her loss, María's enduring contributions and personal service—including her charitable work at the Casa del Pobre—happily brought her impressive recognition. The Republic of Cuba honored her with the Order of Carlos Manuel de Céspedes, the highest award given to individuals for meritorious service. María received notification of the distinction eight months after Antonio's death. The telegram from Cosme de la Torriente, secretary of state for the Republic of Cuba, informed her: "President Mendieta proposes to present to you, in recompense for your meritorious and patriotic services, the national Order of Merit, Carlos Manuel de Céspedes. Effusive felicitations." María's achievement is highlighted by the fact that very few Americans have received this prestigious award. The other recipients that year were all Cubans: Father Gutiérrez Lanza, meteorologist at Belén Observatory; General Mario G. Menocal, former Cuban president; and Mrs. María Reyes, founder of the Patria orphanage.[25]

It should further be noted that María received this recognition shortly after Key West's economy virtually collapsed. The cigar industry had dwindled to almost nothing, and the sponge industry had departed for more lucrative opportunities at Tarpon Springs. While most Floridians prospered during the 1919–1926 Florida Boom, the island city foundered. By the onset of the Great Depression in 1929–1930, catastrophe loomed. Florida historian Charlton Tebeau described the situation: "The boom left [Key West] relatively untouched, and its population declined in the twenties to 12,831 and by 1935 to 12,317." He continued, "By 1933 the city debt was $5,000,000, interest of a quarter of a million was unpaid, and there were no funds for current expenses. In July of 1934 the city asked the governor of the state to declare a state of emergency so that the community could be turned over to the Federal Emergency Relief Administration of the New Deal."[26]

The depths of Key West's despair seemed almost to compel public admiration of María's service, as memories of 1920s criticisms faded away. One year after she received Cuba's highest medal for meritorious service, local civic officials and visiting Cuban dignitaries honored her when Mercedes Hospital celebrated its twenty-fourth anniversary. Key West's principal newspaper described the event—held on October 10, 1935—with specific reference to its guest of honor. "October 10, anniversary of 'El Grito de Yara' was also the anniversary of María Gutsens's accession to the position of matron of Mercedes Hospital in Key West," its article began. "For the past 24 years, Mrs. Gutsens has handled the affairs of this sanctuary for the ill and invalided who are without means and has managed to carry on in the face of desperate conditions and almost impassable obstacles, it is pointed-out. . . . In consideration of her unswerving adherence to her assumed duties and her brave fight to render succor to those who are in less fortunate circumstances than she, a group of visitors from Cuba, members of the commission which came to Key West to take part in the celebration of October 10, presented Mrs. Gutsens with $21, voluntary contribution of the commission." In a conclusion that displayed María's ever-savvy sense of the value of publicity, the article went on to declare, "To express her appreciation for this unlooked for but happily welcomed gift to the institution, Mrs. Gutsens requested the *Citizen* to publish her acknowledgement of the donation."[27]

By that time María had institutionalized the anniversary celebration as a marketing and fund-raising tool for the hospital. Each annual event offered a festive atmosphere that relieved Key West doldrums and sparked positive publicity of the very real charitable work conducted there and ever-greater recognition of the role María had played in ensuring the facility's ongoing existence. In order to underscore her Cuban heritage, build publicity, and guarantee continued support, she took pains to involve Cuban officials, dignitaries, and luminaries in the celebrations. She also made good use of the great honor previously bestowed on her by the Republic of Cuba. An example of the local coverage she generated is an account of the 1938 anniversary:

> Today Mercedes Hospital, a charitable institution, celebrates its 27th anniversary, which incidentally is on the date that the first cry for freedom from Spanish oppression went up in Cuba, but the city is honoring especially Mrs. María Gutsens, 74 years old, who has kept the institution going those long 27 years by daily solicitation.
>
> Tonight 6 o'clock, Mrs. Gutsens told the *Citizen* at the visit of Cuban civic and military officials to her hospital, she will proudly wear the Carlos Manuel de Céspedes medal, the highest honor Cuba bestows—given her in 1934 for her unselfish devotion to the unfortunate of the Mercedes Hospital.
>
> Proud and [as] a happy light shines in her eyes, Mrs. Gutsens recalls the original founding of the hospital in 1911 by 26 women of Cuban descent, two from Havana of whom she is the only one left still connected with the hospital. She remembers too the donation of the building on Virginia Street between Georgia and White by the late Eduardo Gato. "A great and charitable man," she said. "It was named after his wife, Mercedes."

The *Key West Citizen*'s coverage then shifted to a description of María's ecumenical approach to fund-raising and the acquisition of needed supplies, in the process reinforcing how important even small donations were to the hospital's continuing operation:

> Mrs. Gutsens solicits daily among those of both Anglo Saxon and Latin descent to make up the $133 a month needed to keep the institution going.

Plucking a shirt here she will say, "May I have this for those at Mercedes Hospital?" In the same manner she secures parts of bottles of milk, loaves of bread, a little sugar, etc. She is known and loved by all in town.

Ultimately, she stressed her heritage and dedication as providing credibility for her solicitation efforts:

Mrs. Gutsens is the wife of the late Captain Antonio Gutsens who served in the Cuban revolution against Spanish oppression. She came to Key West 50 years ago, fleeing from persecution. Oh, Yes, she remembers very well the event of Cuban liberation, but clearer and dearer to her are those connected with the Mercedes Hospital. "It is my religion," she says summing it all up.[28]

As time passed and María's reputation reached new heights in the Key West community, the publicity associated with the anniversary celebrations focused even more particularly on her, her experiences, and her insights. It touched as well on her continuing fund-raising accomplishments despite the bitter challenge of economic depression, including commitments of public funding from Monroe County and the federal government. Coverage of the twenty-eighth anniversary offers an excellent illustration as it delved into her "errands of mercy":

Marking its 28th year of service to the sick of the community who cannot afford to pay for hospital services Mercedes Hospital tomorrow still see[s] "Mamá" Gutsens as its director. The 75 year old little Cuban lady who was one of the original founders of the institution, gray haired and wrinkled, has been a familiar sight in the city on her errands of mercy. The county contributes to the support of the hospital, but Mrs. Gutsens finds that many other things are necessary for the well being of the inmates and often she gets a can of milk here, a little hominy there to give the patients what they need.

"Times are hard but people are still generous," Mrs. Gutsens says. Everywhere she goes she is called "Mamá" by white and colored alike. She is a symbol of the care of eternal motherhood.

At the hospital at present are five patients who need the care of the hospital very badly. One patient has been there nine years. From time to time it is necessary to call in medical aid and Mrs. Gutsens finds that doctors volunteer their services gladly. At the hospital there are five in charge of the work.

The hospital was originally founded by the Dolores Mayg club for ladies, but one by one the ladies have all dropped out of the work until Mrs. Gutsens is the last left.

Cuban links still held great importance, culturally and economically, to María and to Mercedes Hospital. The anniversary coverage continued,

> In 1934 Manuel Céspedes, president of Cuba, sent Mrs. Gutsens a specially struck medal recognizing her great work. A commission came here to present the medal to her. Numerous American and Cuban flags have been given her by governmental officials. Last year Cuba sent her two beautiful flags, one American and one Cuban. Tomorrow morning they will be gaily draped in the front of the hospital. Spirit of Mercy to the Sick and Poor will have been celebrated once more at the hospital and through little Mrs. María Gutsens.[29]

By the late 1930s, María had managed to secure funding commitments from the city as well as the county. A 1939 proposal then suggested saving Key West and Monroe County money through the additional use of Mercedes Hospital as a rehabilitation center for patients who had undergone operations at the Marine Hospital. A newspaper preserved from that time offers a glimpse of daily operations, as María had framed them from nearly three decades of experience. "Mercedes Hospital is a large place, beautifully aired," its writer related. "There are about 25 beds there, which are badly needed by many patients in town," he noted. "A nurses' aid W.P.A. project will probably be in charge of the Clinic Hospital [the local county hospital]. Heading it could be kindly Miss Martínez who has a real love and talent for her work in hospitalization of the poor." The writer added, "Operations for clinic patients are now performed at Marine Hospital with required hospitalization for a few days or a week after the operation. Sometimes the patients must remain longer. They could then be removed to the Mercedes Hospital and the city and county save the $2 a day fee which is the minimum the Marine Hospital can afford to charge and which it is very kind to make so low to clinic patients." The item concluded, "These plans are still very much in the air, but this column hears the recommendations will soon be made to the county."[30]

María celebrated her thirtieth year as director of Mercedes Hospital in October 1941. Reflecting on her thirty-nine years of service, she allowed herself an uncustomary moment of self-revelation, commenting on her struggle to keep the facility open. "It has been much trouble," she observed, "and many tears." Time had taken its toll by then, and her ability to organize and conduct a community anniversary celebration clearly had diminished. When asked about plans for the thirtieth anniversary she stated simply, "We will have a good dinner and we probably will have visitors." She still labored tirelessly to solicit donations from the public to augment the small amounts of money received from the city and county, until her death, only one month later.³¹

María Valdés de Gutsens's demise came relatively suddenly. She died on November 7, 1941, at her Key West home at 1032 Catherine Street, at the age of eighty-two. The funeral service was held on November 9 at the Mercedes Hospital. Pallbearers from the order of Caballeros de Martí, long associated with women's auxiliaries of the Masonic orders, assisted at the event. An obituary listed her survivors as one daughter, Mrs. Carmelina Betancourt; two grandsons, Antonio and Arsenio Betancourt; and one granddaughter, Mrs. Salina Rodríguez. Several accounts by persons who knew María noted that she and Antonio had no children. Since Carmelina in 1910 was described as a boarder in their home, she probably was a beloved relative whom María treated as a daughter. Gutsens was buried in the Catholic cemetery in Key West.³²

As would have been expected, news of María's passing quickly reached officials in Cuba. One day after her death, the president of Cuba sent his condolences by way of the Cuban Consulate in Key West. In a note transmitted on his behalf, Colonel Fulgencio Batista expressed his regrets upon hearing of the sad news. "The President of Cuba begs me to send to the family of the patriotic María Valdés de Gutsens his sympathy on her death," Batista's secretary specifically informed Consul Berardo Rodríguez Valdés, "and requests that you represent him at the funeral."³³

María's death doomed the Casa del Pobre, Mercedes. Two years after the event the hospital closed its doors for lack of funding. Without the tireless fund-raising of its late matron the facility found itself unable to continue operating with only city and county funding; even those sources of income by then were in dispute as the county accused the city of not contributing its fair share. "Commendable efforts were being made to keep open the Mercedes Hospital at least until the time the proposed municipal hospital on Stock Island is opened, but it seems now that the Mercedes may have to close for lack of funds, and part of that reason, it was declared this morning is traceable to the inactivity of the city council in this matter," a contemporary report commented.

> The city, despite the fact that it had agreed to contribute monthly to the Hospital, has not given it a cent since last March, and when the matter came up last Tuesday night before the city councilmen, all they did was to refer it to the county commissioners.... Now, the commissioners have been contributing $100 monthly to the hospital, without missing a payment, but the action of the city councilmen, as one commissioner put it, "is a little too much." Maximo Valdez, chairman of the county's public welfare committee said to the *Citizen*: Even though the operation of Mercedes Hospital is purely a city

matter, the commissioners have been contributing $100 monthly in the hope of keeping it open until the municipal hospital is completed in order that the sick and needy in Key West may be taken care of [and now] the city councilmen are trying to dump the matter into our laps as though it was up to us to take care of the hospital alone.[34]

Since Mercedes Hospital's closure, Gato's former home has been converted into offices, apartments, and now condominiums. Despite these transformations the spirit of María V. Gutsens reportedly continues to haunt the tenants of the magnificent two-story building. During María's lifetime, the hospital was frequently understaffed, so she would often perform some of the routine nursing tasks, such as changing beds or taking patients' temperatures. Since María's death, building residents have described the apparition of an elderly woman who resembles María, who has tried to take their temperatures when they were ill. The following story numbers as one among many told by former Gato home occupants who have seen or felt María's presence:

> A couple of months after the death of María de Gutsens, a man was checked into the hospital with severe pneumonia. Convinced of his pending death, but unable to move on his own, he thought of his wife and kids and lamented the fact that he would die without being able to express his love to them one last time. As he lay suffering in the middle of the night, a nurse appeared at his bedside and asked if she could be of any assistance. He requested her help in penning a letter to his family and she happily obliged. The two stayed together for about an hour; the man lying in bed and dictating the letter, the nurse patiently writing out the words until he was finished. Upon completion she inserted the letter into an envelope, addressed it and placed it on the windowsill beside his bed. She then stayed by his side until he fell asleep.
>
> The following morning when the man awoke, his condition had improved significantly. When the nurse conducted her rounds in the morning, the gentleman asked if she would summon the night nurse so that he could thank her. "I was the only one here all night," she replied, to which the man went on to describe the nurse who had helped him. "She was a short, stocky lady with white hair and a blue gray dress." The nurse recognized the description. "We used to have a lady here who looked like that, but she has since passed on." The man was insistent she had been there and pointed to the letter she had helped him write.
>
> The nurse picked up the letter and stared in disbelief at the envelope. It was in María's handwriting.[35]

As the story of her ghost suggests, the spirit of María Valdés de Gutsens remains alive in the hearts of Key West residents, including a few individuals who still remember personally her kindness and complete dedication to assisting the poor. Some residents recall relatives who spent their last days in the care of "Mamá." Some have reported seeing a sparkling light in the Gato building. Perhaps—at least one can hope—the sparkling light will inspire others to follow María's example as a true mother to the poor.

Notes

My sincere appreciation to Tom Hambright at the Monroe County Public Library for his research assistance with locating articles and photographs; thanks also to Alicia Scott Ritter and Fred Salinero for their work on recovering the heritage of the Cuban émigrés of Key West.

1. Juan Pérez Rolo, *Mis recuerdos* (Key West, 1933), 51.

2. *Jacksonville Florida Times-Union*, September 24, 1887. For more information on the Cuban immigrant colony of Key West during the nineteenth century, see Consuelo E. Stebbins, *City of Intrigue, Nest of Revolution* (Gainesville, 2007). On Key West's history generally, see Maureen Ogle, *Key West: History of an Island of Dreams* (Gainesville, 2003).

3. *New York Age*, November 3, 1888.

4. Ibid., December 1, 1888. See also Canter Brown Jr., *Florida's Black Public Officials, 1867–1924* (Tuscaloosa, 1998); idem, "Prelude to the Poll Tax: Black Republicans and the Knights of Labor in 1880s Florida," in *Florida's Heritage of Diversity: Essays in Honor of Samuel Proctor*, ed. Mark I. Greenberg, William Warren Rogers, and Canter Brown Jr. (Tallahassee, 1997), 69–81.

5. *New York Age*, December 1, 1888.

6. Monroe County, Florida, marriage records, Book 4, p. 60 (available at Monroe County Courthouse, Key West); 1910 U.S. Decennial Census, Monroe County, Florida (population schedule).

7. *Tampa Tribune*, August 1, 1889; *Jacksonville Florida Times-Union*, July 24 and August 7, 1889; *Palm Beach Post*, February 27, 2002; *Florida Bar News* 29 (March 15, 2002), 1, 8. On Judge James Dean, see Canter Brown Jr. and Larry E. Rivers, "The Pioneer African American Jurist Who Almost Became a Bishop: Florida's Judge James Dean, 1858–1914," *Florida Historical Quarterly* 87 (Summer 2008), 16–49.

8. Brown, *Florida's Black Public Officials*, 63–66; Karl H. Grismer, *Tampa: A History of the City of Tampa and the Tampa Bay Region of Florida* (St. Petersburg, 1950), 204–6; *Key West Historic Tracts, No. 1, Key West, Fla. before the Fire of March 30, 1886, by the New York Sun Man: A Sketch, A Criticism, A Burlesque* (Key West, 1907), 4.

9. Jefferson B. Browne, *Key West, the Old and the New* (St. Augustine, 1912; reprint, Gainesville, 1973), 149.

10. William J. Bigler, *Public Health in Florida—Yesteryear: Florida's Public Health Centennial* (Tallahassee, 1989), 4–6; Canter Brown Jr., "Dr. James Alpheus Butler: An African American Pioneer of Miami Medicine," *Tequesta: The Journal of the Historical Association of Southern Florida* 66 (2006): 49–68; E. Ashby Hammond, *The Medical Profession in 19th Century Florida* (Gainesville, 1996), vi, 93, 602, 652, 708; *New York Age*, September 5, 1912, April 3, 1913, January 8, 22, and February 19, 1914.

11. Browne, *Key West*, 149–50.

12. Ibid.; *Jacksonville Florida Times-Union*, April 7, 1911.

13. *Jacksonville Florida Times-Union*, April 7, 1911.

14. Gerardo Castellanos, *Motivos de cayo hueso* (Havana, Cuba, 1935), 344–45.

15. Ibid.; Browne, *Key West*, 150.

16. *Jacksonville Florida Times-Union*, October 2, 1911.

17. Ibid., October 12, 1911.

18. *Key West Citizen*, November 13, 1966; Castellanos, *Motivos de cayo hueso*, 345.

19. Charlton W. Tebeau, *A History of Florida* (Coral Gables, 1971), 403; *Key West Citizen*, September 12, 1919.

20. Asociación Nacional de Emigrados Revolucionarios Cubanos, *Eduardo Hidalgo Gato: Discurso pronunciado por el Sr. Raoul Alpizar y Poyo* (Havana, Cuba, 1926), 51.

21. Pérez Rolo, *Mis recuerdos*, 51

22. *Key West Florida*, April 12, 1924.

23. Ibid., July 25, 1925.

24. *Key West Citizen*, February 12, 1934; Antonio Gutsens death certificate, #3197, Bureau of Vital Statistics, Florida State Board of Health, Jacksonville.

25. *Key West Citizen*, October 11, 1934 (the English text appears in the article).

26. Tebeau, *History of Florida*, 403.

27. *Key West Citizen*, October 15, 1935.

28. Ibid., October 10, 1938.

29. Ibid., October 9, 1939.

30. Ibid., November 16, 1939.

31. Ibid., October 20, 1941.

32. Ibid., November 7, 1941; 1910 U.S. Decennial Census, Monroe County, Florida (population schedule).

33. *Key West Citizen*, November 8, 1941 (English translation in original).

34. Ibid., August 19, 1943.

35. David L. Sloan, *Ghosts of Key West* (Key West, 1998), 38–46. For more hauntings in the Gato home, see *National Enquirer*, January 29, 1985.

CHAPTER 7

Louise Cecilia Fleming
1862–1899

Medical Missionary

LARRY EUGENE RIVERS

LOUISE CECILIA FLEMING enjoyed a life that lasted only thirty-seven years, but in the time allowed to her, she managed to forge precedents for involvement by African American women in education, church work, and medicine. That she began her life as a slave on a Florida plantation seemingly should have precluded such outcomes, but as the details of experience illustrate, hers was a life built on faith, faith not only in divine providence but also in her ability as an individual and as a woman to contribute meaningfully to the world around her. Lulu, as her friends and colleagues called her, knew heartbreak and disappointment. Still, her faith carried her in directions that could not have been anticipated and in a manner that stands in defiance of our understanding of important conventions of her times.[1]

Figure 13. Louise Cecilia Fleming, c. 1890s. (Courtesy of David Christian.)

Lulu Fleming entered the world on January 28, 1862, just as the nation launched itself into civil war. On that day, however, the conflict likely seemed far removed from the plantation called Hibernia, located at Fleming's Island on the western banks of Florida's St. Johns River, less than two dozen miles upriver from the small town of Jacksonville and only a few miles downriver from the nascent resort community of Green Cove Springs. The shocking reports of guns would echo there in only a matter of months, but for that moment Hibernia lay a world apart from the reality of much of what had become the Confederate States of America.[2]

In the early 1860s Hibernia and the region that surrounded it reflected traditions of Spanish Florida at least as much as they did the Old South. Owned by Lewis (sometimes, Louis) Fleming, the property had come into his hands from his father George Fleming, who had entered Spanish East Florida in the late eighteenth century. As was true of many of his peers, George Fleming's attitudes toward race, color prejudice, and slavery were molded by Spanish custom, as preserved and recast in La Florida. Daniel L. Schafer has termed those attitudes "a mild and flexible system of race relations" within which blacks could rise to property ownership, enjoy some social mobility, and influence public policy. Even after Spain ceded La Florida to the United States in 1821, a good number of pre-cession families remained in East Florida (the area of northeast Florida and the peninsula), their previous attitudes intact along with their ability to influence newcomers from the emerging cotton states to the north.[3]

The Flemings certainly constituted one such family, and sometimes, their attitudes outdistanced those of neighbors. Area planter families who were holdovers from the Spanish era typically permitted slaves to purchase their own freedom, if they could, as well as that of loved ones. Cyrus Forrester, who lived nearby at Magnolia, purchased his freedom in 1848. He subsequently married, raised five children, and by the eve of the Civil War, owned property valued at the considerable sum of $2,400. The Flemings, though, tended to grant freedom rather than to sell it. By 1835 Lewis had freed a slave named Pompey and promptly had installed him as overseer at Hibernia. Given other similar actions by family members, Schafer concluded, "It seems that manumission was a family tradition the Flemings continued whether Florida was a Spanish possession or part of the United States." New Yorker W. J. Stillman visited in 1857 and confirmed the nature of life at Hibernia. "It is worthy to note . . .," he recorded, "that the kindliness to the slaves seems universal on the St. Johns River. It was a kindly and an indulgent community, and that it was a slave-holding society never forced itself on the attention." Of Hibernia, Stillman commented, "I never heard of punishment of a slave or saw a discontented Negro; the black children were the jolliest little creatures that I ever saw and the adults seemed to do as much or as little work as they pleased."[4]

That so many area slaves would soon take advantage of the arrival of Union troops to seek their freedom exposes the exaggeration of Stillman's observations; still, the undeniable facts of persistent interracial marriages—and some interracial relationships outside marriage but involving affection across racial lines—speak directly to the climate of the time. Perhaps the most prominent example of such interracial marriage was slave trader Zephaniah Kingsley, whose African-born wife, Anna Madgigine Jai Kingsley, helped to pioneer modern citrus-growing techniques just downriver from Hibernia at Laurel Grove (today's Orange Park). Following her husband's death in 1843, Anna remained a major holder of Florida property into the post–Civil War era. Jacksonville founder Isaiah Hart meanwhile more or less openly enjoyed at least one, and perhaps several, relationships with family slaves. His attachment to Amy Hickman grew so strong that he directed inclusion of a substantial bequest to her in his last will, probated the year before Lulu's Fleming's birth. He opened that portion of the document with the words, "Farewell Amy. Farewell my children."[5]

The fact of such marriages and relationships, with attendant obligations across racial lines, bore more than passing importance to Lulu Fleming, because available evidence hints that Lewis Fleming was her grandfather. At least, tradition among family descendents suggests as much. The circumstances seemingly were these. Lewis Fleming's first wife, Augustina Cortes Fleming, died during 1832, leaving sons named George Claudius and Lewis (usually seen as Louis) Isador Fleming and a daughter, Augustina Fleming. Lewis remarried in the late 1830s to Margaret Seton but, in the intervening years, appears to have conceived a daughter, Chloe, with a female slave at Hibernia. As Chloe matured, she received favorable treatment from the Flemings and eventually became, as one of Lulu's biographers put it, "a personal maid of the lady of the house." In the late 1850s she formed a relationship with a man said to have been "brought as a slave from the Congo." Their first child, a son named William, arrived in December 1857. A second son, Scipio, followed in 1860. Lulu's birth in 1862 added a daughter to the growing family.[6]

Identification of Lulu's father involves even greater difficulties that parsing her relationship with the white Flemings. He likely did come from the Congo, but little else remains certain. Lulu's friend and supporter William Still, the Philadelphia abolitionist and Underground Railroad supporter, shared a story that offers most of the detail available about the man. "When little Lulu was only about six weeks old her father resolved to go to war," he recorded. "Thus taking his wife and children and as many young slaves as were willing to join the army and fight for liberty, he bravely attempted to carry into execution his bold resolve." Still then recounted Fleming's betrayal by a supposedly Union-sympathizing steamboat captain (he mistakenly refers to the man as "captain of a Union gun-boat") and his imprisonment "in irons" at Jacksonville by Confederate soldiers. "Narrowly did he escape being hanged (some did not escape)," Still added. "Very soon after he was released from his imprisonment he was found in the Union army, fighting against slavery, and for two years he was in the service, and was only released by death without ever seeing his wife and children again."[7]

Despite questions about some of Still's details, his story rings true in essentials. In mid-March loyalties of many area men shifted between the Union and the Confederacy. The principal steamboat captain who touched regularly at Fleming Island was just such a man. Paul Bartolo Canova's steamer *Governor Milton* eventually honored with its name Florida's wartime chief executive John Milton but, as a businessmen, Canova necessarily enjoyed easygoing relations with area Unionists. Those sentiments doubtlessly manifested themselves more publicly after March 11—six weeks after Lulu's birth—when four Union gunboats crossed the St. Johns River bar as a precursor to the Union occupation of Jacksonville the following day. Unfortunately for Lulu's father, the Union withdrew from that town on April 8. Logic suggests that the reoccupation of Jacksonville by the Confederates convinced Canova to trade his cargo of refugees for a measure of Rebel acceptance and forgiveness.[8]

Although Lulu's father cannot be identified with certainty, available documentation does reveal one very plausible candidate. Military records note that that David Flemming "escaped" on July 10, 1862. This escape may have been from Confederate confinement at Jacksonville. Flemming eventually found safety at Mayport, located at the mouth of the St. Johns River and occupied by Union forces. There, on November 11, 1862, he enlisted in Company G, First South Carolina Infantry, one of the nation's first black fighting units. Flemming does not appear to have returned to Florida following his Civil War service.[9]

Chloe Fleming's location in the years immediately following Lulu's birth is similarly difficult to ascertain. Her father, Lewis Fleming, died suddenly in August 1862. Within two months Confederate authorities had ordered the roundup of all St. Johns River–area blacks, while Lewis's son Francis P. Fleming reported in mid-October, "I understand that [Union forces] have carried off all the negroes that they could get hold of." Again following the brief third Union occupation of Jacksonville during March 1863, black troops raided up the St. Johns as far as Palatka. Soon after the fourth and final occupation of Jacksonville in February 1864, Union tax officials seized Hibernia for nonpayment of taxes. The remaining white Flemings, headed by Lewis's widow, Margaret Seton Fleming, withdrew westward to Lake City.[10]

By then, Chloe seems to have settled within Union lines at Jacksonville. Her white half-brother Louis I. Fleming Jr., an Amherst graduate, had practiced law there prior to the war, while another white half-brother Frederick A. Fleming fought with Confederate forces in the vicinity through the conflict. Subsequent events suggest that one or both of them, perhaps at Margaret Seton Fleming's behest, ensured her survival. Chloe and her children would not have felt alone, since thousands of former slaves crowded the community. By February 1864 Esther Hill Hawks had opened there the state's first racially integrated school. Other institutions also emerged. Particularly, black members of Jacksonville's Baptist Church commenced meeting separately from whites. Although a Union hospital operated in their sanctuary during the occupation, the peace brought control of the property to the black members. One account of Lulu's youth noted, "When she was still a child, she would accompany her mother, along with other slaves, with the families that owned them to the church where the white families were members." The account added, "That church was Bethel Baptist Church of Jacksonville."[11]

The immediate post–Civil War years understandably brought more change for Lulu and her family. About 1867 Chloe married laborer Clem (or, possibly, Flem) Hawkins, and soon the couple had returned to Hibernia's vicinity. Margaret Seton Fleming meanwhile had reopened Hibernia as a tourist hotel. She enjoyed moderate prosperity from the initiative, and Hibernia became a customary calling point for tourists enjoying the semitropical wonders of the St. Johns River valley. By 1869 one respected guidebook would label it "one of the best [hotels] on the river." Chloe and her new husband may have assisted in its operation. By decade's end they inhabited a house adjacent to the hotel. Joining them and Chloe's two sons and daughter were two new children. Betsy had arrived in 1868, while Thomas was born in April 1870. Clem Hawkins managed to support his family and to prepare to establish himself on his own. Before the mid-1870s he had saved enough to purchase a farm just across the river in St. Johns County. There, most family members remained centered for decades.[12]

In those years Margaret Seton Fleming may have intervened again to aid Lulu by arranging for her formal schooling at Jacksonville. Lulu's biographer Joseph R. Moss related family lore that "a white lady undertook to see that she received a good education from a normal school in the area." He added, "The indications are that this may well have been the wife of the former owner of Louise Fleming's mother." Margaret enjoyed excellent connections to assist her in arranging for the schooling. For one her stepson Louis Fleming was still practicing law in Jacksonville. As a family member noted, "Lewis Isadore [sic] was devoted to his stepmother, Margaret." Meanwhile, Margaret's son Francis P. Fleming also located in the town following his Civil War service, reading the law with a family friend and gaining admission to the bar in 1868.[13]

Some sources suggest that Lulu's normal school (or teacher preparation) education took her approximately to a tenth-grade level. If so, then she commenced schooling at Jacksonville about 1868, at age six. By that time black educators had already begun to make their mark in the community. None stood out more than did Mary Still, sister of abolitionist William Still. Brought to Florida from Philadelphia in 1866 by the Reverend Charles H. Pearce, presiding elder of the state's African Methodist Episcopal (AME) Church, she already possessed years of experience teaching and ministering to the needy and to black soldiers in coastal South Carolina. At Jacksonville, Mary emerged not only as an AME stalwart but also as an educator. AME Bishop Alexander W. Wayman later described her as "that noblest of women" and insisted that she was "worth her weight in gold as a Christian woman." A church historian added that "she seemed to find her greatest pleasure in relieving the sick and administering to the distressed."[14]

The only normal school for African American children located in Florida in the late 1860s, and the one with which Mary Still associated herself, carried the name the Stanton Institute. Founded in 1868 by the Freedmen's Bureau and designed to draw students from throughout the state, the Jacksonville school aimed at first to offer white as well as black students a top-quality teacher training. A new building, dedicated in the spring of 1869, furthered that goal, but the school could not overcome resistance from white parents to the presence of black children. Many a freedman's family saw the situation otherwise, however, and the institute's student body swelled into the hundreds. As the only black member of the inaugural faculty and although she remained at the school only until 1872, Mary Still exercised influence on the institution's development and philosophy from her position in the primary department. This particularly worked to the advantage of girls, because Still encouraged their active involvement with education and other concerns. "Young women can contribute more to building up their race here than in the North," she wrote in April 1868. "There is a good deal to be done."[15]

Stanton impressed itself deeply on most, if not all, its students, including Lulu Fleming. By 1873 reports suggested that it had already attained status as "one of the most successful schools for freedmen in the country." Alumnus James Weldon Johnson proclaimed, "I judge that Stanton, with respect to rough boys, held its own with any school in the country." The influences extended well beyond the curriculum. The American Missionary Association (AMA), long involved with the needs of freedmen at Jacksonville, furnished funding through the mid-1870s. Afterward, the AME Church through Principal James C. Waters, an ordained minister, continued a religious orientation. Accordingly, each day commenced with chapel exercises. As a visitor commented in 1873, "The students learn ... what most teachers fail to teach, the great lesson of Christianity, as taught in their every day lives as well as on the Lord's Day."[16]

Beyond such formal religious observances, moral causes held sway with Stanton faculty, staff, and students. Temperance may have headed the list. Backed by the AMA and the AME Church, the temperance cause first argued for moderation in the use of alcoholic beverages and then for a complete avoidance of such spirits. As early as 1872 Jacksonville's Bethel Baptist Church, which Lulu attended, was cooperating with the AMA and Stanton in the work of the Independent Temperance Society at Bethel Baptist Church. Two years later the Triumph Lodge, International Order of Good Templars (IOGT), established itself at Jacksonville with male and female leadership. By 1876, the IOGT Grand Lodge of Florida had authorized AME minister Joseph E. Lee to expand the order's network throughout the state. Significantly for Lulu Fleming's future, women continued to occupy key leadership roles in the organization.[17]

Missionary work also appeared as a worthy goal for Stanton's graduates. Mary Still especially praised female mission work in Haiti. "My heart swells with emotion and zeal for the cause that burns within my soul," she wrote in 1874. "I hope that the Lord will bless the late effort, and make it powerful in your hands [those of the AME Ladies of the Mite Missionary Society] to the pulling down of the works of the enemy." Others, though, had begun to look to the mission field of Africa. At the Florida AME Conference annual meeting held at Jacksonville in 1876, a session that Lulu Fleming may have attended, an American Bible Society representative spoke eloquently on that subject as well as the temperance cause. "The Daughters of the Conference and the Missionary Society occupied the seats in front of the pulpit and between the two aisles," conference minutes recorded, "and presented a beautiful scene well calculated to cheer the heart of the Missionary of the cross."[18]

Another influence likely entered Lulu Fleming's life during her Stanton years. Mary Still's sister Caroline Still Wiley Anderson had matriculated at Oberlin College in 1874 following graduation from Philadelphia's Institute for Colored Youth. Soon, she relocated to Washington, D.C., where she entered the Howard University Medical Department. In 1876 Caroline returned to Philadelphia and enrolled in the Women's Medical College. She graduated in

1878, the second black woman to do so. Caroline may have visited sister Mary at Jacksonville during that period, opening the possibility of an early acquaintance with Fleming. If not, Lulu at the least would have received news about Caroline and her accomplishments directly from Mary.[19]

It seems unlikely that, as of the late 1870s, Caroline Still Wiley Anderson's influence had set Lulu Fleming on the road to medical school, but that possibility cannot be entirely disregarded. The era witnessed the beginning emergence in Florida of a black professional class, including attorneys and medical doctors, a fact of which Fleming would have been well aware. Henry S. Harmon, like Anderson a Philadelphian and graduate of the Institute for Colored Youth, won acceptance to the bar at Gainesville in 1869. Numerous others soon followed in the legal profession, notably Harmon's future law partner, U.S. Representative Josiah T. Walls.[20]

Medical practitioners arrived a decade or so later than did the attorneys, but their coming would have been heralded during Fleming's years at Stanton. Alexander H. Darnes deserves particular mention. The St. Augustine native pursued an undergraduate degree at Lincoln University before entering the Howard University Medical Department. He claimed his M.D. degree in 1880 before returning to a Jacksonville practice. James Weldon Johnson recalled Darnes's milestone accomplishment. "Few were the colored people at that time who had the faith to believe," he recorded, "that one of their own number knew how to make those cabalistic marks on a piece of paper that would bring from the drugstore something to stand between them and death." Two years after Darnes arrived at Jacksonville, Dr. William J. Gunn followed his lead at the state capital of Tallahassee. Florida's African American medical community grew thereafter at a reasonable pace, with Jacksonville usually hosting the largest contingent.[21]

Even if Anderson's influence did not stir Lulu Fleming's interest in the medical profession, it—along with the influence of several others—may have put her to thinking about college. A number of African American residents of Jacksonville and regular visitors to that community boasted college degrees by the mid- to late 1870s. Jonathan Clarkson Gibbs, Florida's superintendent of schools during 1873–1874, had graduated from Dartmouth College before attending the Princeton Theological Seminary. Coincidentally, Chloe Fleming's half-brother George Claudius Fleming, who passed away prior to Lulu's birth, had earned a degree at the latter institution in 1853. He previously had received an M.D. degree at the University of Pennsylvania.[22]

Other college graduates merit attention. Perhaps offering a more immediate Jacksonville connection to Lulu, local AME minister and political leader

Joseph E. Lee had arrived prior to mid-decade. Also a graduate of Philadelphia's Institute for Colored Youth and later of the Howard University Law Department, Lee by 1875 sat in the Florida House of Representatives and had begun to claim power in local, state, and national politics. He would have been known to Lulu Fleming from participation in Stanton activities, as well as from his leadership in the state's International Order of Good Templars organization. Providing a direct connection to her, James C. Waters, Lincoln University class of 1870, assumed the Stanton's principalship in 1876—when it became a public school—and served until 1881, when he left to found Allen University. His friend and fellow Lincoln graduate Francis James Grimké also visited, and eventually—with his wife Charlotte Forten Grimké—established a home at Jacksonville.[23]

A fervent Baptist, Lulu also would have enjoyed connections with college graduates through her church. Henry Wilkins Chandler, a Baptist lay leader, had arrived at Ocala by 1876 following graduation from Bates College and the Howard University Law Department. The gifted teacher soon represented Marion County in the state senate. Interestingly for Fleming's future, Reuben S. Mitchell and Susie M. Mitchell located in the 1870s just north of Ocala at Gainesville. Teachers by profession, they had numbered among the early graduates of Shaw University. That Raleigh, North Carolina, institution stood out as the second school for African Americans founded by the American Baptist Home Mission Society. In Florida, the Mitchells quickly expanded their interests to Baptist matters statewide, while R. S. Mitchell entered politics and published a newspaper before becoming a U.S. deputy marshal. The Mitchells' daughter Effie Carrie Mitchell-Hampton subsequently became, in 1907, the first female African American licensed to practice medicine in Florida.[24]

Even if they did not possess college degrees, African American figures of state and national renown contributed to the remarkable Jacksonville world that emerged while Lulu Fleming pursued her education. John Willis Menard stood out among them. An Illinois native, Menard had worked in President Abraham Lincoln's administration before venturing to New Orleans during the Civil War's waning hours. Voters in that city elected him in 1868 to the U.S. House of Representatives, the first black man so honored. Within a short time after the Congress refused Menard his seat, he relocated to Jacksonville, where he claimed a place in the Florida House of Representatives and emerged as the state's leading African American journalist and publisher. "Florida is destined to become the negro's new Jerusalem," he wrote in 1872. "Here then the oppressed colored people of Georgia and intelligent and well-to-do colored men of the North must come and pitch their tents." He continued, "Let them come!" Menard added another accomplishment in 1879 with the publication of a poetry collection entitled *Lays in Summer Lands*. Meanwhile, his wife, Elizabeth, taught in Jacksonville. Following a stint at Stanton in 1874, she joined Mary Still in staffing the public school located nearby in the popular suburb known as LaVilla.[25]

The presence in the Jacksonville vicinity of white figures of prominence additionally encouraged bright young people such as Lulu Fleming to think of larger national and global causes. For one thing several former Union generals and government officials invested heavily in Florida initiatives, bringing their fame and associations deep into the poor and still-isolated state. Henry S. Sanford's activities especially would have come to Fleming's attention. Named by President Lincoln as minister to Belgium in 1861, Sanford in 1870 purchased twenty-three square miles of property on the upper St. Johns River. The town of Sanford was founded two years later on the shores of Lake Monroe, while the general's orange grove had begun to mature in close proximity. The entrepreneur added hotels to lure tourists and, as a temperance advocate, proudly proclaimed Sanford the first "dry" town in Florida. To the state's African Americans, though, Sanford soon represented the worst aspects of northern immigration. As the town of Sanford took life, the *Jacksonville Republican* accused its founder, in light of his attitudes toward his laborers, of instituting a species of slavery at Lake Monroe. In 1876, questions about the general's character multiplied when he participated in an international conference called by King Leopold II of Belgium to organize the African International Association to "civilize" equatorial Africa.[26]

On the other side of the coin, Lulu's likely acquaintance with another northern settler in the Sunshine State would have emboldened her as a woman and as someone interested in claiming a larger role in the world. Harriet Beecher Stowe gained fame in the 1850s as author of the classic *Uncle Tom's Cabin*. In 1867 she and her brother Charles Beecher, later Florida's superintendent of schools, settled just downriver from Hibernia at Laurel Grove (Orange Park). Soon, Stowe had purchased a home and orange grove on the eastern shore at Mandarin, whence she marketed Florida's virtues to the nation while transforming herself into an attraction to be admired by the steamboat passengers moving up and down the St. Johns. She and her brother meanwhile pursued the cause of education, especially for African American children. If Lulu did not come to know Mrs. Stowe while journeying to and from Jacksonville and Hibernia when school was not in session, she would have encountered her numerous times at Stanton Institute.[27]

How then did these influences affect Lulu Fleming's life? Most significantly,

Figure 14. Harriet Beecher Stowe and family at her Mandarin home on the St. Johns River, c. 1870s. (Courtesy of Florida State Archives.)

while at Stanton she experienced a religious awakening coupled with a yearning to aid those in need. One source suggests that she accepted baptism at Bethel Baptist Church on January 14, 1877, having been "converted" the previous year. Her zeal, though, evidenced itself most profoundly after the area endured that summer and fall a yellow fever epidemic that took the lives of numerous residents, including Margaret Seton Fleming's daughter Maggie Fleming. In the wake of that tragedy, Lulu's commitment deepened. "I entered into the blessed light of His love," she recalled, "wherein to walk is fullness of joy, December 1877." She added, "I was a missionary like Andrew of old from the very day I found the Lord."[28]

Before she could live her new commitment, Fleming had to earn a living. Apparently, she graduated from Stanton in the spring of 1878, or possibly the previous year. Her immediate family still lived on their St. Johns County farm, on the east side of the St. Johns River. Older brother William A. Fleming, who may have attended Stanton during the late 1860s and early 1870s, already participated in county Republican Party politics. He soon would live at St. Augustine, the county seat. By 1882 William only narrowly would lose a race for the Florida House of Representatives. He remained active politically despite the loss, representing his state as late as 1904 as an alternate delegate to the Republican National Convention. Moreover, William increased his standing within the state's African American leadership by furthering the temperance cause. The year 1887 saw him selected as grand secretary of the Good Templars Grand Lodge of Florida, a position that he held for at least three terms.[29]

Circumstances point to William A. Fleming as the connection who arranged a teaching job for Lulu in St. Augustine during 1878. A black principal, Jacob Jordan, recently had taken over the town's "School House No. 1 (Colored)" from white AMA teachers. His goal involved hiring an all-black faculty. As a graduate of the state's leading normal school, Fleming easily fit the bill. She and Jordan found common cause, and within a matter of a year or two she rose to the position of "First Assistant." She remained, seemingly happily, through the spring of 1882. Through those years she attempted to live her faith and faith-born commitments to the extent possible, including by teaching a Sunday school class at her local Baptist church. "While teaching in Florida . . . ," William Still observed, "sympathizing deeply with the two most needy and lowly classes in the community where her field of labor belonged, instead of devoting her leisure time to such amusements and recreation as are generally hailed with delight by the average young and thoughtless teachers, Lulu was found with a devotion which was as rare as it was Christ-like, doing with all her might what her hands found to do, in aid of the aged and infirm and the poor little orphan children."[30]

The event that set Lulu Fleming on her future professional course occurred in the spring of 1882 while she remained in St. Augustine. "I met in my Sabbath-school Dr. Kellsey, of Brooklyn, N.Y., who became deeply interested with the manner in which I expounded the Word of God to my class, which consisted of the pastor of that church, the licensed ministers and the adults generally of the school," she explained, adding,

> This gentleman, who was then in the rear of the room, came up and introduced himself to me, asking if I were a Floridian, and then he asked where I was educated. I told him. He thought I should have a higher course, as my heart was so much interested in missions. I told him my mother had edu-

cated me to the extent of her means, and that I was now on life's ocean for myself. He said, "I will see if I can't help you if you care to attend college."[31]

The Reverend Rufus B. Kelsay of Brooklyn's Sixth Avenue Baptist Church honored his promise. A native of New Jersey who had lived during his youth in Philadelphia, he had held important pastorates in New Jersey and Maryland, including Baltimore's High Street Baptist Church, before accepting the pulpit at prestigious Sixth Avenue Church. By 1882 he had lived in Brooklyn for seven years and was well positioned to offer assistance to a young person in need. In Lulu's case he did so by organizing "a company of young ladies" who belonged to his congregation and interesting them in Fleming's cause. With funds provided by the company, Lulu—about October 1, 1882—entered the Normal Department at Raleigh's Shaw University.[32]

At Shaw, Lulu Fleming flourished. During the first year she helped to support herself by teaching in the university's "model school." By the 1883–1884 academic year, however, she had qualified as an "assistant teacher" on the university level and had transferred from the Normal Department to the Scientific Department. This fact hints that she had already decided to pursue medical training. If so, she may have intended to use that training in a specific missionary field abroad. William Still explained, "In 1883 . . . while in school, Africa was laid on her soul." Still believed that Fleming's interest at that point extended only to "trying to have others become interested and go," but Lulu during the winter and spring of 1885, her final year at Shaw, unsuccessfully sought an African missionary appointment through the Women's American Baptist Foreign Missionaries Society. By then she had transferred from the Scientific Department to the Estey Seminary Course, housed—as the school's catalogue boasted—"in one of the finest school edifices in the State of North Carolina." She graduated as class valedictorian on May 27, 1885.[33]

While no missionary appointment came to Lulu Fleming in 1885, the interest in Africa she developed at Shaw is easily understood. As the historian David Killingray observed, "Africa was the persistent geographical focus of African American missionary thought throughout the nineteenth century." Reconstruction's end, Killingray insisted, "stimulated a renewed interest among many African Americans for a return to Africa and for missionary activities in the Continent." Mission boards proliferated among Baptist, African Methodist, and Presbyterian congregations. Building upon a Southern Baptist tradition of mission work in West Africa that extended back to the 1840s, black Baptists in the South organized the Baptist Foreign Mission Convention in 1880. In this era numerous institutions of higher learning in the United States, including

Shaw, trained young men and women for missionary service. African missionary training, though, received its greatest attention in Great Britain, including at Charles Haddon Spurgeon's Pastors' College, associated with London's Metropolitan Tabernacle, which admitted African Americans as early as 1875.[34]

While the African missionary movement developed within the African American community, the Congo commanded the attention of the world. Just after Lulu began her second year at Shaw, Henry S. Sanford pushed the subject forward in the United States by visiting President Chester A. Arthur on King Leopold's behalf. This visit, on November 29, 1883, resulted in action by Arthur that in effect endorsed Leopold's "philanthropic" and private International Association of the Congo. Sanford thereafter pressed for public support for Leopold's Congo initiatives, claiming that the king was creating a "Canaan for our modern Israelites," by which he meant, in his words, "an outlet . . . for the enterprise and ambition of our colored people in more congenial fields than politics." Before Lulu concluded her second year at Shaw, the United States recognized Leopold's claim to the Congo—the first country to do so. Slightly less than one year afterward, in February 1885, a gathering known as the Berlin Conference offered international sanction for Leopold's proposed Congo Free State. Two days after Fleming graduated from Shaw, Leopold proclaimed the Congo Free State. He assumed the title King-Sovereign and thereafter ruled as an absolute monarch.[35]

As Leopold acted, Fleming faced questions about her own future. Unable as a female Baptist to obtain a missionary appointment to Africa, her principal alternative involved returning to her native state. No employment awaited her at Hibernia, so she ventured instead to Jacksonville. William Still reported simply that she "returned to her former field in Florida." The fact that she did not assume a teaching position underscores her reinforced commitment to church and missionary work. Fortuitously, Jacksonville's Bethel Baptist Church at that very moment was welcoming a new minister, the Reverend J. Gardner Ross, a Massachusetts-born intellectual who had graduated in 1877 from the Newton Theological Seminary before accepting the pastorate at the Webster Street Baptist Church in New Haven, Connecticut. As a Baptist minister, he embraced two causes especially. The first was missionary work, a fact that he exemplified by his service as corresponding secretary and president of the New England Baptist Missionary Convention. The second cause was that of temperance.[36]

Subsequent events suggest that Ross helped to encourage Lulu's connections with the increasingly strong Jacksonville temperance movement, although she possessed longtime relationships of her own, including through her brother William A. Fleming. Another key figure was William H. Artrell, the Bahamian-born educator who in 1885 accepted the principal's job at Stanton Institute (then sometimes called the Jacksonville Graded School) and also assumed the position of Chief Grand Templar of Florida, International Order of Good Templars. However she came to his attention, Artrell retained Lulu's services as an organizer. The Black Templar historian David M. Fahey wrote that her efforts involved lecturing "from church to church." He related one instance of her success: "W. M. Artrell described one exhausting expedition that he and his wife, Victoria, undertook in order to institute a new lodge in an out-of-the-way Florida village on a wintry evening in 1886." He observed,

> St. Nicholas lay across the St. Johns river, four miles from Jacksonville. L. C. Fleming, a young woman recently returned from school in North Carolina, had ... persuaded twenty-seven people there to sign a charter petition. After the Artrells crossed the river by steam ferry, a mule-drawn dray carried them to meet the new recruits at a Baptist church. On the return journey through the pine woods they endured a pouring rain, followed by a wait in the chill for the ferry, which was late. They got home at two in the morning and had to rise at six to begin a new day's work.[37]

Through the Good Templars' Grand Lodge of Florida, Fleming soon emerged, if only temporarily, as a journalist. That body in January 1886 organized a newspaper with a board of directors composed of AME ministers, IOGT organizers, and Republican political figures Joseph E. Lee and John R. Scott Jr., along with Artrell. AME layman D. S. D. Belliny took managerial responsibility. Named *The Florida Templar*, it aimed at national circulation and influence. The bimonthly publication represented an ambitious effort, David Fahey noted, as it constituted "the only black temperance newspaper in North America." Lulu's association with the organ appears to have dated from its inception, a fact that brought her some notice nationally. By May 1886, however, rifts within the Grand Lodge of Florida had prompted Lee's resignation, and the *Templar* entered a troubled period. How many months thereafter Fleming remained in its employ cannot be ascertained, but her service there and the paper's questionable future served as a backdrop for dramatic events in her life during the summer of 1886.[38]

Those events traced their origins, indirectly, to the late 1870s. After British explorer David Livingstone and American journalist Henry M. Stanley had drawn public attention to Central Africa, Livingstone's admirers H. Grattan Guinness and his wife, Fanny E. Guinness, had launched the Livingstone Inland Mission to establish missionary outposts in the Congo basin. They trained their missionary volunteers at their East London Institute for Home and Foreign Missions and, by the mid-1880s, operated seven stations on the Congo River. The first carried the name Mukimvika and was located at the river's mouth on the Atlantic Ocean. In order of ascent up the river, the others operated at Palabala, Banza Manteka, Mukimbungu, Lukunga, Leopoldville, and Equatorsville. By that time, however, the Guinnesses had begun to experience serious challenges. "It had so grown and developed," Fanny Guinness recorded, "that we felt it could no longer be managed as a subsidiary branch of our East London Training Institute." Guinness acknowledged also that financial burdens and the death toll on missionaries from tropical diseases factored substantially in their thinking. As the problems mounted, J. N. Murdock of Boston, Massachusetts, approached the couple on behalf of the American Baptist Missionary Union (ABMU). An agreement ensued whereby most of the stations passed to the American group. This occurred in 1885, about the time Lulu Fleming graduated from Shaw University.[39]

Black Baptists in the United States, and likewise white Baptists, answered the ABMU's call for cooperation. By late March 1886 the Baptist General Association of Western States and Territories had managed to train and transport medical missionary Theophilus E. S. Scholes and "mechanic" companion the Reverend J. E. Ricketts to Banana Point, Congo Free State, which lay across the river from the mission station at Mukimvika. As various Baptist societies joined to aid the cause, the Woman's Baptist Foreign Missionary Society learned of Fleming's expressed interest in African missionary work and, in June 1886, contacted her at Jacksonville to gauge her willingness, as Fleming expressed it, "to go as their *first* representative to that far off dark land." She accepted quickly. "I felt happy," she related, "and free from the sin of omission of duty." Bethel Baptist Church Pastor Ross encouraged his congregation to contribute funds. Soon, friends at Shaw University had organized the Hayes & Fleming Foreign Mission Society. They aimed to support Lulu and Liberia-bound fellow alumnus J. O. Hayes through the auspices of the National Baptist Foreign Mission Convention.[40]

Happy acceptance of the daunting challenge of Congo missionary work did not mean an immediate transatlantic relocation for Fleming. To prepare herself for duties she would be expected to perform, perhaps originally including direct assistance to Scholes, Lulu determined to further the health-related studies that she had pursued as a Shaw undergraduate. That institution operated the Leonard Medical School, but its policy of spurning female students compelled Fleming to look elsewhere for assistance. Leonard typically recommended that women attend either the medical school at Howard University or the Women's Medical College of Pennsylvania. At Jacksonville, Mary Still or her sister, Dr.

Caroline Still Wiley Anderson, may have endorsed the Women's Medical College. In any event Lulu began attending lectures at that Philadelphia institution in the fall of 1886 and continued her studies there through the next spring. Understandably, friends and family took great pride in her commitment to missionary work and her pursuit of a medical education. Brother William recognized this fact in March 1887 when he named his newborn daughter Lulu C. Fleming.[41]

Given the focus of this essay on Fleming's experience as a woman in the American South during the mid- to late nineteenth century, the details of her first African sojourn must await a later telling, save for a number of cogent points. First, her departure from the United States in mid-March 1887 took her initially not to the Congo but to London. Her friend and associate missionary, Nora Antonia Gordon, a graduate of Atlanta's Spelman Seminary, later traveled there from Boston on the Cunard Line, and it must be assumed that Fleming did the same. In London she arranged for Bywater, Tanqueray, & Co. to manage her financial affairs. Likely, she also attended, as did Gordon, the Guinnesses' East London Institute, studying the Congo and its missionary challenges. If she did, she did not tarry long. The newly christened missionary arrived at Banana Point on May 16 and at her intended station at Palabala four days later.[42]

Since Fleming called Palabala home for the next four years, it merits description. Located 120 miles from the coast and five miles south of the lower Congo branch, it stood as one of the region's most important settlements. "Palaballa has been in the kingdom second only to one in all Congo," she observed. The community was one of the first inland points for upriver travelers because of required portage around the Congo's shoal waters. Lulu described it as "pleasantly situated on a plateau seventeen hundred feet above the level of the sea." In 1887 its five-acre ABMU complex contained twelve buildings, she wrote, "including outhouses." Fleming added, "There are six native towns near the station, the farthest of which is only forty minutes' slow walk." The place, she insisted, reminded her of Florida. "The climate seems quite like that of my own beloved birth State," she informed William Still. "I think if the country is ever cleared up, as our Florida is being done," she continued, "the climate will be even superior to Florida."[43]

As illustrated by letters to William Still, Lulu drew on her journalistic experience to promote missionary endeavors in the Congo to a wide Baptist and African American audience. In New York prior to her Boston departure she had seen fellow Floridian and Stanton student T. Thomas Fortune, who then edited the *New York Freeman*. She promised to send him "tidings from 'Our

Fatherland'" and did so. Her initial letter was dated July 12, 1887, and published on September 3. Her William Still letters also found their way into print. One dated October 6, 1887, appeared in the AME Church's *Christian Recorder*, for example. Fortune chose to reprint it in the *Freeman*. Other of her Congo writings appeared in the ABMU's *Baptist Missionary Magazine* and in the *American Baptist Missionary Union*. Her annual reports to J. N. Murdock also carried detail of her activities and of the mission work generally, offering excellent material for dissemination by the ABMU.[44]

Fleming's reports and the comments of her colleagues and of visitors made clear her successes, which came despite enormous resistance to her Christian message and even to her efforts to provide basic medical care. Most progress came with men, and that caused her stress as well as disappointment. "Oh how I long to see women reached!" she reported in October 1888 to Dr. Murdock. "Am praying to be freed from my station work in course of the year by the coming of a companion," she added. "This will leave me free to do town and jungle work." She concluded, "The women must be reached in their homes. So must the children." Fleming's hoped-for companion, Nora Gordon, joined her by June 1889, permitting Lulu to expand her activities. Subsequently, medical services commanded a greater proportion of her attention than did teaching. An 1890 sojourner at Palabala noted that fact: "In a native hut at a considerable distance from the rest of the mission work, Miss Fleming teaches between twenty and forty heathen children every morning," he commented. "Miss Fleming also has a dispensary here, where she prescribes for the simpler diseases of the natives," the man continued. "They make a wry face over her doses, but come again for more."[45]

Beyond teaching and serving as a medical missionary, Fleming took responsibility for mentoring both colleagues and Congo residents. In the former category she particularly nurtured Nora Gordon and her talents. Lulu arranged financing for a house and headquarters for them at some distance from the main mission compound, providing an example for the younger woman to emulate. According to one account at least some individuals soon were "[begging] hard that the missionary would stay and teach them all the time." Fleming waxed with pride at Gordon's blossoming dedication and spirit. To evidence that pride she arranged, probably through William Still, for a biographical essay on Gordon to appear in the 1893 compilation *Women of Distinction: Remarkable in Words and Invincible in Character*. Lulu penned the article at Palabala in January 1892. "Pray," she had declared two years earlier of herself and Gordon, "that we may long be spared to work for these, our own brothers and sisters, whose minds and hearts are even darker than their faces."[46]

She took upon herself as well the personal and financial obligation of educating several young people from Palabala at Shaw University. Three youngsters subsequently arrived at Raleigh in 1888 prepared to undertake general studies and missionary training. One, Henry M. Stephen, she described as "the crown prince of Palabala." Stephen proved proficient in carpentry and medical care as well as theological studies and had prepared by 1894 to return to the Congo. A male friend of Stephen's accompanied the "prince." Named Robert Walker, he, too, successfully pursued theological studies before returning to Africa. The third, Stephen's sister, adopted at Fleming's suggestion the name Estey Carolina in recognition of the program and state to which she was sent. By 1892 the young woman had altered her name in Lulu's honor to Estey Carolina Fleming. The missionary and her protégé evidently had grown close, as indicated by the fact that Lulu referred to her in correspondence as "my daughter" and "my girl."[47]

As matters evolved, Fleming's protégés studied at Shaw longer than Lulu managed to remain in Africa. She had hoped to work there at least five years, but circumstances frustrated those dreams. A trip upriver in the summer of 1889 drastically undermined the good health that she had enjoyed up until then. "Owing to the strain of the first part of the year and the roughness of the journey to Vunda and back, having walked most of the way" she explained, "I returned very much reduced." Lulu failed to rebound, although her ever-present optimism kept her hoping for relief. By the summer of 1890 mission doctors had made clear that her health was growing worse. "I must put down my beloved work, for a time," she recorded in January 1891, "and seek rest at home." She added, "I have been fearing this for a long time, as my strength has been so fast declining." Spring saw her exit the Congo. "I traveled alone from Europe on my way home," she lamented, "and very much prefer company."[48]

Fleming arrived in the United States on June 15, 1891, but if ABMU officials believed that her return would prompt her to rest in a traditional sense, she quickly disabused them of the notion. Before her African departure, she had notified them of her hope "to be allowed two years home in which to study medicine, so as to be better able to help these suffering people." She now gained admission to Shaw University's medical and pharmacy programs, subject to undergraduate status. She studied there from November 1891 to late March 1892. The months at Shaw seem to have taxed her constitution further. Despite that, she petitioned for an immediate return to the Congo. ABMU physicians insisted, however, that she wait for three more years until her health was restored and she had rested. Her sudden desire to return to Africa, it should be noted, may have stemmed from family tragedy. Lulu's half-sister Emma M. Hawkins, born in 1875, died at Atlanta on July 29, 1892. The young woman had planned to follow in her older sister's footsteps as a missionary to the Congo and, in order to prepare herself, had enrolled in Spelman Seminary's newly authorized missionary training program. Whatever the cause of her death, Emma did not live long enough to begin her courses.[49]

The loss may well have prompted Fleming to reexamine her own goals and intentions. Shaw records suggest that she did not return for the fall session of 1892. Instead, she apparently spent much of the next year in Florida at her childhood home of Hibernia, attempting to recover her health. A Jacksonville newspaper item dated September 12, 1893, offers a sense of how she otherwise occupied her time: "The services at Bethel Baptist church Sunday night were well attended," it read, "and very interesting."

> Miss Fleming, the well-known African missionary, lectured, which was very interesting. She told of the habits and doings of these people in Africa, and it seemed to be such a pleasure to her to be able to assist these people of the dark continent. Miss Fleming exhibited a lot of clothing and also fancy work done by these people, whom she takes such an interest in. Her lectures are amusing and interesting, and at times very sad, when she begins to tell of her experiences in trying to bring these people to the folds of a crucified Savior. Miss Fleming is a native Floridian, and lives at Hibernia, and the people here are proud of her and the work that she is doing. She is a ready and fluent speaker, and always captures her audience.[50]

Within weeks following the lecture Fleming returned to medical studies. This time, with ABMU assistance, she took courses at the Women's Medical College of Pennsylvania where she had briefly studied previously. Admitted as a second-year student, Lulu fared well and graduated ninth in a class of fifty-two on May 8, 1895. In those years, as one account explained, "She lectured a great deal on Africa, and was warmly commended for her graphic descriptions of the people, customs and country of the 'Dark Continent.'" She associated herself, as well, with the work of Philadelphia's Grace Baptist Church, an institution known as "the Temple." Pastor Russell H. Conwell emerged not only as a friend but also as a champion for her. Fleming explained what that meant in a letter written from Spelman Seminary the month following her graduation. "My Church . . . expects to make me their personal missionary in the Congo and will support me through the dear Ladies who will be glad to cooperate with them in so doing." Lulu added, "My joy was full when my Pastor said the Church would support me." Her "dear Ladies" had contributed individually to her work, in some cases since her first arrival in the Congo. "My Ladies have been faithful to me in the past," she recorded, "and I am unwilling to part with them."[51]

It bears mention that another institution of higher learning beside the Woman's Medical College recognized Fleming's attainments during this period. Her "daughter" Estey Carolina Fleming graduated on March 30, 1894, from Shaw University's missionary training program. Less than two months later, on May 17, 1894, the same school awarded Lulu an honorary master of science degree. Some evidence hints that she may have remained in Raleigh through the summer of 1894, before returning to Philadelphia for her final year of medical school.[52]

Fleming's aim at the time she received her medical degree was to return not simply to the Congo but, at the suggestion of a fellow missionary, to the troubled region served by the missionary station at Irebu on the upper Congo River, located nearly one thousand miles by water into the interior. The Women's Foreign Mission Society ultimately granted her requested appointment on October 2, 1895. Lulu subsequently traveled in a party that included Estey Carolina and her brother, Henry M. Stephen. This time, her itinerary took her to Antwerp, Belgium, then on to Banana Point at the Congo's mouth. At Palabala by December 2, she greeted the new year laboring at Irebu Station.[53]

The problems and challenges that missionaries had faced in Palabala during 1887 had swelled menacingly by 1896 at Irebu. King Leopold's rule and Belgian exploitation had produced misery in much of the Congo. The Belgians had nurtured what amounted to vicious and sometimes deadly slavery in connection with the rubber trade. As a consequence native war repeatedly descended to wreak havoc. In fact, violence touched Lulu personally when, in the summer of 1896, Irebu suffered assault. "It has been a year of trial, especially when the natives attacked the state camp at Irebu, June 28, and also came and pillaged the station," the Reverend Thomas Moody reported. He added, "We were kept from all harm, but it was a very trying time for a month or two." Moody's colleague W. A. Hall offered his own observations: "We began the past year with bright hopes, but before the close of the first half of the year our hopes were almost shattered from the result of a native war," he commented. "The people in the towns around were scattered, . . . our goods destroyed and stolen."[54]

Added to the woes of misery and war as immediate concerns among the missionaries at Irebu were questions regarding financial support. Fund-raising efforts for Congo missionary work increasingly met with frustration. By the spring of 1897 calls circulated for the Baptists' abandonment of Congo work "on account of its difficulties." Fleming felt the financial pinch along with her colleagues. Promised funds failed to arrive in a timely manner, if at all, despite pleas to ABMU officials. When the "difficulties" multiplied with floods and increased violence as 1897 passed toward 1898, hard choices were imposed upon the mission system. By early in the new year Irebu station had been virtually closed and Lulu transferred to Bolengi, two weeks' travel by steamboat above Leopoldville.[55]

At Bolengi, Lulu Fleming reached the end of her service in the Congo and as a missionary. The region found itself beset with epidemics of "sleeping sickness," referred to as "the great scourge of the Congo." The medical missionary from Florida numbered among its victims. For months prior to her departure from the Congo in early 1899, as one report put it, "she was laid aside from active service." At Philadelphia by April, she entered Grace (or Samaritan) Hospital, a facility owned by Grace Baptist Church, to which she belonged. There, "she was lovingly cared for till the end came" on June 20, 1899. Russell H. Conwell took charge of the funeral services, where "a distinguished company of friends and of women physicians, who knew the deceased in her student days" mourned Fleming's passage. Initially interred at Philadelphia's Olive Cemetery, her remains eventually were recommitted to the earth in that city's Mt. Zion Cemetery.[56]

Louise Cecilia Fleming's life largely speaks for itself, but a few words are in order here. While she enjoyed certain advantages from connections with white relations, she nonetheless braved tough odds to pull herself from origins in slavery to acclaim as a medical doctor and African missionary, among other accomplishments. At least in the African American community, those accomplishments were recognized in her lifetime through accounts in newspapers, including white southern newspapers, as well as through the pages of publications such as L. A. Scruggs's 1893 book *Women of Distinction*. Another distinguished author, J. A. Whitted, historian of the Black Baptist Church in North Carolina, in 1908 summed up Fleming's life and service in as articulate a manner as anyone: "Such women as Miss Lula C. Flemming are seldom found," he wrote. "Whatever she undertook to do she did it fearlessly, and 'with all her might.'" He continued, "She soon went beyond human endurance. She not only undertook to administer to the souls of men, but she came back to Philadelphia, took a course in medicine and went back with more zeal and earnestness to administer both body and soul." *Baptist Missionary Magazine* added by way of understatement, "Her decease, untimely as it seems to us, will bring sadness to the hearts of many."[57]

Notes

1. The principal sources on Louise Cecilia Fleming's life are Joseph R. Moss, "The Missionary Journey of Louise 'Lulu' Fleming, M.D." (paper delivered at the Florida Baptist Historical Society annual meeting, May 4, 1996) (xerographic copy in possession of the author); Jerry M. Windsor, "First Fruits from Florida," *Journal of Florida Baptist Heritage* 4 (Fall 2002): 16–23; Ray Jennings, *Zaire Missionary Pioneer: Lulu Cecilia Fleming, M.D., 1862–1899* (Valley Forge, Pa., n.d.); William Still, "Miss Lulu C. Fleming," in *Women of Distinction: Remarkable Works and Invincible in Character*, comp. Lawson A. Scruggs (Raleigh, N.C., 1892).

2. Moss, "Missionary Journey," 1; Still, "Miss Lulu C. Fleming," 197.

3. Daniel L. Schafer, "'A Class of People Neither Freemen Nor Slaves': From Spanish to American Race Relations in Florida, 1821–1861," *Journal of Social History* 26 (Spring 1993): 587–610. On race relations in Spanish Florida, see also Jane Landers, *Black Society in Spanish Florida* (Urbana, 1999); Daniel L. Schafer, *Anna Madgigine Jai Kingsley: African Princess, Florida Slave, Plantation Slaveowner* (Gainesville, 2003). On Hibernia, see Margaret Seton Fleming Biddle, *Hibernia: The Unreturning Tide* (New York, 1974); Arch Fredric Blakey, *Parade of Memories: A History of Clay County, Florida* (Orange Park, 1976).

4. Schafer, "A Class of People," 595–600; Biddle, *Hibernia*, 32–33, 42–43.

5. Daniel L. Schafer, "Zephaniah Kingsley's Laurel Grove Plantation, 1803–1813," in *Colonial Plantations and Economy in Florida*, ed. Jane G. Landers (Gainesville, 2000); idem, "Freedom Was as Close as the River: African Americans and the Civil War in Northeast Florida," in *The African American Heritage of Florida*, ed. David R. Colburn and Jane L. Landers (Gainesville, 1995), 157–84; Larry Eugene Rivers, *Slavery in Florida: Territorial Days to Emancipation* (Gainesville, 2000), 65–84; Canter Brown Jr., *Ossian Bingley Hart, Florida's Loyalist Reconstruction Governor* (Baton Rouge, 1997), 119. See also, Schafer, "A Class of People"; idem, *Anna Madgigine Jai Kingsley*.

6. Telephone interview with David Christian by Canter Brown Jr., November 27, 2006 (notes in possession of the author); Biddle, *Hibernia*, 32–35; William Graham Bland, comp., "St. Margaret's Episcopal Church Cemetery, Clay County, Florida" (undated typescript in Clay County Archives, Green Cove Springs); Moss, "Missionary Journey," 1; William Hicks, *History of Louisiana Negro Baptists from 1804 to 1914* (Nashville, 1915), 221; 1870 U.S. Decennial Census, St. Johns County, Florida (population schedule); 1880 and 1900 U.S. Decennial Censuses, Clay County, Florida (population schedules).

7. William Still, struggling to recall conversations he had had years before about Lulu Fleming's background, confused a good bit of the information that he shared, including the "Union gun-boat" story. He apparently reversed, for instance, the ethnicity of Lulu's parents. "Her mother was half Congo and her father half Caucasian," he wrote (Still, "Miss Lulu C. Fleming," 197–98).

8. Edward A. Mueller, *St. Johns River Steamboats* (Jacksonville, 1986), 204; Arch

Frederic Blakey, Ann Smith Lainhart, and Winston Bryant Stephens Jr., eds., *Rose Cottage Chronicles: Civil War Letters of the Bryant-Stephens Families of North Florida* (Gainesville, 1998), 110–11, 156–58; "Paul Bartolo Canova" at The Photographic Canova Family Tree website www.canova3.com/tree/fampics/i0081/INDEX.HTM; Richard A. Martin and Daniel L. Schafer, *Jacksonville's Ordeal by Fire: A Civil War History* (Jacksonville, Fla., 1984), 75–87.

9. Schafer, "Freedom," 164.

10. Biddle, *Hibernia*, 46–54; Martin and Schafer, *Jacksonville's Ordeal by Fire*, 116–17, 137–46; Edward C. Williamson, "Francis P. Fleming in the War for Southern Independence: Letters from the Front," *Florida Historical Quarterly* 28 (July 1949): 46–47.

11. Francis P. Fleming, *Memoir of Capt. C. Seton Fleming of the Second Florida Infantry, C.S.A.* (Jacksonville, Fla., 1884), 20; Frederick A. Fleming Confederate pension application, #A02015, Florida Confederate Pension Application Files, Florida State Archives, Tallahassee; Martin and Schafer, *Jacksonville's Ordeal by Fire*, 248–66; *Jacksonville Florida Times-Union*, April 24, 1905; Moss, "Missionary Journey," 1; Windsor, "First Fruits," 17–18.

12. 1870 U.S. Decennial Census, Clay County, Florida (population schedule); 1880 U.S. Decennial Census, St. Johns County, Florida (population schedule); Biddle, *Hibernia*, 65–76; Blakey, *Parade*, 124, 150; Daniel G. Brinton, *A Guidebook of Florida and the South, for Tourists, Invalids and Emigrants: With a Map of the St. Johns River* (Jacksonville, Fla., 1869), 59.

13. Moss, "Missionary Journey," 2; Biddle, *Hibernia*, 42; Fleming, *Memoir*, 18, 20; *Jacksonville Florida Dispatch, Farmer and Fruit-Grower*, May 23, 1889.

14. Moss, "Missionary Journey," 2; Charles Sumner Long, *History of the AME Church in Florida* (Philadelphia, 1939), 187; *Philadelphia Christian Recorder*, September 8, 1866, and December 30, 1880.

15. Larry Eugene Rivers and Canter Brown Jr., "'A Monument to the Progress of the Race': The Intellectual and Political Origins of the Florida Agricultural and Mechanical University, 1865–1887," *Florida Historical Quarterly* 85 (Summer 2006): 5–8; "Teachers Monthly School Report," Stanton Institute, February and March 1870, "Stanton Normal Institute... Teachers Names and Residences," May 8, 1870, and "Report of Stanton Normal School," January and February 1871, November 1872, American Missionary Association Papers, roll 86 (Florida roll 2), Amistad Research Center, New Orleans (microfilm available at Henry A. Hunt Library, Fort Valley State University, Fort Valley, Ga.) (hereafter, AMA Papers); *Philadelphia Christian Recorder*, May 16, 1868.

16. *Jacksonville Republican* clippings, c. November 11, 1872, and March 1873, AMA Papers; James Weldon Johnson, *Along This Way: The Autobiography of James Weldon Johnson* (New York, 1933); 34–35; Rivers and Brown, "'Monument to the Progress of the Race,'" 18–19.

17. Joe M. Richardson, *Christian Reconstruction: The American Missionary Association and Southern Blacks, 1861–1890* (Athens, Ga., 1986), 38, 241; Larry Eugene Rivers

and Canter Brown Jr., *Laborers in the Vineyard of the Lord: The Beginnings of the AME Church in Florida, 1865–1895* (Gainesville, 2001), 77, 91, 103–4, 106–7; Richard L. Brown to AMA, May 3, 1872, AMA Papers; *Philadelphia Christian Recorder,* April 13, 1876; *Tallahassee Sentinel,* October 28, 1876. On the Good Templars, see David M. Fahey, *Temperance and Racism: John Bull, Johnny Reb, and the Good Templars* (Lexington, Ky., 1996).

18. *Philadelphia Christian Recorder,* January 7, 1875, and April 13, 1876.

19. Ruth J. Abram, *"Send Us a Lady Physician": Women Doctors in America* (New York, 1985), 111; Gloria H. Dickinson, "Dr. Caroline Still Wiley Anderson, 19th Century African-American Physician," *Women's and Gender Studies Newsletter* 11 (November 1990), n.p.

20. Darius J. Young, "Henry S. Harmon: Pioneer African American Attorney in Reconstruction-Era Florida," *Florida Historical Quarterly* 85 (Fall 2006): 177–96; Peter D. Klingman, *Florida's Black Congressman of Reconstruction* (Gainesville, 1976).

21. Canter Brown Jr., "Dr. James Alpheus Butler: An African American Pioneer of Miami Medicine," *Tequesta: The Journal of the Historical Association of Southern Florida* 66 (2006): 54–58; Johnson, *Along This Way,* 41; Jonathan Hutchins, "William J. Gunn and the Beginnings of the Practice of Medicine by African Americans in Florida," in *Go Sound the Trumpet! Selections in Florida's African American History,* ed. David H. Jackson Jr. and Canter Brown Jr. (Tampa, 2005), 121–36.

22. Brown, *Florida's Black Public Officials,* 92; E. Ashby Hammond, *The Medical Profession in 19th Century Florida: A Biographical Register* (Gainesville, 1996), 193–94. On Jonathan C. Gibbs, see Learotha Williams Jr., "'A Wider Field of Usefulness': The Life and Times of Jonathan Clarkson Gibbs, c. 1828–1874" (Ph.D. diss., Florida State University, 2003).

23. Larry E. Rivers, "'He Treats His Fellow Men Properly': Building Community in a Multi-Cultural Florida," in *Amid Political, Cultural and Civic Diversity: Building a Sense of Statewide Community in Florida* (Dubuque, Iowa, 1998), 111, 116–17; Brown, *Florida's Black Public Officials,* 103–4; Benjamin W. Arnett, *The Budget: Containing Annual Reports of the General Officers of the African Methodist Episcopal Church* (Dayton, Ohio, 1884), 18–19; *Lincoln University College and Theological Seminary Biographical Catalogue, 1918* (Lancaster, Pa., 1918), 8; Brenda Stevenson, ed., *The Journals of Charlotte Forten Grimké* (New York, 1988), 513–21. On Joseph E. Lee, see Gary V. Goodwin, "Joseph E. Lee of Jacksonville, 1880–1920: African American Political Leadership in Florida" (master's thesis, Florida State University, 1996).

24. Canter Brown Jr. and Barbara Gray Brown, *Family Records of the African American Pioneers of Tampa and Hillsborough County* (Tampa, 2003), 47–50; Brown, *Florida's Black Public Officials,* 80, 111; George Patterson McKinney Sr. and Richard I. McKinney, *History of the Black Baptists of Florida, 1850–1985* (Miami, 1987), 108, 117, 157; Nichole West, "Dr. Effie Carrie Mitchell-Hampton, Florida's First African American Female Physician" (undergraduate seminar paper, Florida A&M University, 2005), 3–4, 10 (xerographic copy in possession of the author).

25. John Willis Menard, *Lays in Summer Lands*, ed. Larry Eugene Rivers, Richard Mathews, and Canter Brown Jr. (Tampa, 2002), 91–144; *Philadelphia Christian Recorder*, December 28, 1872; *Jacksonville Tri-Weekly Florida Union*, May 2, 1874; *Webb's Jacksonville Directory, 1876–7* (New York, 1876), 113, 133. On LaVilla, see Patricia L. Kenney, "LaVilla, Florida, 1866–1887: Reconstruction Dreams and the Formation of a Black Community," 185–206, in *African American Heritage of Florida*, ed. Colburn and Landers; Peter Dunbaugh Smith, "Ashley Street Blues: Racial Uplift and the Commodification of Vernacular Performance in LaVilla, Florida, 1896–1916" (Ph.D. diss., Florida State University, 2006).

26. *Savannah Daily Advertiser*, March 2, 1872; *Savannah Daily Republican*, November 20, 1872. On Henry S. Sanford generally, see Joseph Fry, *Henry S. Sanford: Diplomacy and Business in Nineteenth Century America* (Reno, 1982). On Belgian King Leopold II, his interests in equatorial Africa, and his relationship with Henry S. Sanford, see Adam Hochschild, *King Leopold's Ghost* (Boston, 1999).

27. John T. Foster, Jr. and Sarah Whitmer Foster, *Beechers, Stowes, and Yankee Strangers: The Transformation of Florida* (Gainesville, 1999), 46–54, 75, 88–92, 104–7; Charles Edward Stone, *Life of Harriet Beecher Stowe Compiled from Her Letters and Journals* (Boston, 1889), 401–3.

28. "The Death of Miss Lulu C. Fleming, M.D.," *Baptist Missionary Magazine* 79 (1899): 440; Still, "Miss Lulu C. Fleming," 198; Biddle, *Hibernia*, 95.

29. 1880 U.S. Decennial Census, St. Johns County, Florida (population schedule); *Tallahassee Weekly Floridian*, December 19, 1882; *Official Proceedings of the Thirteenth Republican National Convention Held in the City of Chicago, June 21, 22, 23, 1904* (Minneapolis, 1904), 86; *Jacksonville Daily News-Herald*, November 25, 1887, and April 11, 1888; *Jacksonville Florida Times-Union*, April 12, 1888; *Tampa Journal*, April 11, 1889.

30. "History of St. Johns County Public Schools" at the St. Augustine Genealogical Society website www.stauggens.com/SAGS/Stauggen9.html; Gil Wilson, "Searching for the first black teacher in St. Augustine" at http://drbronsontours.com/firstblackteacher.htm; Still, "Miss Lulu C. Fleming," 199.

31. Still, "Miss Lulu C. Fleming," 198.

32. "Rev. Rufus D. Kelsay" [NI0054] at www.freepages.genealogy.rootsweb.com/~thekelsayfamilyt; Varnum Lansing Collins and Frank Pierce Hill, comps., *Books, Pamphlets and Newspapers Printed in Newark, New Jersey, 1776–1900* (privately published, 1902), 257; George F. Adams, *History of Baptist Churches in Maryland Connected with the Maryland Baptist Union Association* (Baltimore, 1885), 80; Still, "Miss Lulu C. Fleming," 198; *Catalogue of the Officers and Students of Shaw University, 1882–1883* (Raleigh, 1883), 7, 12.

33. *Catalogue of the Officers and Students of Shaw University, 1882–1883*, 7, 12; *Catalogue of the Officers and Students of Shaw University, 1883–1884* (Raleigh, 1884), 7, 9; *Catalogue of the Officers and Students of Shaw University, 1884–1885* (Raleigh, 1885), 11, 18, 24–25; Still, "Miss Lulu C. Fleming," 198; Moss, "Missionary Journey," 4.

34. David Killingray, "The Black Atlantic Missionary Movement and Africa, 1780s–

1920s," *Journal of Religion in Africa* 33 (January 2003): 13–17; Susannah Thompson Spurgeon, comp. *The Autobiography of Charles H. Spurgeon, Compiled from His Diary, Letters, and Records,* vol. 4, *1878–1892* (Cincinnati, 1900), 334–35; Evelyn H. Walker, W. Fletcher Johnson, John Rusk, Allen E. Fowler, et al., *Leaders of the 19th Century with Some Noted Characters of Earlier Times* (Chicago, 1900), 265–70. On African American Baptist missionaries to Africa, see Sandy D. Martin, *Black Baptists and African Missions: The Origins of a Movement, 1880–1915* (Macon, Ga., 1989); Walter L. Williams, *Black Americans and the Evangelization of Africa, 1877–1900* (Madison, Wis., 1982). See also Katja Fullberg-Stolberg, *Amerika in Afrika: die Rolle des Afroamerikaner in den Beziehungen zwischen den USA und Afrika, 1880–1910* (Berlin, 2002).

35. Hochschild, *King Leopold's Ghost*, 77–87.

36. Moss, "Missionary Journey," 4; Still, "Miss Lulu C. Fleming," 199; "Rev. J. Gardner Ross, A Brief Account of His Life and Public Service," *Colored American Magazine* 5 (August 1902), 268–69.

37. Fahey, *Temperance and Racism*, 121–24; Rivers and Brown, "'Monument to the Progress of the Race,'" 37–38; *Jacksonville Florida Times-Union*, August 27, 1885; McKinney and McKinney, *History of the Black Baptists*, 114–15.

38. Fahey, *Temperance and Racism*, 122; *Philadelphia Christian Recorder*, March 10, 1887; *Jacksonville Florida Times-Union*, January 28 and May 22, 1886; Jerrell H. Shofner, "Florida," in *The Black Press in the South, 1865–1979* (Westport, Conn., 1983), 101; R. R. Wright Jr., comp., *The Encyclopædia of the African Methodist Episcopal Church*, 2nd ed. (Philadelphia, 1947), 267.

39. Thomas Armitage, *A History of the Baptists: Traced by Their Vital Principles and Practices* (New York, 1887), 826; Mrs. H. Grattan Guinness, *The New World of Central Africa: With a History of the First Christian Mission on the Congo* (London, 1890), 175–201, 389–409; Mr. and Mrs. H. Grattan Guinness, *The Divine Program, or The World's History* (London, 1888), 452–55; Eva N. Dye, *Bolenge: A Story of Gospel Triumphs on the Congo* (Cincinnati, 1910), 12–14.

40. Thomas Lewis Johnson, *Africa for Christ: Twenty-Eight Years a Slave* (London, 1892), 83; Still, "Miss Lulu C. Fleming," 199; William Hicks, *History of Louisiana Negro Baptists from 1804 to 1914* (Nashville, 1915), 221; J. A. Whitted, *A History of the Negro Baptists of North Carolina* (Raleigh, 1908), 53–55.

41. *Philadelphia Christian Recorder*, March 10, 1887; Thomas J. Ward Jr., *Black Physicians in the Jim Crow South* (Fayetteville, Ark., 2003), 8; 1900 U.S. Decennial Census, St. Johns County, Florida (population schedule).

42. *Philadelphia Christian Recorder*, December 8, 1887; *New York Freeman*, September 3 and December 31, 1887; L. C. Fleming to J. N. Murdock, March 12, 1889, Dr. Louise "Lulu" Cecilia Fleming Correspondence, American Baptist Historical Society, Valley Forge, Pennsylvania (hereafter, Fleming Papers); L. C. Fleming, "Miss N. Antonia Gordon," in Scruggs, *Women of Distinction*, 217–22; Benjamin Brawley, *Women of Achievement* (Chicago, 1919), 43–48.

43. *New York Freeman,* September 3, 1887; *Philadelphia Christian Recorder,* December 8, 1887.

44. *Jacksonville Tri-Weekly Florida Union,* May 3, 1873; *Jacksonville Evening Metropolis,* February 9, 1912; *New York Freeman,* September 3 and December 31, 1887; *Philadelphia Christian Recorder,* December 8, 1887; Still, "Miss Lulu C. Fleming," 198–202; Moss, "Missionary Journey," 5; Fleming to Murdock, October 12, 1888, March 12 and October 11, 1889, January 10, 1890, and January 10, 1891, Fleming Papers.

45. Fleming to Murdock, October 12, 1888, and January 10, 1890, Fleming Papers; Samuel Norvell Lapsley, *Missionary to the Congo Valley, West Africa, 1866–1892* (Richmond, Va., 1893), 61–63.

46. Fleming to Murdock, January 10, 1890; Fleming, "N. Antonia Gordon," 220; Fannie Roper Feudge, "Children of Central Africa," *The Gospel in All Lands* (June 1890), 245.

47. Fleming to Murdock, October 12, 1888, and October 11, 1889, Fleming to "Dear Brethren," August 18, 1894, H. M. Stephen to "A.B.M.U.," August 18, 1894, Fleming Papers; Moss, "Missionary Journey," 5–6; *Catalogue of the Officers and Students of Shaw University, 1890–91* (Raleigh, 1891), 17, 22; *Catalogue of the Officers and Students of Shaw University, 1892–1893* (Raleigh, 1893), 12, 15, 18; *Catalogue of the Officers and Students of Shaw University, 1893–1894* (Raleigh, 1894), 11–13; *Twenty-First Annual Catalogue of the Officers and Students* (Raleigh, 1895), 23, 32.

48. Fleming to Murdock, October 11, 1889, January 10, 1890, and January 10, 1891, Fleming to "Dr. Mabie," June 15, 1895, Fleming Papers.

49. Jennings, *Zaire Missionary Pioneer,* n.p.; *Catalogue of the Officers and Students of Shaw University, 1890–91,* 24; *Catalogue of the Officers and Students of Shaw University, 1891–1892* (Raleigh, 1892), 12–13; "Deercreek Cemetery Information" (typescript, n.p., n.d.), 10 (available at Clay County, Florida, Archives, Green Cove Springs, Florida; xerographic copy in possession of the author); Emma M. Hawkins tombstone inscription, Mt. Olive Baptist Church Cemetery, Orangedale, Florida.

50. *Catalogue of the Officers and Students of Shaw University, 1892–1893,* 11, 15–20; *Jacksonville Evening Telegram,* September 12, 1893.

51. Moss, "Missionary Journey," 6; *Forty-Fifth Annual Announcement of the Woman's Medical College of Pennsylvania* (Philadelphia, 1894), 29; *Forty-Sixth Annual Announcement of the Woman's Medical College of Pennsylvania* (Philadelphia, 1895), n.p.; *Philadelphia Examiner* clipping, July 6, 1899, and "Woman's Medical College of Pennsylvania: Minutes of Faculty Meetings, June 1888–June 1896" (typescript, n.d.), 289–90, 344–45, Lulu Cecilia Fleming file, Archives and Special Collections, Drexel University College of Medicine, Philadelphia, Pa.; L. C. Fleming to "Dr. Duncan," June 15, 1895, Fleming Papers. On the Reverend Russell H. Conwell, see Agnes Rush Burr, *Russell H. Conwell and His Work: One Man's Interpretation of Life* (Philadelphia, 1917).

52. *Catalogue of the Officers and Students of Shaw University, 1892–1893,* 22; Shaw

University, Raleigh, *Twenty-First Annual Catalogue of the Officers and Students, 1894–1895* (Raleigh, 1895), 25, 32; Fleming to Duncan, June 15, 1895, Fleming Papers.

53. Fleming to "Mr. Mabie," July 1, 1895, Fleming to Henry Richards, December 2, 1895, Fleming Papers; Moss, "Missionary Journey," 7; *Philadelphia Examiner* clipping, July 6, 1899; *Baptist Missionary Magazine* 76 (July 1896): 411; idem 77 (January 1897): 7; and idem 77 (July 1897): 452.

54. *Baptist Missionary Magazine* 77 (July 1897): 411. On deteriorating conditions in the Congo during the mid- to late 1890s, see Hochschild, *King Leopold's Ghost*. See also Edmund D. Morel, *The Congo Free State: A Protest against the New African Slavery; and an Appeal to the Public of Great Britain, of the United States, and the Continent of Europe* (Liverpool, 1903); Morel, *Red Rubber: The Story of the Rubber Slave Trade Flourishing on the Congo in the Year of Grace 1906* (London, 1906).

55. *Baptist Missionary Magazine* 77 (May 1897): 207, 409; idem 78 (July 1898), 308; idem 80 (March 1900), 111; Fleming to Duncan, October 27, 1896, Fleming Papers; Moss, "Missionary Journey," 7.

56. *Philadelphia Examiner* clipping, July 6, 1899; *Baptist Missionary Magazine* 79 (1899): 440; Jennings, *Zaire Missionary Pioneer*, n.p.; Moss, "Missionary Journey," 7.

57. Whitted, *History of the Negro Baptists of North Carolina*, 54–55; *Baptist Missionary Magazine* 79 (1899): 440.

CHAPTER 8

Adella Hunt Logan
1863–1915

Educator, Woman's Suffrage Leader, and
Confidant of Booker T. Washington

TERRANCE D. SMITH & SALLY J. ZEPEDA

ADELLA HUNT LOGAN, a Georgia-born woman of African descent, arrived in life during a time of civil war and died in the next century within one month of the passing of the greatest black leader of her generation, a man with whom she had enjoyed a long personal and professional relationship. In the course of that life, Logan carved for herself an enduring place in the history of her times. Her interests and influences spanned a variety of fields, although she left her special mark in education and as an advocate for woman's suffrage. She witnessed the bright promise of the Emancipation Proclamation and the Reconstruction era and saw the birth of Jim Crow racial prejudice and discrimination. Logan fought against that evolution despite origins in privilege

Figure 15. Adella Hunt Logan, c. 1902. (From Culp, *Twentieth Century Negro Literature*.)

and family ties that stretched across the racial divide. Little wonder that her friend W. E. B. Du Bois memorialized her during her lifetime. She epitomized to him, biographer David Levering Lewis has observed, a fusion of the "intuition, compassion, artistic prowess and grace" of African Americans and "a social order in which people of color and women of whatever color were ruled by a class of white men whose authority derived mainly from the accident of color or gender." Adella Hunt Logan was, Du Bois reflected, "Princess of the Hither Isles."[1]

The circumstances of Adella Hunt's entry into the world were unusual though not unique. She was born at or near Sparta, Georgia, in February 1863. This seat of beautiful homes and comfortable living lay in the middle of Hancock County, a political subdivision situated halfway between Macon to the southwest and Augusta to the northeast. The region could claim status as the heart of Georgia's plantation belt, and slaves outnumbered whites two to one. Still, traditions and persistent complications of the area's slave system permitted a few white men, as one historian explained, "to father the child of a slave, raise the child as his own, and leave her [after slavery's end] the bulk of his estate." This fact, in turn, permitted the child to "[wrap] herself in the cloak of her father's wealth and prestige." Kent Anderson Leslie has offered us, as one example, the remarkable story of Hancock's Amanda America Dickson, whose white father left her "the wealthiest black woman in the South."[2]

Although she would not attain wealth to the same degree as Dickson, Adella Hunt drew upon a heritage and upbringing not too dissimilar from the circumstances of Dickson's life. Her grandmother Susan Hunt had been "a free mulatto–Cherokee Indian woman" who had entered into "a permanent monogamous relationship" with Nathan Sayre, a public prosecutor, legislator, and judge who lived at Pomegranate Hall in Sparta's southeastern section. Three children resulted from the relationship, one of whom—a daughter, Mariah Hunt—by the early 1850s also had entered into "a permanent relationship with a white man." That person was Henry Alexander Hunt, a younger son of a family that operated a plantation near Mt. Zion, a few miles north of Sparta. Since Mariah's light skin tone would have permitted her to pass as white, she and Hunt may have married legally despite statutory proscriptions against interracial marriage, perhaps even in a ceremony conducted by her father, Judge Sayre. To the Hunts, eight children would be born. Adella came as the fourth child and second daughter.[3]

Adella entered a world in the process of transformation. By early 1863 fears of slave rebellion—an abortive attempt actually occurred—had tightened restrictions on all of the county's black residents, ushering in drastically altered patterns of local race relations. One-time slave Samuel Simeon Andrews described the scene to an interviewer during the 1930s:

> With changed expression he told of an incident during the Civil War: Slaves, he explained had to have passes to go from one plantation to another and if one were found without a pass the "patrollers" would pick him up, return him to his master and receive pay for their service. The "patrollers" were guards for runaway slaves. One night they came to Aunt Rhoda's house where a crowd of slaves had gathered and were going to return them to their masters; Uncle Umphrey the tanner, quickly spaded up some hot ashes and pitched it on them; all of the slaves escaped unharmed, while all of the "patrollers" were badly injured; no one ever told on Uncle Umphrey and when Aunt Rhoda was questioned by her master she stated that she knew nothing about it but told them that the "patrollers" had brought another "nigger" with them; her master took it for granted that she spoke the truth since none of the other Negroes were hurt.

The interviewer observed in closing, "He remembers seeing this but does not remember how he, as a little boy, was prevented from telling about it."[4]

The transformation continued and in certain respects accelerated when General William Tecumseh Sherman's troops ravaged Middle Georgia and Hancock County in 1864. Sparta and Mt. Zion avoided destruction, but its horrors could be seen by all who ventured near. "About three miles from Sparta we struck the 'Burnt Country,' as it is well named by the natives, and then I could better understand the wrath and desperation of these poor people," Eliza Frances Andrews, a young white woman, recorded. "There was hardly a fence left standing all the way from Sparta to Gordon," she continued. "The fields were trampled down and the road was lined with carcasses of horses, hogs, and cattle that the invaders, unable either to consume or to carry away with them, had wantonly shot down to starve out the people and prevent them from making their crops." She added, "The stench in some places was unbearable. . . . I almost felt as if I should like to hang a Yankee myself."[5]

If Adella's first two years witnessed such dramatic turns, the peace in 1865 added more. At Mt. Zion, to which her father returned after Confederate army service, joy initially pervaded the slave quarters. "When it wuz over with an' our white mens come home," one-time slave Henry Rogers recollected, "all de neighbors . . . livin' on plantations 'round us had a big dinner over at my white peoples' the Hunts, an' it sho wuz a big affair." That joy soon turned for many into concern and then despair. "The freed people who stayed in rural Middle Georgia after 1865 remained in the same repressive environment in which they had been enslaved, as promises of free land soon proved a chimera," Adella's granddaughter Adele Logan Alexander explained. "They faced the scorn of former slaveholders who, in losing the bitter war, had also lost much of their wealth, honor, dignity, and cherished way of life." In fact, to this day the county bears the burden of the war, especially in terms of the decline of agriculture, particularly the cotton industry, following eventually upon the war's end. Sparta soon reflected the decline. "[It was] a community that was no longer wealthy, no longer the crown jewel of the richest plantation county in Middle Georgia," a historian observed. "By the 1880s Sparta was the county seat of a farming community that remained in the midst of an agricultural depression from which it never recovered. . . . Before the Civil War, Hancock County led the state in successful agriculture, but the times had changed."[6]

Fortunately for Adella, she and her siblings belonged to what has been described as a "notable elite," from whose ranks emerged any number of individuals willing to challenge the racial conventions of their day and the obstacles that confronted not only black women but all women. Henry Alexander Hunt—although his economic circumstances and prospects may have been diminished by the Civil War, Emancipation, and agricultural depression—nonetheless could provide for them. "I was not born a slave, nor in a log cabin," Adella recalled. Instead, she was raised by a loving mother in a comfortable house near her father's home. "[Grandmother] had a secure home and the continuing support, protection, and guidance of not only her mother and other 'colored' relatives but her white father as well," Adele Logan Alexander observed. Indeed, Alexander traces Adella's lifelong interest in political affairs to her father's nurturing. "Her father used to talk politics to her when she was a little girl," a friend declared. Alexander pointed out how unusual was this situation. "Only a few white girls in Georgia . . . engaged in political debate with their fathers. Politics was not considered something that fell within a woman's sphere of interest and understanding." She continued, "For a rural white Georgian such as Henry Hunt to 'talk politics' with his nonwhite daughter would have been even more of an anomaly."[7]

Among the benefits bestowed upon Adella by her father and family was education. "To tell the truth," she later insisted, "I got my education by no greater hardship than hard work, which I regard as exceedingly healthful." A friend declared that her early schooling was "of a private nature," perhaps referring to teachings received from a white aunt. As noted by Alexander, Adella's brother Henry A. Hunt Jr. felt that the children only required "Discipline, *discipline*, DISCIPLINE, the first, second, and third requisites for all training worth having." Fortunately, within years of the peace Sparta was graced with the presence of a black school. The Bass Academy—named for its benefactor, county school superintendent W. H. Bass—had been launched by the Freedmen's Bureau and assisted by the American Missionary Association. Located within walking distance of Adella's home, it apparently was humble in appearance. In a likely reference to the academy, brother Henry described "the little, unpainted school house that was open for three months each year." Inside, Henry explained, "On those crude benches, [he and his brothers and sisters] caught in some miraculous way the desire for book learning and the determination to get it."[8]

Likely through the encouragement of her Bass Academy teacher-mentor Richard Carter, one of Atlanta University's first graduates, Adella by 1879 had set her sights on furthering her education at that growing institution of higher learning. Carter requested State Representative W. J. Northern to arrange for her admission on a free tuition scholarship, and given Adella's family connections, Northern proved more than willing to accommodate the request. With that encouragement and after a summer spent teaching, the sixteen-year-old woman departed for the state capital. There, she required only two years to complete her studies in the normal (that is, teaching) department. She graduated in 1881, according to friend Daniel Wallace Culp, "as a bright member of one of its brightest classes." Culp added, "Two years of teaching in an American Missionary School in a South Georgia town, where she was also a city missionary, prepared her for more advanced work, which opened to her at Tuskegee, Ala."[9]

As Culp observed, Adella's two years as a teacher in Albany, Georgia, led to recognition of her skills as an educator and to career opportunities. First, Atlanta University invited her to return to teach at that school. Instead, she chose in 1883 to accept an appointment at the Tuskegee Normal and Industrial Institute (now Tuskegee University), founded in 1881 by Booker T. Washington and located in Tuskegee, Alabama. Quickly, Washington came to admire her abilities. Miss Adella H. Hunt, an associate of both recorded, "was then a teacher who had the faculty of touching a responsive chord in a student." During 1883–1885 she served as an English and social sciences teacher as well as librarian. In the latter capacity she commenced organization of "one of the largest libraries on women's suffrage." That endeavor, the results of which are still maintained at Tuskegee University, suggests a very early commitment to what would become one of her special causes.[10]

As she immersed herself in the institute's work during these early years, she also found a colleague who would become a dear friend. Ohio-born Olivia A. Davidson had arrived at the school two years prior to Adella and instantly had caught Washington's eye. As the principal recollected, "Miss Davidson and I began consulting as to the future of the school from the first." So close did their relationship become that the two married in 1885, and the happy union endured until Davidson's early death four years later. In 1883, though, Davidson was the person to whom Washington turned when Hunt initially declined Tuskegee's overture, an invitation that, seemingly, originated with Davidson. "I think highly of the recommendation [for Hunt's employment] but very much fear that she will not leave her present position for the model school," he informed Davidson. "She closes her present school soon so I shall write and mention the matter to her now." Once Hunt's service at Tuskegee commenced, the relationship between the two women ripened. "From the first she fitted into the activities and spirit of the school," Daniel Wallace Culp commented, "and became Miss Davidson's right hand helper."[11]

Hunt's relationship with Davidson led directly to her career advancement at about the time of Davidson's marriage to Washington. With his wife otherwise occupied, Washington designated Hunt as "Lady Principal" in Davidson's stead. "In this position Miss Hunt emphasized the academic side of the school and also urged the physical development of the girls," Culp noted. "Her own line of teaching was the normal training of student teachers," he continued. "Her services were constantly in demand for Peabody and other teachers' institutes in Georgia and Alabama."[12]

As lady principal, Hunt supervised young teachers-in-training in addition to performing her teaching duties. As Culp suggested, her responsibilities also involved traveling throughout the southern states to conduct in-service education programs for teachers who taught at substandard segregated schools. Several of Washington's surviving letters speak to the overall success of her efforts. In 1888, for instance, he reported to Solomon Palmer, state superintendent of education for Montgomery, Alabama, about State Teachers' Institutes conducted by Hunt and S. E. Courtenay.

> [These institutes] were held in Union Springs, Bullock county, and Greensville, Butler County, August 6th and 13th, respectively, continuing in one session one week at each place. The subjects discussed were Reading, Language, Writing, Arithmetic, Geography, Grammar, Physiology and Hygiene.... It was the aim to make the Institutes as practical and useful as possible, so in connection with these exercises a plan of topics on the branches was presented and explained, together with simple means of illustrations.... In the evenings lectures were given on the 'Work of the Public Schools.' In the discussion of this subject it was shown that useful knowledge, a cultivated mind, and a right way of using it, are the ends to which the Public Schools

should direct their attention. . . . These Institutes stimulate the teachers to renewed efforts in improving their work. The attendance at both Institutes was very good."[13]

Through these outreach activities, as well as through personal contacts with students and educators generally, Hunt gained a reputation as one of the South's leading authorities on the subject of education for African American children. Culp would highlight this fact in his 1902 work *Twentieth Century Negro Literature; or, A Cyclopedia of Thought on the Vital Topics Relating to the American Negro by One Hundred of America's Greatest Negroes*. He not only included a biographical sketch but also Adella's essay "What Are the Causes of the Great Mortality among the Negroes in the Cities of the South, and How Is That Mortality to Be Lessened." In it, she expounded on education as a necessity for uplift. "The system of education in vogue in Southern cities will work slowly because up to the beginning of the twentieth century, school attendance has not been made compulsory," she averred:

> There are no truant schools, no reform schools. Idleness tends to vice. Idleness and vice are in no way conducive to health and longevity.
>
> Many Negroes do not want education for themselves nor for their children. These people swell the death lists in Southern cities' health offices to such distressingly large numbers. They are often cared for and buried by funds from the city treasury. Would it not pay to try compulsory education? To try teaching them to help themselves, to save themselves?
>
> To say that the home life of the masses must be improved is but another way of saying they must be educated. Among the most potent forces in the uplift of a people are the school, the press, the courts and the church.
>
> Under a system of compulsory education, the Negro would much sooner learn to observe the laws of health and thus to extend his life.[14]

Personal reasons certainly factored by 1902 into Hunt's perceptions about the need for and benefits of education. These derived from her marriage in 1888 to a Tuskegee colleague and their subsequent commencement of parenthood. Her husband, Warren Logan, had been born in 1859 at Greensboro, North Carolina. He studied as a young man at Virginia's Hampton Institute (where he befriended Booker T. Washington) and emerged as a protégé of the school's head, General Samuel C. Armstrong. Subsequently, as Logan put it, "I studied Latin, Greek, geometry and book-keeping." Following six years teaching in Maryland, he had accepted Washington's invitation to join him at Tuskegee. He taught or, as he declared, "[had] a hand in the training of the students." His principal responsibilities, though, involved serving as treasurer. "Mr. Warren Logan . . . has the ability to teach the student the value of a dollar by making him sacrifice almost beyond the point of endurance," a fellow Tuskegee employee recorded. "At the same time, with a smile and a cheerful disposition, he would make the student feel that his burden was light." Washington believed that, in drawing Logan to Tuskegee, he had gained an asset far greater than a teacher and employee. "Mr. Warren Logan . . . ," he wrote in 1901, "now for seventeen years has been the treasurer of the Institute, and the acting principal during my absence. He has always shown a degree of unselfishness and an amount of business tact, coupled with a clear judgment, that has kept the school in good condition no matter how long I have been absent from it. During all the financial stress through which the school has passed, his patience and faith in our ultimate success have not left him."[15]

Little information has survived regarding Adella and Warren's relationship other than that it appeared to others, at least in the beginning, as reasonably successful. Adele Logan Alexander stated simply, "Logan was a mulatto who looked almost as white as his wife. The couple had nine children." Alexander hinted, however, that Adella's attitudes at times may have strained the marriage. "Adella Hunt Logan was a willful woman," she observed, "who rarely avoided controversy." It helped, as Alexander stated, that Warren was "an educated person whose racial and social background resembled [her] own." Adella could be described as a person who "had acquired a little money and property," but Warren boasted assets as well. By 1891 he owned "one-third interest in 2,200 acres of land, eight mules, wagons, household furniture, etc." Accordingly, the Logans raised their children in comparative luxury, in the house they occupied next door to Washington's Tuskegee home. Son Warren, born in January 1890, joined them first, followed over the next two decades by eight brothers and sisters. Six of the children would survive to adulthood.[16]

Adella's ties with the woman who, in 1891, would become Booker Washington's third wife drew her closer to community activism during the first years of her marriage. Margaret Murray Washington had been born at Macon, Georgia, at about the same time as Logan was born in nearby Sparta. She had graduated from Fisk University before coming to Tuskegee as a teacher in 1889. By the following year she had entered upon the duties of lady principal, Adella's former position. Over time their friendship brought a great deal of community outreach and involvement in cultural affairs. A high point was the 1895 organization of the Tuskegee Woman's Club, an entity that aimed to serve "the general intellectual development of women." An aggressive force for improvements within the local African American community, the club, according to one of

Figure 16. Margaret Murray Washington, c. 1920s.
(Courtesy of UCR/California Museum of Photography.)

Margaret's biographers, "held weekly mothers' meetings, providing child care and offering classes and lectures to adult women." Additionally, "The club took special interest in the poor workers on a nearby plantation. The club opened a school for the children, ran boys' and girls' clubs, and began a newspaper-reading club for men." Historian Deborah G. White, referring to the Tuskegee Woman's Club's success, asserted that the organization "exemplified the spirit and work of black Woman's Clubs."[17]

Given that Adella had retired from active employment at the Tuskegee Institute on her marriage (although, as will be seen, not from all teaching and other responsibilities at the school), she found considerable time to contribute to causes such as those espoused by the Tuskegee Woman's Club. These activities broadened her horizons and her sphere of operations during an era when such clubs were creating great momentum for change among women, both white and black. As one scholar of the subject observed, "[These clubs] mushroomed into a major social force before the end of the century, spreading education, culture, and changes in the legal and political system like spores on the wind." In line with that dynamic, Adella moved from leading monthly discussions at the Tuskegee Woman's Club to deep involvement in national causes and organizations. Woman's suffrage stood high among these causes.[18]

The issue of suffrage rights for women had ignited beginning in 1870, one year after Wyoming had pioneered extension of the franchise. In that year drafters of the Fifteenth Amendment to the U.S. Constitution effectively elevated the battle for human rights by excluding right-to-vote protections for women. As post-Reconstruction attempts by white officials to restrict voting rights for African American men touched state after state, questions of women's voting rights became enmeshed with racial politics. In the South and elsewhere, whites feared that if black women could vote, then the black vote would become too powerful. As a result in the late 1800s and early 1900s competing and conflicting perspectives about the suffrage movement emerged. The predominant one insisted that "suffrage strategies and ideas [should reflect] those of middle-class white suffragists." The suffrage movement thereupon became even more important for African American women. "As the woman suffrage movement progressed into the early twentieth century and the racial oppression of Black people intensified," historian Dulcie Straughan explained, "African American suffragists moved further away from the abstract nineteenth-century argument that suffrage was a human right that all people deserved, to focus more on what they perceived as the real issue—that African American women needed suffrage even more that white women, because Blacks were more heavily oppressed."[19]

Adella first actively campaigned for suffrage through the Tuskegee Woman's Club. Her position at Tuskegee and her stature as a public intellectual within the Tuskegee Institute gave her credibility in moving the message forward. She and Margaret Murray Washington pursued their pro-suffrage path, it should be noted, with Booker T. Washington's support. Among the numerous articles that Logan authored for state and national journals, she enjoyed excellent exposure in the *Colored American*, the national journal sponsored by Washington. In that essay she proclaimed, "Government of the people, for the people, and by the people is but partially realized so long as woman has no vote. If white American women with all their natural and acquired advantages need the ballot, that right protective of all other rights, how much more do black Americans, male and female, need the strong defense of a vote to secure their right to life, liberty, and the pursuit of happiness?"[20]

To further her woman's suffrage campaign, Adella engaged the Tuskegee community in several ways. For example, in 1900 she "organized a political parade for her civics class at about the time for the kick-off of Republican President McKinley's reelection campaign . . . [and she] coached the debate team, which focused on the question of women voting." That any black woman would engage in such public demonstrations of opinion ran markedly counter to prevailing practice. Marjorie Spruill Wheeler, in her study *New Women of the New South*, commented upon that fact. "A few black women living in the South, including Margaret Murray Washington and Adella Hunt Logan of Tuskegee, were prominent suffragists," she wrote. "But these women were discriminated against by white suffragists of the North, who feared their participation would alienate potential support among white Southerners; and they were completely excluded from suffrage organizations in the South by white women who were either opposed to black suffrage or (at best) feared that participation of African American women would totally discredit their cause in the minds of most Southern whites."[21]

Near the century's end Logan was to run headlong into just this sort of opposition. Because of her light skin color, she had managed to join the white National American Woman Suffrage Association (NAWSA), deemed the most significant organization advocating voting rights for women. When she did, only a few of its leaders and members realized that she was black. Then, in 1897 Logan approached Susan B. Anthony for permission to address the association—as a black woman—at its national convention. This proved too much for Anthony and many of her supporters. The nation's most prominent woman's suffrage leader rejected Logan's request outright. "I would not on any account," she insisted, "bring on our platform a woman who had a ten-thousandth part of a drop of African blood in her veins." Ironically, Logan eventually became Alabama's only NAWSA life member.[22]

Such opposition based upon race failed to deter Logan from her pursuit of the vote. She persisted not simply as a woman but also as someone concerned about children and generations to come. She had become convinced that "blacks needed the vote to obtain for their children adequate school facilities, a fair 'share of the public-school funds,' and just and humane treatment under the law." Even in the last years of her life and despite marital complications and medical issues, Adella Hunt Logan remained steadfast to the cause. In just one of many examples, she advocated passage of a law that would have required a statewide suffrage referendum in Alabama. As so often happened with the causes that she promoted, the bill that she backed went down to defeat.[23]

Adella may have summarized her sentiments about woman's suffrage most eloquently in an essay published in 1912. It appeared in *The Crisis*, the journal of the National Association for the Advancement of Colored People (NAACP), thanks to the support of her friend W. E. B. Du Bois, who edited the publication. "More and more colored women are studying public questions and civics," she began. "As they gain information and have experience in their daily vocations and in their efforts for human betterment they are convinced as many other women have long ago been convinced, that their efforts would be more telling if women had the vote." She continued,

> Adequate school facilities in city, village and plantation districts greatly concern the black mother. But without a vote she has no voice in educational legislation, and no power to see that her children secure their share of public-school funds....
>
> They know, too, that officers, as a rule, recognize few obligations to voteless citizens....
>
> They must wait while they besiege their legislature. Having no vote they need not be feared or heeded....
>
> Not only is the colored woman awake to reforms that may be hastened by good legislation and wise administration, but where she has the ballot she is reported as using it for the uplift of society and for the advancement of the state....
>
> Colorado [which granted women the vote in 1893] has never had a better school than her women have made. Judge Ben[jamin Barr] Lindsey is as popular with colored women voters as he is with white women voters. The juvenile court over which he presides gives the boys a square deal regardless of color.[24]

Logan's work for woman's suffrage constituted just one facet of her public activities from 1888 to 1915; her other endeavors illustrated that white opposition to black woman's suffrage and the participation of black women in national suffrage organizations did not deter her from seeking cooperation and understanding across the color line. She associated early on with the NAACP, although the National Association of Colored Women (NACW) offered her a greater field for activity. Founded in 1888 with the goal of forming alliances with all women regardless of race, creed, nationality, or traditions, NACW especially offered critical opportunities for black women because the white-dominated National Council of Women prohibited African Americans from joining that organization. Still, NACW adopted the theme of inclusiveness as one of its top strategic priorities to advance its overall mission and to gain the right to vote for black women.[25]

The mission of inclusiveness led NACW women to seek a union of their organization with the National Council of Women, and Logan helped to achieve that goal. Most notably, in December 1899 she authored for the NACW publication *The National Association Notes* a compelling article explaining the multiple benefits to be derived from the merger. She insisted on the importance of the union for African Americans "because we are American women and the council exists to promote the welfare of all women in the country." She further explained, "We shall be better understood, and, we trust, more highly esteemed, by the people of other races and nations, if we are given opportunities to work in sympathy with them, rather than be left out of their plans altogether." As a fundamental point, she argued, all must understand that "ignorance of each other is at the bottom of the prejudice existing between the races."[26]

Efforts toward unity as espoused by Adella Hunt Logan ultimately succeeded. In 1901, NACW joined forces with the National Council of Women. Mary Church Terrell, NACW president, declared in the *National Notes*, "The National Association of Colored Women has been baptized into fellowship with the National Council of Women by the tears of our sisters of the more favored race, and feeling confident that the bond of union between the white women and the colored women of this country has been greatly strengthened thereby." The proactive, if controversial, approach and influence of Adella Hunt Logan to further unity between the two organizations had resulted in improved race relations.[27]

One intellectual aspect of Adella's pursuit of woman's suffrage rights and of her association with NACW reflected for her a larger cause; that is, throughout her work she developed the theme of the black woman as a role model. In the spirit of advancing the race, she and other NACW leaders strove to educate the public about the great accomplishments of specific black women. Those to whom they pointed, all NACW members, symbolized a "great nation and great civilization" despite the fact that they were relatives of slaves. Accordingly, each issue of *The National Association Notes* focused on a prominent and successful black woman. The monthly feature provided a sense of pride and dignity for its readership and, over time, offered recognition to, among others, Adella Hunt Logan, Olivia Davidson Washington, Julia Layton, and Josephine Silone-Yates. This initiative enjoyed a degree of success. "As I review the work of the women of my race during the past 80 years," one reporter declared about *The National Association Notes*, "I see 'nobly done' written above their endeavor."[28]

Other areas of concern also commanded Logan's attention. She served, for instance, as a local, state, and national spokeswoman for the welfare and rights of rural African American women and the plight of the poor. Meanwhile, she continued to apply herself for the betterment of the Tuskegee Institute and its students. She possessed a persistent passion for educating and molding the minds of young people. Her work and her extensive knowledge base provided a solid foundation on which she built an outstanding reputation for sound curriculum development. Her students, she determined, would receive a well-rounded and quality education. Booker Washington honored Logan's expertise. Particularly, he requested that she evaluate the teaching faculty at Tuskegee Institute. She accepted that challenge, and she reviewed literature of professional criticism. She also provided guidance for teachers and constructive feedback for the professional growth and development of faculty members.[29]

While pursuing her state, regional, and national goals, Logan kept a careful watch on the home front and upheld its importance. She especially followed the traditions of elite black women by believing in the ideals of clubwomen and in her role as housewife. She credited her knowledge of domestic skills to the education she had obtained at Atlanta University. One aspect that Adella valued was the art of cooking and preparing healthy meals for her family. She wrote numerous publications on healthy living, parenting, what to eat, "establishing a good home," and the "Gospel of the Tooth-Brush." These priorities she managed to incorporate as part of the schoolwide curriculum at Tuskegee. She then carried her concerns and insights beyond the school and city to regional and national audiences. Her essay on mortality among African American residents of southern cities has already been mentioned. As another example she presented at an 1897 Atlanta University conference a paper entitled "Prenatal and Hereditary Influences." Her perspective on the family—which she considered a powerful, formative, and nurturing factor—suggested that heredity influences "were central to all human experience and could be traced back through many generations." She argued further that "the deeds of parents would be seen in their children and we are today reaping what was sown, not by our fathers alone, but their fathers and grandfathers." According to conference minutes, this presentation led Logan into an "animated discussion" with famed educator Lucy Craft Laney of Augusta, Georgia, additional testimony to her willingness to take controversial stands.[30]

As has been discussed, Adella Hunt Logan's work centered on five major themes: inclusion, righting social wrongs, black women as role models, women's self-improvement, and strength through unity. Certain points should be underscored concerning several of these. With respect to the first, her vision and the theme of inclusiveness expanded to all aspects of her life, in particular to urging churches and community organizations to embrace the concept.

Given her firm belief that the two greatest influences on human growth and development were the church and state, this activity logically flowed from her other work. The effort ultimately led in 1899 to the involvement of clergy at the NACW biennial convention, held that year in Chicago. Commenting on the development, President Mary Church Terrell insisted, "If our ministries, all over the country, would preach at least one sermon of the week on what the National Council of Women has done and is trying to do, it would aid materially in making our convention a success." She added in words that could have been uttered by Logan: "Our women bear the heaviest burdens of the church. Through the pastor, it should come to our assistance, whenever it can consistently and conscientiously do so."[31]

The theme of inclusiveness takes on special importance in light of the onset of the Jim Crow era and Adella Hunt Logan's passion for "righting social wrongs." Many scholars have observed that the dawn of the twentieth century represented a period of deteriorating race relations with the imposition of segregation laws in the South and elsewhere. That Logan could maintain equilibrium, not unlike her mentor Booker T. Washington, and a magnanimous attitude toward whites speaks volumes for her wisdom and leadership. Black Americans and, particularly, black women could not progress, she understood, unless some cooperation could be established between leaders on both sides of the racial divide.[32]

Additionally, Adella Hunt Logan, as a prolific author of several health-conscious publications, also elevated the theme of the self-improvement of women. Embedded in her thinking was a rekindling of the Victorian ideal of womanhood—that women should exert their influence on their husbands and children and, through them, on society at large—as a model for black women. One of her most popular published articles, "The Morning Toilet," stresses, for example, the importance of dressing nicely in the morning so that a woman's husband and children would view her positively. Other topics of her publications ranged from proper etiquette to poetry quotations. In the final analysis, the self-improvement theme assisted many to make the transition from young girls into respected women.[33]

Further, the direction in which Logan and her associates led the NACW helped to shape the theme of strength through unity. In February 1902, Josephine Yates, newly elected NACW president, expressed sentiments also held by Adella. "In union lies our greatest strength," she declared, "hence with great interest we view the amount of effective organization that is being done by our women, and the wonders it is working in all parts of our land." Yates and Logan both also understood the importance of effective communication in fostering a sense of unity and establishing common goals and objectives. By 1901, the efforts of these women would lead club members from eleven states, governed by the national office, to foster "an interchange of strength and opinion which makes for a successful effort in both."[34]

Despite her contributions and the lasting nature of her public service, it became evident as the decade of the 1910s unfolded that the challenges Adella faced in life were taking their toll. These included, among others, the deaths of three children; the diagnosis of another of her children with tuberculosis; and struggles associated with her racial identity, her own health problems, and rumors that her husband had become "embroiled in a romance." As she observed in one essay, a woman's compounding frustrations could lead her "to cry, to swear, or to suicide." These words proved prophetic.[35]

As Adele Logan Alexander explained, "[Adella] was beset with health problems and personal crises and became deeply depressed because she could not tolerate the racist and sexist society in which she lived and the people who refused to treat a woman of color as their equal. Her life spiraled downward [and] she became increasingly despondent." In early October 1915 Booker Washington intervened to secure Adella admission to J. H. Kellogg's highly regarded sanatorium at Battle Creek, Michigan. She had endured, he told Kellogg, a nervous breakdown. Washington himself then entered a decline that was to prove terminal. Logan rushed back to Tuskegee, but Washington died soon thereafter on November 14. In testimony to the friendship that had endured between the two educators, George Washington Carver eventually would paint two murals honoring their lives and legacies. With Booker Washington's passing Adella's depression understandably deepened, a condition exacerbated when her husband, Warren Logan, was passed over in the selection of Washington's replacement as head of the Tuskegee Institute. It all proved too much. On December 10, 1915, Adella Logan committed suicide, jumping from a top floor of Tuskegee Institute's main academic building in the presence of administrators, teachers, visitors, students, and two of her own children.[36]

Adella Hunt Logan accomplished much throughout her life and career. She helped to bring the woman's suffrage movement to the forefront in the South, especially for African American women; contributed to the field of education; and provided leadership for regional and national organizations supporting these efforts. She made indelible contributions at the Tuskegee Institute as a teacher, librarian, and lady principal; yet, she was motivated to uplift not only the students who attended the Tuskegee Institute but also the citizens of rural

Alabama. Serving in a larger arena, Logan publicized the plight of women in national forums, and she elevated the women's platform by showing the inequality of women of color. Her tragic death cannot negate the value of her contributions.

Notes

We are grateful to Daria Willis for her generous guidance in securing information about Adella Hunt Logan. Ms. Willis is author (as Daria Willis Joseph) of "Adella Hunt Logan: Educator, Mother, Wife, and Suffragist, 1863–1915" (master's thesis, Florida A&M University, 2007) and currently is expanding that work as a doctoral dissertation at Florida State University.

1. Adele Logan Alexander, *Ambiguous Lives: Free Women of Color in Rural Georgia, 1789–1879* (Fayetteville, Ark., 1991), 194; David Levering Lewis, *W. E. B. Du Bois: The Fight for Equality and the American Century, 1919–1963* (New York, 2000), 19.

2. 1900 U.S. Decennial Census, Macon County, Alabama (population schedule); Alexander, *Ambiguous Lives*, 1–45. On the life and times of Amanda America Dickson, see Kent Anderson Leslie, *Woman of Color, Daughter of Privilege: Amanda America Dickson, 1849–1893* (Athens, Ga., 1996). On black privilege in Georgia during the antebellum era, also see Whittington Bernard Johnson, *Black Savannah, 1788–1864* (Fayetteville, Ark., 1996).

3. Adella Hunt Logan's granddaughter Adele Logan Alexander has offered an excellent study of Adella's family background in *Ambiguous Lives*. See also Adele Logan Alexander, "How I Discovered My Grandmother, and the Truth about Black Women and the Suffrage Movement," *Ms.* (November 1983): 29–33.

4. George P. Rawick, *The American Slave: A Composite Autobiography*, 41 vols. (Westport, Conn., 1972–1979), 17:13.

5. Eliza Frances Andrews, *The War-Time Journal of a Georgia Girl, 1864–1865* (New York, 1908), 32–33.

6. Alexander, *Ambiguous Lives*, 138, 142–43; Leslie, *Woman of Color*, 81.

7. Joseph, "Adella Hunt Logan," 54; 1870 U.S. Decennial Census, Hancock County, Georgia (population schedule); Daniel W. Culp, ed., *Twentieth Century Negro Literature; or, A Cyclopedia of Thought on the Vital Topics Relating to the American Negro* (Atlanta, 1902), facing p. 199; Alexander, *Ambiguous Lives*, 151–52. On the notable black elite see, among other works, Willard B. Gatewood, *Aristocrats of Color: The Black Elite, 1880–1920* (Bloomington, Ind., 1990); Janette Thomas Greenwood, *Bittersweet Legacy: The Black and White "Better Classes" in Charlotte, 1850–1910* (Chapel Hill, 1994); Jacqueline M. Moore, *Leading the Race: The Transformation of the Black Elite in the Nation's Capital, 1880–1920* (Charlottesville, Va., 1999).

8. Culp, *Twentieth Century Negro Literature*, facing p. 199; Alexander, *Ambiguous*

Lives, 167–68; Leslie, *Woman of Color*, 176. For more on Henry Alexander Hunt Jr., see Donnie D. Bellamy, "Henry A. Hunt and Black Agricultural Leadership in the New South," *Journal of Negro History* 60 (October 1975): 464–79. On Bass Academy, see Eileen B. McAdams, "Hancock County Public Schools," www.georgiagenealogy.org/hancock2/schools.html.

9. Alexander, *Ambiguous Lives*, 176–79; Culp, *Twentieth Century Negro Literature*, facing p. 199; *Catalogue of the Officers and Students of Atlanta University* (Atlanta, 1900), 40.

10. Darlene Clark Hine, Elsa Barkley Brown, and Rosalyn Terborg-Penn, *Black Women in America: An Historical Encyclopedia* (Brooklyn, N.Y., 1993), 731; Booker T. Washington, *Tuskegee and Its People: Their Ideals and Achievements* (New York, 1906), 308; *Opelika-Auburn* (Ala.) *News*, May 23, 2000. On Booker Washington and the Tuskegee Institute in its formative years, see, among others, Louis R. Harlan, *Booker T. Washington: The Making of a Black Leader, 1856–1901* (New York, 1972).

11. Booker T. Washington, *Up from Slavery: An Autobiography* (New York, 1906), 81–83, 130–31; Louis R. Harlan, Pete Daniel, Stuart B. Kaufman, Raymond W. Smock, and William M. Welty, eds., *The Booker T. Washington Papers*, vol. 2: *1860–89* (Urbana, 1972), 230; Culp, *Twentieth Century Negro Literature*, facing p. 199.

12. Culp, *Twentieth Century Negro Literature*, facing p. 199.

13. Harlan et al., *Booker T. Washington Papers*, 2:494.

14. Culp, *Twentieth Century Negro Literature*, 199, 201.

15. *Twenty-Two Years' Work of the Hampton Normal and Agricultural Institute at Hampton, Virginia* (Hampton, Va., 1891), 91; Robert Francis Engs, *Freedom's First Generation: Black Hampton, Virginia, 1861–1890* (New York, 2004), 123; Washington, *Tuskegee and Its People*, 308; idem, *Up from Slavery*, 104. On Hampton Institute and Samuel C. Armstrong, see also Francis Greenwood Peabody, *Education for Life: The Story of Hampton Institute: Told in Connection with the Fiftieth Anniversary of the Foundation of the School* (New York, 1918); Robert Francis Engs, *Educating the Disenfranchised and Disinherited: Samuel Chapman Armstrong and the Hampton Institute, 1839–1893* (Knoxville, Tenn., 1999).

16. Alexander, *Ambiguous Lives*, 194–95; *Twenty-Two Years' Work*, 91; 1900 and 1910 U.S. Decennial Censuses, Macon County, Alabama (population schedules).

17. Hazel V. Corby, *Reconstructing Womanhood: The Emergence of the Afro-American Woman Novelist* (New York, 1987), 119; Faustine Childress Jones-Wilson, *Encyclopedia of African American Education* (Westport, Conn., 1996), 509; Culp, *Twentieth Century Negro Literature*, facing p. 199; George Hutchinson, *In Search of Nella Larsen: A Biography of the Color Line* (Cambridge, Mass., 2006), 100; Deborah G. White, *Too Heavy a Load: Black Women's Defense of Themselves, 1894–1994* (New York, 1999), 28.

18. Sandra Haarsager, *Organized Womanhood: Cultural Politics in the Pacific Northwest, 1840–1920* (Norman, Okla., 1997), 3; Dulcie Straughan, *Lifting As We Climb: The Role of* The National Association Notes *in Furthering the Issues Agenda of the National Association of Colored Women, 1897–1920* (Chapel Hill, 2005–2006), 8(3)

(available through Media History Monographs 8 [2006] at http://quicksilver.elon.edu/facstaff/copeland/mhmjour8-2.pdf.

19. Straughan, *Lifting As We Climb*, 55; Rosalyn Terborg-Penn, *African American Women in the Struggle for the Vote, 1850–1920* (Bloomington, Ind., 1998), 54.

20. Adele Logan Alexander, *Homelands and Waterways: The American Journey of the Bond Family, 1846–1926* (New York, 1999), 312.

21. Terborg-Penn, *African American Women in the Struggle*, 194–95; Marjorie Spruill Wheeler, *New Women of the New South: The Leaders of the Woman Suffrage Movement in the Southern States* (New York, 1993), xx.

22. Corby, *Reconstructing Womanhood*, 119.

23. Wheeler, *New Women of the New South*, 108; Alexander, *Homelands and Waterways*, 336.

24. Adella Hunt Logan, "Colored Women as Voters," *The Crisis* (September 1912), 242–43. Tennessee-born Judge Benjamin Barr Lindsey pioneered in his Denver courtroom juvenile justice philosophies and approaches that gained him worldwide attention. See, among other sources, Donald J. Shoemaker and Timothy W. Wolfe, *Juvenile Justice: A Reference Handbook* (Santa Barbara, Calif., 2005), 114.

25. On the NACW, see, among other sources, Tullia Kay Brown Hamilton, "The National Association of Colored Women" (Ph.D. diss., Emory University, 1978); Charles H. Wesley, *The History of the National Association of Colored Women's Clubs, Inc.: A Legacy of Service* (Washington, D.C., 1984).

26. Straughan, *Lifting As We Climb*, 7–8.

27. Ibid. On Mary Church Terrell, see Mary Church Terrell, *A Colored Woman in a White World* (New York, 1980).

28. Joseph, "Adella Hunt Logan," 10.

29. See, for example, Louis R. Harlan, Stuart B. Kaufman, Barbara S. Kraft, and Raymond W. Smock, eds., *The Booker T. Washington Papers*, vol. 4, *1895–98* (Urbana, Ill., 1975), 130.

30. Joseph, "Adella Hunt Logan," 1, 37, 39–40; Alexander, *Ambiguous Lives*, 13; Culp, *Twentieth Century Negro Literature*, facing p. 199, 199–201; *Social and Physical Condition of Negroes in Cities: Report of an Investigation under the Director of Atlanta University and Proceedings of the Second Conference for the Study of Problems Concerning Negro City Life, Held at Atlanta University, May 25–26, 1897* (Atlanta, 1897), 30. On Lucy Laney, see G. T. Williams-Way, "Lucy Craft Laney, the Mother of the Children of the People: Educator, Reformer, Social Activist" (Ph.D. diss., University of Southern California, 1998).

31. Joseph, "Adella Hunt Logan," 8–9.

32. The principal argument for the timing of the Jim Crow era's onset can be found in C. Vann Woodward, *The Strange Career of Jim Crow* (New York, 1966) and its many subsequent editions.

33. Adella Hunt Logan, "The Morning Toilet," *The National Association Notes* 2 (January 1899): 4.

34. Joseph, "Adella Hunt Logan," 11.

35. Alexander, *Homelands and Waterways*, 338.

36. Ibid., 194; Louis R. Harlan, *Booker T. Washington: The Wizard of Tuskegee, 1901–1915* (New York, 1983), 525; Joseph, "Adella Hunt Logan," 55; Monroe N. Work, *Negro Year Book: An Encyclopedia of the Negro, 1916–1917* (Tuskegee, 1916), 363; *Baltimore Afro-American*, November 20, 1915; *New York Times*, November 23, 1915.

CHAPTER 9

Florence Johnson Hunt
1866–1953

Days of Labor of an
African American Woman

FRED R. VAN HARTESVELDT

WHEN HISTORIAN JACQUELINE ANNE ROUSE undertook in the late twentieth century to construct a list of African American "women of impressive accomplishments," she had no difficulty identifying a large number of suitable candidates. Among those Rouse cited was Georgia's Florence Johnson Hunt who, she noted, justifiably could claim truly impressive achievements in education and in social welfare and reform. Nonetheless, despite being a personage of such distinction, Florence Johnson Hunt is now virtually forgotten. As has been the case with other women, her obscurity results partly from the shadow cast by a more famous husband. Henry Alexander Hunt won the Spingarn Medal in 1930, served as a member of President Franklin Delano Roos-

Figure 17. Florence Johnson Hunt, c. 1910s. (Courtesy of Fort Valley State University.)

evelt's Black Cabinet, and built an educational legacy that stands today as the Fort Valley State University, a member institution of the University System of Georgia. As published sources have revealed, he mixed easily with blacks and whites, who largely regarded him with respect. To his credit and during his lifetime as a professional educator and advisor to a president, H. A. Hunt never allowed those around him to forget that Florence worked in tandem with him throughout their married life. Still, his was the public face of their achievements. Like so many wives, Florence remained, seemingly contentedly so, in the background. Historians fail, however, if they permit such a shadow to veil the contributions of an outstanding woman.[1]

From the outset a cogent fact should be remembered: Florence Johnson Hunt managed her impressive accomplishments despite obstacles thrown in her path during the heart of the most intense period of the Jim Crow era of racial discrimination and prejudice. Thus the barriers she had to cross, principally in the first four decades of the twentieth century, were not only those of gender but also of race. As one example, the white-owned local newspaper—reflecting attitudes throughout much of the South—largely ignored the Fort Valley High and Industrial School where she and her husband labored on behalf of a regional community of more than one-quarter million African Americans. Even worse, in 1921 the paper's editor, in noting that Georgia had the largest black population in the Southeast, insisted this merely meant that there were "more niggers who needed lynching." Although the Fort Valley school enjoyed the support of numerous white backers, the simple act of living and progressing in such a community—while promoting the evolution of a struggling school into a vibrant center of education—deserves much more notice than Florence has received. Surprisingly, some writers have even disparaged African American accomplishments in this era. Afrocentrists and their followers regard blacks who struggled with the burdens of racism in that era as too accommodationist, portraying them as little more than dupes of whites. Any careful inquiry into the life and careers of Florence Hunt unquestionably demonstrates that she lived as nobody's dupe.[2]

Florence Hunt's careers also provide excellent context and support for the placement of black women within the patterns associated with Progressive-Era women. They became politically aware and began to fight for reform, especially in education and social welfare. Like their better known white counterparts, they formed clubs and acted in concert. The fact that black women, even in the rural South, formed networks, created organizations, and fought for reform in the Progressive style begs to be better understood, especially since the Progressive movement often is regarded as not having significant black involvement. One of the movement's pre-eminent historians, insofar as Progressivism touched the South, went so far as to divorce it from black aspirations entirely. Instead, he pointed to the Ku Klux Klan as the movement's lineal descendant. Matters, in fact, were far more complicated.³

Florence Johnson was born at Raleigh, North Carolina, on October 23, 1866. She came from a solid, if humble, family. Her parents, Columbus and Eliza A. Johnson, had been owned by a "large slaveholder" in Wake County. Florence apparently came as their third child after sons Edward Austin and Thomas Johnson. At least five other children would follow her. Census takers in 1880 listed Columbus as a "day laborer" and noted that Eliza, of mixed race, was making a living as a cook and washerwoman. Clearly, though, they valued education for their children. When son Edward evidenced "a remarkable aptitude in his studies," they enrolled him in the best school available to them, about which more will be mentioned shortly. By the time Edward prepared to leave for Atlanta University in the fall of 1878, he had earned the seventy-five dollars he carried with him. Columbus and Eliza, unable to read and write, allowed the journey only with trepidation. "My mother and my father," he recorded, "did not think well of my determination to make the trip, five hundred and forty-five miles from North Carolina into a strange country and to live among people whom I did not know."⁴

The school that offered Edward A. Johnson his early education—and that his sister Florence presumably attended as well—was the Washington School. Supported by the American Missionary Association until the mid-1870s, it rose out of the post–Civil War efforts of teacher Fisk P. Brewer, a Yale graduate and classical scholar who later served the University of North Carolina as professor of Greek language and literature and as librarian before going on to an even more distinguished career outside the South. While Brewer remained at the Raleigh school only briefly, he nonetheless affected the institution in lasting ways that would touch Florence Johnson deeply. First, he embraced the emphasis on Christian values in education, including service, advocated by the American Missionary Association. He also pressed for a broad-based education for his students, as opposed to mere industrial training. Finally, he insisted that poverty and need trumped race, thus giving his school a broader focus and outlook than might otherwise have been the case. Racial barriers meant nothing to him. As the *History of the University of North Carolina* noted: "[A] newspaper says that he ruined his usefulness by boarding with a negro for a short while after reaching Chapel Hill. It was alleged too that he invited negroes to his house when teaching at a colored school at Raleigh."⁵

Edward provided the example that Florence required, if she required one, to continue her education at the college level. A student at Atlanta University by 1878, he earned an undergraduate degree in four years. Thereupon he accepted a position as principal of Atlanta's Mitchell Street School. He returned to Raleigh in 1885 to accept the same position at the Washington School, now a public institution. At about that time, Florence made the trip to Atlanta that her parents had feared so intensely when Edward had ventured there seven years earlier. Scant available evidence suggests that she passed her time at Atlanta University as productively as had Edward. She graduated with her bachelor's degree in 1889, prepared to teach.[6]

Beyond preparing her for a career, Atlanta University additionally introduced Florence to the man she would marry. Henry Alexander Hunt had been born in Hancock County, Georgia, also in 1866, one of eight racially mixed children and younger brother to Adella Hunt Logan, profiled in chapter 8. He helped to pay his university expenses by working as a carpenter, but he excelled nonetheless in athletics, academics, and student life. It was said, additionally, that he "became a professing Christian while pursuing his college course." A friend insisted that Henry was "the most popular of his class," and it is no wonder that he caught Florence Johnson's eye. He graduated "with the highest honors of his class" in 1890 with a bachelor of arts degree. After teaching for a short time at Jackson, Georgia, he accepted the principalship of the Charlotte Graded School at Charlotte, North Carolina. He probably did so to be closer to Florence while he earned sufficient funds to permit him to marry. That effort received a boost in November 1891 when he joined the faculty of Biddle University (now Johnson C. Smith University) as superintendent of the Industrial Department. This appointment arose out of new president D. J. Sanders's initiative to hire the institution's first black faculty members, as one commentator put it, "to prove to many members of both races that African Americans had indeed made great strides through education and hard work." Two years later, on June 14, 1893, Florence and Henry married at Raleigh. Three children eventually were born to them: Dorothy (1896), Adele J. (1899), and Hal (1901).[7]

The Hunts' marriage illustrates a pattern then emerging among educated African Americans. Drawn together by love, they established a partnership with the understanding that they jointly would seek to better society and the condition of their people. Thus, Florence Johnson Hunt's activities accelerated greatly subsequent to her marriage. In addition to her responsibilities as a wife and a mother, she worked closely with her husband. First, she supplemented the family income by operating in their home a boarding house that specialized in serving Biddle University personnel. By 1900 she catered to eight lodgers. She also aided Henry as he advanced at the university. For example, when he

Figure 18. Henry Alexander Hunt and Florence Johnson Hunt, c. 1930s. (Courtesy of Fort Valley State University.)

organized the first farmers' conference held in North Carolina, Florence provided ideas and assistance. Their relationship thus was a partnership from the beginning. By 1902 he would tell a friend that "much of whatever success he has attained is attributable [to his wife]."[8]

Florence's commitment to activism may have provided inspiration to Henry A. Hunt's success. Despite the many calls upon her time, she—like many women in the late 1800s and early 1900s—devoted countless hours to worthy causes. Temperance likely stood foremost among them. In 1889 North Carolina

African American women split from a state Women's Christian Temperance Union (WCTU) organization that was dominated by whites, thereby affording North Carolina the distinction of hosting the nation's only black women's temperance union reporting directly to the national body. By 1891 the organization boasted four hundred members in nineteen chapters, including at Raleigh and Charlotte. It continued to flourish thereafter. The date of Hunt's association with the movement cannot be determined, but evidence suggests it began at or before the time of her marriage. In Charlotte she joined with others in various educational campaigns, including placing tracts in hotels, holding temperance rallies, and petitioning Congress to ban the trade in alcohol. Entertainments figured as well in the Charlotte movement, some of which Florence probably held at her commodious home. According to one local historian, "By 1901 the WCTU's activities had expanded to include ministry to prisoners and narcotics abusers as well as 'scientific temperance instruction' in the local schools." The next year Florence edited the organization's state journal.[9]

That was only the beginning of her good work. If Hunt did not participate in the organization of the National Association of Colored Women at the Nineteenth Street Baptist Church in Washington, D.C., in 1896, she affiliated with the group and its leader, Mary Church Terrell, soon after. And Florence's activism led to early recognition from the national body. At its second national convention, held at Chicago in August 1899, she was named state organizer for North Carolina. She would maintain the organizational connection for decades following her relocation to Georgia in the early 1900s.[10]

Meanwhile, the creation of better economic opportunities for African Americans drew Hunt's attention as well. As early as 1891 a national journal reported, "Charlotte is improving very rapidly [and] the colored populace of the city seems to be contributing their share to the city's prosperity." The article noted "handsome and commodious residences and fine church edifices [and] a splendid core of teachers." Historian Janette Thomas Greenwood added, "Biddle [University] especially came to symbolize the progress made by blacks since Reconstruction." Among the projects with which Biddle's leadership and faculty associated themselves was the work of the Coleman Manufacturing Company. Florence's brother Edward A. Johnson served as its vice president. The firm's first grand aim was the erection of a black-owned and -operated cotton mill near Charlotte. When fund-raising proved more challenging than expected, Hunt contributed her own efforts. At the cornerstone-laying ceremony on February 8, 1898, Florence's presence—along with that of her friend Meriah Elizabeth Gion Harris, wife of African Methodist Episcopal Zion (AMEZ)

Church Bishop Cicero Richardson Harris—reflected, according to Greenwood, "the active interest and participation of women of the better class in industrialization."[11]

While Florence and Henry were establishing themselves professionally and starting a family in North Carolina, the institution with which they were to be indelibly associated was being created in Georgia. The Fort Valley High and Industrial School began operating at Fort Valley, south of Macon, about 1890 as an informal school that met in Usher's Temple Colored Methodist Episcopal (CME) Church and then in the Masonic Lodge Hall. Chartered in 1895, it filled a substantial need. Public education in Georgia, especially in rural areas, was abysmal. In Houston County (Peach County, where the school is currently located, was not established until 1924) and the five counties immediately adjoining it lived some 200,000 blacks in 1907. A total of 11,256 black children were enrolled in schools, but only 5,811 (51 percent) attended. The public monthly investment in educating these children came to 39 cents apiece. In five of the counties the local county board of education owned not one "colored schoolhouse." By comparison, 61 percent of white enrolled students attended school, and education spending was $1.34 per pupil per month. More than half of the "white schoolhouses" were county owned.[12]

John W. Davison was tapped to provide the driving force behind the new school, and the fact that his tenure proved problematic would lead to the Hunts' relocation to Georgia. Initially, the board of trustees elected Davison "Principal for Life." He moved quickly to acquire property and, with the help of J. H. Torbert—long to be one of the school's major fund-raisers—convinced the Quaker philanthropist Anna T. Jeanes to contribute a substantial building. When completed, Jeanes Hall operated as a dormitory for women. Such advances initially brought Davison popularity in the white and black communities. His success did not last, however. Financial difficulties and, perhaps more fundamentally, a philosophical dispute over the best course for black education led to discord. Davison introduced academically oriented coursework, but most of the school's white supporters and some of its black supporters felt that vocational training after the manner of Tuskegee Institute offered a preferable model. Probably inevitably, Davison lost the struggle as financial problems mounted. In 1903 he resigned. At that time the school was renting out space in an effort to stave off bankruptcy.[13]

The opportunity that then arose permanently altered the lives of Florence and Henry Hunt and their children. After some debate the Fort Valley High and Industrial School trustees settled on Henry as the leader the school needed.

Not only did he enjoy a good reputation for his work at Biddle, but he also believed firmly that agriculture provided the way out of poverty and discrimination for rural blacks. The question was, could he be talked into uprooting his family and moving to the rural Black Belt of Georgia? The move would involve a dramatic change from the more affluent and sophisticated places where the couple had spent much of their adult lives. To secure Hunt's assent the trustees enlisted the support of a variety of the school's supporters who favored the choice, including George Foster Peabody, a philanthropist and trustee; Wallace Buttrick of the General Education Fund, which contributed financially to the school; and Adella Hunt Logan, Hunt's sister and an aide to Booker T. Washington at Tuskegee Institute. After consultation with Florence, Henry Hunt accepted the position and, on February 9, 1904, the family arrived at Fort Valley.[14]

The condition of Fort Valley High and Industrial School at the time of the Hunts' arrival bode none too well for its future. To begin with, the institution had only 145 students and an annual budget of just $840. Florence, for whom the transition proved traumatic, described the difficulties they encountered, with even the elements seemingly working against them. She wrote later of "that dark, chilly, rainy February night of the Hunts' arrival at Fort Valley." Her first impressions were less than favorable:

> The old gray horse and the buggy waiting at the station. The lifting of two small girls and a boy from the buggy to be 'toted' down in the arms of stronger boys. The water standing around the old house. The rooms, so large, so empty and bare. The old log barn. The old laundry stood right along side the principal's house, Anna T. Jeanes Hall dormitory partially completed. The three-room school building across the road. The deep cellar surrounded by a three-foot brick wall and filled with water. The beginning of another building. The school grounds, a sand bed, millions, billions, trillions of pebbles, but trees, shrubbery, lawns—where, oh where, were they!
> The big pond between the School and Central of Georgia Railway so near. Men, women, children paddling in the water, riding in bateaux, shooting the bull frogs. At night the croak of the frogs, the yell of the drinkers, gamblers on the railroad banks, green slimy puddles of water, mosquitoes, malaria, typhoid.[15]

Hunt goes on to offer her thoughts about the necessity of black schools becoming community centers with responsibilities far beyond simply educating youths, a philosophy that helped her to make the transition and that constituted the core principles behind her future activities. In this context, she noted the lack of gardens and poorly preserved food that resulted in poor nutrition; the absence of public health: "flies, gnats, sore-eyed children, no nurses, no colored doctors; children late, even two hours late, to school and excused at noon to take lunch to the fields; school terms reduced to two months because the labor of youths was needed; and Christmas Eve to January first—fire crackers, drinking, shooting, swearing, fighting, going to jail." Although Florence Hunt would always play a major part within the academic program of the Fort Valley school, social outreach understandably became her greatest contribution.[16]

The Hunts first undertook to stabilize the school, not an easy task. Florence remembered, for example, an occasion in the spring of 1904 when the local sheriff confronted her as she worked in her new flower garden. The man, who sported "long hair . . . shaggy beard, [and a] stocky build," intimidated the physically small woman. He had come to seize the school horse, which had been put up as collateral for a loan prior to the Hunts' arrival. Gyp, the horse, provided critically needed assistance in the farming of school grounds in order to feed students and faculty. She pleaded with the officer not to take the horse. She insisted that her husband, who was away at that time, would resolve the financial matter as soon as he returned. Making little headway with the sheriff, she fortunately managed to send a student to the fields to warn that the horse must not be brought back to the barn. Finally, as darkness fell the sheriff gave in, recognizing he could not seize a horse that he could not find. Florence's charm, however, had worked a lasting result. "Until his death," she recalled, "his attitude toward the school was friendly." Gyp eventually was redeemed and served the school for many years.[17]

Not all whites were so supportive, as numerous examples show. To cite one, when the Chapel Hall burned in the years soon after the beginning of the Hunts' Fort Valley residence, slate roofing exploded. The white community, anxious about African American reaction to the tightening racial controls of the Jim Crow era, became convinced that an arsenal had been concealed on campus. Guards were posted, and a citizens' committee investigated. Not surprisingly, the slate was found to be the cause of the explosions. "The guards quietly went away," Florence observed. "No more was heard of the magazine housed in the roof of the 'Niggra school.'"[18]

Black hostility had to be overcome as well. Because the Hunts represented "the new educated Negro," Florence recollected, many local blacks "looked at [us] so hard, so silently, with the eye of suspicion and fear." To the Hunts, regular church attendance was more civic duty "than a way of expressing any fervent religious devotion." The region's rural population, in contrast, embraced fundamentalism in religion and—despite the Hunts' best efforts to secure justice and decent treatment for blacks—feared that the newcomers' efforts constituted mere proselytizing in disguise. Local preachers fanned the concerns. "Only patient, persistent kindness from Mr. Hunt and his wife, the doing of good for evil," one man recorded, "could ever have triumphed over such bigotry and meanness as was visited upon these two people whose only crime was befriending the friendless."[19]

These obstacles notwithstanding, the one and a half decades following the commencement of Henry Hunt's tenure as principal at Fort Valley saw the partnership between him and Florence produce amazing progress. Although rural areas stood at a disadvantage when seeking philanthropic support, the Hunts succeeded well at drawing money from people with such prominent names as Peabody, Rosenwald, Rockefeller, Carnegie, Huntington, and Jeanes. That fact, in turn, permitted them to build buildings and support educational growth. By the years immediately following World War I, the annual budget had grown to $80,000. During those first years Henry Hunt often pursued out-of-state fund-raising. His wife sometimes traveled with him but also ventured out on her own to contact supporters and find necessary funds. Mostly, though, the institution remained central to her. She proudly reminisced about not only the buildings built but also the improvements to the town, such as the opening of an artesian well. This well made pure water conveniently available, and production of garden vegetables greatly increased. Meanwhile, her home was remodeled and piped water added. "Water, baths," she exclaimed. "Oh joy!"[20]

While—as will be seen—Florence committed herself to community service, she neglected neither education-related nor administrative labors required to run Fort Valley High and Industrial School. Her titles and duties varied and overlapped from time to time, but she had no sustained break in responsibilities to the school from her arrival there in 1904 until her husband's death in 1938. She began as a teacher of stenography and English. In the second decade of the century she taught literature. Then in the 1920s and early 1930s she served as director of girls' industries, which entailed "Supervision of Girls Industries—Huntington and Jeanes Hall, Infirmary, Laundry and Teachers of Sewing, Cooking, Handicrafts." After 1933 she served as assistant principal and member of the governing board. In the mid- to late 1930s—when her husband spent much of his time in Washington, D.C., as assistant governor of the Farm Credit Board—she dominated the administration of the Fort Valley institution despite officially sharing the assistant principal role with a man, Frank Horne (uncle of the well-known Lena Horne). She directed serious problems to Henry Hunt by telegram, and he wired back strategic direction. Otherwise, Florence Hunt dealt with the logistics of running the place.[21]

By the mid-1920s the story of Fort Valley's turnaround at the hands of Henry and Florence Hunt had received widespread attention. "The Fort Valley High and Industrial School, Georgia, . . . had its beginnings thirty years ago," one national publication proclaimed in a fashion echoed by others. For "its new life upon its present broad foundations," the publication's author knew exactly where to place the credit. This progress resulted, he stated, as "the result of the consecrated wisdom of a Negro layman and his wife, Mr. and Mrs. H. A. Hunt." He concluded, "They are both thoroughly practical and constructive leaders, who know how to relate the theory of books to the practice of industry."[22]

One key element of their success required local, regional, and national outreach. In line with Florence Hunt's personal desires and from its beginnings, the Fort Valley High and Industrial School had intended to make itself part of the community, giving and getting support. She helped to bring that goal to fruition. To win community support she and her husband attacked local problems in every possible manner. For one thing, with faculty members they started Sunday school participation in order to win over the children while still facing suspicion from adults. Direct interaction between the community and the school began with the first Thanksgiving and a community rally, similar to the functions Florence had sponsored as a member of the North Carolina Colored Women's Christian Temperance Union. The rally provided an opportunity to ask community members to contribute to the school. Although the records of the first such event were lost to fire, the receipts were remembered as "very meager indeed." The rally became an annual and far-more-successful event, however, that continued through the Depression until 1939 when the school became a state-sponsored institution. The Hunts also initiated a May Day party that included singing, dancing, and a maypole. By the 1930s these and other activities and advances had won community favor. By then, black public school classes competed to see which could raise the most money for what had become the Fort Valley High and Normal School.[23]

Under the Hunts' leadership the school, however desperately it needed community financial support, rejected even the appearance of merely taking without giving. Florence shared with Henry the work of running Sunday schools, Thanksgiving rallies, and May Day celebrations, while additionally performing an enormous amount of community service. This service in time reached out to all Georgians and addressed national concerns, but despite an increasingly busy schedule, she found time to attend locally to those in need. Friends accordingly remembered her fondly as "giving special attention to the aged and infirm, little children, families handicapped by ignorance, poverty and illness."[24]

While Henry Hunt was focused more particularly on education and the development of agricultural extension, Florence Hunt took the lead in their charitable and health-related initiatives. As Henry acknowledged, "Perhaps the most outstanding and, possibly the most useful service of the Fort Valley School, is to be found in its unique community work." As mentioned earlier and from the very start, they recognized the school's responsibility for changing the life, attitude, and atmosphere not only of the immediate community but also of the more remote districts. Their diligence paid off over time, and Fort Valley High and Industrial School emerged as a rare source of hope and help for the Middle Georgia black community. The effort, understandably, proved personally and financially expensive for the Hunts. Years later even one of the school's white founders, while praising their success, nonetheless felt compelled to comment upon the degree of their sacrifice.[25]

Florence Hunt's early efforts naturally were limited by available resources, but one of the first was her Christmas Tree celebration, which grew from a children's program into an annual community festival. Contributions were sought from around the country and came from as far away as Massachusetts. The school was decorated; musical programs were offered; and those involved sometimes were invited downtown by white audience members who were impressed by student performances. On Christmas Day the school opened and presents were given to those in need. Children received fruit, toys, and candy. Adults took home tobacco, coffee, and other foodstuffs. Coffee and sandwiches were served and carols sung. On occasions when more donations were received than were used at Christmas, the extra was kept to help those later found to be in need. A talented organizer with years of experience behind her, Florence did not lack for assistance in this worthy cause. When she wrote about how the eyes of the children "sparkled and danced," little doubt can be entertained about her motives for and joy in the Christmas Tree, a celebration that continued until she left the school.[26]

Health care loomed as an even more vital community need. In the early years of her stay at Fort Valley, as Florence reported, "Ill health was thought to be a natural state.... This was particularly true of the women folks." Peach County did not have a hospital until 1953. African Americans were not guaranteed attention even if they traveled to a more distant medical facility. Therefore, they often turned to folk medicine, and Hunt's contempt for the "root Doctor and conjure woman" was open. Accordingly, Florence offered first the Hunt home and then the Fort Valley High and Industrial School infirmary as centers for health advice and basic care. She and other teachers started mothers' meetings at a time when no black nurses or doctors served the community. Slowly, dependence on folk treatments and patent medicines gave way to more understanding of such issues as vaccinations, hookworm treatments, tonsillectomies, and balanced diets. A public health nurse began to work in the community after World War I. As would be expected, Florence arranged for her headquarters office to be hosted by the school.[27]

The necessity for more effective health care occupied Hunt's attention thereafter. Especially, she added to the list of her fund-raising efforts a campaign to build a proper medical facility. Progress came slowly, but in 1934 the school opened a brick infirmary, named for Hunt in acknowledgment of her central role in its creation. Although offering limited services, the infirmary could handle emergencies and provide first aid. The extension of health-care services to the region grew with the initiation of weekly health clinics attended by those, white and black, who had little or no access to regular hospitals. Local doctors of both races participated. The infirmary soon was bustling, as published reports suggested. "During the month of March [1936] there were twenty-four cases, sixteen operations on tonsils and eight other bed patients," one report noted. "In addition 196 students and teachers as well as twenty-one of the community folk were given treatment." Nor were all the problems minor. At the end of 1936 Ida Mae Jordan's grandfather brought her to the infirmary with burns over much of her body. The doctor who was summoned saw no hope of survival. The child rallied, however, and eventually recovered. Her family could pay nothing, but there was no question under Florence's guidance of denying her the help the infirmary could provide.[28]

Central for Florence Hunt with regard to the welfare of children were twin causes: educating children and educating parents in proper child care. The Fort Valley High and Industrial School provided primary education for black children who enjoyed scant other opportunities to learn. The school operated in the Gano Building. To sustain the program Florence in 1909 organized a mothers' club that became the Gano Parent-Teacher Association. The club boasted a countywide organization and gave black parents a means of exerting at least some influence over local education. The PTA participated actively, contributing to Christmas activities and other community programs. Hunt also helped to find homes with northern Quaker families for black girls who had gotten pregnant and who lacked family support in Georgia. She took on the additional responsibility of locating money for their education or vocational training.[29]

Hunt's interest and activity on behalf of children went beyond the Middle Georgia community where she lived. As mentioned, even before coming to Fort Valley she, like Progressive women all over the United States, involved herself with a network of reform-oriented women's organizations. Once settled in Fort Valley, Hunt worked increasingly on causes adopted by the Georgia Federation of Colored Women's Clubs. Organized June 21, 1902, it incorporated in October 1921. Florence likely joined soon after her arrival in Georgia, although a 1936 report observed that she had "worked with the Georgia Federation for 20 years." Like its white counterpart, the federation sponsored a variety of reforms but focused on youth and education. Alice D. Carey, president from 1913 to 1921, led an effort that resulted in the establishment of a reform school for boys in Atlanta. Although a fund was initiated early in the 1920s to create a similar facility for black girls, a decade later little progress had been made. The lack of progress did not reflect an absence of need. As the *Macon Telegraph* reported as late as the end of 1938, "A large number of Negro delinquent girls now is being kept in county jails or stockades with adult criminals."[30]

Hunt, in the capacity of federation executive secretary, took an early role in the organization's efforts to create a proper training school for delinquent young women. In June 1929 it invested $750 in ten acres located on the Old Savannah Road in Macon as a site for the school. The purchase did not, however, provide sufficient land and, unfortunately, the site could not be expanded or sold. More than ten years later the federation still owned it. In 1930, Hunt and her husband hosted Addie W. Hunton of New York, who had helped to pioneer the work of the Young Women's Christian Association, an organization in which black women were attempting with only mixed success to create an autonomous presence. While visiting in Georgia, Hunton traveled around the state with Hunt. They visited a number of towns and schools, advocating the creation of the training school and seeking support for it.[31]

Hunt emerged in 1931, somewhat to her surprise, as the central figure in the effort to build the school. Despite the Great Depression, it was a good year for her and her family. Henry had gotten a $1,400 grant from the Rosenwald Fund for the study of Danish agricultural education. As a result, the couple departed for Europe. Plans called for them to leave at the beginning of June and visit Germany, Switzerland, Italy, France, and England as well as Denmark. They expected the trip to last four months. While in Denmark, though, word reached Florence of her election as ninth president of the Georgia Federation—the first chosen in absentia. Her sense of duty almost overwhelmed the pleasures of her trip. She came close to panic over the logistics of balancing the responsibilities of the presidency with her obligations to the Fort Valley High and Normal

School. Fortunately, her husband managed to calm her with assurances that both jobs would wait until she returned home from the trip of a lifetime.[32]

By the fall of 1931 President Hunt had appointed the organization's cabinet, drawing women from all over Georgia, and had launched her campaign to build the school. Following a racially mixed meeting in Macon convened to support the project, an invitation from Wesleyan College brought the cause to that prestigious campus. "Macon soon had more clubs," Florence recalled, "than any other Georgia city." Her diligence paid off quickly. As of the spring of 1932 the federation had raised $3,000 for the training school. It arranged to purchase for $2,000 a new site, consisting of 131 acres on Camp Wheeler Road about five miles from Macon. To build the school the group turned to the Works Progress Administration, a New Deal agency that undertook construction projects. Their application was rejected because the property at that time remained in private hands. Hunt then arranged for the Bibb County Board of Public Welfare (Macon is the county seat) to take ownership, though the county rejected any responsibility for running the school. The federation agreed to raise any funds needed. The WPA thereupon consented to pay for the building, which was completed in 1936.[33]

As it turned out, though, the struggle had only begun for Florence and the federation. The state left the school vacant for two years. During that time it suffered damage from vandalism, until two supportive white families were moved in to provide protection. In December 1938 the Macon Junior Chamber of Commerce, perhaps prompted by Florence and her white supporters, publicly denounced the situation and called for implementation of the school plan. The proposal went directly to the state director of public welfare. The DeKalb County grand jury issued an appeal the next year, expanding the call to the Atlanta area. According to the *Macon Telegraph*, the continuing failure to use the facility was "due to lack of money." Florence Hunt's account differed: "The Bill [to fund the school] went before the Legislature four times. The first time the answer came, the Bill passed, but was lost. The second time there was an insufficient amount available. The third time the Bill was vetoed." Finally, in 1943, the legislature, with Governor Ellis G. Arnell's support, allocated $25,000 annually for operations plus $5,000 for equipment. By year's end the school readied itself to accommodate about thirty girls and six teachers. Graduates were to be qualified for "the highest type of domestic work." Thanks in part to Florence's leadership, the fate of such girls, who in previous times would have been "locked up in jails, made cooks at prison camps, and put to work on the public streets of their towns," brightened considerably. Publicly at least, Hunt enjoyed and graciously shared her success: "To me it is not only a victory of the

Georgia Federation of Colored Women's Clubs, but it is an interracial achievement as well. Whites and blacks worked together all over the state." Privately, however, she certainly had hoped for more.[34]

As if her crowded calendar needed more commitments of time, the 1930s evolved as a demanding period for Hunt in other ways. The Depression made fund-raising for Fort Valley High and Industrial School both more difficult and more necessary. The institution had become a junior college in 1926 and was renamed Fort Valley High and Normal School with the introduction of a full teacher training program. Hunt traveled widely in the North on behalf of the institution, speaking to women's and youth groups and church conferences, and making contact with longtime friends of the institution. She also oversaw the sale of student-made handicrafts at, for instance, the General Convention of the Episcopal Church in Atlantic City during October 1935. When it seemed that the school would fail for lack of resources, the Hunts—with Florence as Henry's active partner—managed to obtain support from the American Church Institute. Somehow, thanks to their mutual endeavors, there always was just enough to stay afloat.[35]

Additionally, her husband's renown had continued to grow. In 1930 he received the respected Spingarn Medal from the National Association for the Advancement of Colored People in recognition of his long service in agricultural education for blacks. In 1932, he accepted appointment as assistant to the governor of the Farm Credit Administration, thereafter spending much of the years 1933–1938 in Washington, D.C. There, he gained recognition as part of Franklin D. Roosevelt's Black Cabinet. Henry retained his position as principal of the Fort Valley High and Normal School, but much of the burden of managing the school fell upon Florence's shoulders during those years. She joined the governing committee in 1934 and took over in 1937 as academic director. Her emergence into public exercise of authority did not occur without criticism. Their arrangement came under fire as autocratic by the late 1930s, and calls for change were sounded. Before any action could be taken, however, Henry Hunt died, on October 1, 1938.[36]

For Florence Hunt much changed. As she declared in a letter to the *Fort Valley Message* concerning her husband's death: "My days of labor with the School now cease but not my interest and love and ambition, for the success of the work in its manifest detail." She left the principal's house, where she had lived since 1904, and moved down the street from the school to a private apartment in the home of her businessman son. She died on September 24, 1953, at age eighty-seven. She was buried, at her request, beside her husband on the campus of what was by then Fort Valley State College. As Peach County's most recent historian observed: "She was a great lady."[37]

Florence Johnson Hunt devoted her life to service. She played an extremely significant role in the creation and development of the institution that is today Fort Valley State University. She has received little credit for this accomplishment due to the prevailing gender attitudes of the time, though one cannot say that her husband was unduly praised or that he failed to acknowledge her as a partner in the work. Even more significantly, she extended the role of the school as a social service center and provider to many thousands of black Georgians who, without her endeavors, would have lacked not only education but very fundamental elements of quality of life such as basic medical care. Her work for youth through women's clubs puts her squarely in the midst of the Progressive movement, though she carried the ideals further in time than usually is recognized in accounts of the movement's influence. No one could have regarded her life as trivial, even had she not faced the barriers of the Jim Crow system and the attitudes that supported it. She did face and overcome them, thereby leaving Georgia and the world better places.

Notes

I thank my friend and colleague Donnie D. Bellamy for information, advice, and encouragement on this essay; and Wilmetta Jackson, archivist at the Hunt Memorial Library of Fort Valley State University, for help with source materials.

1. Jacqueline Anne Rouse, *Lugenia Burns Hope: Black Southern Reformer* (Athens, Ga., 1989), 5; personal interview with Frances Tabor Hoskin by the author, September 19, 2007 (notes in possession of the author); *Fort Valley Message*, March 1938; *Macon (Ga.) Telegraph*, February 9, 1931.

2. Clipping related to growth of Negro population of central Georgia from *Fort Valley Peachland's Journal & Leader Tribune*, c. 1921, in Heritage Collection, Hunt Memorial Library, Fort Valley State University (hereafter, Heritage Collection); W. T. B. Williams, "Fort Valley High and Industrial School," *Southern Workman* 143 (November 1910): 627; Donald L. Grant, *The Way It Was in the South: The Black Experience in Georgia*, ed. Jonathan Grant (Athens, Ga., 1993), 241; Clarence E. Walker, *You Can't Go Home Again: An Argument about Afrocentrism* (New York, 2001), 59–61.

3. Rouse, *Lugenia Burns Hope*, 5, 55; Rebecca S. Montgomery, *The Politics of Education in the New South: Women and Reform in Georgia, 1890–1930* (Baton Rouge, 2006), 74; Dewey W. Grantham, *Southern Progressivism: The Reconciliation of Progress and Tradition* (Knoxville, Tenn., 1983), 414–16.

4. Florence Johnson Hunt tombstone inscription, Fort Valley State University, Fort Valley, Ga.; 1880 U.S. Decennial Census, Mecklenburg County, North Carolina (population schedule); Thomas O. Fuller, *Pictorial History of the American Negro* (Memphis, 1933), 288–89; Edward A. Johnson, "A Student at Atlanta University," *Phylon* 3 (2nd qtr. 1942), 135.

5. Elizabeth Reid Murray, *Wake, Capital County of North Carolina* (Raleigh, N.C., 1983), 608; Howard N. Rabinowitz, *Race, Ethnicity, and Urbanization: Selected Essays* (Columbia, Mo., 1994), 98; J. W. Hood, *Report of the Superintendent of Public Instruction of North Carolina, for the Year 1869* (Raleigh, N.C., 1869), 17–18; Kemp P. Battle, *History of the University of North Carolina*, vol. 2, *From 1868 to 1912* (Raleigh, N.C., 1912), 10; Heather Andrea Williams, *Self-Taught: African American Education in Slavery and Freedom* (Chapel Hill, 2005), 189. On the American Missionary Association and freedmen's education in the South, see Joe M. Richardson, *Christian Reconstruction: The American Missionary Association and Southern Blacks, 1861–1890* (Athens, Ga., 1986); Maxine D. Jones, "'They Are My People': Black American Missionary Association Teachers in North Carolina during the Civil War and Reconstruction," *Negro Education Review* 36 (April 1985): 78–89. On the development of Raleigh's schools for freedmen and their children, see Charles L. Coon, "The Beginnings of the North Carolina City Schools, 1867–1887," *South Atlanta Quarterly* 12 (July 1913): 235–47; J. M. Barbee, *Historical Sketches of the Raleigh Public Schools, 1876–1942* (Raleigh, N.C., 1943).

6. Johnson, "Student at Atlanta University," 135–36, 139–40, 143–44, 147–48; Willard B. Gatewood Jr., "Edward A. Johnson (Edward Austin), 1860–1944," in *Dictionary of North Carolina Biography* (Chapel Hill, 1979–1996) (available online at http://docsouth.unc.edu/church/johnson/bio.html; Joseph J. Boris, ed., *Who's Who in Colored America* (New York, 1927), 105; *Catalogue of Officers and Students of Atlanta University* (Atlanta, 1900), 40.

7. Donnie D. Bellamy, *Light in the Valley: A Pictorial History of Fort Valley State College since 1895* (Virginia Beach, Va., 1996), 28–30; Daniel W. Culp, *Twentieth Century Negro Literature; or, A Cyclopedia of Thought on the Vital Topics Relating to the American Negro* (Naperville, Ill., 1902), facing p. 395; Janette Thomas Greenwood, *Bittersweet Legacy: The Black and White "Better Classes" in Charlotte, 1850–1910* (Chapel Hill, 1994), 149; 1900 U.S. Decennial Census, Mecklenburg County, North Carolina (population schedule); 1910 U.S. Decennial Census, Houston County, Georgia (population schedule). On Henry A. Hunt, see also Donnie D. Bellamy, "Henry A. Hunt and Black Agricultural Leadership in the New South," *Journal of Negro History* 60 (October 1975): 464–79.

8. Frank Horne, "Henry A. Hunt, Sixteenth Spingarn Medalist," *The Crisis* 37 (August 1930): 261; 1900 U.S. Decennial Census, Mecklenburg County, North Carolina (population schedule); Culp, *Twentieth Century Negro Literature*, facing p. 395; Glenda Elizabeth Gilmore, *Gender and Jim Crow: Women and the Politics of White Supremacy in North Carolina, 1896–1920* (Chapel Hill, 1996), 43–44.

9. "North Carolina Civil Rights Time Line" at www.king-raleigh.org/history/NC CivilRightsTimeLine.htm; Greenwood, *Bittersweet Legacy*, 103–4, 229–30; David J. Whitener, *Prohibition in North Carolina, 1715–1945* (Chapel Hill, 1946), 115. On the rise of the temperance movement within the African American community of the post–Civil War South, see David M. Fahey, *Temperance and Racism: John Bull, Johnny Reb, and the Good Templars* (Lexington, Ky., 1996).

10. *Minutes of the Second Convention of the National Association of Colored Women Held at Quinn Chapel, 24th Street and Wabash Avenue, Chicago, Illinois, August 14th, 15th, and 16th, 1899* (Chicago, 1899), 1–24; "History of the National Association of Colored Women's Clubs, Inc.," www.nacwc.org/about/history.php. On the National Association of Colored Women's Clubs generally, see Elizabeth Lindsay Davis, comp., *Lifting As They Climb: An Historical Record of the National Association of Colored Women* (Washington, D.C., 1933); Charles Harris Wesley, *The History of the National Association of Colored Women's Clubs: A Legacy of Service* (Washington, D.C., 1984); Beverly Washington Jones, *"Quest for Equality": The Life and Writings of Mary Eliza Church Terrell, 1863–1950* (Brooklyn, N.Y., 1990).

11. G. F. Richings, *Evidences of Progress among Colored People* (Philadelphia, 1905), 481–85; Greenwood, *Bittersweet Legacy*, 143. For more on the Coleman Manufacturing Company, see Allen Edward Burgess, "The Coleman Manufacturing Company, 1896–1904" (Ph.D. diss., Duke University, 1977); J. K. Rouse, *The Noble Experiment of Warren C. Coleman* (Charlotte, N.C., 1972). On the subject of economic advancement of North Carolina African Americans generally, see Robert C. Kenzer, *Enterprising Southerners: Black Economic Success in North Carolina, 1865–1915* (Charlottesville, Va., 1997).

12. Grant, *Way It Was*, 241; Rebecca S. Montgomery, *The Politics of Education in the New South: Women and Reform in Georgia, 1890–1930* (Baton Rouge, 2006), 66; Williams, "Fort Valley High and Industrial School," 627–68. The principal source on the history of Fort Valley, Ga., is Billy Powell, *Echoes from the Valley* (Macon, Ga., 2006). The principal source on the history of the Fort Valley State University and its predecessor institutions is Bellamy, *Light in the Valley*.

13. Grant, *Way It Was*, 241; Bellamy, "Henry A. Hunt and Black Agricultural Leadership," 465–66; idem, *Light in the Valley*, 19–23; Willard Range, *The Rise and Progress of Negro Colleges in Georgia, 1865–1949* (Athens, Ga., 1951), 183; James D. Anderson, *The Education of Blacks in the South, 1860–1935* (Chapel Hill, 1988), 123–24.

14. *Fort Valley Message*, December 1938; Range, *Rise and Progress*, 183; Horne, "Henry A. Hunt," 261.

15. Florence Johnson Hunt, "Memoirs of Twenty-Five Years," in H. A. Hunt, "The Fort Valley Normal and Industrial School," in *Down Where the Need Is Greatest: A Record in the Field of Negro Education* (New York, n.d.), 23. Unfortunately, the original of Florence Hunt's memoirs has been misplaced in the Hunt Memorial Library of Fort Valley State University, but it is quoted extensively in Henry Hunt's contribution to *Where the Need Is Greatest*.

16. F. Hunt, "Memoirs," 26.

17. "Mrs. Hunt Looks Back 30 Years," *Fort Valley Message*, November 1934.

18. Ibid.

19. Adele Logan Alexander, *Ambiguous Lives: Free Women of Color in Rural Georgia, 1789–1879* (Fayetteville, Ark., 1991), 163; F. Hunt, "Memoirs," 26; *Fort Valley Message*, March 1938; George A. Towns, "Henry Alexander Hunt," *Fort Valley Message*, December 1938.

20. Range, *Rise and Progress*, 184–85; Montgomery, *Politics of Education*, 64–65; F. Hunt, "Memoirs," 26.

21. Frank Horne, ed., "Outline of the Program of Studies," Fort Valley Publications, Number 1 (transcript in Hunt Papers, Heritage Collection); Donnie D. Bellamy, "Henry A. Hunt," in *The Dictionary of Negro Biography*, ed. Rayford W. Logan and Michael R. Winston (New York, 1983), 493.

22. Theodore DuBose Bratton, *Wanted—Leaders! A Study of Negro Development* (New York, 1922), 165.

23. "Our School and Community," *Fort Valley Message*, November 1935; H. Hunt, "Fort Valley Normal and Industrial School," 29; *Fort Valley Message*, December 1929; Hoskin interview.

24. Torn, undated pages from *Fort Valley Message,* Heritage Collection.

25. H. Hunt, "Fort Valley Normal and Industrial School," 27–28; *Fort Valley Message*, May 1934 and March 1938; E. Franklin Frazier, "A Community School: Fort Valley High and Industrial School," *Southern Workman* 54 (October 1925), 463; Williams, "Fort Valley High and Industrial School," 631.

26. *Fort Valley Message*, January 1931, December 1932, and December 1936.

27. Florence J. Hunt, *From Root Doctor to Nurse* (Fort Valley, Ga., n.d.), n.p.; *Fort Valley Message*, May 1934; Bellamy, *Light in the Valley*, 42–43; F. Hunt, "Memoirs," 26.

28. *Fort Valley Peach*, May 29, 1931; H. Hunt, *Down Where the Need Is Greatest*, 28–29; F. Hunt, *From Root Doctor to Nurse*, n.p.; Bellamy, *Light in the Valley*, 42–43; "Fort Valley Normal and Industrial School, Annual Report of the Acting Principal to the Board of Trustees," May 16, 1936, Heritage Collection; *Fort Valley Message*, May and December 1936.

29. Frazier, "Community School," 463; Governor Treutlen Chapter, Daughters of the American Revolution, Fort Valley, Georgia, comp., *History of Peach County, Georgia* (Atlanta, 1972), 35; *Fort Valley Message*, December 1929.

30. Bellamy, *Light in the Valley*, 44; Rouse, *Lugenia Burns Hope*, 5; Wesley, *History of the National Association of Colored Women's Clubs*, 292; Davis, *Lifting As They Climb*, 130; Asa H. Gordon, *The Georgia Negro: A History* (Spartanburg, S.C., 1972), 208; *Macon* (Ga.) *Telegraph*, December 16, 1938.

31. Mrs. H. A. Hunt, "A Dream Comes to Life: Address Delivered at the Opening of Training School for Delinquent Colored Girls, Macon, Georgia, November 2, 1943," *The Herald: Official Journal of the Georgia Teachers' and Educational Association* 10

(February 1944), 3; *Macon* (Ga.) *Telegraph*, June 15, 1929; *Fort Valley Peach*, December 23, 1930.

32. *Fort Valley Peach*, May 29, 1931; Wesley, *History of the National Association of Colored Women's Clubs*, 293; F. Hunt, "Dream Comes to Life," 3; Gordon, *Georgia Negro*, 208.

33. F. Hunt, "Dream Comes to Life," 3–4; Davis, *Lifting As They Climb*, 130–31; *Macon* (Ga.) *Telegraph*, December 16, 1938, and November 9, 1943.

34. *Macon* (Ga.) *Telegraph*, March 20, 1941, and November 9, 1943; F. Hunt, "Dream Comes to Life," 3–4; *Fort Valley Peach*, May 29, 1931.

35. *Fort Valley Message*, December 1932 and November 1934; Alva Tabor, "Mr. and Mrs. Hunt As I Knew Them" (typescript, n.d., Heritage Collection), n.p.

36. Bellamy, "Henry A. Hunt and Black Agricultural Leadership," 474–75; "Henry Alexander Hunt," *Journal of Negro History* 24 (January 1939): 135; Bellamy, "Henry A. Hunt," in *Dictionary of Negro Biography*, 493; Hoskin interview.

37. Powell, *Echoes from the Valley*, 35.

CHAPTER 10

Selena Sloan Butler
1872–1964

Atlanta Club Leader, Reformer, Educator

DAVID H. JACKSON JR.

SELENA SLOAN BUTLER, considering her heavy community involvements and enduring legacies, has received peculiarly little scholarly attention, even given the relative scarcity of scholarship on southern women of the late nineteenth and early twentieth centuries, especially African American women. Several studies written on African American clubwomen and their organizations fail to accord her adequate treatment despite the fact that she emerged as a national leader. Jacqueline Anne Rouse, in her interesting study on Lugenia Burns Hope, examined her subject's Atlanta community work and discussed other women who worked with Hope but made no mention of Butler. Similarly, a more recent study by Allison Dorsey discussed community formation in Atlanta. Although this was a dynamic within which Selena Butler played a

Figure 19. Selena Sloan Butler, c. 1902. (Courtesy of Georgia Women of Distinction.)

significant part, Dorsey also made no mention of Butler. A few passing references here and a few short sketches there constitute the remainder of history's attention to her.[1]

Yet, as this essay explores, Selena Sloan Butler's record merits a review that captures her remarkable life and situates her accomplishments in historical context among Atlanta's black elite. The fact remains that Selena Sloan Butler became a leading pioneer of women's activism in the early twentieth century, working during her lifetime with a variety of influential organizations. She particularly served the National Association of Colored Women (NACW), the National Association of Afro-American Women, and the Georgia Federation of Colored Women's Clubs. Beyond that, she held membership in Sigma Gamma Rho Sorority and the Atlanta Neighborhood Union, while founding what would become the black Parent-Teacher Association. Additionally, she furthered the work of the Georgia Commission on Interracial Cooperation (CIC), the Ruth Chapter of the Order of the Eastern Star, and the Chautauqua Circle of Atlanta, before helping to organize and lead the Phyllis Wheatley Branch of the YWCA in Atlanta. Last but not least, she established the first Gray Ladies Corps for African American women. In aiming to bring Butler's accomplishments to the forefront, this chapter focuses primarily on her public life as she worked through such organizations to help "uplift the race." It further places Butler and her family among the South's black middle class of the late nineteenth and the twentieth centuries.[2]

Selena Sloan Butler's life spanned very critical times in African American history. Born near the end of Reconstruction in Thomasville, Thomas County, Georgia, on January 4, 1872, she passed her formative years during an era when African Americans were making considerable political, educational, and social gains. Then, she lived through what Rayford Logan has called the nadir of African American history, when many of the advances blacks had made during Reconstruction were systematically taken away by political reversals and, ultimately, the rise of Jim Crow racial discrimination. Afterward, African Americans had to contend with discrimination based in newly enacted laws; economic exploitation through mechanisms such as peonage and the convict-lease system; disfranchisement; racial violence including lynchings; and legal retrenchments mandated by the courts.[3]

The situation in the Peach State proved especially horrendous, and an examination of the lynching plague blacks faced there can help to make the point. By 1900 almost one-third of Georgia cities held majority black populations, yet the state led the nation with 505 lynchings perpetrated between 1882 and 1923. Ironically, whereas most southern states reached the peak of lynching violence between 1880 and 1900, the Peach State stood out as the only southern state to deviate from this trend. More Georgia blacks were lynched between 1900 and 1920 than in the previous twenty years; that is, during the "Progressive Era" conditions for black Georgians worsened instead of becoming better.[4]

As Selena Butler grew to understand, any breach in Georgia's code of racial etiquette could lead to swift and irrevocable punishment, as was true in much of the South. Black men and women were lynched—if not because of mistaken identity—for alleged larceny and, especially, suspicion of assaulting white women. For instance, George Reed—charged with *attempting* to assault Mrs. J. M. Locklear, a white woman, in January 1901—was lynched by a mob of 150 men at Rome. Afterward, the perpetrators riddled his body with scores of bullets. Significantly, Mrs. Locklear had failed to identify Reed in a lineup. Mobs routinely broke into jails and took prisoners. About three months after Reed's death, Walter Allen, another black man of Rome, was charged with assaulting a fifteen-year-old white girl named Blossom Adamson. Subsequently, Allen was taken from jail by four thousand people who, according to a report, "battered down the prison doors and hanged him to an electric light pole." After this the ritual of shooting the corpse ensued and an estimated "thousand bullets entered the negro's body." Allen never wavered in maintaining his innocence.[5]

Even more appalling were instances where blacks were killed simply because they were suspected of larceny. The penalty paid by Groveton's Charley Jones serves as an example. He was lynched on May 7, 1914, for allegedly stealing a pair of shoes. Soon afterward Valdosta's Ceasar Sheffield was taken from prison and shot to death. He had been charged the previous day with stealing meat from a smokehouse. As these instances illustrate, Selena soon learned that, at least in Georgia at that time, a black person's life was not always worth more than a pair of shoes or a piece of meat.[6]

These lessons continued to be taught well into Butler's adulthood. The year 1906 was unsettling and offered particular challenges for Atlanta blacks, as the city became the scene of the "most sensational riot" in the South. Progressively more blacks had moved to the city from rural areas looking for better opportunities, and some white residents—who considered the newly arrived Atlantans to be more lawless and immoral than longtime African American residents—had grown alarmed. Three local newspapers—the *Constitution*, the *Journal*, and the *Georgian*—began running inflammatory stories about black crime and black men allegedly attacking white women. Many of these stories were either untrue or grossly exaggerated. Meantime, Clark Howell and Hoke Smith, white Democrats opposing each other in a divisive campaign for the

U.S. Senate, engaged in race-baiting that stirred racial strife. Conditions quickly deteriorated before Selena's eyes.[7]

Cataclysm ensued. On September 22, 1906, a white man climbed atop a box located on one of Atlanta's major streets and waved a newspaper bearing the headline: "THIRD ASSAULT." After drawing the attention of passersby, he yelled, "Are white men going to stand for this?" The crowd responded: "No! Save our women! Kill the niggers." This led to an orgy of violence against African Americans that lasted five days. Thousands of whites roamed the streets, some attacking every black person they saw. Black businesses were destroyed and, as white men armed themselves, white policemen began arresting blacks for possessing arms to defend themselves. African Americans were indiscriminately beaten, tortured, and killed. In the end one white person and twenty-five blacks died. Hundreds more suffered injuries. None of the white terrorists was ever brought to justice.[8]

Other influences beyond rising tides of racial discrimination and violence also touched Selena, among them Thomasville, where she spent her early years. While remaining a sleepy southern community during the summers, it pulsed with vibrancy during the winter months when affluent northern visitors and sportsmen descended upon the area to enjoy its restorative air, good hunting, and favorable climate. This, coupled with the town's size relative to surrounding rural areas, created a far different atmosphere than prevailed in many Georgia towns. Regarding size, in 1880—when Selena was around eight years old—Thomas County held 12,213 black residents, who comprised nearly 60 percent of the population. Thomasville's blacks made up a similar percentage. By 1900 African Americans totaled 56 percent of the county, and 62 percent of the city, population.[9]

Fortunately for Selena, during her youth Thomasville enjoyed relatively easy race relations as compared to other cities in southwest Georgia. Even with a majority black population, by 1909 no lynching had taken place in the town and only one had occurred in the county, that an act roundly condemned by blacks and "the better element of white citizens." By contrast Quitman, located in Brooks County twenty-six miles to the east, experienced more lynchings than any other county in southwest Georgia, the entire state, and possibly the entire South, according to scholar John Dittmer. This was the general setting from which Selena Sloan emerged intent upon working to uplift her people.[10]

While it would be misleading to suggest that most African Americans in Thomasville enjoyed a comfortable lifestyle, the city did boast a fairly robust black professional, artisan, and business class. Frederick Douglass and Booker

T. Washington, each of whom visited Thomasville at least once, noted the progress being made there by black people. Indeed, African Americans owned an impressive amount of property and a number of homes, and adhered to Washington's philosophy of economic development. One observer noted that middle-class black homes "are invariably painted, the yards neatly fenced, [and] the surroundings generally beautified by shrubs and flowers." Thomasville blacks filled the professions of real estate dealers, physicians, nurses, dentists, pharmacists, teachers, and preachers, to name just a few. There were also a number of African American–owned businesses: a drugstore, nearly two dozen grocery stores, a hotel, a dairy, barber shops, and several other enterprises. In addition, local blacks established schools, churches, orphanages, fraternal orders, hospitals, homes for the elderly, mutual-aid organizations, and literary societies.[11]

On occasion Thomasville blacks also banded together and, within certain limits, took public action when they felt disrespected by whites. For example, one observer noted that a boycott took place after "a leading millinery store inaugurated the custom of not allowing any Negro customer to try on a hat," instead decreeing that the woman "must be satisfied with viewing it on the head of the white clerk." However, "when a colored minister's wife was refused this privilege the minister took the incident to his congregation. As a result the firm lost all its colored patronage and soon went into the hands of a receiver." African Americans responded similarly when a white doctor and a white dentist discriminated against them. One person recalled that Thomasville's black community turned "against all white doctors" and "exclusively patronize[d] its own dentist." Having developed in this environment and witnessed these kinds of acts, Selena Sloan's determination to serve her race surely sharpened.[12]

Selena Mae Sloan did not grow up surrounded by material possessions or other trappings of affluence. Her mother, Winnie Williams, was of African and Native American descent, while her white father, William Sloan—who supported Selena, her elder sister, and her mother—did not live with them. Williams, like many other blacks during the era, encouraged her daughters to secure an education. Selena became an exceptional student. Even though her mother unfortunately died during her youth, the eager pupil nonetheless continued her schooling and managed to excel. Although schooling options for blacks in Thomasville were limited, Selena received her early education from a missionary- operated elementary school within the county. A local pastor, who had served as her mother's minister, recognized her abilities and later paid for her to attend Spelman Seminary (now Spelman College) in Atlanta, named in honor of Mrs. John D. Rockefeller's mother, Lucy Henry Spelman.[13]

Whereas despite its seasonal vibrancy Thomasville generally had the pace of a small town, the Atlanta that Selena encountered was markedly different. From 1890 to 1940 the city grew from around 65,000 to 302,000 people. During that period the black population never fell below 31.3 percent, an aberration from most other southern urban areas. Only Memphis and New Orleans contained more African Americans than Atlanta did when Selena arrived for school. The city meanwhile became a New South industrial leader, dubbing itself the "Gate City of the South." Growth and prosperity led some people to see Atlanta as a place of opportunity for blacks.[14]

In 1881 Sophia Packard and Harriet Giles, two well-to-do white Bostonians, viewed Atlanta in exactly that manner and, as they desired to start a school in the South for African American women, they ventured to the city. Consequently, with assistance from African American minister Frank Quarles of the Friendship Baptist Church, Packard and Giles opened Spelman Seminary in the basement of Quarles's church. The location held significance since Friendship, founded by Quarles in 1862 one year before the Emancipation Proclamation was implemented, was the second oldest independent black church in Atlanta. In February 1883 Spelman moved from the church basement to a nine-acre site that already contained a few frame buildings and an old barracks. The founders eventually interested Mrs. John D. Rockefeller in the school. She thereafter took a personal interest in Spelman and became its benefactor. In 1884, around the time that Selena would have been enrolled, the name officially changed to Spelman College.[15]

In its early years Spelman provided industrial training for girls, but it quickly added a grammar school, high school, "domestic arts school," nurse-training school, and normal school. The institution eventually focused on training African American women for leadership roles, although teacher training constituted its earliest mission. After an 1884 visit, John D. Rockefeller Sr. was so impressed that he paid off the debt on the property, providing Spelman with a degree of financial security. In fact, Spelman soon would boast thirty teachers, eight hundred students, a $10,000 endowment, and a physical plant valued at $350,000. Thus, Selena Sloan Butler enjoyed more advantages than many students at minority schools in the late nineteenth century. Having enjoyed excellent preparation for a vocation as a teacher and a leader, she graduated in 1888 at the age of sixteen. Initially, she worked as an English and elocution teacher in Atlanta before relocating to Tallahassee, Florida.[16]

Sloan's Florida sojourn reflected not only the quality of her pedagogical skills but also her increasing capacity and maturity. Albeit young and inexperienced as an educator, she still was offered a position beginning in July 1891 at the Florida State Normal and Industrial School (now Florida A&M University). While at the Tallahassee institution during the 1891–1892 school year, she made a memorably positive impression on those she taught, demonstrating the quality of her education. "Miss Selena M. Sloan, proprietress . . . in Tallahassee, Fla.," Monroe A. Majors observed in *Noted Negro Women; Their Triumphs and Activities* published in 1893, "is a living example of the excellence of Georgia teachers." He added, "She is a charming young woman, and is an inspiration to any girl with whom she comes in contact." The same writer opined that "Georgia cherishes a remarkable pride in her, and she deserves the esteem of everyone." Majors's comments also evidenced that, at an early date and before she married, Selena had established herself as a "noted" person among black women.[17]

Marriage did lie on Selena's horizon, however. While in Atlanta she had met Henry Rutherford Butler, a native of Cumberland County, North Carolina, located near Fayetteville. Edward Randolph Carter, who in 1894 published a useful history of African Americans in Atlanta entitled *The Black Side*, provided insight on Selena's future husband. Butler had come into the world on April 11, 1862, destined to become successful. He had attended Lincoln University in Pennsylvania from 1881 to 1887 and graduated with an A.B. degree. Although possessing very little money, he enrolled in Nashville's Meharry Medical College. He excelled at the school, with one of his contemporaries praising him for winning "the H. T. Noel gold medal for being the most proficient in operative surgery and dissecting." Five days after receiving his medical degree in 1890, Henry left Nashville for Atlanta with twenty-five dollars in his pocket. There he established a successful medical practice with Dr. Thomas Heathe Slater. Slater had been born in Salisbury, North Carolina, on December 25, 1865, the year the Civil War ended. A classmate of Henry Butler's, he had attended Lincoln University and Meharry Medical College, where the men maintained a close friendship. Just as Butler won a gold medal for surgery, Slater won "the gold" for "excellence in obstetrics."[18]

Butler and Slater became Atlanta's first black physicians. When they set up their practice a number of prominent blacks in the city even warned them that "there was no future for a Negro doctor in Atlanta." Some African Americans believed black doctors were not as qualified as white ones. Others felt that the mere presence of black physicians threatened the social order and would bring about white retribution. Undaunted, Butler continued to excel professionally and later completed postgraduate work at Harvard University Medical School during 1894–1895, where he took a special course in surgery and diseases of children. Already, in 1890, he and Slater had opened a lucrative pharmacy named Butler, Slater & Company. Their business, one source insisted, was the "first drug store established by colored men in Ga." and "the largest retail drug business of any colored drug establishment in the United States." As a contemporary explained, Dr. Butler and his partner "were the pioneer druggists of the Negro race in the State of Georgia, and hence hold the first pharmacy license ever issued to Negroes in the history of the State of Georgia."[19]

Selena Mae Sloan married Henry Rutherford Butler on May 23, 1893, and commenced a new life chapter that would see her emerge eventually into public life. First, though, the couple built their lives together in Atlanta. Mrs. Butler meanwhile stopped working outside the home, a common evolution within many elite black families of the time. The couple had one child, Henry Rutherford Butler Jr., born on November 1, 1899, when Selena was in her late twenties. When young Henry approached school age, Selena could not locate a suitable preschool for him, so she started a kindergarten in her home. Others emulated her example.[20]

The Butlers formed a part of the rising black middle class, or new black elite. As historian Darlene Roth put it, Henry and Selena "enjoyed relatively high social status." Overall, their behavior aligned with Victorian ideals prevalent during the period. By the time the couple married in 1893, Henry had become a well-established businessman. As a successful surgeon and entrepreneur, Henry would have appeared to Selena as a man who would be a good provider, and little or no evidence has surfaced that, at the time of the marriage, she was looking for any business or professional standing outside a marital relationship. Paula Giddings has noted that, for many college-educated women of that time, "marrying men of achievement was also an integral part of their determination to fulfill themselves as women."[21]

Women in Selena's position of prominence and economic security—once married—enjoyed some flexibility in choosing to do and say things outside the home "without reference to dire economic need, or concern that they might threaten their husbands' self-worth." Women such as Margaret Murray Washington, Mary Church Terrell, and Ida B. Wells-Barnett followed this pattern. Echoing this point, progressive black clubwoman Fannie B. Williams noted that "every colored man who succeeds in business brings his wife . . . a little nearer to that sphere of chivalry and protection in which every white woman finds shelter." Many black Victorians—including Selena Butler—understandably desired shelter and flexibility.[22]

When it came to utilizing their options for flexibility protected by economic and social shelter, women such as Selena often acted forthrightly. Particularly, the Butlers lived during a time when successful blacks were expected to serve as "race men" and "race women" and to help "uplift the race." The Butlers took this charge seriously, involving themselves in the community. They meanwhile took on many trappings of the black elite and lived by strict rules of etiquette, manners, and dress. Elite blacks prided themselves on having big homes with nice libraries. An elegant home became so important to the social life of so-called "aristocrats of color" that they spent what often appeared to others as a disproportionate amount of their resources on their homes. Indeed, considerable status came along with owning a nice home, and many black aristocrats did just that.[23]

The Butlers were no exception. A contemporary described their residence as "a beautiful home on Auburn [A]venue." An examination of the residences of other prominent blacks paints a picture of what the house may have been like. African Methodist Episcopal (AME) Church Bishop Henry McNeal Turner lived in Atlanta during this era in a home with twenty rooms. One observer noted that "the interior of his residence resembled that of an old style New England library, for books and papers and pamphlets and manuscripts... were scattered in every part of his house." Similarly, Alonzo Herndon, a successful barber, became the city's largest African American property owner by 1900. Herndon later founded the Atlanta Life Insurance Company and became Atlanta's first black millionaire. His imposing home, designed by a local black architect and built in 1910, was a two-story, fifteen-room Beaux Arts mansion.[24]

It also appears that Selena and Henry followed black elite patterns in their church affiliation. They attended Big Bethel AME Church, one of the "big three" black churches in Atlanta. Big Bethel, Friendship Baptist, and First Congregational Church dominated the scene because of the prominence of their ministers, their social activism, and their size. To be sure, a number of elite blacks, especially the light-skinned ones, tried to distinguish themselves by the church they attended. The so-called "old black elite" typically joined the Episcopal, Congregational, Presbyterian, Methodist Episcopal, or Catholic Church. In some cases, the particular church attended carried more significance than the denomination. The AME Church, the AME Zion Church, and the Baptist Church all had elite members. The ministers of churches attended by the black aristocracy were generally well educated and the members generally had high status.[25]

Like many other black male professionals, Henry Butler also became heavily involved in African American fraternal associations. He joined Sigma Pi Phi, the Boulé, and Omega Psi Phi fraternity. He also served as grand master of the Masons (Prince Hall Affiliation) for more than fifteen years; belonged to the Odd Fellows, the Elks, and Woodmen of the World; and was a leader among the Knights of Pythias. Membership in so many organizations provided obvious benefits in terms of attracting patients to his medical practice. Racial conditions may have necessitated his involvement, but community involvement had also become a hallmark of his family.[26]

Selena meanwhile complemented her husband by involving herself as a pioneering community activist and an organizer. As was expected of black Victorians, she joined a social club, the Chautauqua Circle, one of Atlanta's oldest and most exclusive clubs for black women, formally organized on September 8, 1913. Members were college-educated or married to prominent local men, and a large number were natives of either Atlanta or Georgia. Selena Sloan Butler served as president and remained a member for twenty-five years. The National Chautauqua Movement—an influential development in popular adult education that had operated at Lake Chautauqua, New York, since 1874—had inspired the formation of Atlanta's Circle. Henrietta Curtis Porter, a founding member of the Atlanta club, became the guiding force ensuring the Circle's strict adherence to the philosophies of the National Chautauqua Movement. The Chautauqua Circle held monthly meetings that consisted of cultural programs, discussions, and lectures on a variety of topics, including education, literature, international issues, civil rights, race relations, economics, health, art, religion, science, and politics.[27]

Reflecting attitudes typical of many black clubwomen of the era, most women associated with the Circle expressed little interest in woman's suffrage. "The socially superior Chautauquas politely entertained the question 'Should Women Have the Right to Vote?' at their first recorded regular meeting in 1913," Darlene Roth related, "but could not have been very interested in it, as they failed to record the outcome of their debate in the minutes." Roth goes on to assert that in 1919, "when the women's suffrage question was all but settled, the question reappeared in Chautauqua discussions, but this time with a compelling racial emphasis: 'Resolved: That the Responsibility for the Political Condition of the Negro Rests Upon the Women of the Race.'" Ultimately, a spirited debate on the subject ensued, and the pro-suffrage position barely won.[28]

Henry encouraged and supported Selena's work inside and outside the home. The same could not be said for all black men. In general, black men accepted the predominant white male perspective that a woman's "place" was in the home with children, an attitude that often caused friction within families and relationships. In 1908 an anonymous black writer in *Colored American Magazine* gave African American men advice on "How to Keep Women at Home." He expressed dismay over women who worked outside the home and urged black men to organize and convene to resist the trend. "Women are getting very bold, and instead of using the freedom that civilized men are allowing them, for adding to the comforts of man," he warned, "they are abusing them."[29]

However, conditions in the South generally did not permit black men to provide adequately for their families unless their wives worked to supplement the family income. Many women took umbrage at black men's stay-at-home arguments, feeling that they limited not only the progress of women but also the overall advancement of the race.[30]

Selena Butler already had addressed this sort of thinking head-on. "It is argued by most people that women's specific and only mission is that of maternity and obeying the injunction of the wise man, 'Train up a child in the way it should go,'" she had commented in the *Spelman Messenger* in 1897, "[but,] since so much is expected of her, is it not right that she should be given opportunity for development in the highest and broadest sense, that her physical, mental and moral nature may be prepared to fill the highest and noblest calling allotted her?"[31]

Selena Butler also challenged arguments of whites that African Americans were their inferiors and did not have a history worth mentioning. Indeed, after Reconstruction ended, white psychologists, historians, social workers, ministers, and criminologists specializing in "scientific racism" engaged in concerted efforts to gain control over the perception of blacks, efforts that persisted throughout most of Butler's life. Some of their ideas emerged from the application to human society of British scientist Charles Robert Darwin's theories of evolution and "natural selection," especially by sociologists William Graham Sumner and Herbert Spencer. For white racists African Americans stood at the bottom of society because of their innate inferiority not because of a social and legal system that worked to oppress them. Educated blacks such as Selena Butler oftentimes found themselves defending the race against such charges.[32]

This was a situation that should be underscored. Many white interlocutors made the case for black inferiority. For instance, in 1900 Charles Carroll published a 382-page book titled *The Negro a Beast, or, In the Image of God*, ostensibly the result of fifteen years of "study." As the title indicates Carroll set out to "prove" that African Americans were subhuman and made more in the image of "beasts" than of "God." Carroll concluded that "the low order of the Negro's mentality—his lack of inventive skill—is demonstrated by his meager accomplishments in his undomesticated state, which has been shown, are confined to the fashioning of a few rude weapons of stone; while the greater achievements of the domesticated Negro are due solely to the influence of man" (meaning, of course, the "white man"). Carroll concluded, "If from any cause he [the black man] is relieved of this influence and is thrown upon his own resources in the forest, he soon relapses into savagery and descends to the use of stones for weapons." Similarly, Buckner Payne, a Nashville publisher, wrote that African Americans were destined to remain at the bottom of society, as evidenced by a history that "is as blank as that of the horse or a beaver."[33]

Selena did not shy away from responding to such arguments. "It is amusing as well as provoking," she declared on one occasion, "to hear intelligent men and women, speaking on the Negro, begin with the savage period of his life, forgetting or not knowing or ignoring the fact that he once occupied a stage of civilization to which other races bowed before he lapsed into barbarism." Butler felt that, in order to counter such claims effectively, African American teachers needed to "study the past and current history of your race and with pride tell it to your pupils in the classroom or to your children as you sit around the fireside." She asked, "If you do not do this, who will?"[34]

She continued with other advice: "Hang upon the walls of your homes pictures of men and women of your own race who have given a chapter that deserves to be recorded in the history of the civilized world." Black people, she asserted, "should appreciate everything that represents the achievement of our people, whether modern or ancient. Then, fill your libraries with books that are the product of the Negro brain." If black Americans followed her instructions, she "prophesied" that "almost every child of the succeeding generation will speak with as much pride of his race and the Negro blood in his veins as does the Anglo-Saxon of his race and the blue blood which comes to his veins."[35]

Black women in particular found themselves the target of white people's vitriol and derogation, a circumstance that helped to spark some of Butler's earliest activism. In particular, her organized community involvement can be traced to her participation in the black women's club movement. A major catalyst in the formation of black women's clubs was a defamatory letter written by James W. Jack, president of the Missouri Press Association, on March 6, 1895. Jack had been sending letters to Florence Belgarnie of Great Britain, the secretary of an antislavery society and a supporter of the black race. In the March 6 letter he asserted that "the Negroes of this country were wholly devoid of morality, the women were prostitutes and were naturally thieves and liars." Belgarnie forwarded copies of this letter to leading African American men and women, hoping that they would respond. They did with much vigor: it remained very important for individuals such as Selena to counter negative stereotypes about African American women because, if unanswered, they might be assumed to be true.[36]

Selena certainly responded by her actions. She worked with, among other groups, the National Association of Colored Women (NACW) and served as a delegate to its founding convention. Its motto "lifting as we climb" well articulated the group's purpose. Founded in 1896, a year after Jack's letter, the NACW by 1917 consisted of more than one thousand clubs and represented some fifty thousand women in twenty-eight federations. Compared to other organizations in the black community, the NACW, on the whole, displayed an especially strong commitment to the idea of service to the race. Most NACW members were middle-class, educated women who worked diligently to uphold Victorian and Protestant mores. More than 65 percent worked as educators, as had Butler; others were hairdressers, clerks, seamstresses, or businesswomen. Of the total membership, 75 percent were married but only about 25 percent had children.[37]

The main mission of the NACW was to give black women such as Butler an avenue to help in elevating the masses of blacks because, if they did not, they risked being pulled back into the lower class. Most clubs engaged in a variety of activities dictated by the community's immediate needs. Some established and operated medical clinics, settlement houses, reading rooms, day-care centers, and homes for delinquent children. Others worked to outlaw lynching, or established schools, orphanages, kindergartens, and homes for the elderly. The work of the NACW and its affiliates illustrates its members' belief that black educational advancement was important to eliminate prejudice against blacks. However, their social standing led many of these women to adopt snobbish, condescending, and maternalistic attitudes toward the disadvantaged and the poor. As Gerda Lerner noted, the welfare activities of the NACW "show[ed] strong class prejudices on the part of club women and reflect[ed] a patronizing, missionary attitude in dealing with the poor." On the positive side, however, black women such as Selena seem to have been more successful than white women in bridging class lines.[38]

Butler's role in the women's club movement extended beyond membership and cooperation. When Mrs. L. B. Norris of Marietta called for Georgia women to meet in 1902, Selena already was well respected in Atlanta and the state, and when the Georgia Federation of Colored Women's Clubs organized on June 21, 1902, she was offered and accepted its presidency. Ultimately incorporated in October 1921, the Georgia Federation became the state affiliate of the NACW and the regional affiliate of the Southern Federation of Colored Women's Clubs, an umbrella group founded in 1889 by Booker T. Washington's wife, Margaret Murray Washington. Under Selena's leadership, the federation embraced the motto. "Not to be ministered unto but to minister." As with the national group, the Georgia Federation's motto expressed the women's desire to serve their race. The colors adopted were royal blue and white. The group's expressed purpose, historian Charles Wesley explained, was to "raise the standard of the home; and to work for social, moral, economic and religious welfare of women and children."[39]

The early years of the Georgia Federation's existence under Selena Butler's leadership proved crucial to the organization's survival and expansion. Working with her after the organizational meeting was Mrs. S. C. J. Bryant as secretary and Addie Waits Hunton as state organizer. Selena held the presidency for two years before being succeeded by Mattie Norris. This state group served as the parent organization for local clubs in Georgia including ones at Atlanta, Macon, Savannah, Fort Valley, Albany, and LaGrange, among others. The Georgia Federation's activities focused on health-related issues, child welfare, and better social relations throughout the state. "They have been supporters of every good cause and have taken the lead in arousing racial pride, by keeping alive the noble and heroic deeds of black men and women," one writer observed. Butler's leadership meanwhile had laid the foundation for the group and helped pave the way for future generations of African American women to follow.[40]

Selena also worked with the Atlanta Neighborhood Union and, presumably, the Gate City Free Kindergarten Association. Lugenia Burns Hope, wife of John Hope—first black president of Atlanta Baptist College (now Morehouse College) and later of Atlanta University (now Clark Atlanta University)—headed this organization. The Neighborhood Union formed in 1908 seeking to raise "the standard of living in the community and to make the West Side of Atlanta a better place to rear our children." The women adopted the motto "Thy Neighbor as Thyself" and engaged in a number of reform activities geared toward Atlanta blacks. With Butler's support, the Neighborhood Union raised funds for a playground for children; placed children in orphanages, homes, and reformatories; purchased a settlement house; conducted domestic science classes; and addressed the overall physical and social improvement of children. According to Jacqueline Rouse, "The ultimate goal of the union was to organize neighborhoods in each section of the city and establish settlement houses in each neighborhood, where the 'people could gather for their meetings, clubs and classes and feel that they were their very own.'" John Dittmer assessed the group's effectiveness. "The work of the Neighborhood Union cut across social and economic lines," he concluded, "it was perhaps the best example of self-help through community action in the South."[41]

The examples of the Neighborhood Union and the Gate City Free Kindergarten Association help to highlight that a part of Butler's early community involvement grew out of personal experiences. After Henry Jr. entered Yonge

Street Elementary School, Selena sought ways for parents to become involved in their children's education. In 1911 she "organized the first black Parent-Teacher Association in the country," located at her son's elementary school. After this organization began to flourish, Butler went on to establish the Georgia Parent-Teacher Association in 1919. Just seven years later she created the National Congress of Colored Parents and Teachers (NCCPT). Selena strove to coordinate the policies and programs of her group with those of the white national Parent-Teacher Association (PTA). She established the National Congress "to function only in those states where separate schools for the races were maintained." For the most part the black PTA served African Americans in the South, where most blacks lived and where racial segregation became most entrenched. However, one scholar has argued that "black PTAs, unlike their white counterparts, were central to the establishment of a school system for African Americans in the South and were unified by a political agenda to promote integrated schools and interracial cooperation."[42]

NCCPT activities compelled Butler to travel widely, since the group held annual conventions all over the country and its members dealt with a variety of issues and topics. For instance, the group met at Florida A&M College in Tallahassee, Florida, on July 28–31, 1935, hosted by the Florida Congress of Colored Parents and Teachers led by its president Mrs. E. B. Baker. President J. R. E. Lee of Florida A&M extended "a most cordial invitation to our National to meet on the campus of this famous College," a notice proclaimed, "and assures us that every arrangement will be made to make our convention a success and the stay of our delegates pleasant." Members chose "Homemaking Education" as the theme for that year's program, and delegates had to pay one dollar to attend. A number of topics were covered including homemaking education, developing social responsibility in the community, and reports of departments and national chairwomen, as well as problems from specific localities and a report on the status of their work. In 1970, a few years after Selena Butler died, the black and white PTAs finally merged, forming the National Parent-Teacher Association. Butler was elevated to national founder status along with two white women, Phoebe Hearst and Alice McLellan Birney (also from Georgia).[43]

While one easily might assume that these organizations could have consumed all of Selena's energy and capacity, she still found time to serve Atlanta's black Young Women's Christian Association (YWCA) and the Atlanta-based Georgia CIC. The YWCA African American branch, founded on September 4, 1919, grew out of black exclusion. An interracial group of women and men, the membership elected Mrs. Peter James Bryant, wife of the pastor of the Wheat Street Baptist Church, as its first president. Butler, who attended the

Figure 20. The Yonge Street Parent-Teacher Association, c. 1919. (Collection of the author.)

inaugural meeting, headed the financial committee. Sometime later the group adopted the name Phyllis Wheatley Y and moved to the city's near west side. The Y became a major agency for social activity and social welfare for Atlanta blacks, especially as they related to young girls and women.[44]

Organized in 1919, the interracial CIC worked primarily in the South and established an educational program that focused on race relations at state and local levels. Will W. Alexander, a former Methodist minister and YMCA worker, led the group. Other prominent whites and some blacks, including Selena, joined with Alexander. The group hosted ten-day schools for blacks and whites to train leaders in promoting interracial work. The CIC labored to end lynching, gain suffrage for all citizens, ensure equal participation in government welfare programs, and guarantee justice under the law. It carried on a program of education and research on southern problems, and devoted considerable attention to health, education, and agriculture. The CIC never advocated racial equality, however, nor did it challenge segregation. Instead, "it signified a recognition on the part of middle-class whites of the emergence of a black bourgeoisie with whom they could ally in attempts to ameliorate the 'race problem' upon which progress in the South seemed perennially to founder." What is more, as Jacquelyn Dowd Hall has informed us, it represented "an acknowledgement that white violence could have extremely disruptive social consequences if blacks fought back, turned to the federal government for protection, or chose migration as an alternative to victimization."[45]

The direction of Selena's life of contributions and activities shifted dramatically in 1931 when her husband, Dr. Henry R. Butler, died in Atlanta. The traumatic event prompted Selena to move to England in order to live with her son, Henry Jr. He had also become a physician, having completed his medical school training at Harvard. An Ivy League degree in hand, he had joined his father's practice in Atlanta. Being of a younger generation, however, Henry did not feel the same attachment to the South as did his father, especially after he spent years outside the region, and he relocated. As it turned out World War II compelled son and mother to return to their native land, but not to Georgia. Instead, they moved to Fort Huachuca, Arizona, where he served in the army hospital. During that period Selena organized the first Gray Lady Corps for African American women, named for the gray veils they wore. Gray ladies served local military and veterans' hospitals by counseling, comforting, and transporting patients. Butler continued to develop parallel institutions for blacks, especially when they faced exclusion from white groups.[46]

When Henry Jr. married and relocated to Los Angeles, California, Selena elected to return to Georgia. As might have been expected, she reestablished herself in Atlanta and became active once again in the community. By 1953 her health had begun to fail, however. So, she moved to Los Angeles in order that Henry Jr. and his wife could tend to her. Selena Sloan Butler lived with her son for a little more than one decade before dying of congestive heart failure on October 7, 1964, at the age of ninety-two.[47]

Although few people today know of her many accomplishments, Selena Sloan Butler was recognized during her lifetime for her charitable service and philanthropy, especially as it related to child welfare. President Herbert Hoover appointed her to serve on his 1929 White House Conference on Child Health and Protection, while Spelman College and the American Red Cross, among others, honored her in one way or another. Her portrait now hangs in the Georgia State Capitol, and a park carries her name. Appropriately, it is located next to the Henry Rutherford Butler Elementary School, formerly the Yonge Street School, where her son had studied and where she had founded the first PTA for African Americans. In 1995, Mrs. Butler was inducted into the Georgia Women of Achievement, an honor she so well earned and deserved through her remarkable life of service to others.[48]

Notes

1. Jacqueline Anne Rouse, *Lugenia Burns Hope: Black Southern Reformer* (Athens, Ga., 1989); Allison Dorsey, *To Build Our Lives Together: Community Formation in Black Atlanta, 1875–1906* (Athens, Ga., 2004). See also Donald L. Grant, *The Way It Was in the South: The Black Experience in Georgia* (New York, 1993); Darlene R. Roth, *Matronage: Patterns in Women's Organizations, Atlanta, Georgia, 1890–1940* (Brooklyn, N.Y., 1994), 77–78; Alton Hornsby, *A Short History of Black Atlanta* (North Richland Hills, Tex., 2006), 102–3; Darlene Roth, "Selena Sloan Butler," in Darlene Clark Hine, Elsa Barkley Brown, and Rosalyn Terborg-Penn, eds., *Black Women in America*, vol. 1 (Bloomington, Ind., 1993), 210–11.

2. Elizabeth Lindsay Davis, *Lifting As They Climb: An Historical Record of the National Association of Colored Women* (Washington, D.C., 1933), 269–70; Roth, *Matronage*, 77–78; see Georgia Women of Achievement website and look up Selena Sloan Butler at www.georgiawomen.org/_honorees/butlerss/index.html.

3. Rayford Logan, *The Negro in American Life and Thought: The Nadir, 1877–1901* (New York, 1954); John Hope Franklin and Alfred Moss, *From Slavery to Freedom: A History of African-Americans*, 7th ed. (New York, 1994), 356.

4. John Dittmer, *Black Georgia in the Progressive Era 1900–1920* (Urbana, Ill., 1980), 2, 131.

5. *Chicago Record*, January 4, 1901, and *Chicago Record-Herald*, April 2, 1902, reprinted in Ralph Ginzburg, ed., *100 Years of Lynching* (Baltimore, 1988), 36, 44–45.

6. *Montgomery Advertiser*, May 8, 1912; *Atlanta Constitution*, April 18, 1915.

7. Franklin and Moss, *From Slavery to Freedom*, 314; Darlene Clark Hine, William C. Hine, and Stanley Harrold, *The African-American Odyssey*, 2nd ed., (Upper Saddle River, N.J., 2003), 385. See also Gregory Mixon, *The Atlanta Riot: Race, Class, and Violence in a New South City* (Gainesville, 2005); David F. Godshalk, *Veiled Visions: The 1906 Atlanta Race Riot and the Reshaping of American Race Relations* (Chapel Hill, 2005); Dorsey, *To Build Our Lives Together*, 147–66.

8. Franklin and Moss, *From Slavery to Freedom*, 314; Hine, Hine, and Harrold, *African-American Odyssey*, 385; Dorsey, *To Build Our Lives Together*, 147–66. See also Mixon, *Atlanta Riot*; Godshalk, *Veiled Visions*.

9. Titus Brown, "The African American Middle Class in Thomasville, Georgia, in the Age of Booker T. Washington," *Journal of South Georgia History* 15 (Fall 2000): 57, 69; Joe M. Richardson, "Allen Normal School: Training 'Leaders of Righteousness,' 1885–1933," *Journal of South Georgia History* 12 (Fall 1997): 1, 3; W. Fitzhugh Brundage, *Lynching in the New South: Georgia and Virginia, 1880–1930* (Urbana, Ill., 1993), 118, 270–80.

10. Brown, "African American Middle Class," 57, 69; Richardson, "Allen Normal School," 1, 3; Brundage, *Lynching in the New South*, 118, 270–80. On Thomas County, Georgia, see William Warren Rogers, *Thomas County, 1865–1900* (Tallahassee, 1973);

idem, *Transition to the Twentieth Century: Thomas County, Georgia, 1900–1920* (Tallahassee, 2002).

11. Brown, "African American Middle Class," 55, 56, 71–72.

12. Ibid., 66–67.

13. Roth, "Selena Sloan Butler," 210. See also Georgia Women of Achievement website and look up Selena Sloan Butler at www.georgiawomen.org/_honorees/butlerss/index.html. The most prominent school for elite blacks in Thomasville was Allen Normal and Industrial School, founded and operated by the American Missionary Association. However, it is unlikely that Selena attended this school because it did not open until 1886. Selena graduated from Spelman in 1888; therefore, it is reasonable to assume that she spent at least two years at Spelman before finishing her studies. Selena probably already lived in Atlanta when Allen Normal opened. See Richardson, "Allen Normal School," 1–26; Brown, "African American Middle Class," 63, 68–69, and Rogers, *Thomas County 1865–1900*, 233–44.

14. Roth, *Matronage*, 18, 20–21, 45–46.

15. Alton Hornsby says that Friendship Baptist was the oldest independent black church in Atlanta, but Allison Dorsey says it was founded after, and grew out of, First Baptist Church in Atlanta. See Hornsby, *Short History*, 11, 62; Dorsey, *To Build Our Lives Together*, 58–59.

16. Hornsby, *Short History*, 63; Monroe A. Majors, *Noted Negro Women; Their Triumphs and Activities* (Jackson, Tenn., 1893), 327; Beverly Guy-Sheftall, "Black Women and Higher Education: Spelman and Bennett Colleges Revisited," *Journal of Negro Education* 51 (Summer 1982): 279–80; Roth, *Matronage*, 78. See also Georgia Women of Achievement website and look up Selena Sloan Butler at www.georgiawomen.org/_honorees/butlerss/index.html.

17. Majors, *Noted Negro Women*, 327; *Jacksonville Florida Times-Union*, May 27, 1892; Ledell W. Neyland and John W. Riley, *The History of Florida Agricultural and Mechanical University* (Gainesville, 1963), 34; Michael Bailey, "The Early Women of Florida Agricultural and Mechanical University" (graduate seminar paper, Florida A&M University, 2003), 4 (xerographic copy in possession of the author); Records of the State Board of Education, Record Group 491, Series 252, Minute Book No. 2, p. 201, Florida State Archives, Tallahassee. At the State Normal School Sloan worked within a liberal arts tradition influenced by Oberlin College, Oberlin, Ohio. See Reginald Ellis, "Nathan B. Young: Florida A&M College's Second President and His Relationships with White Public Officials," in David H. Jackson Jr. and Canter Brown Jr., eds., *Go Sound the Trumpet! Essays in Florida's African American History* (Tampa, 2005), 154–57.

18. Edward R. Carter, *The Black Side; A Political History of the Business, Religious, and Educational Side of the Negro in Atlanta, Ga.* (Atlanta, 1894), 137–38; *Lincoln University College and Theological Seminary Biographical Catalogue, 1918* (Lancaster, Pa., 1918), 34; H. F. Kletzing and William H. Crogman, *Progress of a Race; or, The Remark-*

able Advancement of the Afro-American Negro (Naperville, Ill., 1912), 550–52; Hornsby, *Short History*, 87.

19. In 1903 Dr. Henry R. Butler organized and became the first president of the Atlanta State Savings Bank, an all-black enterprise. The bank had assets of $600,000, and highly respected men such as Alonzo Herndon, David T. Howard, and Benjamin J. Davis Jr., served on its board of directors. Butler, along with other prominent black men, including John Hope, Hugh H. Proctor, and William A. Hunton, helped organize the YMCA (black) in Atlanta. Butler served as president of the Masonic Relief Association and became organizer and first president of the Georgia Medical Society for Colored Physicians, founded on December 19, 1893. In addition, Henry became the first treasurer of the National Medical Association when that group organized in Atlanta in 1895. He worked as superintendent of the Fair Haven Infirmary in Atlanta and was the first African American to serve on the regular contributing staff of the *Atlanta Constitution*. As special correspondent he wrote articles for more than ten years under the headline "What Colored People Are Doing." Kletzing and Crogman, *Progress of a Race*, 550–52; Hornsby, *Short History*, 84, 87; Thomas J. Ward Jr., *Black Physicians in the Jim Crow South* (Fayetteville, Ark., 2003), 109, 220; Carter, *Black Side*, 134–36; Joseph J. Boris, ed., *Who's Who in Colored America* (New York, 1927), 33; Frank L. Mather, *Who's Who of the Colored Race, 1915,* vol. 1 (Chicago, 1915), 54; John A. Kenney, *The Negro in Medicine* (Tuskegee, Ala., 1912), 26–27; Dorsey, *To Build Our Lives Together*, 113.

20. Boris, *Who's Who in Colored America*, 33; See also Georgia Women of Achievement website and look up Selena Sloan Butler at www.georgiawomen.org/_honorees/butlerss/index.html.

21. Paula Giddings, *When and Where I Enter: The Impact of Black Women on Race and Sex in America* (New York, 1988), 113; Kletzing and Crogman, *Progress of a Race*, 552; Roth, *Matronage*, 78.

22. Giddings, *When and Where I Enter*, 112–13; Fannie B. Williams, "Woman's Part in a Man's Business," *Voice of the Negro* (November 1904), 545; Kletzing and Crogman, *Progress of a Race*, 552.

23. David H. Jackson Jr., *A Chief Lieutenant of the Tuskegee Machine: Charles Banks of Mississippi* (Gainesville, 2002), 19.

24. Daniel W. Culp, *Twentieth Century Negro Literature; or, A Cyclopedia of Thought on the Vital Topics Relating to the American Negro* (Naperville, Ill., 1902), 221; Mungo M. Ponton, *Life and Times of Henry M. Turner* (Atlanta, 1917), 47, 55, 123, 134, 135. See also Stephen W. Angell, *Bishop Henry McNeal Turner and African-American Religion in the South* (Knoxville, Tenn., 1992), 39, 284; Willard Gatewood, *Aristocrats of Color: The Black Elite, 1880–1920* (Bloomington, Ind., 1993); E. Franklin Frazier, *Black Bourgeoisie: The Rise of a New Middle Class* (New York, 1957); National Park Service, "A National Register of Historic Places Travel Itinerary: Herndon Home," www.nps.gov/nr/travel/atlanta/her.htm; Alexa B. Henderson, *Atlanta Life Insurance Company:*

Guardian of Black Economic Dignity (Tuscaloosa, Ala., 1990), 164; Hornsby, *Short History*, 83; Juliet E. K. Walker, *The History of Black Business in America* (New York, 1998), 190.

25. Dorsey, *To Build Our Lives Together*, 58; Jackson, *Chief Lieutenant*, 20–21. Darlene Roth says that Selena Butler attended First Congregational Church in Atlanta. Clement Richardson, John Kenney, and Joseph J. Boris, among other contemporaries, however, recorded that Henry Butler attended Big Bethel. Mrs. Butler could have changed her church affiliation at some point or, in an unlikely scenario, she may have attended a different church than her husband. See Roth, *Matronage*, 78; Clement Richardson, *National Cyclopedia of the Colored Race* (Montgomery, Ala., 1919), 111; Kenney, *Negro in Medicine*, 27; Boris, *Who's Who in Colored America*, 33.

26. In 1906, white Pythians in Georgia secured an injunction to prevent the black Knights of Pythias from using the same name, ritual, and regalia as their group. Led by Henry Butler, African Americans took the case to state court but lost. Butler's efforts did not go unnoticed, however. According to one observer, "He was one of 'Georgia's strong men' in the fight against being crushed by the white Knights of that State, and when some of the lodges were afraid to hold their meetings he went from lodge to lodge night after night, encouraging the members to hold out and not give up." Although Georgia whites continued to oppose them, black Knights won a U.S. Supreme Court ruling in 1912 that allowed them to continue to function as Pythians. Mather, *Who's Who of the Colored Race*, 54; Ephie A. Williams, Smith W. Green, and Joseph L. Jones, *History and Manual of the Colored Knights of Pythias, North America, South America, Europe, Asia, Africa, and Australia* (Nashville, Tenn., 1917), 978; Richardson, *National Cyclopedia*, 111; Dittmer, *Black Georgia*, 56.

27. Roth, *Matronage*, 77.

28. Ibid., 64.

29. "How to Keep Women at Home," *Colored American Magazine* 14 (January 1908): 8.

30. Cynthia Neverdon-Morton, *Afro-American Women of the South and the Advancement of the Race, 1895–1925* (Knoxville, Tenn., 1989), 2–3.

31. Selena Sloan Butler, "Heredity," *Spelman Messenger*, June 1897.

32. Sylvester Johnson, *The Myth of Ham in Nineteenth-Century American Christianity: Race, Heathens, and the People of God* (New York, 2004), 95–96.

33. Charles Carroll, *The Negro a Beast, or, In the Image of God* (Miami, 1900), 114, 124–136; Johnson, *Myth of Ham*, 35.

34. Butler, "Heredity," 2–3.

35. Ibid., 2–3.

36. Beverly Jones, "Mary Church-Terrell and the National Association of Colored Women, 1896 to 1901," *Journal of Negro History* 67 (Spring 1982): 22–23.

37. Kevin K. Gaines, *Uplifting the Race: Black Leadership, Politics, and Culture in the Twentieth Century* (Chapel Hill, 1996), 214, 217; Neverdon-Morton, *Afro-Ameri-*

can Women of the South, 3; Davis, *Lifting As They Climb*, 269–70; Roth, "Selena Sloan Butler," 211; Stephanie J. Shaw, "Black Club Women and the Creation of the National Association of Colored Women," in Darlene Clark Hine, Wilma King, and Linda Reed, eds., *"We Specialize in the Wholly Impossible": A Reader in Black Women's History* (Brooklyn, N.Y., 1995), 433–47; Giddings, *When and Where I Enter*, 95, 108; Gatewood, *Aristocrats of Color*, 237–46, 269; Jones, "Mary Church-Terrell and the National Association of Colored Women," 20–33; Gerda Lerner, "Early Community Work of Black Club Women," *Journal of Negro History* 59 (April 1974): 158–67; Angela Davis, *Women, Race & Class* (New York, 1983), 127–36. For primary documents see Gerda Lerner, *Black Women in White America: A Documentary History* (New York, 1973), 433–58; Cynthia Neverdon-Morton, "The Black Woman's Struggle for Equality in the South," in *The Afro-American Woman: Struggles and Images*, eds. Sharon Harley and Rosalyn Terborg-Penn (reprint ed. Baltimore, 1997), 43–57; Deborah Gray White, *Too Heavy a Load: Black Women in Defense of Themselves, 1894–1994* (New York, 1999), 21–141.

38. Rouse, *Lugenia Burns Hope*, 4; Neverdon-Morton, *Afro-American Women of the South*, 6; Stephanie J. Shaw, *What a Woman Ought to Be and to Do: Black Professional Women Workers During the Jim Crow Era* (Chicago, 1996), 166–88; White, *Too Heavy a Load*, 21–141; Gatewood, *Aristocrats of Color*, 243; Lerner, "Early Community Work," 160, 167; Giddings, *When and Where I Enter*, 97, 98; Gaines, *Uplifting the Race*, 220–22; Rosalyn Terborg-Penn, "Discrimination against Afro-American Women in the Woman's Movement," in Harley and Terborg-Penn, *Afro-American Woman: Struggles and Images*, 17–27.

39. Charles Harris Wesley, *The History of the National Association of Colored Women's Clubs: A Legacy of Service* (Washington, D.C., 1984), 292.

40. Wesley, *History of the NACW*, 292–95.

41. Roth, *Matronage*, 78; Giddings, *When and Where I Enter*, 135–36; Rouse, *Lugenia Burns Hope*, 66–67; Lugenia Burns Hope, "The Neighborhood Union, Atlanta, Georgia: A Black Settlement House," 500–3, in Lerner, *Black Women in White America: A Documentary History*; Dittmer, *Black Georgia*, 65. The Gate City Free Kindergarten was founded by middle-class African American women in Atlanta such as Lugenia Burns Hope and Selena Butler because they realized that black mothers who worked outside the home needed facilities at which to leave their preschoolers during the school day. Alonzo Herndon became so impressed with the goals and accomplishments of the group that he purchased a building and gave it to the association to be used as both a school and a playground for the children. This was significant because, as Jacqueline Rouse related, "the city of Atlanta did not provide a single playground or park for Black children." With the additional space they acquired, the kindergarten was enlarged into a day-care center. Although no direct evidence links Selena Butler to this organization, she likely supported this endeavor because she too experienced difficulties in finding a suitable preschool for her son when he was small. Also, the work of

this group dovetailed with the work of the Neighborhood Union of which Mrs. Butler was surely a part. See Rouse, *Lugenia Burns Hope*, 28–30.

42. Roth, "Selena Sloan Butler," 211; see Georgia Women of Achievement website and look up Selena Sloan Butler at www.georgiawomen.org/_honorees/butlerss/index.html; Christine Woyshner, "Black Parent-Teacher Associations and the Origins of the National Congress of Colored Parents and Teachers, 1896–1926" (paper presented at the annual meeting of the American Educational Research Association, New Orleans, Louisiana, April 2000), 3–4 (xerographic copy in possession of the author); Guy-Sheftall, "Black Women and Higher Education," 280; William W. Cutler III, *Parents and Schools: The 150-Year Struggle for Control in American Education* (Chicago, 2000), 112.

43. Official Call, Ninth Annual Convention of the National Congress of Colored Parents and Teachers, issued by the National Office, Atlanta, Georgia, 1935(?) (copy in possession of the author). See also "Resolution honoring Selena Sloan Butler and directing that her portrait be placed in the State Capitol; and for other purposes" found at the Georgia State Legislature site www.legis.state.ga.us/legis/1999_00/fulltext/lc194528.htm; Roth, "Selena Sloan Butler," 211; "The New Georgia Encyclopedia," www.georgiaencyclopedia.org.

44. Hornsby, *A Short History of Black Atlanta*, 102–3; Rouse, *Lugenia Burns Hope*, 1–2, 96–107.

45. Franklin and Moss, *From Slavery to Freedom*, 356; Dittmer, *Black Georgia*, 207–8; Rouse, *Lugenia Burns Hope*, 109–16; Jacqueline Dowd Hall, *Revolt against Chivalry: Jessie Daniel Ames and the Women's Campaign against Lynching* (New York, 1993), 62–63.

46. Roth, "Selena Sloan Butler," 211.

47. *Atlanta Daily World*, October 8 and 10, 1964.

48. Ibid; www.georgiaencyclopedia.org.

CHAPTER 11

Gertrude Dzialynski Corbet
1874–1931

"Miss Dynamite," A Jewish Woman in
Public Life in the Progressive-Era South

CANTER BROWN JR.

THE STORY OF GERTRUDE DZIALYNSKI CORBET is one of a woman who found the courage and direction to defy the conventions of her time—including, to a certain extent, limitations that arose from her status as a Jewish woman—to help pave the way in the Progressive-Era South to women's full participation in social, political, and professional life. Refusing to accept the status quo, she labored successfully as a women's rights activist, confidant of public officials, political consultant, attorney, civic leader, businesswoman, and proud adherent of her Jewish faith and heritage. Much about her life may surprise, from her origins to its conclusion. But every step of the way and in an intriguing fashion she evidenced what an intelligent and determined woman

Figure 21. Gertrude Dzialynski, c. 1914. (From *Jacksonville Florida Times-Union*, February 4, 1914.)

could achieve at a time when and in a place where her life path might have been expected to be very different.[1]

While Gertrude Corbet's experiences and contributions centered in Florida, she was born on October 17, 1874, in Savannah, Georgia.[2] Her father, Philip Dzialynski, a widower, had come to know her mother, Mary Cohen, in that city during the final months of the Civil War. The couple married in May 1865. A merchant, Philip embraced Savannah's Jewish community, assuming a leadership role at Congregation B'nai B'rith Jacob and helping to organize the Hebrew Collegiate Institute. Business reverses, though, compelled the Dzialynskis to relocate to Florida in 1870. The trip offered a return home for Philip. His family, having immigrated from Prussian Poland, had established itself in the state two decades earlier.[3]

The move allowed Philip to rebuild his personal finances, admittedly always volatile for a country merchant, well before Gertrude's birth. He worked first for Mary's merchant brother Jacob R. Cohen. At Bartow, a frontier village and county seat located approximately forty miles east of the village of Tampa, he gained familiarity with the region's cattle industry. An emerging economic dynamo tied to a beef-hungry Cuban market, the trade had begun to produce piles of Spanish gold doubloons for local owners, a boon for a poor and underpopulated state and region. Philip chose, astutely, to secure his future prosperity with strong connections to this lucrative business. His intellect, humor, honesty, and commitment to public service soon earned him respect, friends, business, and a seat on the Polk County Commission.[4]

Ties to one leading cattleman proved especially important to the Dzialynskis and soon prompted their relocation from Bartow. Jacob Summerlin, Bartow's principal developer, shifted his attention in the early 1870s to another cattle town located slightly more than fifty miles to the northeast called Orlando. Jacob R. Cohen also invested in the place. When Summerlin chose in the spring of 1874 to dispose of his Orlando store, Cohen arranged for Philip and Mary to assume ownership. On a personal level the couple thrived, particularly with the discovery in early 1874 that Mary was pregnant. Realizing the dangers of childbirth in a frontier environment, however, Mary returned to Savannah that fall for Gertrude's birth.[5]

Orlando offered baby Gertrude her first Florida home; yet, a town sixty miles to its south-southwest, and ten miles south of Bartow, would exert a far greater influence upon her. Fort Meade, where Philip purchased a store in 1876, served as the cattle kingdom's center. It had emerged in the 1870s as a relatively affluent economic and cultural island in a sparsely populated and mostly poor frontier. In the next decade the community took on a more cosmopolitan air as

Figure 22. Fort Meade, Florida, school class, 1885, with Gertrude Dzialynski, back row, white collar, standing second to the right of the doorframe on the left. (Collection of the author.)

well-to-do English families built winter homes there. By age eleven Gertrude could play lawn tennis, enjoy cricket matches, walk gaslit streets, and hear father Philip's tales of fox hunts and horse racing—diversions balanced by cattle drives down Main Street and visits by Seminole Indians. The mix led to lively times and fascinating social opportunities. Gertrude's sister-in-law Bertha Zadek Dzialynski, for one, recalled those years at Fort Meade as "the happiest period of my life."[6]

As Gertrude grew to adolescence, she absorbed a multifaceted education. As to formal studies, the condition of local schools prompted Philip initially to employ a governess for his several children. In the mid-1880s, though, he and other local men built a schoolhouse and staffed it with qualified teachers. Gertrude naturally joined the student body. Literary expression seemed her greatest interest. "As a young woman," one family member recalled, "she wrote a number of short stories and plays."[7]

Gertrude fared well at the Fort Meade school until 1889, when her parents dispatched the fourteen-year-old to the East Florida Seminary at Gainesville, a modest predecessor of the University of Florida. Their action coincided with local teacher William R. Thomas's decision to join the seminary's faculty.

Gainesville would offer a home to Gertrude in future years, but her first stay extended for only one school term. She excelled in her courses save for mathematics. Her social standing, however, exceeded her academic performance. As an observer noted of the May 1889 honors ceremony, "The young ladies did not compete for the prizes, but they were the recipients of numerous bouquets of beautiful flowers, in fact Miss Dzialynski's bouquet bearers formed quite a large procession."[8]

The budding scholar returned home at a time when the family's fortunes had suffered from the effects of a bitter freeze, a fact that changed the course of her education. After her parents sold what assets remained to them in Fort Meade, they resettled at Bartow and operated a leased boarding house. Jacob Summerlin had just given the community a state-of-the-art brick school building, fully equipped. Gertrude enrolled in the Summerlin Institute by January 1890 and ultimately graduated from there, probably in December 1891. Then, Tampa and the prospects of "a business course" beckoned to her. She enrolled in the Tampa Business College and Literary Institute in January 1892. Gertrude's formal education reached its conclusion when she finished the course eight months later.[9]

Paralleling the young woman's formal education was an equally and perhaps more important informal one. Significantly, the Fort Meade area's frontier environment forced women to be self-reliant. A "Cracker," or "plain folk," culture where many men accepted little responsibility for daily attention to family support necessitated as much. A few women even emerged as community leaders. A Dzialynski neighbor Cuthbert Rockner, for instance, served as the town's key developer during the mid- to late 1870s and early 1880s, an activity in which Philip and Mary participated. Rockner's cattleman-husband meanwhile was assassinated by a fellow cattleman in 1877 as he and Philip rode horseback together a few miles from town.[10]

Gertrude's mother proved one of those self-reliant women and a businesswoman of ability. Mark I. Greenberg's study of Savannah's Jewish community highlighted "women's absence from the business world" except for keeping boarders, a practice that occurred principally in the homes of "recent immigrants." Few boarders were housed at one time, though, in most residences. In contrast and beginning in 1881, Mary Dzialynski operated her large Fort Meade home as the town's principal commercial hotel. "My mother-in-law was an excellent hostess in a quiet, dignified way," Bertha Dzialynski observed, "and with her large, comfortable home and staff of trained servants, entertainment was more or less easy for her." Bertha added of Mary, "She was a brilliant and cultured woman and a student of national and international affairs."[11]

Operation of "The Dzialynski House" carried additional significance for Gertrude's future life beyond allowing her to witness firsthand her mother's success. Philip's ties to Democratic power brokers had been forged through tests of the Civil War and Reconstruction. Within a few years of his arrival in Polk County, he had risen to leadership positions within the local party, and by the 1880s, candidates and incumbents streamed to Fort Meade to rekindle friendships with him, enjoy Mary's hospitality and, very importantly, court financial support from area cattlemen. Three governors maintained particularly close ties to the Dzialynskis: William D. Bloxham (governor 1881–1885 and 1897–1901); Edward A. Perry (governor 1885–1889); and Henry L. Mitchell (governor 1893–1897). Mitchell, in fact, partnered in an orange grove with Philip as early as 1878, while Bloxham also invested in local property. That Philip's brother Morris served Jacksonville—the state's emerging first city and business center—as its mayor during the early 1880s and remained an influential Democrat thereafter served only to bolster Philip's attractiveness to men of power.[12]

Gertrude thus matured breathing air suffused with politics but also with respect for her Jewish faith and heritage. Florida's small Jewish community looked upon Philip as "a Hebrew scholar," and he traveled the state accordingly. As examples, at Tallahassee in 1890 and the next year at Jacksonville he led Yom Kippur services. The family delighted in Christmas trees and Philip contributed to the Methodist building fund, but he also exposed Fort Meade to Jewish traditions and ceremonies. In 1877, daughter Jennie married Louis Herzog, with Gertrude—they called her "Gertie"—looking on. As one account related, Philip "performed the Jewish part of the ceremony." Bertha Dzialynski recalled that, when Fannie Dzialynski wed Myer Greenfield in 1888, the family "invited all relatives, friends, and all the Florida 'crackers' in the neighborhood." As would be expected, "the service was performed by the father of the bride" under a "canopy which stood in the center of the hall [and which] was tastefully draped in laces, flowers, etc." Gertie and sister Minnie looked lovely as bridesmaids. Thus, while usually distant from an organized congregation, the Dzialynskis met their religious obligations as Jews through practices that they could perform as a family or as individuals. When possible they availed themselves of community-oriented services but thrived nonetheless on personal practices.[13]

Women outside the family and Fort Meade community influenced Gertrude as well, particularly upon her move to Tampa in January 1892. Florida, generally speaking, remained hostile to women's causes, but Tampa offered, without much exaggeration, a different world. Racially and culturally mixed and sometimes volatile, its population and sophistication had swelled by the 1890s thanks to railroad and resort development. A study of Tampa women contains a chapter on the late 1800s entitled "Amazing Change." The author hit the mark exactly. Local women as early as 1880 had demanded voting rights. Fifteen years later Florida's first woman's suffrage organization convened there, electing Tampan Eleanor Chamberlain its president. For years Chamberlain had penned a suffrage and women's rights column for the *Tampa Journal* newspaper. One biographer commented that Eleanor "seemingly found nothing but depravity in men's rule and no help except in 'womanly wisdom.'"[14]

Women engaged in a variety of public and business roles in late nineteenth-century Tampa, although journalism appeared particularly attractive. Julia Magbee, Lucie Vannevar, and Mary Taylor made their marks as owners, publishers, editors, correspondents, columnists, and reporters. Gertrude knew at least one Tampa female journalist before her arrival there. Nellie Beck, having written for several Bartow newspapers as well as having delved into other forms of community activism, had moved to Tampa in 1889 to take an editorial position with the *Tampa Journal*. As a newspaperwoman and a Florida commissioner for the 1893 Chicago World's Fair, she traveled widely. She had been acquainted with the Dzialynskis since at least 1884 and, when at Bartow after 1889, she naturally stayed at their boarding house. In 1892 Nellie became co-owner of the *Tampa Tribune* and launched her own magazine, *The Tampian*. She later helped to edit the *Tampa Daily Times* and the *Tampa Morning News* before returning to Bartow as editor of the *Bartow Courier-Informant*.[15]

Enjoying regular exposure at Tampa to activist women, Gertrude also possessed an entrée to the highest levels of local political life. Her brother and sister-in-law, George I. P. and Bertha Dzialynski, had moved there from Fort Meade, and she lived with them. Bertha's cousin Bertha Brown Glogowski, a Gainesville native and daughter of Prussian-born Tobias and Pauline Brown, also resided in Tampa with her husband, the merchant Herman Glogowski. Weeks after Gertrude settled in town, Herman won a fourth and final term as the city's mayor. In 1896 he would help to found there Congregation Schaarai Zedek, serving as its first board chairman and supervising construction of its synagogue.[16]

Travel and exposure to different places, peoples, and environments must be added to Gertrude's arsenal of influences. By age twenty-one she could count Savannah, Orlando, Fort Meade, Bartow, and Tampa as having offered her homes. Beyond that, the Dzialynski family typically spent much of each summer in Savannah and New York City, where Philip purchased merchandise for his stores. There, a cosmopolitan world distinct from that of frontier Florida beckoned to Gertie. After sister Fannie's 1888 marriage, the Dzialynskis added

Beaufort, South Carolina, to their itineraries. Not only did the Greenfields live there; so, too, did relations of Gertrude's mother, Mary.[17]

Upon this foundation of diverse, complicated, and sometimes surprising building blocks, Gertrude built her career. Her initial goal involved becoming an attorney. First, in September 1892 and following graduation from Tampa Business College, she took a "stenographer and typewriter" job with the prominent law firm of Wall & Wall. The *Tampa Tribune* (which is to say, Nellie Beck) observed, "She has the ability to make a good lawyer and we should be glad to see her enter the profession." A reversal of family fortunes and her father's increasingly fragile health compelled her return to Bartow by 1893, but she was back in Tampa by March 1894. Recognized by that time as one of Bartow's "most intelligent and cultured young ladies," she took a position with rising legal star Thomas M. Shackleford, then four years away from appointment to the Florida supreme court. In the year or two that followed, Gertrude blossomed in Tampa's challenging atmosphere, lending her talents to a variety of interests and causes. She even found time, according to one account, to support a fund-raising effort to purchase an organ for the local Episcopal church. "The last recitation was given in costume by Miss Dzialynski," the *Tribune* reported. "Hager was the subject." It added, "The recitation and the costuming were both dramatic and meritorious, Miss Dzialynski evidently being an amateur genius in strict histrionic efforts."[18]

What might seem at first glance to have been a productive and carefree period for Gertrude during 1894–1895 appears very differently upon closer examination. The national economic depression that resulted from the Panic of 1893 dealt a major blow to the regional economy, especially to the lucrative phosphate mining industry that had developed in southern Polk County since the late 1880s. Having lost much of what they had managed to hold on to after earlier reversals, Philip and Mary Dzialynski now found themselves nearly destitute, at least in terms of available cash. They relocated in July 1894 to Beaufort, South Carolina, where Gertrude's sister Fannie and brother-in-law Myer Greenfield could take care of them. Florida's economy thereafter suffered a massive and enduring blow in February 1895 with what still is known as "the Great Freeze." In its aftermath Philip and Mary returned to the Sunshine State. They established themselves at Jacksonville, where brother Morris could aid them. Philip passed away there, widely mourned, on January 15, 1896.[19]

As it turned out, her father's death left twenty-one-year-old Gertrude Dzialynski with principal, albeit not entire, responsibility for her mother's welfare, a responsibility she bore resolutely until her own death. In need of enhanced income, she accepted in 1896 a legal secretary's position at Gainesville with prominent attorney William Wade Hampton. They likely had met through Thomas Shackleford as a result of investments made by Hampton in Tampa-area properties. A prominent Democrat, Hampton may deserve credit for bringing Gertrude to the attention of State Superintendent of Public Instruction William Nichols Sheats, formerly of Gainesville. Sheats soon employed her as his personal stenographer. Thus, by late 1897 Gertrude had set up a new home at the state capital of Tallahassee. It did not hurt her prospects that family friend William D. Bloxham again was serving as governor or that her uncle Jacob R. Cohen had become one of the town's principal businessmen and civic leaders.[20]

Gertrude's two-year Tallahassee sojourn allowed her not only to care for her mother but also, possibly, to fulfill her professional dream of the early 1890s. "Gertrude was a brilliant woman and ambitious," sister-in-law Bertha Dzialynski explained. "Not content to settle down to a mediocre job as stenographer, she secured a position in Tallahassee, studied law at night school, and in 1898 was admitted to the bar." Bertha continued, "She was among the first women to be accorded this privilege in Florida, if indeed she was not herself the first." Official documentation of this accomplishment has not been identified. Tallahassee's newspapers for the period have disappeared, as has Leon County's attorney's registration book. Florida supreme court records suggest that Dzialynski did not seek admission in 1898 to that panel's bar. A study of Florida's first women lawyers acknowledged the possibility of her bar admission that year, but the lack of documentation compelled the study's authors to officially recognize Louise Rebecca Pinnell, who took the oath in October 1898, as the state's first female lawyer. The two women eventually would find themselves friends and would associate closely as activists for reform.[21]

Even if Gertrude achieved bar admission in 1898, she endured more than two decades of frustration before managing to commence legal practice. Bertha explained, "She went to Jacksonville and opened an office but she was too far in advance of the times. Clients shied away from a woman lawyer and there was no alternative but to close the office." Seemingly, this attempt occurred in 1899. Compelled to support her mother, Gertrude soon returned to Gainesville, where Mary operated a boarding house called the Commercial Hotel out of her rental home. Meanwhile, her daughter apparently returned to W. W. Hampton's employ as a legal secretary. "My mother-in-law was land-poor and in bad health," Bertha commented, "but Gertrude was making a good salary and supported the home in which she and her mother lived." She did so by commencing a career as a legal reporter. As the years passed she gained, one account observed, "wide experience in the legislature, in the circuit and federal courts, and in reporting public speakers." One highlight occurring during the period saw Gertrude "summoned to New Orleans for the somewhat onerous task of reporting a woman's convention, that of the Daughters of the Confederacy." Commented the organization's national secretary, "I have never before had such efficient assistance."[22]

Offering support to the possibility of Bertha having achieved bar admission in 1898, authorities at Gainesville and the East Florida Seminary recognized during this period her ability to further the education of that institution's students. As niece Ruth Hope Dzialynski Leon put it, "She became the first woman faculty member of East Florida Seminary." In 1899 and again in 1901 Gertrude held classes in phonography (also known as Pitman shorthand) as a part of the school's "complete business course." The University of Florida, successor to the East Florida Seminary, has honored her (as Gertrude D. Corbet) for her service by naming the ground floor west of its Jennings Hall for her. The dedication refers to Dzialynski as "an instructor at the East Florida Seminary, one of the first woman attorneys in Florida, and a leader for women's suffrage."[23]

The door to further opportunity finally opened for Gertrude in 1904, and the individual who turned the knob may have been either her Uncle Morris or else her Gainesville employer W. W. Hampton. Both men were, in the words of the times, "prominent in public affairs." Particularly, in 1904 they aided the successful campaign of Jacksonville's Napoleon Bonaparte Broward for governor. Through one or both of them, Gertrude agreed to support Broward, serving the candidate as his personal secretary. She then joined the new governor's staff as a personal secretary in January 1905.[24]

From 1904—if not before—until her death, Gertrude lived and breathed politics. She did so despite facing obstacles as a woman and while retaining a fine sense of humor. One unexpected challenge to her composure presented itself early when Governor Broward asked her to stand in the receiving line at the governor's inaugural reception. The story reveals much about her character and personality. "She had a new dress for the reception and to wear with it she had a large picture hat trimmed with roses," Bertha Dzialynski related. "I packed her trunk, a large square packing trunk, and to protect the roses on her hat I put her silk hose between them." She continued,

> On the day of the reception Gertrude put on her hat evidently without glancing into a mirror. As she stood in the reception line she was quite pleased to note that her hat was attracting a great deal of attention. Each

woman looked fixedly at it and even the men seemed to look at it curiously. When she reached her room and removed her hat she found a pair of rolled hose between two of the roses!

Bertha added, "She used frequently to tell the story on herself and laugh heartily, for she cared nothing whatever for clothes and was never self-conscious about her appearance."[25]

Details of Gertrude's service for Governor Broward remain sketchy, likely because most documentation remained in the governor's personal papers and later was destroyed. Subsequent events suggest that—at the least—he encouraged her substantive input on certain matters, including politics. The years also brought her close acquaintanceship with many of his closest supporters, individuals who later would call upon or recognize her considerable talents. These men included brothers William J. Bryan and Nathan P. Bryan, who had managed the governor's campaign, and also State Senator Thomas F. West of Pensacola who, during 1913–1917, would serve as Florida's attorney general and, during 1917–1925, as a member of the state supreme court. Before pursuing the topic of contacts she made while working for Broward, it should be noted that one pleasant aspect of Tallahassee society for Gertrude stemmed from access to his and her own family members. Most importantly, her sister Etta in 1902 had married Louis E. Cohen, a capital city pharmacist. Doubtlessly, their presence buttressed her social life while affording needed assistance with her mother's care.[26]

Of the political figures who would come to Dzialynski's aid or otherwise call upon her talents, Thomas F. West was first. In May 1907 Dzialynski's Uncle Morris died at Jacksonville. This event apparently placed Gertrude in a financial bind in terms of her ability to support her mother on a relatively small state-government salary. West offered the young woman a position as legal secretary with his Pensacola firm of Smithwick and West. By September she and future Florida attorney Minnie E. Kehoe had founded the Florida Law Reporting Association. "The new firm," the partners boasted, "proposes to do expert reporting anywhere in the state, and is prepared to answer calls on short notice." Gertrude also quickly immersed herself in the local political scene by recording and transcribing, presumably at West's direction, the public statements of U.S. Senator Stephen Mallory, a Pensacola resident. Up for reelection in 1908, Mallory anticipated Broward's entry into the Democratic primary where the election would be decided. Gertrude hoped that Broward would run and in August 1907 thought she had found a key that might open the way for the candidacy. "Some little ripple of talk has been created by the expression of Senator Mallory that he was not in sympathy with the prohibition movement," she reported to Broward on August 31. Encouraged by local politicians to communicate the information to William J. Bryan in anticipation of Bryan's participation in the race, Gertrude first pushed Broward. "I have not written to Mr. Bryan," she related to the governor, "nor shall I before hearing from you. (I am thoroughly an 'administration man')." She added, "I am giving you this for your own information, and in the hope that you might use it in a campaign yourself."[27]

The governor failed to take the course that Dzialynski desired, but she nonetheless seemed to have anticipated involvement in a Broward campaign. First, Broward temporized on Gertrude's desire to press prohibition as an issue in a potential senatorial race, noting to her in early September that he did "not feel that it is proper, perhaps, as Governor of the State, voted for by many of the wets, as well as the drys, to take an active part in a campaign on the subject." Broward took care, however, to express his thanks for her efforts on his behalf. "I appreciate very much your writing that you give me this information that I might use it in a campaign for myself," he wrote. "I do not care to write any more on that line for the present, but I assure you that I appreciate the position taken by you." He added, "Probably I will be able to say more to you later on." The subsequent conversation may well have taken place in late October or early November when Gertrude visited the capital city. Reportedly, the purpose of her visit was to spend time "with her Tallahassee friends." One particular "Tallahassee friend," the state's governor, may have informed her at that time of his plan to endorse his friend and former campaign manager William J. Bryan in the run against Senator Mallory.[28]

Matters then took an unexpected turn that ushered Dzialynski into a new phase of her career and a new stage upon which to further it. Late in 1907 Senator Mallory suddenly took ill, and, on December 23, passed away. Only two days were required for Broward to appoint William J. Bryan to fill the vacancy. That Gertrude already was assisting Bryan in his campaign may be inferred from the fact that he immediately employed her as a personal assistant at the Capitol. Events thereupon moved quickly. On the U.S. Senate payroll by January 9, 1908, Gertrude enjoyed less than three months' tenure before—on March 22, 1908—Senator Bryan succumbed to typhoid fever. A few days later Broward signaled his intention to seek the Democratic senatorial nomination in the upcoming primary. Three weeks afterward—on April 21, 1908—Gertrude left the Senate's payroll and returned with her mother to Pensacola.[29]

Whether Dzialynski aided Broward's 1908 campaign remains open to question, but had he taken her pro-Prohibition advice, the results might have turned out more to his liking. Renowned as a Progressive, Broward managed in the multi-candidate field to find himself painted into an unpopular corner as a pro-corporation man by his friend Duncan U. Fletcher, the Progressive mayor of Jacksonville. Meanwhile, Broward continued to shy away from the increasingly popular temperance cause, although national reformer Carry Nation attempted to bridge the political divide by introducing him to a Miami crowd as "our dry governor." In a June runoff, the apparently more-Progressive man won, with Broward trailing by four thousand votes.[30]

Broward had not finished with senatorial races in 1908, but at that point the future was anything but clear for Dzialynski. Again pressed to support her mother's needs, she returned to work as a legal stenographer in Pensacola. Circumstances again required her to travel considerably through the Panhandle region of North Florida. This dynamic increased by fall 1909 when she secured the position of court stenographer for the Tallahassee district of the U.S. District Court for the Northern District of Florida. Credit for this professional tie likely went to Amos E. Lewis, Senator William J. Bryan's former chief of staff who, in July 1909, had secured the position of commissioner for the Northern District of Florida.[31]

Logic and one small piece of evidence suggest that, in early 1910, Dzialynski returned to the Broward camp for a second senatorial campaign. Frustrated with his second-place showing in the 1908 contest, Broward in January 1910 announced his candidacy against incumbent James P. Taliaferro. A hard-fought contest resulted in a June 22 win by Broward. The slight surviving evidence of Gertrude's involvement comes from the fact that, on primary day, her mother, Mary, was living at Tallahassee with Etta and Louis Cohen, rather than with Gertrude at Pensacola. This would have been quite understandable were Gertrude "on the road" with her candidate. If so and if Gertrude planned to return to Washington in January 1911, her hopes crashed on October 1, 1910, the day Broward died at Jacksonville of complications stemming from gallstone problems. The funeral came three days later, and as the state mourned, so too—in all likelihood—did Gertrude.[32]

Dzialynski's involvement with Governor Broward's political life and the impact of his death find their echoes in the steps she subsequently took. If she had not already relocated her residence to Jacksonville at the time of his death, she did so soon afterward. Mary again lived with her. Gertrude found employment this time as a stenographer with two of the city's most prominent Democratic businessmen, real estate broker Samuel F. Gammon and attorney J. T. G. Crawford. Crawford would go on to serve in 1920 and 1929 as a Democratic national committeeman from Florida. With offices in the city's bold new ten-story skyscraper, the Atlanta National Bank Building, she again immersed herself in politics, this time focusing more directly on a woman's role and her right to vote. She succeeded remarkably and, by 1913, had achieved the position of secretary of the Women's Democratic League of Duval County.[33]

In 1913 political rewards also began to flow to Dzialynski, in recognition of her considerable abilities as well as her party ties. With Democratic President Woodrow Wilson in the White House as of early March following sixteen years of Republican rule, Gertrude soon received the position of office deputy for corporate taxation in the headquarters of H. H. Lewis, U.S. collector of internal revenue for Florida. With the backing of U.S. Senator Nathan P. Bryan, who eventually had stood in for Governor Broward following his death, she rose further with appointment in January 1914 as Florida's deputy collector of internal revenue for federal income taxation. Dzialynski remained in responsible appointive positions with the Internal Revenue Service for approximately four years. She administered not only income tax matters but also inheritance tax issues, eventually assuming the title of deputy collector of revenue for Florida.[34]

Freed by her federal salary from immediate financial cares, Gertrude now embraced political entrepreneurialism, as a sideline but enthusiastically. She established in Jacksonville's Barnett Bank Building a printing and political consulting business called the Eureka Multigraphing Service. "Having recently purchased and set up a complete multigraph equipment," she announced in March 1916, "I am prepared to do all sorts of campaign work." Detailing her potential services further, she described, "Of course we don't do book work, but letters and circulars, etc., we will write, address, seal, stamp and mail,—taking charge of the whole process from the time the copy is sent to us until we put the completed work in the post office." A variety of state and local candidates availed themselves of her services. Her activities quickly extended to political advice and strategy. "My excuse for butting in," she informed one client, "is that it has to be done and I seem to be the goat." Evidencing her excitement, she soon took to signing correspondence, "Yours in the fight, 'Miss Dynamite.'"[35]

Gertrude's principal 1916 client may have been Senator Bryan. As a stenographer she recorded a series of debates between the incumbent and his main challenger, Governor Park Trammell. After one such encounter at Tallahassee in March, she informed a Bryan supporter, "The debate turned out not to be a debate but a slaughter." She added, "The Colonel [Bryan] was at his best and Park, to judge from the manner and the matter of his speech, was depending entirely on his looks." The now-veteran political observer concluded by noting, "I do intend to hand this [a newspaper clipping on a Trammell speech] to the colonel the next time I see him, with the suggestion that he use it as indicated above." A miscue singled out by Gertrude served, in her mind, as ideal anti-Trammell fodder for the newspapers. "Now then," she lectured the Bryan supporter, "couldn't the Miami Metropolis pull off something like this: "Gov. Trammell is reported to have said, in his speech at Tallahassee Friday. . . ." She went so far as to suggest an editorial comment for the paper. "The Governor is either ignorant or is willfully deceiving the people of this state, the facts of the matter being, etc. etc."[36]

Whatever value her services proved to Senator Bryan, they were not enough to forestall the popular governor from election to the senate. With Bryan's defeat came the likelihood of Gertrude's dismissal from federal employment once Trammell took his oath of office. Accordingly, in January 1917 or shortly thereafter, she departed the Office of Internal Revenue and returned to life as a working stenographer. She managed to keep the Eureka Multigraphing Company in operation into 1917 with the assistance of manager A. E. Brown. Before year's end, however, it had closed.[37]

Although faced once again with picking up the pieces of her professional life while maintaining her mother in security, Gertrude could now look to the future confident of dependable assistance and support. On September 19, 1915, she had married John Archibald Corbet, a native of Scotland who worked for the Clyde Steamship Line. "For one of her matter-of-factness and spinster years, it was all very romantic," Bertha recorded of their meeting. "She was returning on a boat from New York and by chance became rather well acquainted with the purser, Mr. Jack Corbett, an exceedingly fine man." The union proved a happy one, although, given Gertrude's independent nature, it likely helped that Jack remained away a good part of the time. Available evidence suggests that his absence may have been extended during World War I by service in the British military. If so, he had returned by 1918, apparently none the worse for wear. The couple had no children. It appears clear, in any event, that Gertrude's choice of a Christian husband was due to factors other than a loss of interest in Jewish religion. As will be seen, her future actions argue strongly against an interpretation of the union as a sign of assimilation or as reflective of a diminished Jewish identity.[38]

Her departure from the IRS, Jack's return home, and the war's end combined to launch Gertrude into a flurry of political, professional, and civic causes. While earning a living as legal secretary for prominent Jacksonville attorney L. R. Milton, she pursued numerous avocations. In December 1918, for example, she assumed the office of corresponding secretary of Jacksonville's influential Martha Reid Chapter, United Daughters of the Confederacy. Members later elected her their president. The next year she and attorney friend Louise Pinnell helped to organize the Jacksonville Business and Professional Woman's Club. Louise presided in 1920, with Gertrude following her in 1921. In December 1920 she also had aided organization of the Duval County Law Enforcement Committee. She associated in its Prohibition enforcement work with former Florida First Lady May Mann Jennings.[39]

Politics, as always, played its part in filling Gertrude's busy schedule. The Nineteenth Amendment to the U.S. Constitution, ratified in August 1920, conferred the vote upon women. It surely filled Gertrude's heart with pride that the women voters of her hometown, Fort Meade, cast the first lawful ballots in the state. For her part, she set about creating a Florida State League of Women Voters. Gertrude chaired the arrangements committee for its organizational meeting held at Jacksonville in the spring of 1921 and personally called the session to order. An account announcing the proceedings noted,

> Mrs. J. A. Corbet, temporary chairman, who called the meeting and who is in charge of the program, states that the league is in no sense a woman's party, but quite the contrary. While the organization is composed of women electors, these women are urged to inform themselves on all public questions, on proposed legislation, and matters in their own communities.

Gertrude, May Mann Jennings, and others followed in April by creating the Duval County League of Women Voters. Gertrude presided over it in 1924–1925, leading demands for representation for women on the state Democratic Executive Committee. Reportedly, she subsequently served as a Florida member of the Democratic National Committee.[40]

In the time remaining to her, Gertrude also practiced law. Having never forgotten her professional dreams of the 1890s, she determined in the immediate post–World War I era to reclaim the status of attorney. Accordingly, in 1921 she took and passed the state bar examination, an innovation since 1898, and soon opened a law office in the fashionable Bisbee Building. For a number of years she fared well, with the *Jacksonville Florida Times-Union* insisting that she "enjoyed a splendid reputation" as an attorney. After the sudden death of her husband, Jack, in September 1925, though, she suspended her practice. Whether this resulted more from an immediate financial need or from Florida's economic bust of 1926 cannot be ascertained. In any event, her services remained much in demand, and she accepted a prestigious posting with A. P. Adair of Jacksonville's Cooper, Knight, Adair, Cooper & Osborne law firm.[41]

Gertrude's final years passed pleasantly and relatively quietly. She involved herself deeply with her temple, Jacksonville's Congregation Ahavath Chesed.

Her Uncle Morris had helped to found it, and father, Philip, often had led services there. She worked especially with the Temple Sisterhood, over which she had presided during 1924–1925. That involvement did not mean that Gertrude withdrew entirely from politics, however. In one example of political service she joined in 1929 a state committee to push adoption of a credit union law in Florida, one of only two women active on the panel. The measure, aimed at assuring the egalitarian concept then known as "economic democracy," met with legislative approval after, in a credit union historian's words, "This committee covered the state like a blanket."[42]

Still, the passage of time brought health concerns, which grew as the Depression year of 1930 passed to an even more challenging 1931. Gertrude Dzialynski Corbet passed away at Jacksonville, aged fifty-six, on January 24, 1931. She was buried the next day in the city's Temple Cemetery. The *Jacksonville Journal*, in an obituary entitled "Long Life of Work Is Ended by Death," asserted no understatement when it noted, "Mrs. Corbet had always taken an active part in all political and public affairs." Her sister-in-law, on the other hand, may have summarized her life most cogently. "Gertrude Dzialynski was a brilliant woman and ambitious," Bertha Dzialynski commented. She added, "[Gertrude was] not content to settle down to a mediocre job."[43]

Gertrude Dzialynski Corbet's life speaks to us meaningfully over the span of nearly a century. She drew strength from every facet of life, particularly including a Jewish faith to which she remained constant and devoted, while evidencing repeatedly a willingness to step outside the norm to question and, at times, reject gender- and culturally based restrictions upon her actions as a woman. Life outside the Jewish community may have encouraged Gertrude to be more daring and flexible. On the other hand, from within the same community came support and, over time, recognition and reinforcement. She earned respect and stirred pride across religious, cultural, and gender lines. She evidenced the great potential of a woman who dared to be different.

Notes

1. The lives and experiences of Jewish women in the nineteenth and twentieth centuries have received increasing attention from historians and other scholars in recent decades. See, for example, Jacob R. Marcus, *The American Jewish Woman, 1654–1980* (New York, 1981); Charlotte Baum, Paula Hyman, and Sonya Michel, *The Jewish Woman in America* (New York, 1981); Jacob R. Marcus, ed., *The American Jewish Woman: A Documentary History* (New York, 1981); June Sochen, *Consecrate Every Day: The Public Lives of American Jewish Women, 1880–1980* (Albany, N.Y., 1981);

Mark I. Greenberg, "Savannah's Jewish Women and the Shaping of Ethnic and Gender Identity, 1830–1900," *Georgia Historical Quarterly* 82 (Winter 1998): 751–74; Mark K. Bauman, "Southern Jewish Women and Their Social Service Organizations," *Journal of American Ethnic History* 22 (Spring 2003): 34–78. See also Mark K. Bauman, ed., *Dixie Diaspora: An Anthology of Southern Jewish History* (Tuscaloosa, 2006).

2. Ruth Hope Leon, "The History of the Dzialynski Family" (typescript, n.d.), collection of the Jacksonville Historical Society, Jacksonville (xerographic copy in possession of the author); Canter Brown Jr., "Philip and Morris Dzialynski: Jewish Contributions to the Rebuilding of the South," *American Jewish Archives* 44 (Fall–Winter 1992), 539. The latter essay is revised, updated, and reprinted in Bauman, *Dixie Diaspora*, 209–35 (subsequent references will be to this version). Other helpful sources on the Jewish experience in Florida during the nineteenth and early twentieth centuries include Samuel Proctor, "Pioneer Jewish Settlement in Florida, 1764–1900," in *Proceedings of the Conference on the Writing of Regional History in the South with Special Emphasis on Religious and Culture Groups* (New York, 1956), 116–31; Natalie H. Glickstein, *That Ye May Remember: Congregation Ahavath Chesed, 1882–1982, 5642–5742* (Jacksonville, Fla., 1982); Henry Alan Green and Marcia Kerstein Zerivitz, *Mosaic: Jewish Life in Florida: A Documentary Exhibit from 1763 to the Present* (Coral Gables, 1991); James B. Crooks, "Jacksonville Jewry after the Fire: 1901–1919," *Northeast Florida History: The Journal of the Jacksonville Historical Society* 1 (1992): 71–79; Elaine Fantle Shimberg, *Congregation Schaarai Zedek: 1894–1994, 5655–5755* (Tampa, 1994); Mark I. Greenberg, "Tampa Mayor Herman Glogowski: Jewish Leadership in Gilded Age Florida," in *Florida's Heritage of Diversity: Essays in Honor of Samuel Proctor*, ed. Mark I. Greenberg, William Warren Rogers, and Canter Brown Jr. (Tallahassee, 1997), 55–68; Canter Brown Jr., *Jewish Pioneers of the Tampa Bay Frontier* (Tampa, 1999); Richard W. Sapon-White, "A Polish Jew on the Florida Frontier and in Occupied Tennessee: Excerpts from the Memoirs of Max White," *Southern Jewish History* 4 (2001): 92–122; Chris Monaco, "A Sugar Utopia on the Florida Frontier: Moses Elias Levy's Pilgrimage Plantation," *Southern Jewish History* 5 (2002): 103–40; Canter Brown Jr., ed., "A Prussian-Born Jewish Woman on the Florida Frontier: Excerpts from the Memoir of Bertha Zadek Dzialynski," *Southern Jewish History* 7 (2004): 109–54; Daniel R. Weinfeld, "Samuel Fleishman: Tragedy in Reconstruction-Era Florida," *Southern Jewish History* 8 (2005): 31–76; Chris Monaco, *Moses Levy of Florida: Jewish Utopian and Antebellum Reformer* (Baton Rouge, 2005).

3. Brown, "Philip and Morris Dzialynski," 209–15.

4. Ibid., 215–18; Brown, *Jewish Pioneers*, 34–35, 54. On the early history of Bartow and Polk County, see Canter Brown Jr., *Florida's Peace River Frontier* (Orlando, 1991); idem, *In the Midst of All That Makes Life Worth Living: Polk County, Florida, to 1940* (Tallahassee, 2001).

5. Brown, "Philip and Morris Dzialynski," 218–19. On Jacob Summerlin, see Joe A. Akerman Jr. and J. Mark Akerman, *Jacob Summerlin: King of the Crackers* (Cocoa, Fla., 2005).

6. Canter Brown Jr., *Fort Meade, 1849–1900* (Tuscaloosa, 1995), 52–120; Brown, "Prussian-Born Jewish Woman," 122.

7. Leon, "History of the Dzialynski Family," 3; Brown, *Fort Meade*, 97.

8. *Jacksonville Florida Times-Union*, January 9, May 24, and June 25, 1889; Record Book No. 2 (1876–1899), Vol. 1, East Florida Seminary Records, 1861–1905, University of Florida Archives, Gainesville; Mary Ann Burg, Kevin McCarthy, Phyllis Meek, Constance Shehan, Anita Spring, Nina Stoyan-Rosenzweig, and Betty Taylor, *Women at the University of Florida* (Naples, Fla., 2003), 1–3. On the history of the East Florida Seminary and the early history of the University of Florida, see Samuel Proctor, "The University of Florida: Its Early Years, 1853–1906" (master's thesis, University of Florida, 1958); Samuel Proctor and Wright Langley, *Gator History: A Pictorial History of the University of Florida* (Gainesville, 1986).

9. Brown, "Philip and Morris Dzialynski," 225–26; Bertha Zadek Dzialynski, "Within My Heart" (typescript, Jacksonville, 1944), 129 (collection of Jewish Museum of Florida, Miami Beach; xerographic copy in possession of the author, courtesy of Perry Coleman, Jacksonville); unidentified June 1934 clipping in Summerlin Institute scrapbook, Polk County Historical and Genealogical Library, Bartow, Fla.; Dorinda Garrard, Polk County Historical and Genealogical Library, to the author, February 3, 2006, in possession of the author; *Tampa Tribune*, October 5, 1891.

10. Brown, *Fort Meade*, 66–67. On the emergence of self-reliant women in the Fort Meade vicinity, see Canter Brown Jr., *Women on the Tampa Bay Frontier* (Tampa, 1997).

11. Greenberg, "Savannah's Jewish Women," 757–59; Brown, *Fort Meade*, 70; idem, "Prussian-Born Jewish Woman," 120.

12. *Jacksonville Florida Weekly Times*, August 21, 1884; Brown, "Prussian-Born Jewish Woman," 119–20; idem, *Fort Meade*, 86; idem, "Philip and Morris Dzialynski," 223–25; *Tampa Sunland Tribune*, April 30, 1878.

13. George I. P. Dzialynski questionnaire, Dzialynski family file, Local History Biography Collection, Hayden Burns Public Library, Jacksonville; *Bartow Polk County News*, October 10, 1890; *Jacksonville Evening Telegram*, October 14, 1891; *Bartow Informant*, June 9, 1881; *Tampa Sunland Tribune*, November 24, 1877; *Bartow Advance Courier*, May 30, 1888; Brown, "A Prussian-Born Jewish Woman," 123, 141.

14. Doris Weatherford, *Real Women of Tampa & Hillsborough County from Prehistory to the Millennium* (Tampa, 2004), 75–139; *Tampa Sunday Tribune*, March 27 and May 1, 15, 22, 1994. On Tampa women, see also Nancy A. Hewitt, *Southern Discomfort: Women's Activism in Tampa, Florida, 1880s–1920s* (Urbana, Ill., 2001); Susan D. Greenbaum, *More Than Black: Afro-Cubans in Tampa* (Gainesville, 2002).

15. *Tampa Journal*, August 1, 1889; Donald B. McKay, *Pioneer Florida*, 3 vols. (Tampa, 1959), 3:741–42; *Tampa Guardian*, August 4 and September 22, 1886; *Tampa Sunday Tribune*, June 10, 1951; *Tampa Weekly Tribune*, June 29, 1993; *Tampa Morning Tribune*, January 9, 1896; *Bartow Informant*, January 26, 1884; *Bartow Advance Courier*, November 23, 1887; *Tampa Journal*, November 21, 1889; *Daily Tampa Tribune*, Sep-

tember 5, 1892; Bentley Orrick and Harry L. Crumpacker, *The Tampa Tribune: A Century of Florida Journalism* (Tampa, 1998), 28–29, 35, 69; Weatherford, *Real Women*, 101, 118–21; Mary Kavanaugh Oldham Eagle, ed., *The Congress of Women: Held in the Woman's Building, World's Columbian Exposition, Chicago, U.S.A., 1893* (Chicago, 1894), facing p. 232.

16. Dzialynski, "Within My Heart," 129; Greenberg, "Tampa Mayor Herman Glogowski," 55–68.

17. Dzialynski, "Within My Heart," 75, 77; *Tampa Sunland Tribune*, May 20, 1880, March 26, 1881, May 4, and 18, and June 29, 1882; *Bartow Courier-Informant*, January 2, 1891.

18. *Daily Tampa Tribune*, September 14, 1892; Dzialynski, "Within My Heart," 129; *Tampa Weekly Tribune*, March 9 and 16, 1894; *Bartow Courier-Informant*, March 7, 1894; Walter W. Manley II, Canter Brown Jr., and Eric W. Rise, *The Supreme Court of Florida and Its Predecessor Courts, 1821–1917* (Gainesville, 1997), 340–43; *Tampa Morning Tribune*, May 30, 1895.

19. Brown, *Florida's Peace River Frontier*, 312–18, 321–25; Brown, *In the Midst*, 179–88; *Tampa Weekly Tribune*, July 13 and November 30, 1894; Brown, "Philip and Morris Dzialynski," 225–26.

20. Dzialynski, "Within My Heart," 129; *Makers of America: Florida Edition* (Atlanta, 1909), 130–34; *B. Bruce George v. The Seaboard Air Line Railway*, 52 *Florida Reports*, 461 (1906), 462–67; William N. Sheats, *Bi-ennial Report of the Superintendent of Public Instruction of the State of Florida for the Two Years Ending June 30, 1898* (Tallahassee, 1899), 417, 425; *Jacksonville Evening Metropolis*, November 9, 1901; *Jacksonville Florida Times-Union and Citizen*, November 6, 1901. For interesting perspectives on William N. Sheats as Florida's superintendent of public instruction, see Reginald Ellis, "Nathan B. Young: Florida A&M College's Second President and His Relationships with White Public Officials," 153–72; and David H. Jackson Jr., "Booker T. Washington's Tour of the Sunshine State, March 1912," in David H. Jackson Jr. and Canter Brown Jr., eds., *Go Sound the Trumpet! Selections in Florida's African American History*, 173–99 (Tampa, 2005).

21. Dzialynski, "Within My Heart," 129–30; Wendy S. Loquasto, ed. and comp.,—*150—: Celebrating Florida's First 150 Women Lawyers* (Charlottesville, Va., 2000), 1, 17–18.

22. Dzialynski, "Within My Heart," 130, 141; *Jacksonville Florida Times-Union and Citizen*, June 13, 1899; 1900 U.S. Decennial Census, Alachua County, Florida (population schedule); *Weekly Tallahassean*, March 21, 1902; *Pensacola Journal*, September 29, 1907.

23. Leon, "History of the Dzialynski Family," 3; "Schools and Teachers," *Phonography Magazine* 15 (October 1901), 193; Burg et al., *Women at the University of Florida*, 79.

24. Daniel Decatur Moore, ed., *Men of the South: A Work for the Newspaper Reference Library* (New Orleans, 1922), 275; *Jacksonville Florida Times-Union*, November

21, 1928; Dzialynski, "Within My Heart," 129–30. On Governor Napoleon Bonaparte Broward, see Samuel Proctor, *Napoleon Bonaparte Broward: Florida's Fighting Democrat* (Gainesville, 1950; reprint ed., Gainesville, 1993).

25. *Jacksonville Florida Times-Union*, January 5, 1905; Dzialynski, "Within My Heart," 130–31.

26. Gertrude Dzialynski to N. B. Broward, August 31, 1907, and Broward to Dzialynski, September 6, 1907, Napoleon Bonaparte Broward Papers, Box 5A, P. K. Yonge Library of Florida History, University of Florida; Proctor, *Napoleon Bonaparte Broward*, 203; Walter W. Manley II and Canter Brown Jr., *The Supreme Court of Florida, 1917–1972* (Gainesville, 2006), 36–41; Alachua County Marriage Records, Book D, 823, Alachua County Courthouse, Gainesville; *Weekly Tallahassean*, March 21, 1902; *Jacksonville Florida Times-Union*, January 7, 1905.

27. Dzialynski to Broward, August 31, 1907; *Pensacola Journal*, September 29, 1907.

28. Broward to Dzialynski, September 6, 1907; *Tallahassee Weekly True Democrat*, November 1, 1907; Proctor, *Napoleon Bonaparte Broward*, 268–69.

29. Proctor, *Napoleon Bonaparte Broward*, 274–75; *Annual Report of the Secretary of the Senate Submitting a Full and Complete Statement of the Receipts and Expenditures of the Senate from July 1, 1907, to June 30, 1908* (Washington, D.C., 1908), 24–30; Dzialynski, "Within My Heart," 130.

30. Proctor, *Napoleon Bonaparte Broward*, 274–84; Wayne Flynt, *Duncan Upshaw Fletcher: Dixie's Reluctant Progressive* (Tallahassee, 1971), 48–53.

31. 1909 Pensacola city directory, 178; ibid., 1910, 160; *Tallahassee Weekly True Democrat*, September 3 and October 22, 1909; *Annual Report of the Secretary of the Senate*, 24; *Register of the Department of Justice and the Courts of the United States, Twenty-First Edition* (Washington, D.C., 1913), 74.

32. Proctor, *Napoleon Bonaparte Broward*, 296–307; 1910 U.S. Decennial Census, Leon County, Florida (population schedule).

33. 1911 Jacksonville city directory, 392; ibid., 1912, 499; ibid., 1913, 459; J. T. G. Crawford at The Political Graveyard, Index to Politicians, www.politicalgraveyard.com/bio/crawford.html; *Jacksonville Florida Times-Union*, February 4, 1914.

34. *Jacksonville Florida Times-Union*, February 4, 1914; *Tampa Daily Times*, February 6, 1914; Leon, "History of the Dzialynski Family," 4; 1917 Jacksonville city directory, 305.

35. Gertrude D. Corbet to J. M. Carson, March 2, 7, and 13, 1916, Misc. Corr., 1915–1916, James Milton Carson Papers, Richter Library, University of Miami, Miami; 1916 Jacksonville city directory, 402; ibid., 1917, 305, 376.

36. Corbet to Carson, March 13, 1916. On the 1916 U.S. Senate race in Florida, see Stephen Kerber, "Park Trammell and the Florida Democratic Senatorial Primary of 1916," *Florida Historical Quarterly* 58 (January 1980): 255–72.

37. 1917 Jacksonville city directory, 305, 376; ibid., 1918, 274; Leon, "History of the Dzialynski Family," 3–4.

38. Dzialynski, "Within My Heart," 131; *Jacksonville Florida Metropolis*, September

20, 1915; *Jacksonville Florida Times-Union*, September 13, 1925; 1916 Jacksonville city directory, 402; ibid., 1917, 305; ibid., 1918, 274.

39. *Jacksonville Florida Times-Union*, December 6, 1918, June 3, 1919, March 10 and April 14, 1920, April 23, 1921; Linda D. Vance, *May Mann Jennings: Florida's Genteel Activist* (Gainesville, 1985), 112, 175; Leon, "History of the Dzialynski Family," 4.

40. Brown, *In the Midst*, 264; *Jacksonville Evening Metropolis*, March 20 and 30, 1921; *Jacksonville Florida Times-Union*, March 17, April 1, 2, 29, 1921, and February 20, 1924; *Jacksonville Journal*, February 20, 1924; Leon, "History of the Dzialynski Family," 4. On the origins and evolution of the Florida State League of Women Voters, see Joan S. Carver, "First League of Women Voters in Florida: Its Troubled History," *Florida Historical Quarterly* 63 (April 1985): 383–405.

41. *Jacksonville Florida Times-Union*, April 24, 1921, September 13, 1925, and January 26, 1931; 1923 Jacksonville city directory, 340; ibid., 1927, 335; Dzialynski, "Within My Heart," 131.

42. *Jacksonville Florida Times-Union*, October 9, 1924; Dzialynski, "Within My Heart," 129; Brown, "Philip and Morris Dzialynski," 530; Roy F. Bergengren, *The Fight for Economic Democracy in North America, 1921–1945* (New York, 1952), 145–46.

43. *Jacksonville Florida Times-Union*, January 26, 1931; *Jacksonville Journal*, January 26, 1931; Dzialynski, "Within My Heart," 129; Brown, "Philip and Morris Dzialynski," 530.

CHAPTER 12

Eartha Mary Magdalene White
1876–1974

The Gentle Community Activist

CAROLYN WILLIAMS

OFTEN REFERRED TO AS "Jacksonville's Angel of Mercy," Eartha Mary Magdalene White devoted her adult life to providing services for, generally improving the quality of life of, and ultimately, enhancing the status of African Americans in Jacksonville, Florida. Although her labors extended through much of the twentieth century and involved a variety of endeavors, she began by working with her mother to feed the hungry and create a home for indigent elderly black people. She then established a community center that continues today as one of the most important homeless shelters in the region. White's charitable work led to political activism, including encouraging African American women to vote, seek office, and lobby behind the scenes to solicit the sup-

Figure 23. Eartha M. M. White and Clara White, c. 1910s. (Courtesy Eartha White Collection, Thomas G. Carpenter Library, University of North Florida.)

port and assistance of prominent politicians. By the end of her long and active life, her fellow Jacksonvillians revered Eartha White as one of the most influential women in the city. Most of all she demonstrated that she had lived up to the motto handed down by her mother, Clara: "Do all the good you can, in all the ways you can, in all the places you can, for all the people you can, while you can."[1]

Eartha White's life began at Jacksonville on November 8, 1876, and from its start complications abounded. She recorded in the family Bible that her mother was Clara English White and her father was Guy Henry Stockton. Clara had been born a slave in 1845 on a plantation lying north of Jacksonville on Amelia Island in Nassau County, owned by Robert Harrison. Harrison had joined Loyalist families that settled on the island in the early 1800s when Florida still belonged to the Spanish Empire. Clara English's mother and father, Adam English and Jane Drummond, along with her paternal grandfather had been given to Harrison's wife, Mary Magdalene Cooper Harrison. Jane English later was auctioned in Jacksonville, and her daughter did not see her again until after the Civil War. Clara grew up at Silver Springs in Marion County near Ocala after being gifted to Mary's nephew Colonel Charles Cooper. During the Civil War Clara married Lafayette White, a former South Carolina slave who by then was serving as a Union army soldier. White was fighting in the same unit—the 34th Regiment, Company D, United States Colored Troops—as Adam English, Clara's father. After the peace in 1865, the Whites joined English and other black Civil War veterans and their loved ones who settled in Jacksonville.[2]

The circumstances under which Guy Henry Stockton fathered Eartha are uncertain. He had been born about 1855 in Gadsden County, located in the heart of Florida's Panhandle and a prosperous center of its plantation belt. His white parents, William Tennent and Julia Telfair Stockton, traced their lineages through old and distinguished families. They were able to support a handsome lifestyle. William served the Confederate States with distinction but, seemingly, never fully recovered his health after wartime. He died at Quincy, the county seat, on March 4, 1869, leaving Julia a widow with four sons and two daughters. She moved the family to Jacksonville in 1870, where her daughter Mary lived with her husband, Florida's Episcopal Bishop John Freeman Young. There Julia maintained her home as a boarding house, calling it "The Priory" in a nod to her tenant son-in-law's standing within the church. Her children matured there, with sons John N. C. Stockton and Telfair Stockton growing to become two of the city's and the state's most influential businessmen and political figures. Meanwhile, Guy Stockton's life does not seem to have been as successful. The eldest among them, Guy lived at home, still unmarried, as late as 1880. He worked as a clerk. His whereabouts thereafter are not known.[3]

Although Eartha White knew that Lafayette White was not her father, whether she knew that Clara White was not her biological mother is not clear. Clara's testimony when she petitioned to receive Lafayette's Civil War pension reveals that she was not, and it raises questions about the circumstances of Eartha's origins that, most likely, will never be answered definitively. Reports circulated widely that Clara had twelve children, all of whom died before reaching maturity. However, she declared in 1896 that Bertha, her last biological child, was given or taken away soon after Lafayette died in 1881. The people who took the child were white and moved to Washington, D.C. As far as Clara knew, Bertha remained alive at the time of the interviews. Further, census records from 1870 located an eight-year-old boy called George, presumably a son, in the White home. Ten years later, the census takers failed to note Bertha's birth, but they did find in the home four-year-old Eartha Mary Magdalene White, who is referred to as the couple's daughter and yet is listed as a mulatto.[4]

The nature of Clara White's sentiments toward her children merits speculation. She evidently allowed Bertha to be taken away to provide her with a better environment and perhaps a better chance of survival than was enjoyed by her children who had died. This action, it can be argued, might not have represented a very profound decision for Clara, who had been given as a child to a white family. In any event Clara apparently felt some bond with her former owners, as suggested by the fact that Clara gave her adoptive daughter the name of her former owner, Mary Magdalene Cooper Harrison. Clara later stated that she and Lafayette White kept Eartha because she (Clara) had promised to keep the child. The consensus among those who have examined the question is that Eartha's biological mother was a young woman named Mollie Chapman. Likely, Clara's promise was made to Mollie. The only thing known about her is that, by 1896, she had died. Since her name fails to appear in the record following Eartha's birth, she probably passed away soon after that event, leaving her baby to the Whites.[5]

Many of the details of Eartha's upbringing have gone unrecorded, although glimpses of her youthful influences offer some insight. During Eartha's childhood Clara White worked as a domestic servant, like many other black former slaves and their female descendants. Meanwhile Lafayette worked as a drayman. Following his death, the family circumstances must have grown more challenging. Yet, Eartha reported that families employing her mother were kind to her and Clara. Thus, she witnessed and experienced what arguably was the most positive side of the paternalistic relationship forged in slavery (between white slaveholders—masters and mistresses—and their bond servants), ties that evolved into patterns of behavior between employers and free servants after the "peculiar institution" had been abolished. Clara also worked at times, in addition to other situations, as a maid in Jacksonville's principal tourist accommodation, the St. James Hotel. There she and Eartha would have come into contact with well-to-do northerners who sometimes became acquainted with members of the hotel staff and who occasionally offered them some pecuniary or other assistance.[6]

Beyond these factors, broader influences touched Eartha as well. Particularly, as she grew to adulthood, Jacksonville came to represent something very special to African Americans in terms of hope and opportunity. Already described soon after the Civil War as the state's "Yankee headquarters," it emerged from wartime devastation as a center for tourism and business. Black residents aided these developments, not only with their physical labor but also through their entrepreneurship, government service, educational initiatives, and creative contributions. A middle class developed that included figures of renown such as African Methodist Episcopal Bishop Daniel A. Payne and his circle of associates and acquaintances. Along with the economic progress came increasing sophistication and broader horizons for many.[7]

The changes at Jacksonville accelerated through the 1880s. The writer, editor, and publisher T. Thomas Fortune, who departed the city in 1878 when Eartha was two years of age, returned twelve years later to a far different scene than the one he had left. "It is a new world to me," he informed friends. Fortune added, "The colored people of no city I have visited have better opportunities to make rapid and sustained progress than those of Jacksonville, or are making such progress. They are a credit to the race and the State." Significantly for Eartha, women played influential roles within the city's African American community, and those roles were not limited to domestic service, education, or church work. By way of example, a nationally circulated black newspaper boasted in 1895 that "Mrs. Rhina G. Geter, an Afro-American, paid the largest individual assessment for paving [Jacksonville's] Bridge street, $438.87." It noted as well, "The *Daily American,* of the same city, says that Afro-Americans own some $600,000 worth of real property in Jacksonville."[8]

Opportunities awaited at Jacksonville not only for well-to-do members of the black community, but also for those who made up for a lack of financial means with hard work and steady determination. An example involving the St. James Hotel, where Clara sometimes worked, helps to make the point. Established by northern entrepreneurs in 1869, the St. James became the most important resort hotel in Florida. As its reputation grew, so too did the number of good jobs. James Weldon Johnson, a Jacksonville native, knew this from intimate experience, for his father James Johnson labored at the hotel as head waiter. "My first definite thought about the hotel was that it belonged to my father," he recorded. "I am struck with wonder at the endless rows of tables now revealed, the glitter of silver, china, and glass, and the array of napkins folded so that they look like many miniature white pyramids," he continued. "One of [the waiters] tucks a napkin under my chin and serves me as though I were a princeling." Johnson concluded, "My father snaps his fingers, waiters jump to carry out his orders, and guests smile him their thanks. He lords it over everything that falls within my ken. He is, quite obviously, the most important man in the St. James Hotel."[9]

Opportunity and experience for African Americans, such as Clara White, who were determined to make their way in the world, also arose out of the steamboat industry. As Jacksonville's reputation grew in the 1870s and 1880s, tourism flourished. One facet of that industry involved steamboats that transported sightseers to partake of regional points of interest and natural beauty. While the vessels traveled numerous waterways, the majestic St. Johns River provided the industry's central focus. Regular runs took tourists upriver to resort communities such as Green Cove Springs, Palatka, DeLand, and Enterprise. Some moved farther, by way of connections via the Oklawaha River, to Clara White's old Marion County home at Silver Springs. The steamship companies engaged African Americans to perform the manual labor and domestic chores on these vessels, as well as actually to operate them. Clara, for instance, worked occasionally as a stewardess aboard various boats, bringing her both income and connections. Since the customers and many staff members rotated between summer seasonal resorts in the North and winter spots in Florida (as also was the case with visitors at the resort hotels), she found herself able to board young Eartha during summer months in the Northeast. In fact, after Jacksonville's infamous 1888 yellow fever epidemic, Eartha and Clara remained for a time in the North.[10]

Before Eartha ventured North, however, she already had arrived at school age. The progress that Jacksonville's African American residents had witnessed economically, politically, socially, and culturally was reflected in educational opportunities. They especially benefited from two schools. The Stanton Institute claimed precedence as the first one established that became a permanent institution; it had opened its doors in the late 1860s with sponsorship from the Freedmen's Bureau and the American Missionary Association. By the mid- to late 1870s the school had earned increased respect, although by the time Eartha would have commenced classes there in the early 1880s, following kindergarten instruction from famed Florida educator Mary Still in the Sabbath school conducted at Mt. Zion AME Church, Stanton's fortunes had declined under the principalship of Daniel Wallace Culp. "He was a poor teacher," James Weldon Johnson recalled. Moreover, "As an administrator he had no success." "The school got to be a sort of go-as-you-please institution, and many parents took their children out and sent them elsewhere." Then, in October 1883 an arsonist destroyed the facility. Either before or after that event, Clara transferred Eartha from Stanton to the Cookman Institute. Founded in 1873 as "the first school of higher education of Negroes established in the State of Florida," it enjoyed support from the northern Methodist Church. As Stanton fell on hard times, Cookman enjoyed rosy prospects. During that period, Eartha pursued her studies there for several years.[11]

Stanton and Cookman did not represent the only formal educational influences that molded the future community activist. As mentioned, Eartha during the 1880s increasingly spent time in the North, particularly during and after 1888. Consequently, she received a significant portion of her secondary education in New York. There, she attended schools that specialized in musical training (the National Conservatory of Music) and cosmetology (Madam Hall Beauty School). The musical training proved particularly important for her, as it paved the way to a burgeoning career on the stage. A lyric soprano, she joined in the 1890s a performing group called the Oriental American Opera Company managed by Jacksonville native John Rosemond Johnson, brother to James Weldon Johnson. The company broke new ground as the first African American company to perform light opera as well as popular tunes. Eartha debuted with the company at the Palmer Theater on Broadway in New York City in 1896. She then toured with it through a variety of locales in the United States and Europe.[12]

During this time, as Eartha passed her twentieth birthday, she fell in love and soon planned to marry. Her fiancé was James Lloyd Jordan of South Carolina, a railroad employee. The couple scheduled the nuptials for June 1896 in Jacksonville. Meanwhile, Eartha traveled with the Oriental American Opera Company and they communicated by letter. The romance, though, ended in tragedy. Jordan grew ill, likely with tuberculosis. He died in May 1896 with Eartha yet performing with her company. The event seems to have worked a lasting influence on the young woman. After the death of her fiancé, she opted to return to Jacksonville and alter the course of her life. Her new path turned her first to teaching and business ventures and finally to her life work in philanthropy.[13]

White commenced this new course by supplementing her education. First, she enrolled in the Florida Baptist Academy, a school founded by Jacksonville's

Figure 24. Eartha M. M. White (bottom row, second woman from left) as a member of the Oriental American Opera Company, 1892. (Courtesy of Eartha White Collection, Thomas G. Carpenter Library, University of North Florida.)

influential Bethel Baptist Church. Later, she again attended Stanton, probably because by then it offered teacher training (or normal) instruction. Besides its curriculum, Stanton may have enticed Eartha from personal and professional connections. Before 1896 James Weldon Johnson had graduated from Atlanta University and returned to Jacksonville to assume the position of Stanton principal, for reasons including that his mother Helen Dillet Johnson once had taught there. Under his supervision the school added more advanced grades, eventually becoming the first public school to provide secondary (high school) instruction for African Americans in North Florida. John Rosemond Johnson meanwhile also had returned to the city to work as music director of Bethel Baptist Church and the Florida Baptist Academy.[14]

While completing her education Eartha witnessed long-lasting changes then underway in Florida and the South that touched the African American community deeply. Where black men previously had served in political offices at municipal, county, and state levels, by the early 1890s a Democratic legislature had chipped away at the underpinnings of black political strength. The 1889 imposition of a poll tax as a prerequisite for voter registration dealt a particularly harsh blow. These actions left no African Americans in the state legislature and black councilmen in office in only a handful of the state's larger towns, most of which now saw only a single black official serving at a time. Meanwhile Jim Crow racial discrimination and segregation advanced seemingly everywhere. Citizenship rights promised to black people by the Thirteenth, Fourteenth, and Fifteenth Amendments to the U.S. Constitution were being curtailed severely, particularly in southern states such as Florida. The federal courts, upon whom black citizens depended for protection, essentially abandoned the field. In the infamous *Plessy v. Ferguson* decision in 1896, the U.S. Supreme Court voiced its willingness to condone these local and state actions. This decision endorsed the "separate but equal" principle, an oxymoron as proved by the progress of history during the first half of the twentieth century.[15]

At Jacksonville black politicians generally faced increasing roadblocks to elective and appointive positions and—by the end of the twentieth century's first decade—had been removed from office altogether, save for a handful of federal appointees who survived only to 1913. George Eugene Ross, for example, was the last black man to serve on the Jacksonville city council, holding his seat from 1901 until 1907. Sixty years passed thereafter before African Americans again would be elected to the city government. Interestingly, two of the first three African Americans elected to the city council in 1967, after the six-decade hiatus—Mary Singleton and Sallye B. Mathis—were women. Since Eartha White had played—as will be seen—such an important role in promoting the participation of black women in Jacksonville politics during the preceding decades, she obviously deserves a substantial measure of the credit.[16]

Years passed after White's return to Jacksonville before she could engage in political activism and direction, and the events of that period demand our attention first. Eartha may have embarked on a teaching career even before her graduation from Stanton. She commenced instruction of children in 1896, founding a school in the small hamlet of Bayard near Jacksonville. White had learned at Stanton that educational facilities for African Americans, particularly in small towns and rural areas, were appallingly inadequate and that, accordingly, teachers were required to be particularly resourceful. Eartha rose to the challenge. She acquired property by gift from Bartolo Genovar of St. Augustine upon which she built a school. She then arranged for the donation of needed supplies. Thus sheltered and otherwise provided for, she taught at her rural school until near the century's close. Meanwhile she further evidenced her caring nature through nursing sick soldiers brought to Florida as a result of the Spanish-American War of 1898. By then she had learned that she could make a difference.[17]

A growing reputation as a teacher then led White back to the Stanton Institute as the twentieth century dawned. The move represented a promotion as well as recognition of her abilities. The school, under James Weldon Johnson's guidance, had progressed markedly, boasting a faculty of "twenty or more" teachers. A surviving account from those years suggests its importance. "Stanton stands dear to the hearts of Jacksonville's entire colored population," the account observed. "It is the literary birthplace of thousands of those who bear the distinction of not being illiterate, as well as of many who have won higher distinction as being successful pursuers after higher learning, and who are today found holding their own in the professional business and social world." Tragically, Jacksonville's Great Fire of May 3, 1901, destroyed the venerable institution. Johnson subsequently led efforts for its reconstruction and reopening by February 1902. "The opening of this school will bring true happiness to hundreds of homes in the city," observed a local newspaperman. In the new school Eartha labored successfully, sensitively molding young minds and hearts for more than a decade.[18]

Even while teaching Eartha found time for additional exercise of her talents, and the venue she chose involved the founding of a business that would aid the African American community. Specifically, in 1901 she accepted a position as clerk of the newly formed Afro-American Industrial and Benefit Association, the predecessor of the Afro-American Life Insurance Company. Chartered on April 1, 1901, the concern had grown out of a suggestion made by the Reverend J. Milton Waldron of the Bethel Baptist Church. At his behest, seven men met at the church parsonage "on a bleak wintry night of January 14" to discuss "the unhealthy surroundings, the presence of poverty and the absence of adequate relief in times of dire distress" among African Americans. A history of the company noted that the men "discussed prayerfully among themselves ways and means of alleviating the suffering, giving care and treatment to the sick and providing for the respectable burial of the dead." Establishment of a burial fund for African Americans represented its first initiative. From this small beginning the fund evolved into the first insurance company started in Florida by African Americans. Ultimately, the Afro-American Insurance Company became one of the most successful black businesses in the region, employing hundreds of agents in Florida and beyond. It also produced one of the first African American millionaires in the state, Abraham Lincoln "A. L." Lewis. He, in turn, would play an important role in the life and career of Eartha White.[19]

Eartha's personal and professional ties to A. L. Lewis may have begun prior to the Afro-American Industrial and Benefit Association's foundation, and they also may have led her to an early acquaintance with an influential national leader. In 1900, the year before the company was founded, Lewis attended the first meeting of the National Negro Business League in Boston. According to White's biographer Carmen Godwin, Eartha accompanied Lewis. Reportedly the only woman present, she met with Booker T. Washington, head of the new organization. Godwin states, "Washington served as a major figure of inspiration to White and she would emulate his philosophy of social and moral uplift of the black race." Eartha's subsequent contributions provided ample evidence to support this assertion. Her life was filled with activities to improve the material conditions and the general political and social status of African Americans.[20]

Already imbued with Washington's spirit and drive in 1901, Eartha literally may have saved the Afro-American Industrial and Benefit Association from collapse soon after its founding, displaying thereby integrity, loyalty, and personal courage of the first order. In May 1901 as Jacksonville's Great Fire consumed most of the city, including association's offices, "Miss Eartha M. M. White, who was Clerk in the Home Office at that time, made a daring entry into the Home Office, and with courageous bravery salvaged from the flames such as she could gather of the books and records of the Company," a company historian related. "This act of heroism saved to the Company the only valuable books of records of the Home Office, the loss of which without this daring service would have been an irreparable loss." Its records intact thanks to White, the association prospered as Jacksonville rebuilt. "The Afro-American Benefit Association is fast becoming the favorite institution of its kind in the city and State," a local man noted in December 1903. Two years later it could claim credit for having actually become "the favorite institution of its kind in the city and State." As a Jacksonville newspaper explained in September 1905, "The Afro-American Industrial and Benefit Association was organized five years ago by colored men. Wonderful progress has been made since then. . . . At present there are fifty branches of this association in Florida, and new ones are being established each week. The people are heartily co-operating with the plan first inaugurated by the founders."[21]

Using the Jacksonville connections she had forged by the early 1900s, Eartha could begin to involve herself directly with those most in need. As she embarked on her long career of philanthropy and political activism, though, the racial climate continued to harden. As Jacksonville was becoming a New South city, characterized by impressive economic and political growth and overall progress for whites, the Jim Crow system meanwhile meant greater disfranchisement of and discrimination against black residents. As this process advanced, disenchantment followed. By the early 1900s, for instance, James Weldon Johnson would describe the city as a "100% cracker town." The Johnson brothers and future labor and civil rights leader A. Philip Randolph, among others, left during this period. They became part of the first Great Migration of African Americans northward from the South.[22]

Racial segregation accompanied racial discrimination, enhancing the frustration of African Americans such as Eartha White. To cite one example, the year the Afro-American Industrial and Benefit Association was founded also saw the Jacksonville city council enact its first ordinance mandating racial segregation on the city's main form of public transportation, the trolleys. African Americans protested by boycotting the streetcars, filing litigation, and establishing a competitive streetcar line. These actions were initially successful, resulting in some delay of comprehensive enforcement, but proved soon enough to be of no avail. Legally enforced racial segregation prevailed by mid-decade. This represented the first of many restrictions that resulted from the separate but unequal system of segregation that would make Jacksonville a typical Jim Crow–era southern city.[23]

Still, frustrations and resentments over discrimination and segregation paled as a concern for Eartha and many others as maintenance of the "southern way of life" brought patterns and sometimes waves of racial violence. Florida surprisingly led the way, experiencing more lynchings per capita from the mid-1880s through the mid-1930s than any other state. Reverberations followed within the African American community. James Weldon Johnson's departure from Jacksonville, for example, was hastened in 1901 after a white mob nearly killed him. Also illustrating the point, in 1912 Booker T. Washington visited the city as part of a statewide tour to promote the Negro Business League. During that time Jacksonville endured turbulence because of the lynching of two black men, and the Tuskegee educator heard over his own voice "the howl of the mob." Washington, thought by many to have accommodated himself to the era's white supremacist policies, denounced these murders. Just a few years afterward, Jacksonvillians founded their first chapter of the National Association for the Advancement of Colored People (NAACP) in part as a protest against the mounting racial violence in the city.[24]

Women, including Eartha, may have particularly feared the explosive and potentially deadly impact of this climate. Early NAACP leaders, especially female leaders, reacted in alarm to the fact that white government officials condoned racial hatred and violence. Margaret McCleary, the Jacksonville branch secretary and a person well known to Eartha, reflected this outlook as it touched upon women. "The white women down here are forming a 'home guard,'" she wrote. "They are to learn to shoot and protect themselves, presumably against

'Negros.'" She continued, "[Governor Sidney J.] Catts wrote one of the women giving permission to form a home guard. He said it was very necessary for white women to learn how to shoot and defend themselves, for as they already know such, the brutal assault by the 'Negro fiend.'" McCleary concluded, "So with white women and men armed, our chances of life and liberty are very poor."[25]

In this era of racial violence and discrimination, Eartha White carved out a unique position as a community activist through accomplishing an extraordinary volume of community service and by astute political maneuvering. The Great Fire of 1901 first called her to action after city officials stalled in providing desperately needed services for African Americans. White and other black leaders accordingly mobilized to help members of their community begin recovery and rebuilding. Soon after the conflagration Eartha attended a meeting at her church, Bethel Baptist, intended as a forum for discussion of the revitalization of the Union Benevolent Association, a group originally formed in 1875 to provide assistance for indigent African Americans. As it turned out, Eartha and her mother, Clara, led the revitalization effort by raising funds to build a senior citizens' shelter. Called the Colored Old Folks Home, it opened in 1902. Eartha White served as its president and chief fund-raiser.[26]

From her position at the Old Folks Home, White then helped to organize the City Federation of Women's Clubs to provide a united front in addressing critical problems. Historian James Crooks observed that "by 1916 [the federation] comprised sixteen groups" including the colored Young Women's Christian Association, the Brooklyn Improvement Club (an organization addressing the need of a predominantly African American community in the city), the J. H. Blodgett Improvement Club (named in honor of the prominent African American businessman Joseph H. Blodgett), the Colored Old Folks Home, and the Mary E. Smith Club (organized in 1896 as the Afro-American Woman's Club and named subsequently after the group's founder). The City Federation of Women's Clubs, similar to a white organization named the Woman's Club of Jacksonville, "had departments concerned with the condition of young women, children, health and hygiene, domestic science, the social sciences, business, education, temperance, juvenile courts, art, music, religion, literature and suffrage." It helped to establish or facilitate "the first playground, 'Wilder Park,' in the black community, improvements for the county jail, particularly for black men and women," the first social worker in the black community, and two school nurses for black schools.[27]

The City Federation of Women's Clubs, reflecting Eartha's principles and orientation, also cooperated with the white women's clubs. May Mann Jennings, wife of former Governor William S. Jennings, characterized during World War

I the cooperation forged between the two races: "We are on friendly terms with the colored people of this city and will try in every way to assist the colored women all over the state. . . . I think wherever there is better understanding there is better co-operation," she continued. "There has never been a time in the history of the world when the organized efforts of womanhood counted for so much as now." Jennings especially recognized White's contributions: "She is an exceedingly bright and energetic woman, and seems never to be weary in well doing." She added, "The people of Jacksonville owe her a great deal more than they realize."[28]

White's horizons quickly expanded from the local to the state level. Particularly, in 1908 she assisted in the organization of the State Federation of Colored Women at a St. Augustine gathering. Soon that assembly had endorsed a direction for its labors that must have pleased White tremendously. "The building of a home for delinquent girls has been decided upon as the special work to be accomplished by the State Federation of Colored Women," an account of its 1911 annual meeting proclaimed. Meanwhile, in 1910 the Jacksonville Woman's Club "sparked the formation of Associated Charities which included African American women." Eartha became the first African American "friendly visitor" who assisted needy people in the black community. Her cooperative interaction with white clubwomen again mirrored the manner in which she operated for the rest of her life.[29]

Women's activism evolved for Eartha into women's political activism, an understanding of which requires a very brief look at Florida's experience. White women's participation in Florida partisan politics arose in good part as a reaction to the enfranchisement of African American men. In contrast, involvement by black women came as a response to obstacles to black men's involvement in local and state politics. Even then, women's political activism touched the Florida region later than some other parts of the country. Southern white women came late to the suffrage movement due in part to the extreme conservatism of the region, including in gender politics, and in part to the association of the women's rights movement with the abolitionist campaign. Not surprisingly, the first women's rights convention in the South did not take place until nearly four decades after the women's movement began.[30]

Moreover, the woman's suffrage movement among white women from the beginning was tinged with racism. Tampa's Ella C. Chamberlain, who organized and presided over Florida's first woman's suffrage group, reflected this outlook: "I am a free-born American woman. . . . I deny that my brother can properly represent me." Chamberlain added, "How can I, with the blood of heroes in my heart, and with the free and independent spirit they bequeathed me, quietly submit to representation by the alien and the Negro?"[31]

Even this racist orientation aimed at ensuring white supremacy did not warm most southern white men to the woman's suffrage movement. Initially, the men discouraged white women from striving for the vote. Eartha's congressman, Frank Clark, manifested this attitude. He helped lead opposition to woman's suffrage, supporting his position on biblical grounds. Clark maintained "that this whole woman suffrage movement was dominated by a socialist Negro radical element that aimed at overturning the United States." Consequently, the congressman concluded that woman's suffrage would "let an avalanche of Negro votes, destroy the American home, pull [white] women down from the high and honored social position and soil her noble character with the filth of masculine politics." In the face of such opposition, woman's suffrage activity in Florida waned within several years after its birth in the early 1890s; between 1897 and 1912 it lay mostly dormant. By the early 1900s a few woman's enfranchisement clubs were however active in Duval County. The first, the Florida Equal Franchise League, was organized in January 1912. The members avoided using the term *suffrage* because of the intensity of feelings against women obtaining the vote.[32]

Opposition to woman's suffrage persisted despite the rebirth of some organized support, and Florida's legislative leadership continued to reflect that position into the second half of the twentieth century. Increasingly malapportioned and dominated by conservative—and usually white-supremacist—politicians living in North Florida (as opposed to the somewhat more moderate leaders resident in the peninsula), the legislature balked, despite the efforts of a small number of women activists, at supporting approval of the Nineteenth Amendment during the 1910s and afterward. Even though the state would dispatch a woman to the U.S. House of Representatives from a peninsular district in 1928, legislative resistance continued unabated. Not until 1969, during the second wave of feminism (jump-started, like the first stage, by the black rights movement), did Florida's solons symbolically vote to approve the woman's suffrage amendment.[33]

When white women ultimately began to vote and organize politically, they did so on a segregated basis and made clear their intention to support white supremacy based on Democratic Party power that had become institutionalized by the early twentieth century. White women were encouraged to vote to increase the rolls of white voters. The goal of the first League of Women Voters in the area, the League of Democratic Women, was "to further the education of all white women in citizenship to support needed legislation." Moreover the league vowed to leave "no stone unturned to preserve white supremacy."[34]

Meanwhile, in order to support a drastically reduced cadre of black male electors, African American women in the South and nationwide actively participated in the woman's suffrage campaign. While African American women in the North criticized northern feminists for the growing racism of the woman's suffrage movement, southern black activists condemned the racism of the region while accommodating to the hardening racial climate supported by state and national laws and policies. Ultimately, black women suffragists and voters in the South, like their northern counterparts, formed their own separate organizations.[35]

As can be illustrated by the careers of Eartha White and her contemporary Mary McLeod Bethune, black women sometimes followed different paths to the same goal. Historian Maxine Jones compared the political styles and contributions of African American activist women in late-nineteenth- and early-twentieth-century Florida. "Mary McLeod Bethune championed social justice and sought to remove the barriers that prevented Florida's African Americans from participating as full citizens," Jones observed. "She frequently spoke out against lynching, barriers to voting, insufficient funding for public education," and she denounced all forms of discrimination and racial injustice. On the other hand, Bethune, "maintained that interracial cooperation at all levels was essential for improvement in race relations and she facilitated interracial interaction whenever she could."[36]

Jones saw White somewhat differently. "Eartha White accomplished much in meeting the needs of the black community with a leadership style quite different from that of Bethune." White adhered to Booker T. Washington's philosophy: although she "sought to dismantle racism and discrimination, she was not outspoken and did not vocally challenge the system." White "used her influence with Jacksonville's powerful whites and policy makers to achieve for blacks those opportunities and services that they were denied." In furthering these efforts, she "established a network of supporters across the state." Jones qualified however that "although cautious, White was not necessarily accommodating." Jones concluded Eartha was unique in that "she was active in politics at a time [early twentieth century] when race and gender kept thousands from voting in Florida."[37]

While Jones captured the essence of White's style, Eartha in fact acted in a multidirectional, if not multidimensional, manner. As African American men were being pushed out of effective participation in partisan politics, black people responded in a number of ways. Some organized or revitalized political associations, such as the Republican clubs that had been started in the period after passage of the Reconstruction acts in 1867. Others involved themselves in civil rights organizations and activities. More than a few concentrated on economics. Eartha White did all of these.[38]

By the turn of the twentieth century, as access to the polls increasingly was denied to people of color in Florida and racial violence had touched most of the state, White devised a political modus operandi that, as Jones suggested, combined Booker T. Washington's example of stressing moderation and cooperation with whites with self-help and collective activity to protect blacks' lives and secure their rights—with her own unique perspectives. One important expression of this position involved the Colored Citizens' Protective League, which White helped to establish in 1900. Later and among other things, she joined with southern black women as well as whites to denounce lynching.[39]

These efforts evolved out of Eartha's work as a clubwoman. The early years of the century had seen clubs, committees, and organizations proliferate, and World War I escalated their level of activity. For example the Council of National Defense established a Woman's Committee in response to women's desire to contribute to the war effort. That committee, in turn, employed Alice Dunbar Nelson to engage southern black women. Florida was one of few southern states to receive Nelson, who gained favorable impressions of the state's women, particularly Eartha White. After a 1918 visit Nelson concluded, "Florida is so well organized I told them they hardly need me at all." That August—shortly after her participation as the only "colored delegate" at the Committee of the Council of National Defense in Washington, D.C.—White received appointment as chairwoman of Florida's black women's department.[40]

One key to White's success was the effective and productive relations she formed with receptive whites, without compromising her principles. May Mann Jennings recorded her pleasure in working with Eartha during the war. "I am exceedingly interested in the war work among the Negro women of Florida," she declared in 1918, "and I have a great deal of pleasure in cooperating with Eartha M. M. White, president of the City Federation of Jacksonville." At the same time Eartha continued to work actively with the Republican Club of Jacksonville, which she helped to organize in 1918 before women gained the vote. Biographer Godwin goes so far as to describe White as "an ardent Republican." Eartha also championed the use of the vote by women once they acquired this right. Having early labored as an active precinct worker, she also earned recognition for her leadership and hard work as head of the Negro Republican Women Voters. This organization, formed in 1920, permitted expression of partisan differences as well as responses to the deliberate exclusion of black women from organizations such as the Democratic League of Women Voters. These activities placed White in the forefront of the state's woman's rights and African American rights movements. "The Duval County Republican Party passed a resolution thanking Eartha," Godwin noted, "who they referred to as 'the energetic faithful committee representative, leader of the Colored Women Voters.'"[41]

By the time black women could vote, the harassment of black men at the polls had become common in Jacksonville; yet, the poll tax and other laws that restricted black political participation did not apply to women. Therefore, African American women saw the election of 1920 as an opportunity to increase the rolls of black voters and make the black vote count. They also believed that officials would be less likely to harm black women voters. The local NAACP, in the meantime, encouraged black men "to back the colored women up and stand together to defy the throng" of whites.[42]

After the Nineteenth Amendment to the Constitution was ratified, many white southern males continued to discourage white women from voting. For example on August 28, 1920, a Jacksonville newspaper editor declared, "The women have been enfranchised and many of the white women, we think probably the majority of white women of Florida, did not wish the ballot." He went on to speculate, "A large number of these will probably show their disgust not only by remaining away from the polls, but also [by] refusing to qualify as voters." Despite such disparaging remarks about white women's attitudes toward suffrage, the white community urged white women to vote for the Democratic Party to outweigh the black female vote. "We are confident," the editor closed, "that no such reluctance to vote will be found among the negro women."[43]

Other factors besides public opinion worked against the black female vote. To further discourage black voters of both genders, white men across the South revived the Ku Klux Klan (weakly reborn in 1915 at Stone Mountain, Georgia). In October 1920 this phenomenon struck Eartha's home ground. Despite a protest from the NAACP to the sheriff and mayor of Jacksonville, the Klan marched in the city. Blacks turned out as well and shouted at the Klansmen. Fortunately, no serious physical violence occurred that day.[44]

Election day 1920 brought Eartha physically and defiantly to the forefront in the face of such opposition. Election officials tried one final tactic to prevent black women from voting, by decreeing that those desirous of casting a ballot must wait in line until all the white women had voted. To keep them in the voting lines, Earth White organized a lemonade brigade and otherwise strove to maximize voting strength. On that first day, African American women exercising their elective franchise numbered in the thousands. The election produced relatively few Republican votes, however, allowing the Democrats handily to "win" the 1920 elections in the city and the South generally. Still, the Republicans won the national election and began the Republican domination of the presidency until the election of Franklin Delano Roosevelt in 1932.[45]

In spite of the disappointing result of their first experience as voters, black women leaders in Jacksonville and the South, Eartha among them, generally continued to conduct voter registration drives and otherwise encourage voting. Godwin cites a 1928 letter to Nannie Helen Burroughs, president of the National Association of Colored Women, in which White expressly reiterates her commitment to continue the struggle for black votes despite Jim Crow legislation and poll taxes. "I am interested as ever, doing all I can for the cause," she wrote. "I have organized throughout the State groups known as committee men and women to see that people register and pay their poll taxes." By that year Eartha chaired the National League of Republican Colored Women. Her contributions to the party's success in the 1928 presidential election—which had included Herbert Hoover's breaking of the "Solid South" by taking five southern states, including Florida—were acknowledged on November 23, 1928, by the Republican National Committee. "We have indeed won a tremendous victory," they informed her, identifying her as a key player in producing votes, "and under the sound business leadership of Mr. Hoover will understandably show marked progress during the next decade."[46]

The nature of White's relationships with other political figures offers helpful insights. Although a highly visible Republican, partisanship did not preclude her from forming positive and productive relations with Democrats, relations that bore fruit. For example, during both world wars Eartha engaged in extensive work with the Red Cross to aid soldiers and their families. During World War I she served in several capacities, including as director of War Camp Community Services and as recreation coordinator for soldiers in Savannah, Georgia. Additionally, she formed a local baseball team to entertain the troops. These activities, which required an ability to collaborate across the color line, were vitally important. "She was . . . the only woman to participate in the Southeast War Camp Community Service held in Jacksonville," her biographer Godwin observed, "and the only African American invited by President Woodrow Wilson to attend a White House meeting of the Council of National Defense (a planning body set up in 1916 to deal with industrial mobilization)."[47]

White continued to undertake cooperative activities across the color line as World War II commenced, but she likely no longer did so as a Republican.

During the Great Depression of the 1930s she had joined a growing number of African Americans who began either to turn toward the Democrats or else to regard them in a far more positive light than previously. This resulted largely from national developments, particularly the actions of President Franklin D. Roosevelt's wife, Eleanor Roosevelt. Eartha's relationship with Mary McLeod Bethune probably facilitated her personal involvements with Mrs. Roosevelt. By the 1930s Bethune had come to be regarded as a key African American leader, particularly by influential whites such as the Roosevelts. Meanwhile Bethune had continued to associate closely with her longtime friend and colleague Eartha White. Likely due to Bethune's influence as well as White's own national prominence, the Clara White Mission, a Jacksonville charitable enterprise started by White, became a major headquarters of New Deal programs. The "mission served as the African American community's center of relief," a historian commented, "and was the Works Progress Administration (WPA) office of employment and cultural operations."[48]

Many consider the Clara White Mission as White's most important and enduring contribution to the Jacksonville community. Some have even likened it to Chicago's famous Hull House. Her work in this area began in the early 1920s, soon after the death of her mother, Clara. Ultimately, she located the mission in an area infamous as a center of vice and crime. "Ashley Street," because of the mission's presence, in time transformed itself into a "symbol of hope." The resources of the WPA during the New Deal particularly helped Eartha to fulfill her personal mission of "finding employment and helping people to better themselves through training programs." The mission offered a number of services, including a free employment agency, a writers' project, a sewing room to employ women, a training program for domestic service, and a training shop for blind people that provided instruction in Braille, basket and cane chair weaving, and beadwork. Many of these activities continued beyond the end of the WPA and became the basis of a wide range of services and resources that the mission offers to the present day.[49]

Another level of personal and political commitment led White to further engagement in partisan politics and more extensive relations with political leaders, involvements that would last to her life's end. This concerned her relationship with the NAACP, an organization that she strongly advocated from its inception. A chapter of the civil rights organization was organized at Jacksonville in 1917, one of the first such chapters in Florida and, for that matter, in the South. White worked closely over the decades that followed with Simuel S. McGill, an attorney and leading civil rights activist, in its activities. McGill played an important role for the NAACP as lead counsel in major Florida court cases. His most controversial case involved African American men accused of murdering an elderly white man in the 1930s. After several difficult years McGill won his case when, in 1940, the U.S. Supreme Court in *Chambers et al. v. Florida* banned police violence against an accused. Justice Hugo Black found for the majority that police techniques that "fill[ed] the petitioners with terror and frightful misgivings" ranked tantamount to torture. An extant photo of White and McGill with one of the defendants literally illustrates her support of this brand of political activism.[50]

White also actively supported another longtime friend who grew to national prominence in the 1920s and 1930s, labor organizer and civil rights activist A. Philip Randolph, who had grown up in Jacksonville. In particular, she helped him to plan his proposed March on Washington in 1941 protesting discriminatory treatment against African Americans by the U.S. government. President Roosevelt's actions forestalled the march, but the threat of it prompted the president to issue Executive Order 8802 prohibiting discrimination in federal employment. In 1963, when the famous March on Washington did take place, eighty-seven-year-old Eartha was on hand to applaud her friend and colleague Randolph, who served as the grand marshal of the momentous event.[51]

As the civil rights movement evolved in the 1940s and 1950s, White continued to contribute toward black empowerment. In 1958, for example, she helped to combat one notorious method of disfranchisement by distributing a list of possible "Jim Crow" questions to black voters to help them pass the "literacy requirements" of the local voter registration office. Meanwhile, she continued her efforts to promote the role of women in political life. A significant vehicle for these actions was the League of Women Voters, a Jacksonville chapter of which had organized in 1943. Eartha White became one of the first black women to join this group, which promoted registration of black voters. One major obstacle to black voting was removed in 1946 when—thanks to a lawsuit filed by Daniel W. Perkins, a Jacksonville African American attorney and friend of Eartha's—Florida found itself forced to overturn its Democratic Party whites-only primary system. Because of this system African Americans had not been allowed to vote in the primary elections that, in a one-party state, essentially decided who was to serve in office. Subsequently, more African Americans began to register as Democrats.

Eartha White's party affiliation at that time is not known with certainty, but it is safe to speculate that she had become a Democrat. Certainly, she worked during the last decades of her life with Democratic political leaders. One local Democratic politician who became a particular supporter of White's was Florida congressman and Jacksonville native Charles Bennett. In the 1960s when White undertook the last major project of her life, the Eartha M. White Nursing Home, Bennett played a major role in getting state approval of project funding. She learned of the award through a letter from him. In addition, he demonstrated his esteem and admiration by including a sketch of her life in a book he authored.[52]

Although perhaps the most important, Charles Bennett was not the only white politician who eventually acknowledged White's contributions. In time she received accolades from a broad spectrum of leaders, from Jacksonville Mayors Hayden Burns, who took a hard line enforcing the laws of segregation in the early 1960s, to Hans Tanzler, who was the first to work with black council members and who exercised strong leadership in promoting positive race relations as the city struggled to desegregate. The ultimate accolade from a politician came at a White House reception during the Richard Nixon administration in 1970. There, ninety-four-year-old Eartha White received the Lane Bryant Award for Volunteer Service in recognition of "outstanding community service performed in 1968." In fundamental respects, however, it offered a concrete symbol of a life spanning nearly a century spent in service to others.[53]

Eartha Mary Magdalene White passed away at Jacksonville on January 18, 1974, and was buried by grieving friends, loved ones, and admirers at the city's historic Old City Cemetery. She had stood at the forefront of the woman's suffrage and civil rights movements. She had shown courage as well as dedication to the interests of others. She had persevered against the odds and created enduring legacies, using political involvement as a vehicle for her philanthropy. She had offered a model for Florida women of all colors. She had challenged and had inspired. From modest beginnings, she had risen to change her world.

Notes

1. Quotation from Daniel Schafer, "Eartha M. M. White: The Early Years of a Jacksonville Humanitarian," 6 (typescript at Special Collections Department, University of North Florida Library, Jacksonville) (hereafter, UNF Special Collections). The principal available sources on Eartha Mary Magdalene White include Carmen Godwin, "'To Serve God and Humanity': Jacksonville's Eartha Mary Magdalene White (1876–1974)" (master's thesis, University of Florida, 2001); E. Lynne Wright, *More Than Petticoats: Remarkable Florida Women* (Guilford, Conn., 2001), 54–63; E. Murrell Dawson, "Faith-Filled Legacies: Four Twentieth Century African American Women Who Helped Forge Florida's Future," in *Go Sound the Trumpet! Selections in Florida's African American History*, ed. David H. Jackson Jr. and Canter Brown Jr. (Tampa, 2005), 232–35; Maxine D. Jones and Kevin M. McCarthy, *African Americans in Florida* (Sarasota, 1993), 72–74.

2. Eartha Mary Magdalene White family Bible, White Papers, UNF Special Collections; Schafer, "Eartha M. M. White," 3; Eartha M. M. White death certification, Florida Bureau of Vital Statistics, Jacksonville; William Gladstone, *Men of Color* (Gettysburg, Pa., 1993), 198, 213. On the settlement of black Union soldiers in and near Jacksonville, see Patricia L. Kenney, "LaVilla, Florida, 1866–1887: Reconstruction Dreams and the Formation of a Black Community," in *The African American Heritage of Florida*, ed. David R. Colburn and Jane L. Landers (Gainesville, 1995), 185–206.

3. *Makers of America: An Historical and Biographical Work by an Able Corps of Writers*, vol. 2 (Atlanta, 1909), 332–37; 1870 U.S. Decennial Census, Gadsden County, Florida (population schedule); 1880 U.S. Decennial Census, Duval County, Florida (population schedule); *Webb's Jacksonville Directory, 1876–7* (New York, 1876), 132; *Webb's Jacksonville Directory, 1878–9* (New York, 1878), 148.

4. Schafer, "Eartha M. M. White," 3–11; 1870 U.S. Decennial Census, Duval County, Florida (population schedule); 1880 U.S. Decennial Census, Duval County, Florida (population schedule). Biographer Carmen Godwin states her belief that the story of Bertha White was a "fabrication" because Eartha never mentioned it. Godwin, "'To Serve God and Humanity,'" 7.

5. Schafer, "Eartha M. M. White," 7; Godwin, "'To Serve God and Humanity,'" 7.

6. Schafer, "Eartha M. M. White," 7; Godwin, "'To Serve God and Humanity,'" 7.

7. Canter Brown Jr., *Ossian Bingley Hart, Florida's Loyalist Reconstruction Governor* (Baton Rouge, 1997), 174; idem, "Bishop Payne and Resistance to Jim Crow in Florida During the 1880s," *Northeast Florida History* 2 (1994): 23–39; Kenney, "LaVilla," 185–206; Larry Eugene Rivers and Canter Brown Jr., *Laborers in the Vineyard of the Lord: The Beginnings of the AME Church in Florida, 1865–1895* (Gainesville, 2001), 125, 130; Rivers and Brown, "'The Art of Gathering a Crowd': Florida's Pat Chappelle and the Origins of Black-Owned Vaudeville," *Journal of African American History* 92 (Spring 2007): 169–76.

8. *New York Age*, May 10, 1890; *Cleveland Gazette*, July 13, 1895. See also Barbara Ann Richardson, "A History of Blacks in Jacksonville, Florida, 1860–1895" (D.A. diss., Carnegie-Mellon University, 1975).

9. T. Frederick Davis, *History of Jacksonville, Florida, and Vicinity, 1513–1924* (St. Augustine, 1925; reprint ed., Jacksonville, 1990), 487–88; James Weldon Johnson, *Along This Way: The Autobiography of James Weldon Johnson* (New York, 1933), 16.

10. Edward A. Mueller, *First Coast Steamboat Days* (Jacksonville, 2005); Schafer, "Eartha M. M. White," 11–13.

11. Larry Eugene Rivers and Canter Brown Jr., "A Monument to the Progress of the Race: The Intellectual and Political Origins of the Florida Agricultural and Mechanical University, 1865–1887," *Florida Historical Quarterly* 85 (Summer 2006): 5–9, 24; Johnson, *Along This Way*, 61; John T. Foster Jr. and Sarah Whitmer Foster, "The Last Shall Be First: Northern Methodists in Reconstruction Jacksonville," *Florida Historical Quarterly* 70 (January 1992): 267, 271–72, 274–79. For more on black education in postbellum Florida and the institutions specifically cited, see Laura Wallis Wakefield,

"'Set a Light in a Dark Place': Teachers of Freedmen in Florida, 1864–1874," *Florida Historical Quarterly* 81 (Spring 2003): 401–17; Murray D. Laurie, "The Union Academy: A Freedmen's Bureau School in Gainesville, Florida," *Florida Historical Quarterly* 65 (October 1986): 163–74; E. Bruce Rose, "The Influence of the Peabody Fund on Education in Reconstruction Florida," *Florida Historical Quarterly* 55 (January 1977): 310–20; John T. Foster Jr. and Sarah Whitmer Foster, "Aid Societies Were Not Alike: Northern Teachers in Post Civil War Florida," *Florida Historical Quarterly* 73 (January 1995): 308–24; Sarah Whitmer Foster and John T. Foster Jr., "Chloe Merrick Reed: Freedom's First Lady," *Florida Historical Quarterly* 71 (January 1993), 279–99; Gerald Schwartz, "An Integrated Free School in Civil War Florida," *Florida Historical Quarterly* 61 (October 1982): 155–61; Audrey Thomas McCluskey, "Ringing Up a School: Mary McLeod Bethune's Impact on Daytona," *Florida Historical Quarterly* 73 (October 1994): 200–17.

12. Wright, *More Than Petticoats*, 57–58; on John Rosemond Johnson's career and the history of African Americans generally in American music, see Eileen Southern, *The Music of Black Americans: A History*, 3rd ed. (New York, 1997); Henry T. Sampson, *The Ghost Walks: A Chronological History of Blacks in Show Business, 1865–1910* (Metuchen, N.J., 1988). On Florida's and Jacksonville's roles in producing pioneers of African American entertainment, see Rivers and Brown, "Art of Gathering a Crowd," 169–90.

13. Schafer, "Eartha M. M. White," 15; Godwin, "'To Serve God and Humanity,'" 12.

14. Schafer, "Eartha M. M. White," 18; George Patterson McKinney Sr. and Richard I. McKinney, *History of the Black Baptists of Florida, 1850–1985* (Miami, 1987), 107–11; *Jacksonville Evening Telegram*, March 24, October 13, and October 20, 1892, October 5, 1893; Johnson, *Along This Way*, 121–22, 125–30. Florida Baptist Academy relocated in 1918 from Jacksonville to St. Augustine, where it became the Florida Normal and Industrial College in 1944. That year it was moved to Miami where, in 1950, it received its current name, Florida Memorial College. McKinney and McKinney, *History of the Black Baptists*, 145–50.

15. Canter Brown Jr., *Florida's Black Public Officials, 1867–1924* (Tuscaloosa, 1998), 54–69. On the *Plessy v. Ferguson* decision and its implications see, among others, Keith W. Medley, *We As Freemen: Plessy v. Ferguson* (Gretna, La., 2003); Harvey Fireside, *Separate and Unequal: Homer Plessy and the Supreme Court Decision That Legalized Racism* (New York, 2004). On the challenges faced by African Americans in Florida in the post-Reconstruction era see also Arnold Marc Pavlovsky, "'We Busted Because We Failed': Florida Politics, 1880–1908" (Ph.D. diss., Princeton University, 1973); Jerrell H. Shofner, "Custom, Law and History: The Enduring Influence of Florida's Black Codes," *Florida Historical Quarterly* 55 (January 1977): 277–98; Wali R. Kharif, "Black Reaction to Segregation and Discrimination in Post-Reconstruction Florida," *Florida Historical Quarterly* 64 (October 1985): 161–73.

16. Brown, *Florida's Black Public Officials*, 121, 155; Edward N. Akin, "When a Minority Becomes the Majority: Blacks in Jacksonville Politics, 1887–1907," *Florida His-*

torical Quarterly 53 (October 1974): 123–45; Abel A. Bartley, *Keeping the Faith: Race, Politics, and Social Development in Jacksonville, Florida, 1940–1970* (Westport, Conn., 2000), xv–xvii, 21, 130–32. See also Barbara Walsh, *New Black Voices: The Growth and Contributions of Sallye Mathis and Mary Singleton* (Jacksonville, 1990).

17. Godwin, "'To Serve God and Humanity,'" 16–17; Wright, *More Than Petticoats*, 58.

18. Godwin, "'To Serve God and Humanity,'" 13–14; *Jacksonville Evening Metropolis*, January 31 and March 20, 1902; *Program for Benefit Piano Fund, Stanton High School, and Brief History of School, December 3 and 4, 1917* (Jacksonville, 1917), 5; Wright, *More Than Petticoats*, 58. For more on the Great Fire of 1901 as it affected Jacksonville's African American community and, especially, Edward Waters College, see Shirletta J. Kinchen, "The Experience of Pioneering Women Educators," in *Go Sound the Trumpet!*, ed. Jackson and Brown, 148–50.

19. *Fortieth Anniversary, Afro-American Life Insurance Co., Jacksonville, Florida: 1901–1941* (Jacksonville, 1941), 3–5. See also Marsha Dean Phelts, *An American Beach for African Americans* (Gainesville, 1997); Russ Rymer, *American Beach: A Saga of Race, Wealth, and Memory* (New York, 1998).

20. Godwin, "'To Serve God and Humanity,'" 14. Grayce Bateman offers excellent material on Eartha White's many contributions to the Jacksonville community. See Bateman, *Grayce Reminisen[c]es: 40 Years with the Clara White Mission, Inc. 1945–1985* (Jacksonville, 1994). This life of service also was captured in the program entitled *75th Diamond Birthday Observance of the Useful Life of Eartha Mary Magdalene White, Doctor of Humanities* (Jacksonville, 1951) (available at UNF Special Collections).

21. *Fortieth Anniversary, Afro-American Life Insurance Co.*, 6; *Jacksonville Evening Metropolis*, December 10, 1903, and September 18, 1905. For an interesting look at one pioneer black physician's experience with A. L. Lewis and the Afro-American Industrial and Benefit Association during this period, see Canter Brown Jr., "Dr. James Alpheus Butler: An African American Pioneer of Miami Medicine," *Tequesta: The Journal of the Historical Association of Southern Florida* 66 (2006): 49–81.

22. Johnson, *Along This Way*, 89. For information about the New South concept of the Progressive Era in Jacksonville and elsewhere in Florida see James Crooks, "Jacksonville in the Progressive Era: Responses to Urban Growth," *Florida Historical Quarterly* 65 (July 1986): 52–71; idem, *Jacksonville after the Fire, 1900–1910: A New South City* (Gainesville, 1991), 89; Kharif, "Black Reaction"; Thomas Muir Jr., "William Alexander Blount: Defender of the Old South and Advocate of the New South," *Florida Historical Quarterly* 67 (April 1989): 469–70. The first twentieth-century migration of blacks from the South commenced before World War I and included a significant number of those whom W. E. B. Du Bois referred to as the "Talented Tenth." For information about this exodus see Carole Marks, *Farewell—We're Good and Gone: The Great Black Migration* (Bloomington, Ind., 1989); Nicholas Lermann, *The Promised Land: The Great Black Migration and How It Changed America* (New York, 1991); Joe W. Trotter Jr., *The Great Migration in Historical Perspectives: New Dimensions of Race, Class, and*

Gender (Bloomington, Ind., 1991); James N. Gregory, *The Southern Diaspora: How the Great Migrations of Black and White Southerners Transformed America* (Chapel Hill, 2005); Robert Cassanello, "Violence, Racial Etiquette, and African American Working-Class *Infrapolitics* in Jacksonville during World War I," *Florida Historical Quarterly* 82 (Fall 2003): 155–69.

23. *Jacksonville Florida Times-Union*, November 9, 1901, February 26, October 18, and November 9 and 24, 1905; *Indianapolis Freeman*, November 30, 1901; *Charlotte* (N.C.) *Star of Zion*, December 12, 1901; *Washington* (D.C.) *Colored American*, October 10, 1903; *Pensacola Journal*, October 28, 1905; Shira Levine, "'To Maintain Our Self-Respect': The Jacksonville Challenge to Segregated Street Cars and the Meaning of Equality, 1900–1906," *Michigan Journal of History* (Winter 2005): 1–20, www.umich.edu/~history/papers/winter2005/levine.html).

24. Arthur F. Raper, *The Tragedy of Lynching* (Chapel Hill, 1933), 28; Johnson, *Along This Way,* 45; David H. Jackson Jr., "Booker T. Washington's Tour of the Sunshine State, March 1912," in *Go Sound the Trumpet!*, ed. Jackson and Brown, 189–93; Robert W. Saunders Sr., *Bridging the Gap: Continuing the Florida NAACP Legacy of Harry T. Moore, 1952–1966* (Tampa, 2000), 8–10.

25. Quoted from Godwin, "'To Serve God and Humanity,'" 20. On the life and career of Florida's demagogic governor Sidney J. Catts, see Wayne Flynt, *Cracker Messiah: Governor Sidney J. Catts of Florida* (Baton Rouge, 1977).

26. Crooks, *Jacksonville after the Fire*, 90.

27. Ibid.

28. Godwin, "'To Serve God and Humanity,'" 18–19.; Linda D. Vance, *May Mann Jennings: Florida's Genteel Activist* (Gainesville, 1985), 104.

29. Crooks, *Jacksonville after the Fire*, 90; *Jacksonville Evening Metropolis*, May 28, 1908, and July 18, 1911.

30. The following studies, among others, illuminate the origins of the suffrage movement in Florida: A. Elizabeth Taylor, "The Woman Suffrage Movement in Florida," *Florida Historical Quarterly* 36 (July 1957): 42–60; Kenneth R. Johnson, "The Woman Suffrage Movement in Florida" (Ph.D. diss., Florida State University, 1966); idem, "Florida Women Get the Vote," *Florida Historical Quarterly* 48 (January 1970): 299–312. See also Elna C. Green, *Southern Strategies: Southern Women and the Women Suffrage Question* (Chapel Hill, 1997). Excellent local studies offering helpful context are Nancy A. Hewitt, *Southern Discomfort: Women's Activism in Tampa, Florida, 1880s–1920s* (Urbana, Ill., 2001); and Doris Weatherford, *Real Women of Tampa and Hillsborough County from Prehistory to the Millennium* (Tampa, 2004).

31. Quoted in Johnson, "Florida Women Get the Vote," 301. The statement reflects the general anti-black and nativist orientation of the national woman's suffrage movement at the turn of the twentieth century. The Florida Woman Suffrage Association was affiliated with Susan B. Anthony's National American Woman Suffrage Association. See Carolyn Summer Vacca, *A Reform against Nature: Woman Suffrage and the*

Re-thinking of American Citizenship, 1840–1920 (New York, 2004), 45–104; and Doris Weatherford, *A History of the American Suffragist Movement* (Santa Barbara, Calif., 1998), 155–94.

32. Taylor, "Woman Suffrage Movement," 45.

33. Johnson, "Florida Women Get the Vote," 305 n. 22. On Florida's malapportioned legislature, see William C. Havard and Loren P. Beth, *The Politics of Mis-Representation: Rural-Urban Conflict in the Florida Legislature* (Baton Rouge, 1962). On Florida's first woman representative in the U.S. Congress, see Sally Vickers, "Congresswoman Ruth Bryan Owen: The Spirit of Florida," in *Florida's Heritage of Diversity: Essays in Honor of Samuel Proctor*, ed. Mark I. Greenberg, William Warren Rogers, and Canter Brown Jr. (Tallahassee, 1997), 123–36; idem, "Ruth Bryan Owen: Florida's First Congresswoman and Lifetime Activist," *Florida Historical Quarterly* 77 (Spring 1999): 445–74.

34. Joan S. Carver, "First League of Women Voters in Florida: Its Troubled History," *Florida Historical Quarterly* 63 (April 1985): 383–407; *Jacksonville Florida Times-Union*, October 5, 1920. See also Allen Morris, "Florida's First Women Candidates," *Florida Historical Quarterly* 63 (April 1985): 406–22.

35. Rosalyn Terborg-Penn, "Discontented Black Feminists: Prelude and Postscript to the Passage of the Nineteenth Amendment," in *The Black Studies Reader*, ed. Jacqueline Bobo, Cynthia Hudley, and Claudine Michel (New York, 2004), 65–78; Sharon Harley and Rosalyn Terborg-Penn, *The Afro-American Woman: Struggle and Images* (Port Washington, N.Y., 1997), 17–27, 43–57; Ida B. Wells-Barnett, *Crusade for Justice: The Autobiography of Ida B. Wells* (Chicago, 1970), 229–30; and Paula Giddings, *When and Where I Enter: The Impact of Black Women on Race and Sex in America* (New York, 1984), 159–70.

36. Maxine D. Jones, "'Without Compromise or Fear': Florida's African American Female Activists," *Florida Historical Quarterly* 77 (Spring 1999): 478–79. Also see Christopher A. Linson, "Something More Than a Creed: Mary McLeod Bethune's Aim of Integrated Autonomy as Director of Negro Affairs," *Florida Historical Quarterly* 76 (Summer 1997): 20–41.

37. Jones, "'Without Compromise or Fear,'" 487.

38. The first Republican Party organization in Jacksonville was the Union Republican Club, organized by Loyalist and future Republican governor Ossian B. Hart in 1867. Blacks were invited to join this club, and Jonathan Gibbs—a black native of Philadelphia, graduate of Dartmouth, and Presbyterian minister—served on the executive committee. Brown, *Ossian Bingley Hart*, 193–94, 178–79. On Gibbs, see Learotha Williams, "'A Wider Field of Usefulness': The Life and Times of Jonathan Clarkson Gibbs" (Ph.D. diss., Florida State University, 2003).

39. Godwin, "'To Serve God and Humanity,'" 14.

40. Ibid.; *Washington Bee*, May 25, 1918.

41. Vance, *May Mann Jennings*, 104; Godwin, "'To Serve God and Humanity,'" 23.

42. Godwin, "'To Serve God and Humanity,'" 23; Paul Ortiz, *Emancipation Betrayed: The Hidden History of Black Organizing and White Violence in Florida from Reconstruction to the Bloody Election of 1920* (Berkeley, 2005), 215–16.

43. *Jacksonville Florida Times-Union*, August 28, 1920, quoted in Morris, "Florida's First Women Candidates," 408.

44. Godwin, "'To Serve God and Humanity,'" 23. Also see Ortiz, *Emancipation Betrayed*, 215–16; Walter W. Manley II and Canter Brown Jr., *The Supreme Court of Florida, 1917–1972* (Gainesville, 2006), 9. For information on the Ku Klux Klan in Florida, see Michael Newton, *The Invisible Empire: The Ku Klux Klan in Florida* (Gainesville, 2001); David Mark Chalmers, *Hooded Americanism: The History of the Ku Klux Klan* (Durham, N.C., 1987), 225–29.

45. Ortiz, *Emancipation Betrayed*, 211–20; Godwin, "'To Serve God and Humanity,'" 23; *Tampa Morning Tribune*, June 22, 1921; Brown, *Florida's Black Public Officials*, 68–69.

46. Godwin, "'To Serve God and Humanity,'" 23; Michael Gannon, ed., *The New History of Florida* (Gainesville, 1996), 288–89.

47. Godwin, "'To Serve God and Humanity,'" 20.

48. Ibid., 26. One of many interesting sources for understanding the impact of the New Deal on the South's black residents is John Egerton, *Speak Now against the Day: The Generation before the Civil Rights Movement in the South* (New York, 1994).

49. For an extensive discussion of the Clara White Mission, see Bateman, *Gracye Reminisces*.

50. The photo is located in the UNF Special Collections Department. Also see Manley and Brown, *Supreme Court of Florida*, 85–86, 139–40; J. Clay Smith Jr., *Emancipation: The Making of the Black Lawyer, 1844–1944* (Philadelphia, 1993), 281, 310 n. 106.

51. Godwin, "'To Serve God and Humanity,'" 32. Randolph indicated his high esteem for Eartha White in a letter he sent on her seventy-fifth birthday in which he stated, "I have known her practically all of my life and have the deepest respect and admiration and affection for her and all the great work she is doing." *75th Diamond Birthday*, 19. On A. Philip Randolph see, among others, Jervis Anderson, *A. Philip Randolph: A Biographical Portrait* (Berkeley, 1986); Sally Hanley, *A. Philip Randolph: Labor Leader* (New York, 1989); Andrew Edmund Kersten, *A. Philip Randolph: A Life in the Vanguard* (Lanham, Md., 2007).

52. Charles E. Bennett, *Twelve on the River St. Johns* (Jacksonville, Fla., 1989), 137–48.

53. James Crooks, *Jacksonville: The Consolidation Story, from Civil Rights to the Jaguar* (Gainesville, 2004), 3–4, 63–67; James B. Crooks, "Jacksonville before Consolidation," *Florida Historical Quarterly* 77 (Fall 1998): 141–62; idem, "Jacksonville's Consolidation Mayor: Hans G. Tanzler, Jr.," *Florida Historical Quarterly* 80 (Fall 2001): 198–224; Godwin, "'To Serve God and Humanity,'" 34.

CHAPTER 13

Elizabeth Benton Moore
1878–1932

Education and Community Activism
at Georgia's Dorchester Academy

DAWN J. HERD-CLARK

THE EARLY 1900S OFFERED extremely limited economic opportunities for African American women, with racial and gender discrimination heightening their problems. More than a few black women, however, refused to allow these circumstances to define them; rather, they persisted to create their own legacies. Elizabeth Benton Moore, a longtime teacher and missionary, serves as a prime example. As principal of Georgia's Dorchester Academy, a rural school for African American children located near Midway immediately south of Savannah, she furthered her vision of an accredited, self-sufficient educational facility that would challenge students through high academic standards and

Figure 25. Elizabeth Benton Moore, c. 1927.
(Courtesy of Georgia Archives, Vanishing Georgia Collection.)

demanding extracurricular activities. That Moore did this in the late 1920s highlights her ability to overcome challenges. That she embodied a twentieth-century legacy of the American Missionary Association (AMA), a Reconstruction-era arm of the Congregationalist Church still operating in the South, may surprise even more.

Although this glimpse at a southern woman's activism and significance concentrates on Elizabeth Moore's involvement with Dorchester Academy, a look at the trail that led her to the school in 1925 offers much-needed context. She was born in Nashville, Tennessee, during August 1878. Her young parents, George R. and Fannie Benton, lived next door to Fannie's family, headed by her parents, Rice and Elizabeth Moore. Elizabeth was the Bentons' first child. Husband George worked as a tanner at Rice Moore's Nashville shop. Beyond these bare facts, little is known of the family. One of Fannie's brothers shared that he was the product "of a [nearly] white mother and a black father, both slaves." This presumably was the case with all the Moore children. The brother mentioned what must have been a significant early influence on them: "the efforts of Christian women who had lifted him up, and educated him to be a worker for his race." The impact of these AMA teachers and missionaries proved so profound that the Moores and Bentons passed along to their children a sense of obligation "to be a worker" for their race. They also, the brother declared, "called in Christ's name for the means to carry on the work."[1]

Fannie's brother George W. Moore and his wife, Ella Sheppard Moore, influenced Elizabeth Benton Moore tremendously because they reared her for all or most of her childhood. Because of their impact on Elizabeth's life, they deserve particular attention. By the time of Elizabeth's birth, George Washington Moore was twenty-three years of age and ministering at Nashville. Also a student at Fisk University in 1878, he graduated three years later. By then he had pushed himself well along the way in the ministry, achieving office by 1881 as recording secretary of the Congregationalist Church's Central South Conference. He soon would take a leave of absence to pursue a master's degree in theology at Oberlin College in Oberlin, Ohio. With his degree in hand by 1883, he returned to Nashville. Soon he accepted the pastorate of Lincoln Memorial Church in Washington, D.C., as well as a professorship of biblical history and literature at Howard University. Through these prestigious assignments, Moore came to know during the 1880s and early 1890s most of the principal African American leaders, notably Frederick Douglass, former U.S. Senator Blanche K. Bruce, and recent Fisk graduate W. E. B. Du Bois.[2]

Moore ultimately left the nation's capital for a Nashville assignment with the AMA. He labored well more than a decade as field missionary for the AMA, emerging by the 1910s as superintendent of southern church work. He built a spacious and comfortable house at 926 Seventeenth Avenue North—facing the Fisk campus—and involved himself closely with affairs at his alma mater. He traveled as well, and by 1905, according to one source, "had visited Europe as a delegate to several international gatherings." By that point George W. Moore stood high in the ranks of African American leadership in the nation and the world. "His eloquence as a speaker, his sagacity as an adviser, and his sympathy as a friend have made him preeminently successful in his responsible position," a colleague declared.[3]

However great George W. Moore's influence on Elizabeth's life, that of his wife, Ella Sheppard Moore, proved even more profound. A remarkable woman by anyone's standards, she had met and overcome considerable challenges by the time she and George W. Moore married in 1882. Born twenty-nine years before her marriage, she had witnessed her slave mother being sold away from the family, as well as impoverishment in 1866 following Civil War disruptions and the death of her father, Simon Sheppard. She had utilized her musical talent to bring her financial security, becoming a music teacher at Fisk University. There, in the early 1870s, she helped to found Fisk's famed Jubilee Singers. Over time she emerged as the group's "backbone and trainer." After her marriage she became her husband's partner, rather than simply his spouse. John W. Cromwell noted, for example, that the Reverend Moore's tenure at Washington's Lincoln Memorial Church "was a thorough success, due in no small measure to the personality of his wife, Ella Sheppard Moore." Booker T. Washington agreed. "In all the work which [Lincoln Memorial] attempted to do for the masses of the coloured people in Washington," he recorded, "Mr. Moore was greatly assisted by the labours and counsel of his wife." In time, Ella also gained a reputation independent of her husband through activism and writing. Among other things she took on responsibility for preserving and disseminating the history of the Jubilee Singers as well as advancing good causes such as the needs of colored women and girls.[4]

The timing and circumstances of how the Moores came to take charge of Elizabeth remain obscure, but one source indicates that they cared for the child "from infancy." Most likely they took her after their 1882 marriage, when Elizabeth would have been age four. If so, then she accompanied them to Washington before, at fifteen, returning to Nashville and the Moore home on Seventeenth Avenue. In that comfortable residence, she would have enjoyed a life filled with music and singing, for George and Ella excelled at both. Elizabeth additionally was touched, moment by moment and day by day, by living examples of decency, dedication, and commitment, especially within the context of Congregationalist Church doctrine and the work of the AMA. Meanwhile, she received an excellent formal education under the Moores' sponsorship, one that led her to enroll at Fisk about 1894. Four years later she graduated and commenced her own life of service. As will be seen though, she never forgot her affection for or sense of obligation to the Moores, and she carried their name as her own for the rest of her life.[5]

The facts of Elizabeth's early career years are little better known than those of her upbringing. Her first employment after graduation from Fisk seemingly was as matron at the Albany Normal School at Albany, Georgia, an AMA-sponsored institution (now Albany State University). By 1900 she had transferred to Macon County, Alabama, where the AMA maintained a mission school called the Cotton Valley School, located midway between Cotton Valley and Fort Davis. This site lay not far south of Tuskegee and about midway between Montgomery and Columbus, Georgia. The AMA took special pride in the institution, describing it as a "unique and fruitful school" with a "record of transformations." Even though the facility received supervision directly from Booker T. Washington and the Tuskegee Institute, its mission nonetheless demanded commitment. As one source put it, teachers there required "great wisdom and patience."[6]

From Cotton Valley, Moore returned to Nashville. The date of the relocation cannot be established with certainty, but it was prior to 1910. She again lived with George W. and Ella Moore. At first Elizabeth taught in the Nashville public schools, but by 1912 she held the position of director of domestic science for the city's school system. Indications are that she spent at least one summer during the period in New York City attending Columbia University's summer program for teachers. In the meantime she continued to pursue AMA missionary work. The year 1914 brought tragedy, however, as her Aunt Ella died at the age of sixty-three. Soon, Elizabeth had relocated with George Moore to Martin, Florida, situated near Ocala in Marion County. There the well-regarded Fessenden Academy operated under AMA sponsorship. She may well have taught at the academy until her relocation to Georgia in 1925. By that time, as an AMA official declared, she had good character, appearance, and success as a teacher, plus an ability to discipline. Beyond that, he insisted, she possessed ambition, energy, enthusiasm for her work, and perseverance.[7]

The Dorchester Academy, to which Moore journeyed in the mid-1920s, already had enjoyed more than a half-century of accomplishment in partnership with the AMA. Established in 1869 near the Old Midway Church in Liberty County, Georgia, it aimed to provide instruction to African American children in the absence of public schools. The facility benefited greatly beginning in 1874 from the services of Floyd Snelson, an Atlanta University graduate. He initiated construction of a school building and barely saw its completion prior to leaving in September 1877 for African missionary work. Another new building, completed in 1879, coincided with the school's renaming as Dorchester Academy in honor of community residents whose ancestors originally had settled in Dorchester, Massachusetts. At that point the school began providing secondary education. A series of principals managed its affairs thereafter, struggling with funding shortfalls and some persistent community hostility. Despite a 1901 fire that destroyed the teachers' home, girls' hall, dining room, kitchen, laundry room, and other buildings, the school claimed an enrollment within two years of 450 pupils. Its reputation for the training of minority teachers well established, the school in subsequent years became increasingly involved in agriculture on state, regional, and national levels. This focus resulted in the hosting during 1923 of an agricultural conference convened jointly by the Georgia State College of Agriculture and the U.S. Department of Agriculture.[8]

Local black citizens remained very reliant on Dorchester Academy when Moore became principal, for the state and county continued to refuse to meet their educational needs. Georgia's 1877 constitution mandated segregated schools, and equal funding was not provided for black education despite the U.S. Supreme Court's "separate but equal" ruling in the 1896 *Plessy v. Ferguson* decision. In Georgia in 1926, a mere eleven accredited high schools operated for blacks, only one of which was public. Although African Americans regularly paid taxes, the state in 1930 spent $35.42 on educating each white child and only $6.38 per black child. In Liberty County a Rosenwald school named the Liberty County Training School, established in 1928, offered only elementary grades. While other county-run schools existed, most provided inadequate education. These were one-room facilities open a maximum of five or six months each year, if that long, and their teachers had little more than a grammar school education. Dorchester Academy stood out as the only first-rate school and the only high school in the area for black children. AMA Superintendent of Education Fred Brownlee visited the area early in Moore's administration. "There isn't a decent school house within ten miles of the academy," he reported, "and such as there are run for three months in shanties with one teacher for six or eight grades."[9]

Like her predecessors Moore faced major obstacles in advancing Dorchester Academy. A chronic shortage of funds headed the list. As it turned out she provided instrumental leadership in helping parents, students, and community members to realize and then honor their fiscal obligations. Although paying tuition always posed a hardship for most Dorchester Academy parents (they did not enjoy the prosperity of the 1920s), they generally did their best after her arrival to make their required contributions. Unfortunately, in 1927 low cotton prices damaged southeast Georgia's economy. One of Liberty County's largest sawmills closed the following year, affecting the livelihood of many parents. In 1929 a hurricane caused severe damage to the region's crops and helped to spread malaria and influenza. The stock market crash, also in 1929, resulted in the closing of several southeast Georgia banks, compounding the financial difficulties.[10]

Despite the financial distress Moore's constant encouragement motivated parents to help the school survive. Significantly, even during difficult economic times AMA school tuition was not reduced. When a local parent asked for free or reduced fees, Moore typically would respond, "How much are you going to do for the school? You sold your cotton for a pretty good price this year, and you have some money in the bank. Why shouldn't you carry part of the load?" When one woman went to register her grandchildren for school, she was surprised at the required one-dollar registration fee. When she protested Moore underscored how important it was for families to support the school and that tuition payments benefited the community as well. To the extent feasible, though, the principal accepted partial tuition payments and granted scholarships. In 1928, one student submitted three bushels of her parents' corn, worth $1.75, as her tuition payment. Additionally, scholarships increasingly were viewed as essential during depressed periods because they saved students' self-respect while helping the AMA to balance its accounts. Moore emphasized nonetheless that charity or tuition breaks should be given only when essential.[11]

Since students directly benefited from their education, Moore encouraged them to support the school by holding special fund-raising events. These occasions quite often had an educational nature and also doubled as social activities for the rural, segregated community. Through them, various classes and campus organizations competed to see who could raise the most money. The 1926 senior class gave a minstrel show and barn dance, to which its members charged ten cents admission; they also hosted a social where all students wore their clothing backwards. Eighth-grade students presented a play entitled "Dorchester Academy," in which they imitated teachers, and additionally held a fake wedding party with female students wearing paper dresses made in sewing class. The children sent out formal invitations and followed with a reception. At a ninth-grade barn dance, tenth graders were invited to participate in a spelling bee. Socials also included gypsy parties, junior and senior proms, and on one occasion, a poverty party. These events frequently included music performed by students and professional musicians, dancing—although the girls and boys rarely were permitted to dance together—and refreshments. There were plays, carnivals, bazaars, and fashion shows as well. To publicize the events Moore frequently wrote stories for the *American Missionary*, the AMA's official organ, and for the *Savannah Tribune*, southeast Georgia's African American newspaper and the official organ of the Masonic Grand Lodge of the state of Georgia. Thereby, she brought the school local, state, and national exposure.[12]

Moore's effective use of the media over time generated many donations from persons near and far, which proved essential to Dorchester's sound financial health. Congregational churches in Savannah and Charleston assisted, as did the Knights of Pythias. Northern "friends" were even more important for the school's economic survival. Many of the gifts were small, prompted by something as simple as a visit. In 1929, for example, Mr. and Mrs. Louis Stoiber, along with a traveling companion from Newark, New Jersey, were so impressed by what they saw that they made a cash donation. After Mr. and Mrs. Paine visited with Dr. George L. Cady, AMA secretary of promotions, they donated Ned, Dorchester's pet mule. Similarly, in 1929 The Servo Club, a service club composed of young girls from Quincy, Massachusetts, sent four dollars.[13]

Tuition and donations helped, but Moore and Dorchester Academy depended greatly on additional revenue sources. The vast majority of its income came from the AMA. That venerable agency particularly furnished money to help with the school's general expenses, including grounds maintenance, repairs, furniture, and teachers' salaries. Dorchester fortunately also benefited during Moore's principalship from support from the Daniel Hand Educational Fund for Colored People; a $2,000 endowment from the Caroline M. Martin Fund; and, in 1929, a $1,000 bequest from the estate of Rebecca P. Fairbanks.[14]

The fact that students faced many poverty-related problems confronted Moore from the day she arrived on campus. The simple act of getting to and from school, for instance, often proved difficult. During Moore's administration the average distance students walked amounted to nearly seven miles per day, and since the area was so low-lying, they frequently had to make their way through and around swamps or bogs. Moore took special pride in one female student who walked seventeen miles each way yet had perfect attendance; this persistent student managed to complete three years of her education in two. Since so many students had to travel long distances to school, they not uncommonly left their homes before sunup and did not return until dark. Many of the young people also lacked adequate clothing and gratefully accepted used items, routinely solicited by the principal from northern benefactors. Although she sometimes sold donated clothing or bartered such items for corn, potatoes, chickens, and the like, Moore habitually gave away clothing to the poorest students.[15]

Moore achieved some success in countering the transportation problem in 1925 when the Walthourville and Allenhurst communities agreed to begin transporting students to Dorchester. Walthourville, sixteen miles from the academy, "engaged" a truck that transported twenty children each day at a cost of sixty dollars per month. Allenhurst, twelve miles away, transported at least fifteen students daily. In 1926 truck service from Groveland also commenced, thus further enhancing the school's influence in the area. The willingness of these communities to provide transportation for their students reflected Moore's emphasis on making local residents more responsible for their own fate and less dependent upon the AMA.[16]

Whatever Moore's successes in meeting such challenges, the economic realities of hard times took their toll and, as a result, attendance dropped during her tenure. In the 1925–1926 school year, 231 students enrolled. The number dropped to 183 in 1926–1927, 172 in 1927–1928, and 140 in 1928–1929 before inching back up to 146 in 1929–1930 and 162 during 1930–1931. Tuition increases may have been a significant factor in the overall attendance decrease. By 1928, the average elementary education tuition charged in an AMA school ran eight dollars per year, a large sum for most area families, many of whom had numerous children. Another problem involved the nine-month academic year, which began in mid-September when children normally were expected to work on family farms. Although Moore and the teachers urged parents to send their children to school on the first day, potential pupils not uncommonly remained at home until mid-October. Additionally, during the 1920s Georgia's African American population decreased through migration prompted by hostile racial conditions including lynchings, "whitecappings," and actions of a discriminatory judicial system. Thus, fewer school-age students were living in Georgia. The stock market crash of 1929 no doubt adversely affected the community profoundly, making funds for tuition even more scarce. While the total number of students registering for school declined, though, the average attendance rate improved.[17]

Despite declining enrollments, under Moore's leadership Dorchester's curriculum expanded. She desired to broaden students' horizons, teaching them more than reading, writing, and arithmetic. Art appreciation, for example, was initiated in 1926 when the AMA sent Mrs. Elizabeth Jacquith, of Talladega College, to teach a weeklong class. Jacquith delivered a series of lectures on famous works and gave demonstrations of art interpretation. The AMA and Moore believed that, through art, students could be educated in "the fundamental nature of things beautiful, in the amenities and graces of life." As was observed, "No one can be considered educated in whom there had not been developed those inner, abiding sources of joy, open to all whose eyes and ears are trained to see the beautiful in God's earth and sky and the beauty in art."[18]

Moore further promoted the arts when she attempted to organize a band, but was thwarted by a lack of funds. Yet the music department improved during her administration. The school frequently held concerts for students and the community, attempting to provide a wholesome and educational entertainment experience. Music teacher Marcella Jones also gave recitals, and student performances were common. Dorchester boasted a singing quintet, boys' sextet, mass choir, and numerous soloists. Students performed at the school, Midway Congregational Church, and numerous other local churches. The musical performances provided students with opportunities to travel, entertain, and most importantly, publicize the school. Their performances brought even more donations to help support the education of African American students in the Liberty County, Georgia, area. Taking one year as an example, in 1929 Dorchester students sang for Oak Grove Congregational Church, Mt. Sinai Church, Cypress Slash Congregational Church, and a Methodist camp meeting, among other appearances.[19]

Indeed, Moore considered public performance important to children's education, and during her administration the number of student public presentations significantly increased. Not only did the programs provide entertainment to the community, but they also taught students to "appear with more ease and grace when in public," thus serving as community-based classrooms for instruction in proper behavior. These "rhetoricals" included essay and poetry readings, musical selections, playlets, and debates. One program included a song selection, "Welcome Sweet Springtime"; a reflection by Dorchester Academy student James Baker; "The Life of Paul L. Dunbar," read by Wilhelmina Morrison; "When the Co'n Po'n Hot," a reading by Eleanor Morrison; the solo "Rose Marie" by Marion Boone; a presentation on the life of Booker T. Washington by Robert Williams; a demonstration of a battery charge by William N. Curry; a reading from *Uncle Tom's Cabin* by Sadie Moore; and a playlet, "Topsy," acted by Annette McTier, Lula Curry, and Charlotte Monroe. Another rhetorical included a debate among the seventh-graders as to whether English was more important than math. The myriad of plays and minstrels provided first-graders through high school seniors chances to perform, while affording an important source of entertainment for the community and fund-raising opportunities for the school.[20]

Moore took advantage of holidays as occasions for such activities. Student plays and minstrels proved popular during those times; accordingly, during her administration holidays became more enjoyable for everyone. Dances typically marked Valentine's Day. Plays about honesty and truthfulness highlighted George Washington's birthday. Easter brought a church program and included spring break. For Halloween 1925 "the lights were covered with yellow paper to give the weird effect of the season. Pumpkin heads adorned the corners of the room giving a ghostly effect over the whole room." The party also included apple bobbing, peanut hunts, popcorn popping, and marshmallow toasting. Armistice Day celebrations brought readings, recitations, songs, and academic drills. The school enjoyed Thanksgiving with a program, church service, and community activities such as dances and bazaars; the Thanksgiving meal often featured barbecue rather than turkey and dressing. Christmas always took a special place in Dorchester hearts. To emphasize the spirit of giving, the school opened the campus store one week prior to Christmas and sold gifts costing from one to ten cents each. This allowed all students to give at least one present. Teachers gave gifts to students as well; each "painstakingly selected for each of his pupils—not one—but several gifts" from a supply room containing clothing and toys sent from northern supporters.[21]

Abraham Lincoln's birthday was another important holiday celebrated by both the school and the AMA. The Lincoln Fund Drive marked the climax of the school's annual fund-raising program. Through the academic year the various classes competed to raise money, and on or around Lincoln's birthday they presented the school with the sum at an annual gala. George White, AMA promotions secretary, became the school's annual anniversary host. Some of the money raised was sent to the AMA to help it continue its missionary activities in the South and West. The rest helped to pay the school's outstanding obligations. The class that raised the most money won either a banner depicting its members as champions for the year or a new American flag. All Dorchester Academy classes strove to merit such prizes. The individual student who raised the most money also won a prize. To raise money, the classes held dances and sold lunches, roasted peanuts, candy bars, pennants, theme paper, and crafts. The school also solicited funds for the drive from area businesses. The Lincoln Fund drive helped to instill a sense of pride among the students by enabling them to give back to the institution and faculty that provided them with an outstanding education.[22]

The principal extended individual attention to certain students on some holidays. Christmas 1930, for instance, brought difficult times for three Dorchester students whose mothers had recently died. To help them through the trying period, Moore served them breakfast. "Their faces beamed with delight as a breakfast, such as mother might have prepared, was set before them," one account observed. "Santa Claus came to the dining room and invited our young guests to a Christmas tree, where he gave gifts to each of them. Not only were the hearts of the children overjoyed, but those of us who had entertained them."[23]

Since the AMA supported both Dorchester Academy and the Midway Congregational Church (MCC), the church served almost as an adjunct to the school and often sponsored activities to assist students. Like many African American churches during the 1920s and 1930s, MCC organizations, including Club Number 7 and the Busy Bee Club, sold dinners, gave parties, and presented programs to support African American education. Dorchester's strong ties to the MCC also permitted Moore to incorporate religious instruction through inviting students, faculty, and guests to give lectures on self-improvement, adult education, the social gospel, and the personal need for religion, as well as other issues. These events regularly occurred during the school's daily or weekly chapel exercises. The students' religious instruction additionally benefited from the work of the Christian Endeavor Society. Although the Christian Endeavor Society had been established prior to Moore's administration, it had languished before she reactivated the chapter. The principal thought it important not only for religious purposes but also as a tool for training future leaders. Students elected officers, held meetings, and learned to speak publicly. Beyond that, the society sponsored projects to help enlighten students and community members.[24]

The MCC represented only one of many Congregational Church ties to Dorchester Academy. Student groups at Moore's urging visited surrounding churches, including the First Congregational Church in Savannah, where they presented religious programs and solicited support. In addition, Dorchester participated at various times in larger Congregational organizations, including the Georgia and South Carolina Congregational Church Conference, Congregational Sunday School conventions, the Georgia Congregational Church Conference, and the South Eastern Convention of Congregational Churches. Outside church activities were not limited to Congregationalists, however. Students also gave programs at Cross Roads Baptist Church, Jerusalem Baptist Church, the Zion Sunday School Convention, Midway Presbyterian Church, Calvary Baptist Church, and Day Memorial Church. In most instances audience members found themselves so impressed with the school's mission, faculty, and student body that they made contributions.[25]

Moore's efforts to broaden the curriculum extended well beyond art appreciation and public presentations. During 1927 she required fifteen minutes of daily physical education. Instructor Miss P. Maxwell divided students into groups with upperclassmen as captains and ensured real physical effort from all. Moore believed that physical education not only had important health benefits for students but also strengthened timid leaders. She did not simply accept participation, though. Student competency had to be demonstrated during each commencement week.[26]

To a greater degree than her predecessors, Principal Moore also attempted to broaden students' knowledge by exposing them to activities and events outside the immediate Dorchester area. Students went to see the opera *Sampson and Delilah,* a recital by Roland Hayes, the Williams Singers musical ensemble, and a "whale which was on display in Savannah." To inform her charges about foreign affairs and to emphasize that "in helping others we are helping ourselves," Moore encouraged them to help the unfortunate in Angola through the Angola Fund. This successful project was undertaken in 1927 when the Liberty County community was suffering from economic depression. Moore also introduced educational movies. The first film shown dealt with forest preservation, another aspect of Dorchester's educational subjects.[27]

These steps represented only the beginning of Moore's influence. In order to better prepare students for life and careers, she encouraged the school to hold weeklong programs to commemorate National Health Week, Race Relationship Week, and Good English Week. During National Health Week teachers emphasized good health habits, students read papers on health during chapel, and special speakers were brought on campus to speak on various health topics. During Race Relationship Week the school presented programs on the relationship between the races and highlighted racial groups with which southeast Georgians rarely came into contact, including the Chinese and Japanese. Good English Week provided the opportunity to emphasize "good English" through the use of mottos and slogans. Moore and Dorchester teachers believed that learning "proper" English was vital to racial uplift and securing good jobs. The literary and debating club, organized in 1925, used Good English Week to expose its ideas.[28]

Although not as important to her as exposure to the liberal arts and religion, Moore also included industrial education at Dorchester. Agriculture became the most important component of the manual training program, as many students lived on farms and would remain there when their formal education ended. The academy planted crops and raised animals to improve the students' agricultural knowledge and raise produce for school consumption. As an illustration, students in 1929, with the assistance of a recently acquired mule and plow, raised a bountiful harvest. Dorchester also sponsored an agriculture con-

Figure 26. Dorchester Academy schoolchildren, c. 1927.
(Courtesy of Georgia Archives, Vanishing Georgia Collection.)

ference for area farmers. The conference and the school's successful farming methods encouraged area farmers to join a Dorchester-sponsored Farmer's Cooperative Marketing Association, which met on campus. By educating farmers in the latest agricultural innovations and techniques, the cooperative empowered a segment of Georgia's African American population suffering through the dire economic circumstances of the Great Depression.[29]

Moore's enhanced curriculum and "innovative" ideas understandably included oratorical and writing contests, among other things. In a 1930 competition open to high school students, the Paines—the couple that had donated Ned, the mule—asked the students to write about how Ned had affected them. The first and second prizes were $3.00 and $2.00, respectively. The Paines were sufficiently impressed to offer prizes for a second contest on the topic of campus life at Dorchester. Students also frequently participated in county and state fairs. Dorchester won first place for its exhibits at the 1925, 1926, and 1927 Liberty County Fairs. In 1925, the academy participated for the first time in the Georgia State Fair and won the third highest ribbon total among competing schools. The next year it claimed the most ribbons. The students' success under Moore's administration further evidenced itself when schools and colleges increasingly began to visit Dorchester for recruiting purposes. President John C. Wright of North Carolina's Brick Junior College and Talladega College President F. A. Sumner were two of many administrators who recruited there.[30]

Moore held her students to high standards, and one of her major goals involved securing school accreditation. When Fred L. Brownlee, AMA corresponding secretary, visited in 1926, he agreed to help. He praised Moore's invaluable work and assured the school's local friends that, because of the wonderful spirit shown by the people who had cooperated with the principal, the AMA planned to help Dorchester Academy become one of the few accredited black high schools in Georgia. Moore then journeyed to Atlanta to learn what steps had to be taken. The academy, it became clear, needed a science department with laboratory equipment and a library with up-to-date reference books. Accordingly, in 1927 she enhanced the science department by the addition of a lab table that accommodated twelve students and lab materials for physics and biology. One year later the Home Missionary Society of Massachusetts sent $200 for the purchase of the 1928 edition of the *Encyclopædia Britannica* and additional reference books. Moore's efforts—as supported by faculty, students, Liberty County residents, and nationwide supporters—helped Dorchester to meet the state's requirements for a standard high school. In 1931, she and math instructor Thomas Collins were enabled to attend the state conference for accredited high schools and colleges at Morris Brown University, a most notable accomplishment for a rural African American school.[31]

Many students considered one of Moore's greatest accomplishments to be the founding of an athletic program. During her tenure the academy's Tigers and Tigerettes—with Shag, their mascot—inaugurated strong football and men's and women's basketball programs. Tennis and swimming too were initiated, but Moore died before the programs had a chance to develop properly. The principal believed that athletics helped mold "character, sportsmanship, manhood and womanhood," energized the community, and, once again, brought favorable publicity.[32]

A more detailed look at these programs offers insight into how Moore perceived their importance. In 1926, early in her tenure, Dorchester competed in a public school track meet at Savannah. Basketball teams also organized in 1926. Initially, students played each other, but eventually they challenged other schools. The boys' team competed against St. Augustine, Brunswick, Selden Institute, Avery Institute, Statesboro High and Industrial School, Allen Normal, Douglas, Georgia Normal, and Colored Memorial High School of Brunswick, Georgia. Although not always victorious, it usually competed well. The Tigerettes, coached by Anna Ledbetter, played their inaugural game on January 6, 1928, against Cuyler High School. Although the Tigerettes went 0–6 their first year, they improved as time passed. Other teams the girls played included Cuyler Opportunity School, Central Park Junior College, Selden Institute, Georgia State College, Voorhees, Statesboro High and Industrial School, and Colored

Memorial High School. When athletic squads traveled to distant schools, the men and women often participated in doubleheaders.[33]

The football program traced its roots to 1927, and other sports followed. Science teacher and coach J. R. Jenkins led the team in its first football game on Thanksgiving Day 1928, hosted at Dorchester against Colored Memorial High School. Although the academy team lost its first few games, victories proved the norm by 1929. Among the schools to challenge Dorchester were Statesboro High and Industrial School, Waycross, Beach High School, and Live Oak. Moore and Jenkins also organized a baseball team. Opponents included Central Park Junior College, Selden Institute, Central High School, Hinesville, Voorhees Institute, Sandhill, Allen Normal, Ebenezer High School, Georgia State, Eulonia, Edward Waters College, and Ways Station. As with the basketball and football teams, the baseball team improved with experience. Tennis was introduced in 1931. The program continued after Moore's death and, eventually, produced several nationally ranked tennis players. Moore also researched the possibility of building a swimming pool, but she died before that idea could be brought to fruition. She attempted as well to develop a girls' indoor baseball team; however, no records document the team's continued existence. Athletics enhanced the students' educational experience on two levels. First, the Tigers and Tigerettes traveled throughout the southeastern United States to compete in athletic competitions, a rare opportunity for poor, rural African American students. Second, before students could participate in athletic competition, Moore required them to demonstrate academic excellence.[34]

The success of Dorchester's athletic program can be attributed to many factors, although Moore's vision of a complete educational experience stands at the top of the list. To that should be added J. R. Jenkins's ability to organize and develop athletes, the school's acquisition of a truck, and the creation of Dorchester's advisory board. The board, established in 1927, advised the school and provided funds that enabled it to participate in various athletic endeavors. Dorchester alumni and locally prominent residents—including Mr. and Mrs. Richard Perry, Dr. and Mrs. I. D. Williams, J. E. Quarterman, Mr. and Mrs. Hill, Dr. Frazier, Sol C. Johnson, and all Dorchester Academy teachers—comprised the board. Mr. and Mrs. Perry donated three and one-half acres adjacent to the school's property to establish the Perry Athletic Field. The board members then paid approximately $25 each to meet the $500 expense of land clearing. Board members then raised additional funds to fence the field and construct bleachers. In line with Moore's philosophy, students built the fence, and the money they earned went toward their board and tuition. After the field's completion in 1931, the board began work on the bleachers. It also purchased team uniforms. Some members became so interested in athletics that they formed the Dorchester Athletic Association in 1930. Moore correctly believed that athletics would bring attention and much-needed revenue to the school. Few Dorchester projects stimulated as much interest as did the athletic teams.[35]

The advisory board, with Moore's encouragement, met monthly, providing "valuable suggestions" and "money to make needed improvements in the school and the student body." Its first major project facilitated construction of a telephone line for the school in 1928. The closest line had run approximately seven miles away, and Moore felt that a school telephone was essential. The board raised $200 of the $323 needed by soliciting funds, holding socials, and sponsoring a Miss Dorchester Academy contest. The success of the Miss Dorchester Academy challenge led to a Mr. Dorchester competition when the board realized that boys could participate in the fund-raising, given that contest winners were the students who raised the most money. The winners received free admittance to all school functions the following academic year. The Hinesville Telephone Company charged the school five dollars per month for the maintenance of the phone lines and the first phone, and one dollar per month for each additional phone.[36]

Moore's ultimate goal centered upon graduating her students, and she directed considerable effort to various activities, academic and extracurricular, leading to that end. Graduation ceremonies already constituted a special component of the Dorchester experience, but Elizabeth Moore elevated the pageantry. The celebration usually consisted of one week of activities, including a stunt night, play, sermon, manual training and domestic arts show, friends and alumni reception, picnic, and closing exercises. During stunt night the physical education department demonstrated several exercises and dances. The high school and primary departments performed plays and operettas that featured more elaborate sets and costumes than the other performances throughout the year. Student presentations at graduations during Moore's tenure included "Diamonds and Hearts," "Golden Day," "The Dust of the Earth," "America, Yesterday and Today," "Aaron Slick from Punkin Crick," "A Grand Carnival in Little Folks Town," "Aunt Deborah's First Luncheon," and "Everybody Happy?" The annual baccalaureate sermon that punctuated the ceremonies usually was delivered by a prominent local pastor. The Reverends E. W. Rakestraw of Asbury Methodist Episcopal Church, Williams of Freedman's Grove Presbyterian Church, C. S. Ledbetter of Plymouth Congregational Church, J. Clyde Perry of the Episcopal Parish of Brunswick, E. Cleveland of St. John's Baptist Church, and Paul Johns of First Congregational Church numbered among the ministers to preach baccalaureate sermons, thus binding them to the school.[37]

Other events accentuated graduation ceremonies. The manual training and domestic arts show allowed students to display their new projects. The friends and alumni reception provided a way to thank the community and former students for their contributions. The annual picnic, established by Moore, provided a social activity for the community, with games, sideshows, and athletic activities frequently serving as highlights of the day. The culminating event was the graduation ceremony, which featured oratorical exhibitions, noted speakers, and the awarding of diplomas. Since only a limited number of students could afford to stay in school for twelve years, classes were small. To honor those who did persist, Moore invited noted Georgians as commencement speakers. Among them were the Reverend Norman A. Holmes of First Congregational Church; John Hope, president of Morehouse College; Dr. George W. Owens of Atlanta; President B. F. Hubert of Georgia State Industrial College; and Mrs. George S. Wilson, national Republican committeewoman of Georgia. The invitations tied even more prominent Georgians to the school. Moore also placed articles in the *Savannah Tribune* and set signs along roads near the academy. A large attendance was important to enable Dorchester to show the progress students had made during the academic year and, almost as important, to make money for the school. Many activities required an admission fee, and classes competed to see who could raise the most money. Moore even established fund-raising quotas for the various classes.[38]

Principal Moore also strove to create an alumni association. She encouraged all alumni and former students to visit the school and see firsthand the changes taking place. To further her plans she collected as many addresses of graduates as she could. Several area alumni joined the advisory board, and many others who had moved away visited, sent donations, and offered words of encouragement. Moore reached her goal in 1929 when Dr. S. F. Frazier was named temporary chairperson of the Dorchester Academy Alumni Association. The association's avowed purpose was to help the school raise scholarship money and to reward students who excelled academically.[39]

Moore not only desired that former students and alumni participate actively in school activities and functions, she also wanted parents to become involved in their children's education. Thus, she revitalized the Parent-Teacher Association (PTA) which had been formed prior to her principalship but had become inactive. To increase attendance at monthly meetings, she targeted prominent parents, hoping that, once they began to participate, others would too. In 1925, the PTA elected the first officers under Moore's administration: president, Mr. J. E. Quarterman; vice-president, Mr. J. A. Ranktow; second vice-president, Mrs. Betsy Lloyd; secretary, Mrs. Lambert; and treasurer, Miss. E. B. Moore.

The PTA raised money and met with faculty to discuss ways to improve education at the institution. The success of the PTA remains open to question, though, since no records exist of its activities after the 1925–1926 school year.[40]

Moore understood that the school needed the support of the entire community in order to reach its full potential, and she took more care than had some previous principals to inform citizens of the benefits the school provided. During her first year, for instance, she insisted that the teachers visit pupils in their homes in order to demonstrate the school's commitment to them. She and the teachers also visited area churches, including Mt. Zion Baptist Church at Waycross, Friendship Baptist Church, and Taylor's Creek Methodist Church where, more often than not, the school's importance received mention and collections were taken for it.[41]

The principal's leadership bore significant fruit, and the community responded to her pleas to help improve the institution. As one Liberty County resident declared, "Liberty County without Dorchester Academy ain't worth a chaw of tobaccer!" Citizens donated time, money, and produce. In 1926, several men's and women's clubs held a huge picnic. The $100 raised helped them to buy a tractor for the school. In 1926 area women's clubs "furnished dishes and silver for the dining hall, utensils for the kitchen and equipment for the laundry." Others "gave sixty cords of wood, chickens, fruit and vegetables." Moore additionally reported, "It is surprising how the fine men and women of this community have rallied to the support of the school this year. Our friends of the North have been more liberal towards us this year on account of the wonderful interest manifested by these good people of Liberty county." One year later Dorchester distributed piggy banks in which citizens could place their spare change, another way of getting community help. Eventually enough money was raised to purchase a gasoline engine that powered the shop machinery, ground corn, and cut wood. In 1928, another example of the community's willingness to assist was demonstrated when Brother Sweat, who previously had donated wood and helped repair buildings, could no longer do strenuous work. Yet, Moore related, "[He] took his ancient horse, some twenty winters old, broke ground and planted peas. All that fall until he was confined to his bed he brought the shelled peas to be used in our dining-room as his bit for Dorchester Academy." The principal repeatedly thanked such donors for their support in letters to the *Savannah Tribune* and through frequent community socials.[42]

Moore's determination and drive not only expanded the curriculum, extracurricular activities, and fund-raising, she also improved physical facilities.

New roofs were placed on the manual training/science and academic buildings during the fall semester of 1926; new furniture also graced both buildings. In 1927 all seven structures on campus—including Snelson Hall, Curtis Hall, the Academic Hall, Laundry, Dining Hall, Chapel, and Manual Training Building—were painted, inside and out, with paint supplied by northern friends at a cost of approximately $1,000. The community helped Moore to pay the $148.96 shipping costs. In the fall of 1927 a new electrical and water pumping system substantially upgraded the campus plant. Most importantly, by 1928 she had secured a sewage system and bathroom facilities. Septic tanks, designed and installed by AMA Superintendent of Buildings and Grounds D. A. Williston, allowed the installation of complete bathroom facilities in Snelson Hall (the boys' dorm), and Curtis Hall (the girls' dorm).[43]

Although Moore's primary responsibility in Liberty County related to heading Dorchester Academy, she filled many other roles locally that illustrated her commitment to civic activism. As liaison for the school, for example, she frequently hosted socials for those in the community who helped Dorchester. She remained active in Congregational Church activities, often attending the Georgia and South Carolina Congregational Church conferences and state Congregational conferences. She was in constant demand as a speaker. The fact that an African American woman frequently was requested as an orator for key events during the 1920s and 1930s is notable. For instance, in 1926 she addressed a group of farmers at the Kinlaw Rosenwald School of St. Mary's and was the featured speaker at Cuyler High School's graduation. She hosted the Liberty County Teacher's Institute, where Dorchester Academy teachers led discussions about the latest educational methods. To introduce economically innovative ideas to the school and community, Moore attended a National Buyers Association meeting, a subsidiary of the National Negro Business League meeting, in New York City. While there, she learned of efforts to get African American schools and hospitals to buy cooperatively, thus reducing their expenses. After Moore's death the cooperative movement expanded to include the Union Brotherhood Society, a burial association, the Dorchester Federal Credit Union, and two farmers' cooperatives.[44]

Elizabeth Moore accomplished much in a short time and, as is true within any institution, her drive to produce concrete results prompted detractors and naysayers. It appears that her personal approach sometimes lacked tact, and she did not always consult with others before acting. Some faculty members went so far as to describe her as "dogmatic and apparently a sort of 'slave driver.'" To what degree these personality issues affected the institution cannot be determined with certainty. It does appear, from what Moore managed to accomplish, that she did not let them stand in her way.[45]

Moore's many contributions to the school and community ended with her unfortunate death in 1932. The *Savannah Tribune* had reported Moore's illnesses in 1926 and again in 1928 and 1929, but without suggestion that they might be fatal. School and community members thus were shocked when, on January 27, 1932, Moore passed away after a two-month illness and an unsuccessful tonsillectomy. She was only fifty-one years of age. Understandably, students, faculty, community leaders, and AMA officials expressed high regard for Moore in the wake of her death. The AMA *Annual Report of 1932* proclaimed "her purposes, ideas and ideals will permeate the life of the academy and its youth for generations to come."[46]

Elizabeth B. Moore's influence in Liberty County, in only six years of service, proved enormous. She guided the community toward self-improvement, self-reliance, and pride. She taught students at Dorchester that "we are as one large family trying to forget our selves in making others happy." She added, "We also appreciate the fact that whatever we are we must make for ourselves and that a well-spent high school career is one of the greatest helps to true manhood and womanhood." Reflecting her own philosophy, Moore often recited the first verse of Maltbie Davenport Babcock's poem "Be Strong":

> Be Strong!
> We are not here to play, to dream, to drift.
> We have hard work to do, and loads to lift.
> Shun not the struggle; face it. 'Tis God's gift.[47]

Elizabeth Moore had set an excellent example for all Liberty County educators to follow, in the process defying racial and gender stereotypes. J. R. Jenkins, who succeeded Moore as principal, accepted her innovative ideas and credited her with inspiring him. Dorchester Academy's 1933 Lincoln Day celebration was dedicated to Moore:

> Immortal Spirit, visible and clothed, but yesterday,
> Mountains of virtues, priceless gifts of these,
> Challenge us to climb, more patiently by day,
> And stop at night, to share thy destiny.[48]

Notes

1. 1870 and 1880 U.S. Decennial Censuses, Davidson County, Tennessee (population schedules); 1900 U.S. Decennial Census, Macon County, Alabama (population schedule); *General Conference of the Congregational Churches in Maine, Fifty-Eighth Anniversary* (Bangor, 1884), 34.

2. 1880 U.S. Decennial Census, Davidson County, Tennessee (population schedule); James G. Merrill, "Fisk University," in *From Servitude to Service: Being the Old South Lectures on the History and Work of Southern Institutions for the Education of the Negro* (Boston, 1905), 206; Nancy C. Curtis, *Black Heritage Sites: An African American Odyssey and Finder's Guide* (Chicago, 1996), 230; *The Congregational Year-Book, 1881* (Boston, 1881), 218; "Negro Graduates of Oberlin College, 1844–1972," Minority Student Records, Record Group 5/4/3, Oberlin College Archives, Oberlin, Ohio; John W. Cromwell, "First Negro Churches in the District of Columbia," *Journal of Negro History* 7 (January 1922): 99; James M. Gregory, *Frederick Douglass: The Orator* (Springfield, Mass., 1893), 158–59. On Nashville's black community, see Bobby L. Lovett, *The African-American History of Nashville, Tennessee, 1780–1930: Elites and Dilemmas* (Fayetteville, Ark., 1999). On Fisk University, see Joe Martin Richardson, *A History of Fisk University, 1865–1946* (Tuscaloosa, 1980); A. A. Taylor, "Fisk University and the Nashville Community, 1866–1900," *Journal of Negro History* 39 (April 1954): 111–26. On W. E. B. Du Bois at Fisk University, see David Levering Lewis, *W. E. B. DuBois: Biography of a Race, 1868–1919* (New York, 1993). On black life in Washington, D.C., during the 1880s and 1890s, see Jacqueline M. Moore, *Leading the Race: The Transformation of the Black Elite in the Nation's Capital, 1880–1920* (Charlottesville, Va., 1999).

3. Cromwell, "First Negro Churches," 99; Merrill, "Fisk University," 206–7; Curtis, *Black Heritage Sites*, 230; Monroe N. Work, *Negro Year Book and Annual Encyclopedia of the Negro, 1913* (Tuskegee, Ala., 1913), 128.

4. Beth Howse, "Ella Sheppard (Moore) (1851–1914)," www.tnstate.edu/library/digital/sheppard.htm; Cromwell, "First Negro Churches," 99; Booker T. Washington, *The Story of the Negro: The Rise of the Race from Slavery*, vol. 2 (New York, 1909), 267–69; Mrs. G. W. Moore, "Historical Sketch of the Jubilee Singers," *Fisk University News*, October 1911, 42; idem, "Needs of the Colored Women and Girls," *American Missionary* 43 (January 1889): 22–25. On the life and career of Ella Sheppard Moore, also see Beth Howse, *Ella Sheppard (Moore), 1851–1914* (Nashville, Tenn., 1987); Jessie Carney Smith, "Ella Sheppard Moore (1851–1914)," in *Notable Black American Women*, ed. Jessie Carnie Smith (Detroit, 1992).

5. AMA, *Annual Report, 1936*, 54, AMA Archives, Amistad Research Center, New Orleans, Louisiana (hereafter AMA, *Annual Report* for a specified year or years); William E. Barton, *Old Plantation Hymns: A Collection of Hitherto Unpublished Melodies of the Slave and the Freedman, With Historical and Descriptive Notes* (Boston, 1899), 26; "Ella Sheppard, Soprano" at www.pbs.org/wgbh/amex/singers/peopleevents/pan

de04.html; *Catalogue of the Officers and Students of Fisk University, Nashville, Tennessee, for 1897–1898* (Nashville, Tenn., 1898), 84.

6. *Catalogue of the Officers and Students of Fisk University*, 84; 1900 U.S. Decennial Census, Macon County, Alabama (population schedule); *American Missionary* 50 (April 1896): 121; Ralph E. Luker, "Missions, Institutional Churches, and Settlement Houses: The Black Experience, 1885–1910," *Journal of Negro History* 69 (Summer–Autumn 1984): 101. On the Cotton Valley School generally, see Woman's Home Missionary Association, *Cotton Valley, Alabama: A School in the Black Belt* (Boston, c. 1901).

7. 1910 U.S. Decennial Census, Davidson County, Tennessee (population schedule); *Catalogue of the Officers, Students and Alumni of Fisk University, 1911–1912*, 113; AMA, *Annual Report, 1936*, 54; Howse, "Ella Sheppard (Moore)"; 1920 U.S. Decennial Census, Marion County, Florida (population schedule); Kevin M. McCarthy, *Black Florida* (New York, 1995), 213–14; Maxine D. Jones and Kevin M. McCarthy, *African Americans in Florida* (Sarasota, 1993), 149, 165. On Fessenden Academy generally, see Joe M. Richardson, "Joseph L. Wiley: A Black Florida Educator," *Florida Historical Quarterly* 71 (April 1993): 458–72.

8. The principal source for information on the Dorchester Academy is Dawn J. Herd-Clark, "Dorchester Academy: The American Missionary Association in Liberty County, Georgia, 1867–1950 (Ph.D. diss., Florida State University, 1999). See also "Dorchester Academy," www.dorchesteracademy.com/timeline.htm. For an excellent study of another AMA-supported school in Georgia (Ballard Normal School, Macon), see Titus Brown, *Faithful, Firm & True: African American Education in the South* (Macon, 2002). For a thoughtful look at the challenges faced by educators of freedmen, see Heather Andrea Williams, *Self-Taught: African American Education in Slavery and Freedom* (Chapel Hill, 2005).

9. Donald L. Grant, *The Way It Was in the South: The Black Experience in Georgia* (Athens, Ga., 1993), 213; *Savannah Tribune*, May 13, 1926; AMA, *Annual Report, 1934–1935*, 42; *Savannah Tribune*, October 4, 1928; *American Missionary* 81 (January 1927): 406; ibid. (April 1927): 540–41.

10. AMA, *Annual Report, 1928*, 26; ibid., *1929*, 35–36; *American Missionary* 82 (April 1928): 176–77.

11. *American Missionary* 80 (January 1926): 403; ibid., 82 (April 1928): 176–77; ibid., 84 (December 1930): 45.

12. One key reason the socials and programs at Dorchester were so successful was because *Savannah Tribune* editor Solomon Johnson published announcements of many school events. *Savannah Tribune*, October 28, 1926, January 27, March 3 and 16, 1927, and February 27, 1930.

13. The Knights of Pythias was a branch of Free Masonry. In 1927 the Knights contributed $12.00 to the school. *Savannah Tribune*, March 30, 1927, and March 28, 1929.

14. Dorchester Academy first received money from the Caroline M. Martin endowment in 1913. During the majority of Principal Moore's administration, the school

received money from the Caroline M. Martin Fund. AMA, *Annual Report, 1925*, 77; ibid., *1929*, 67.

15. "Dawn at Dorchester," n.d., in AMA Archives; *American Missionary* 81 (January 1927): 406.

16. *Savannah Tribune*, October 22 and November 12, 1925, October 28, 1926; *American Missionary* 79 (December 1925): 353–54.

17. *AMA Annual Report, 1930*, 19; ibid., *1931*, 54; *American Missionary* 82 (February 1928), 66–69; Grant, *Way It Was*, 295. White Caps were members of secret vigilante societies that carried out attacks against anyone transgressing social norms. In the South, attacks were usually racially based and intended to hinder black advancement.

18. *Savannah Tribune*, November 4, 1926; *American Missionary* 81 (November 1927): 837–38.

19. *Savannah Tribune*, October 17 and 24, November 7 and 21, 1929.

20. Ibid., March 3, 1927, and March 25 and April 2, 1931.

21. Ibid., November 12, 1925, December 20, 1928, and November 14, 1929.

22. Notes taken from the unpublished memoirs of the late J. R. Jenkins, lent to the author by his wife, Fannie P. Jenkins, and currently in the possession of his daughter, Angela Serike, Columbia, Maryland (hereafter, Jenkins Memoirs); *Savannah Tribune* February 18, 1926.

23. *American Missionary* 85 (December 1931): 1616.

24. Grant, *Way It Was*, 264; *Savannah Tribune*, February 24, 1927, November 29, 1928, November 28, 1929, October 16, 1930, November 27, 1930, and December 9, 1926.

25. Southeastern Georgia Congregational, Baptist, and Presbyterian church record notes, in possession of the author.

26. *Savannah Tribune*, October 20, 1927, and September 20, 1928.

27. Ibid., December 1, 1927, and March 13, 1930.

28. Students and speakers addressed such issues as keeping fit and nail care. Ibid., November 19, 1925, February 20, 1930, and November 26, 1931.

29. AMA, *Annual Report, 1929*, 35–36; ibid., *1930*, 39–40.

30. The 1926 competition was not viewed as worthwhile in retrospect because Dorchester was the only school to enter exhibits. The school's supporters "were in deed sorry at the lack of competition," Moore wrote, "because great preparation had been made to compete with some of the other schools at the fair." *Savannah Tribune*, October 22 and 29, 1925, October 7 and November 18, 1926, October 13, 1927, March 1, 1928, February 13, 1930, and February 5, 1931; AMA, *Annual Report, 1926*, 20.

31. In 1929 the school library had enough volumes to merit cataloguing the collection using the Dewey decimal system. *Savannah Tribune*, March 25, 1926, December 15, 1927, April 12, 1928, February 5, 1931; *American Missionary* 81 (January 1927), 407; AMA, *Annual Report, 1930*, 39–40.

32. *Savannah Tribune*, November 8, 1928; *American Missionary* 82 (April 1928): 176.

33. *Savannah Tribune*, April 29, 1926, and January 5, 1928.

34. Ibid., March 7, 1927, October 18, 1928, and May 7 and June 18, 1931.

35. *American Missionary* 82 (April 1928): 176; *Savannah Tribune*, September 1, 1927, and March 12, 1931.

36. Jenkins Memoirs; *Savannah Tribune*, February 16, 1928, and November 4, 1929; Hinesville Telephone Company to Miss E. B. Moore, October 3, 1928, AMA Archives.

37. *Savannah Tribune*, May 6 and June 3, 1926, May 19, 1927, April 12 and May 10, 1928, and May 21, 1931.

38. Ibid., April 7 and 28, 1927.

39. Ibid., November 12, 1925, December 6, 1926, January 17, 1929, and June 4, 1931.

40. Ibid., November 12, 1925.

41. Ibid., February 11, 1926.

42. *American Missionary* 81 (January 1927): 407; ibid., 81 (April 1927): 541; ibid., 82 (April 1928): 176; *Savannah Tribune*, March 18, 1926, and January 13, 1927; AMA, *Annual Report, 1926*, 20.

43. There seems to have been some problem with installation of the bathroom facilities because another plea was made for sanitary toilets and good bathing facilities in 1927. *Savannah Tribune*, September 6 and 30, 1926, March 30 and October 20, 1927, and September 6, 1928; AMA, *Annual Report, 1927*, 22.

44. Dorchester Academy joined the National Buyers Association, but the benefits to the school are unknown. A cooperative program was also implemented in the community. *Savannah Tribune*, January 28, 1926, March 17, 1927, January 26, 1928, and June 18 and August 27, 1931.

45. Elizabeth B. Moore, Teacher's Records, AMA Archives.

46. *Savannah Tribune*, January 28, 1932; AMA, *Annual Report, 1932*, 54.

47. Maltbie Davenport Babcock, *Thoughts for Every-Day Living from the Spoken and Written Words of Maltbie Davenport Babcock* (New York, 1901), 168.

48. *Savannah Tribune*, January 1, 1931, and February 23, 1933.

CHAPTER 14

Jerenia Valentine Dial Reid
1879–1962

Woman's Work by a Pioneer of African American Nursing

ESTHER SPENCER

JERENIA VALENTINE DIAL REID, Florida's first black registered nurse, offered through her life and labors an excellent example of the dedication and commitment displayed by many daughters and granddaughters of emancipation, qualities for which they unfortunately have not often been remembered. As an African American woman of the middle class, Jerenia not only lived Victorian ideals of womanhood but fully embodied the notion of working to uplift the race by choosing a career of service to others. She skillfully practiced her profession well into the twentieth century, illustrating as she did a surprising geographic mobility. Moreover, wherever Jerenia applied her skills she improved the day-to-day lives of African Americans by addressing health-care

Figure 27. Jerenia Valentine Dial Reid, c. 1920s. (Courtesy of the National Archives.)

needs that otherwise would have gone unattended within a society locked in the grip of racial discrimination and segregation.

Although Jerenia in the early twentieth century became Florida's first black registered nurse, we should not forget that other African American nurses pioneered the path she followed. African American women had been working as nurses since the days of slavery. The practical realities of bondage routinely required women to handle one another's medical needs. Their services, though, often reached across the color line to the benefit of whites. Most particularly, black women tended pregnant women as midwives, saving countless mothers and children of both races from death or crippling disability. Of course, white society declined to classify their work as nursing, preferring to view it simply as the performance of slave or servant duties. Even at the end of slavery and immediately thereafter, black women, whatever their skills and experience, could not enter the profession because nursing schools would not accept them as students. White southern institutions shut their doors to emancipated health-care workers, and the vast majority of nursing schools in the North that eventually did open their classrooms strictly limited the number of African Americans they would accept. These obstacles almost certainly prevented large numbers of black women from receiving formal education in nursing, although by the late 1870s and early 1880s a few individuals had managed to enter the profession of graduate nurse.[1]

Mary Eliza Mahoney stood out as the first black woman to attain the status of graduate nurse. Born free in Boston, Massachusetts, in 1845, she rejected the limitations of domestic work and in the mid-1870s took advantage of the opportunity to study at the New England Hospital for Women and Children. That institution's policies then limited the admission of African American and Jewish students, respectively, to one per year. The newly minted graduate nurse received her degree in 1879, thereby setting the precedent for other black women who would come after her.[2]

Even with that precedent, the training of black graduate nurses trickled rather than flowed. After Mahoney started her nursing career, only a few black women graduated from predominantly white institutions as she had. Some of these graduated from Mahoney's alma mater, the New England Hospital for Women and Children, while others earned their degrees at schools such as the New York Infirmary in New York City and the Washington General Hospital and Asylum Training School for Nurses in the District of Columbia. Although these white institutions afforded blacks an opportunity then nonexistent in the South, their restrictive policies prevented black women from adequately meeting the health-care needs of the African American community.[3]

The lack of nursing programs for black women loomed as part of a bigger crisis, that of insufficient health care for African Americans. The larger society did not meet the medical needs of the black community because many if not most of its members saw African Americans as second-class citizens not deserving of attention or care. The health conditions of African Americans evidenced that attitude. They suffered substantially higher mortality and morbidity rates than did whites. They caught communicable diseases such as tuberculosis, pneumonia, influenza, typhoid fever, and malaria at higher rates and, relatively speaking, died from these ailments in greater numbers. Although both the black and white communities experienced high infant mortality during this period, especially in the South, blacks faced greater losses. These conditions understandably propelled the black community to demand better access to health care.[4]

The solution to the dilemma of the nonavailability of professionally trained black health-care workers emerged only slowly. As racial segregation and discrimination began to take hold in the South, African Americans quickly appreciated that they required their own medical institutions and training programs. Fortunately, some wealthy white businesspeople aided the African American community in this endeavor. Funding for the first black nursing program came from the Rockefeller family. That innovation, thanks to the Rockefellers, emerged at the Atlanta Baptist Female Seminary, the first college exclusively for black women. The school—later renamed Spelman College in honor of Mrs. Rockefeller's mother—opened in 1881, and the nursing program followed in 1886. Soon thereafter similar programs debuted elsewhere. In 1891, for example, the Provident Hospital School of Nursing in Chicago and Virginia's Dixie Hospital Training School began operation. The following year the Tuskegee Institute at Tuskegee, Alabama, began accepting students. By 1907, a total of twelve nurses' training programs served the nation's black community. The establishment of such courses of study benefited the black community directly, enabling many black women to enter the profession. Professional nursing accordingly emerged as a path by which women could participate effectively in uplifting the race.[5]

Against the backdrop of this educational evolution—or, if you will, revolution—Jerenia Valentine's life began. She was born during the immediate post-Reconstruction years in Jacksonville, one of Florida's most populous urban areas. Located in the state's northeastern corner near the mouth of the magnificent St. Johns River, the city had grown prosperous due to the development of timber and transportation industries. By the 1870s it benefited increasingly from yet another source of revenue, tourism. A large black population labored in support of and prepared to take advantage of the city's economic opportunities. The growing weight of the white supremacy movement hindered the progress that blacks could make but did not eliminate all advances, and a modest black middle class coalesced. Some individuals derived their good fortune from truck farming, contracting, carpentry, and land speculation, while black professionals embraced careers in education, commercial affairs, the ministry, and the law.[6]

Although thousands of African Americans participated in Jacksonville's economic and social life, many of the more affluent blacks lived outside the city limits in the adjacent community of LaVilla. African Americans started settling there as the town developed after the Civil War because of its close proximity to jobs in Jacksonville and relatively low cost of living. Employment in hotels; at the port; and in the timber, construction, and railroad industries cemented the attraction of blacks in search of a place to live. James Weldon Johnson, future National Association for the Advancement of Colored People executive director and lyricist of "Lift Every Voice and Sing," numbered among those to whom LaVilla offered a home. His childhood friend Patrick H. Chappelle, the pioneer of black-owned vaudeville, lived there as well. This was the community that greeted Valentine when she came into the world.[7]

Jerenia was born to Tillman and Mary Ann Valentine, prominent members of the local community. Tillman, by the time of Jerenia's birth, well represented the emerging black middle class in Florida. Originally from Philadelphia, he had come to the state as a Union army soldier. Like numerous other African American servicemen, he had stayed after the Civil War. His last military assignment found him as a sergeant stationed at Gainesville. He and Mary Ann Francis married there on November 30, 1865. Within a year or so Tillman, in search of better opportunities, moved his new family toward the Gulf Coast at or near the railroad terminus at Cedar Key. The 1867 opening of Congressional (or Military) Reconstruction, with its requirement of black voting rights, prompted Valentine to assume a prominent role in the black community at his new location, a fact reflected in his 1867 appointment as a Levy County voter registrar. After his term in office ended, he relocated up the Florida Railroad to his old station at Gainesville, where he remained for three or four years. Then, as a civilian and not as a soldier, he decided to settle in LaVilla.[8]

During the decade leading up to Jerenia's birth, Tillman elevated his personal standing and that of his family high in the ranks of the local black middle class. A carpenter by trade, he benefited from Jacksonville's rapid growth. Well utilizing his skills, he soon emerged as not only an artisan but also a contractor.

He had acquired land while in Gainesville and now purchased land in Jacksonville as well. Tillman prospered and reached a level of affluence that most blacks could not attain. His prosperous ventures and landownership soon positioned him as an important figure in the city's and the state's African American communities. The *New York Globe*, edited by T. Thomas Fortune who had also lived during the 1870s at Jacksonville and in LaVilla, commented on Tillman Valentine's success. Fortune first included Valentine among local property holders in an 1883 review of Jacksonville's black elite, then he added, "[Eli] Hart and Valentine are builders standing high in business circles for their integrity and reliability." Moreover, "A military association is in process of organization under the lead of such men as Tillman Valentine and others, which promises much for good in military matters in our State."[9]

Growing prosperity in Valentine's business affairs was matched by a growing family at home. Seemingly, he and Mary Ann waited until they made LaVilla their permanent home to start a family, although the possibility that they lost one or more children at Cedar Key and at Gainesville cannot be discounted. In any event, their first known child, Sarah, arrived in 1872. Son William followed in 1873. This time two years intervened before the birth of a second daughter, Panchita, in 1875. Jerenia, the youngest child, came into the world four years later at Jacksonville in 1879.[10]

Jerenia's childhood in the 1880s introduced her to exciting times and momentous personalities. Prominent men and women from bishops to college-trained educators to visiting dignitaries visited the Valentine home, due in part to Tillman's commitment to Freemasonry. As the years passed the increasing prestige that he, and by extension his family, derived from his business success was reflected in his climb up the ladder of office in Florida's black Masonic hierarchy. At almost the moment of Jerenia's birth, he had become grand master of Florida, a position he held for nearly a decade. The position brought him into contact with even more individuals of renown and prompted him to travel annually outside the state to attend national conventions. In April 1884, for instance, he participated in the Grand Masonic Convention in New York City, the largest black Masonic gathering to that time.[11]

Notably, as Jerenia matured Tillman also maintained positions of influence within the Republican Party. Although he does not appear to have stood for elective office in LaVilla or Jacksonville, he routinely participated in local Republican conventions as a delegate. Such political activity had real significance despite the waning of Republican power on a statewide level, since the party through the 1880s often controlled municipal governments, particularly in towns on or near the St. Johns River. Black officials sometimes comprised the majority of LaVilla's government and would sit on the Jacksonville city council into the twentieth century.[12]

For Jerenia, her father's involvement in Masonry and politics brought many advantages. One was an acquaintance with Florida's first African American physician, a man who offered to young Jerenia a role model for the entry of African Americans into health care. A native of St. Augustine, Alexander H. Darnes had graduated in 1876 from Lincoln University. Thereafter, he had attended the Howard University medical school, claiming his M.D. degree in 1880. Darnes returned to Jacksonville and opened a practice. Within three years of his arrival in Jacksonville, the *Washington* (D.C.) *People's Advocate* could assert of him, "Dr. Darnes... is meeting with more than marked success in his profession." The item continued, "He was recently placed in charge of all the cases of small-pox inside of the county hospital, by the county commissioners. In spite of the poverty and inexperience against which he had to contend, he saved seventy-five per cent of his cases, while the white physicians in the hospital lost seventy-five per cent of theirs." By 1885, when Jerenia had reached age six, Darnes already was climbing, under Tillman Valentine's aegis, the hierarchical steps of Florida Masonry.[13]

As the daughter of prominent and prosperous parents, Jerenia doubtlessly benefited when it came to education. LaVilla and Jacksonville offered the state's best schooling possibilities for black children, and no institution ranked higher on the ladder than did the Stanton Institute. Although surviving evidence fails to record what school she attended, Jerenia most likely matriculated at Stanton because of its quality instruction and proximity to the Valentine home at LaVilla. The likelihood is underscored by the fact that sister Panchita graduated from that institution. Stanton represented to black Floridians more than a good local school. Established in the late 1860s for residents of all of Florida with the mission of training black men and women to teach, it initially welcomed whites as well as blacks. The refusal of white parents to permit their children to attend, however, left its classrooms for black students alone. African Americans believed in the benefit of education, sent their children to the school in large numbers, and when able, provided financial contributions. As Florida's public school system matured, black voters encouraged Duval County officials to adopt the institution as a public school. By the time Jerenia would have attended, they had done so. Stanton thereafter continued to provide African Americans an education that afforded the opportunity for a better life.[14]

At Stanton, Jerenia would have followed a path similar to that traveled a few years earlier by Panchita, who graduated on June 9, 1891. Occasions such as graduations marked special moments for the black community, the members of which came out in large numbers to celebrate the young people and pride in their school. As such, local newspapers typically preserved details of the ceremonies. A glimpse of Panchita's personality can be gained from a notice of the address she gave during the graduation ceremony: "Panchita N. Valentine then laid the block called 'Excelsior,' and told in fine language of the great things that ambition could accomplish." Panchita's graduation address illustrated that the Valentines instilled within their children an ambition to move ahead in life as well as a firm belief in the opportunities that education would bring.[15]

Although education laid the foundation for Jerenia's future profession, her environment also would have influenced her life choices. The yellow fever epidemic of 1888, for instance, affected her and the Jacksonville community directly and painfully. That year's onset of the dreaded "yellow jack" hit Florida's eastern coast and proved particularly deadly at Jacksonville. Understanding the damage the disease could cause, officials—when they found the first documented case at the Mayflower Hotel—condemned the building and ordered it to be burned. Meanwhile, the medical community could not determine the cause of the disease nor provide a cure. Residents who remained free from the disease and who had financial means, particularly whites, left the city in large numbers. Those remaining mostly confined themselves to their homes after authorities ordered a quarantine, except that members of organizations such as the Masons actively aided efforts to raise funds and tend to the sick and needy. Life in Jacksonville changed abruptly. Social interactions came to a standstill because church and community activities ceased. The cessation of business transactions depressed the economy. At the epidemic's peak the death toll reached into the hundreds. Survivors buried bodies of family members and neighbors in mass graves.[16]

The 1888 yellow fever outbreak struck Jerenia with particular force because the disease almost took her father's life. As a Masonic leader Tillman Valentine would have helped to lead early relief and fund-raising efforts. By October 8, however, he lay victim to the pestilence. The degree of his suffering remains unknown, but most likely the Valentine family feared the worst. Fortunately, Tillman recovered and the family did not experience the loss other families endured. Soon, Jacksonville returned to the bustling southern town it previously had been and the Valentines returned to some semblance of normalcy.[17]

Unfortunately, death eventually caught up to the senior Valentine on March 12, 1895. Jerenia had reached or was about to reach only her sixteenth birthday. Not only the Valentines but the entire black community mourned the loss of a fine man of stature who represented the great progress that blacks had registered in their city and state. The *Jacksonville Florida Times-Union,* a white newspaper, reflected broader sentiments when it described him as "an old and respected citizen." The veteran soldier, public servant, and businessman was buried "with Masonic honors and high ceremony by the members of his lodge." Many people in the community attended his funeral and, because of his position in the Masons, other fraternal orders and benevolent societies joined them to pay their respects.[18]

The record does not reveal how the Valentines coped with Tillman's death. Clearly, though, the event left Mary Ann and her children in a financial dilemma, a reality that many families faced on the departure of the father and breadwinner. Records reveal that Jerenia eventually moved in with sister Panchita, perhaps before and certainly after Panchita's marriage to John H. Thompson in 1899. An educated man, Thompson hailed from Alabama and, with his new bride, worked at Jacksonville as a teacher. Jerenia remained in their home until 1900, during which time she finished her secondary education. The whereabouts of her mother and other siblings during this period are not known with specificity. Certain accounts hint that perhaps Jerenia taught briefly in Columbus, Georgia. In any event, having graduated from high school, she embarked on a journey that took her out of Jacksonville for a time.[19]

Valentine left her lifelong home at the turn of the century with a determined purpose: to pursue professional nursing training in the nation's capital. The Freedmen's Hospital, where she studied, already could claim credit as a historic institution that marked an evolutionary period in the United States. Established in 1862 by the secretary of war, it served the great number of blacks who had moved into the city looking for freedom during the Civil War. Dr. Alexander T. Augusta, a major and surgeon in the U.S. Army, took charge of the facility. One of only six black doctors in the army, he became the first black man to head a hospital. In 1868 the hospital also became a teaching institution with the addition of the Howard University Medical School. As such, Dr. Darnes trained there as did several black physicians who followed his lead and opened practices at Jacksonville in the late nineteenth and early twentieth centuries.[20]

By 1900, the Freedmen's Hospital had grown in facilities and in stature. It naturally had seen the construction and implementation of various improvements to further its missions as a teaching institute and as a place that provided care to African Americans. Because the institution catered to blacks, however, the government did not readily provide the hospital with sufficient funding to upgrade when needed. Dr. Austin M. Curtis, the surgeon-in-chief in 1900, had submitted in previous years requests for electric lighting, for example, because he believed the innovation would offer greater efficiency than did gas and also because poor lighting in the operating room made surgery extremely difficult. It took years before the government approved his request. Although the existence of the hospital constituted great progress for African Americans, this delay underscored that white society still looked on them as second-class citizens.[21]

When Jerenia arrived in Washington, the hospital's nursing program was in its infancy. Administrators, in order to establish the Freedmen's Hospital and Howard University Medical School as leading health-care institutions, had inaugurated the Freedmen's Hospital Training School for Nurses on November 15, 1894. The program originally encompassed an eighteen-month course "of lectures, recitation, and practical work in the wards of the hospital." Soon, officials extended the curriculum to two years. Nurses received training in such skills as dressing wounds and applying poultices and leeches; the management of helpless patients; the best method of applying friction to the body and extremities; the practical methods of caring for a sick room; making accurate reports and observations of patients; and many other duties. The Freedmen's Hospital ensured that, given the state of medicine at that time, its students would be fully prepared to perform their duties as nurses when they left the program.[22]

Before Jerenia could be accepted into the program, she naturally had to meet certain requirements. School rules mandated that a student must be aged twenty-one to thirty-five; have a physician's letter stating that she possessed good health; and fill out an application. After acceptance students underwent a one-month probationary period during which they took courses in reading, penmanship, simple arithmetic, and English dictation. The school fortunately housed students at no cost to them during this time, but they did not receive monetary compensation since they had not been fully accepted. Meanwhile, the faculty assessed whether students had the discipline to continue with the rigorous program. At the end of their probation, the superintendent decided which students should continue with their coursework and which would be dismissed. Jerenia's performance obviously sufficed to permit her to carry on.[23]

Valentine officially commenced the nursing program after she signed a contract dedicating herself to the required period of study and agreeing to adhere to the school's rules and regulations. She served her first nine months as a pupil-nurse, working as an assistant in Freedmen's Hospital wards. In her second nine months, she performed whatever duties the superintendent assigned to her. She worked either as a nurse in the hospital or as a nurse overseeing private cases in the homes of the rich and poor of the city. Her work hours ran from 7:30 a.m. to 7:30 p.m., allowing little time for leisure and ensuring her preparation for a career in nursing.[24]

Understanding the financial difficulties that many students faced due to the expense of their education or simply from their position as black women, the administrators provided every student, including Jerenia, with the necessities required to perform her duties: a cap, textbooks, room and board, and five dollars a month to spend as she wished. Regarding the stipend, the school insisted that "this money is not given as pay for services rendered, as the training given and the profession acquired is considered an ample equivalent, but simply to enable young women without pecuniary resources to enter upon their professional career free of debt."[25]

The nursing program, given that it operated from the only hospital catering to blacks in the District of Columbia area, benefited Jerenia greatly by affording her extensive clinical experience. Its doctors saw patients with ailments of every sort. They treated a large number of cases of typhoid fever and, especially, cancer. Surgeon-in-Chief Curtis found this significant because, as he stated, "The relatively large number of cases of cancer in this department is remarkable since the prevailing opinion has been that the descendants of the African race were rarely affected with the disease." Exposed directly to a broad range of maladies and their treatments, Jerenia received practical training that allowed her easily to establish herself as a professional nurse upon her graduation.[26]

Valentine's training commenced under the supervision of Surgeon-in-Chief Curtis and Superintendent Sarah C. Ebersole, but she finished the program under Surgeon-in-Chief Dr. William A. Warfield and Superintendent and Directress Sarah I. Fleetwood. As Jerenia's immediate supervisor, Fleetwood merits further comment. She claimed particular understanding of the program's needs, having been a member of the first class to complete Freedmen's nursing program in 1896. She graduated third of seventeen students. Many of her classmates went on to leadership positions in the field. For instance, Lucy V. Ashton became superintendent of nurses at Douglas Hospital in Kansas City, Missouri. Fleetwood, though, returned to the Freedmen's Hospital after Sarah C. Ebersole retired in 1900, taking over her position as superintendent on February 1, 1901.[27]

Beyond the nursing program and its superintendent, the city of Washington also touched Jerenia profoundly. In 1900, it hosted a large black middle class. In earlier times, as at Jacksonville, this economic stratum had been composed predominantly of clergymen and teachers, but by the early twentieth century, it had expanded to include many businesspeople and professionals. This shift had occurred because blacks had taken advantage of opportunities in academia, permitting them to train in a variety of occupations. Middle-class blacks subsequently gained power and a certain social standing thanks to their education and accumulation of wealth. Howard University particularly enabled blacks access to wealth by providing degrees in law and medicine. Beyond the nursing program, the Freedmen's Hospital held importance to the black community because it was one of the few hospitals where black doctors could intern. Individuals used these institutions as vehicles to reach a status that the majority of blacks could not easily attain.[28]

Her coursework completed, Jerenia graduated from the nursing program on May 4, 1903. The class of fourteen received diplomas at a commencement ceremony held at the Andrew Rankin Memorial Chapel on the Howard University campus. The African American community celebrated the students' accomplishments and Fleetwood's success as the first black superintendent to take "sole charge" of the nursing program. As the *Colored American*, a city newspaper, reported, "Fully an hour before the time fixed for the ceremonies to begin, the friends began to gather, so that at the hour of commencing every seat in the chapel was filled." The ceremony signified progress to all and showed that the younger generation would continue the work of uplifting the black race that the older generation had begun. It also illustrated to white society that black people possessed the intellectual capacity and aspirations to succeed in professional endeavors.[29]

Jerenia, well prepared to start on her professional career, began working soon after graduating from the program. Understanding the needs of her home community, Jerenia moved back to Jacksonville, where public health issues continued to hinder the black community, and became Florida's first black registered nurse. In the recent past, Jacksonville had been plagued with numerous epidemics ranging from yellow fever to typhoid and smallpox. In the year of Jerenia's return, the city experienced a high level of contagious diseases caused by environmental factors, including humid weather and frequent rains that often led to flooding. The constant presence of insects also made the city's population susceptible to communicable diseases. Compounding these problems, the lack of a proper sanitation system, which translated into the presence of stagnant water in many areas; an open sewerage system; rotting garbage; and carcasses of dead animals decaying on the streets, fueled the spread of diseases.[30]

These conditions affected all of Jacksonville but particularly the black community. In 1900, the city as a whole posted a mortality rate of 28.6 deaths per 1,000 people, compared to a mortality rate of 57.2 for the black community. To improve these conditions, the city undertook significant changes. Recovering from a disastrous fire in 1901, it built more buildings of brick, improved the sewerage system by expanding it with an improved drainage system, and placed bulkheads along the St. Johns River.[31]

Although these changes improved the city, statistics underscored that they did not greatly enhance the African American community. The mortality rate for blacks remained 50 percent higher than for the general population, and the number of blacks who died each year continued to exceed the number of black babies born. In fact, many changes did not touch black neighborhoods at all. Most African American communities did not enjoy city water or sewer services, so were forced to use outhouses and privies that bred insects. Since many lived in poverty, they could not afford screens to keep insects away or healthy diets and medical care to combat illnesses. In the absence of city action to ensure public infrastructure in black neighborhoods, the health of African Americans continued to decline.[32]

Given prevailing needs it is not surprising that when Jerenia returned home, she received a warm welcome. Not only was she personally popular, she also represented hope for the future. Most African Americans by then understood the need for more black health-care professionals, especially in surroundings where no registered nurse previously had worked. Thus, on July 27, 1903, the *Jacksonville Evening Metropolis* could announce: "Several inducements are being made to have Miss Jerina [sic] Valentine, the graduated nurse to remain in Jacksonville. This is her native home and there is no reason why she should not do well here in her profession." By December 10, as the newspaper also reported, Jerenia had secured work. "Miss Gerin Valentine, the trained nurse is now attending a patient in Riverside," the *Metropolis* observed, "where she is giving full attention under the direction of Dr. Mitchell." Due to the needs of the Jacksonville community and Jerenia's desire to make a difference, she subsequently gained substantial experience in her first year as a nurse.[33]

Valentine's progress as a nurse owed thanks to the community's medical doctors, white and black. Jerenia worked particularly closely with Dr. Joseph David Mitchell. A veteran member of Jacksonville's medical community and leader in the white medical association, he immediately assisted her in securing work. In fact, Mitchell personally hired her to nurse his patients in the local hospital and in their private homes. The *Jacksonville Evening Metropolis* made this fact clear through its personal columns. On March 11, 1905, for instance, it observed that "Miss J. L. Valentine, the trained nurse, left the city last night for Tampa, to take charge of a case of typhoid fever for Dr. Mitchell." Ten days later the newspaper again offered mention of her movements. "Miss Jerena [sic] L. Valentine, the graduate nurse," it declared, "is attending a case at the Magnolia Hotel, at

Magnolia Springs under Dr. Mitchell." With Mitchell's help, she gained the experience that made her not only Florida's first black graduate nurse but also a well-respected professional.[34]

Jerenia's profession meanwhile afforded her opportunities not available to the majority of black women during that time. Her position sometimes called for her to live in her patients' homes while nursing them back to health. Occasionally, she lived in the homes of whites and, unlike most blacks, she interacted with them as a professional rather than as a servant. Local news organs proudly reported such visitations, countering stereotypes about black inferiority so often espoused in society. "Miss Geneva L. Valentine, the graduate trained nurse," one proclaimed in a typical fashion on February 8, 1904, "is now located at No. 228 Caroline Street, at the home of Mr. and Mrs. Tutson." The range of her activities, though, was broad. Beyond gaining experience in in-home care and the nursing of patients in a hospital setting, Jerenia benefited from the opportunity to work as a surgical nurse. Understandably, on such occasions the community praised her publicly. Essentially, Jerenia emerged as a significant figure in both the black and white communities in Jacksonville because her work touched the lives of so many people.[35]

In the early years of her practice, Valentine also may have taken the opportunity to teach nursing skills to others or, at least, to assist in such teaching. In the aftermath of Jacksonville's Great Fire of 1901 and thanks to a donation of $2,000 from Georgia A. Brewster, officials of the Boylan Industrial Home for Girls established a nursing program. "With the ownership of all the property in the block on which the Boylan Industrial Home is situated," a report of October 3, 1901, asserted, "that institution will have full facilities for giving practical instruction in nurse training and hospital work." As the account indicates, a hospital, the Brewster Hospital, evolved from the innovation. In the summer of 1903, just when Jerenia would have returned home, published updates noted, "Within the past six or eight months this feature of the work [nurse training] at the Boylan Home has been greatly developed." It added, "Dr. J. Seth Hills, Dr. A. W. Smith and Dr. W. C. Smalls [the city's most prominent black physicians] have contributed their professional services at a great advantage." By December 1904 graduates had begun to issue from the Brewster Nursing School and, at least one newspaper insisted, "[were] giving satisfaction."[36]

As Jerenia continued to grow in her profession, her personal life expanded and matured as well. Perhaps most importantly, she decided to marry. The black elite without question supported the institution of marriage and, as a member of this class, Jerenia would have adhered to this ideal. The black aristocracy saw marriage as a necessary tool for maintaining their social and economic status and as a way of proving to white society that they lived by traditional values. Its members also wanted to show that African Americans too believed in marrying, having children, and building a safe and prosperous community; like whites they, too, were deserving of happiness.[37]

Jerenia's profession understandably afforded her local prominence, and her marriage to Charles A. Dial in 1906 would have cemented her upper-class status within the Jacksonville African American community. Charles at the time worked as a porter for the Southern Express Company, a Georgia corporation organized by railroad and resort mogul Henry Bradley Plant. Charles's position, while it might appear modest to modern readers, placed him in contact with important figures, even leaders of the United States. His responsibilities at times also may have included overseeing the sleeping cars of both whites and blacks and facilitating the pickup and delivery of goods. His duties allowed him to travel and to network. Not surprisingly, Florida native A. Philip Randolph would organize sleeping-car porters into the nation's most powerful black labor union and source for civil rights activism. Dial thus held a well-respected position within the black community.[38]

The nuptials occurred on December 12, 1906. Jerenia and Charles exchanged their vows at the home of family friends "General and Mrs. Taylor" (likely clerk of the Jacksonville Board of Health Charles D. Taylor and his wife, Anna K. Taylor), with the ceremony taking place in the parlor under an arch of evergreens. The bridal party included friends Gusster Randall and Arthur E. Campbell. Jerenia's sister Panchita walked the bride down the aisle. The *Evening Metropolis* described Jerenia as "a handsome bride [of] commanding height and of rare beauty of figure, her fashionably fitting gown of white chiffon, with hand embroidered chrysanthemums, with veil draped from the rear made her the object of universal compliments." She certainly left an impression on the townspeople, while her wedding served to illustrate her status and economic standing. Such weddings brought out many members of the community who wanted to experience the joyous event while acknowledging the popularity and position of the parties. "The parlor halls and porch [were] crowded," observed a published report. The couple received over three hundred gifts from those in attendance. In the process Jacksonville expressed thanks to Jerenia for her valuable presence in the city.[39]

A new era of life now opened for Jerenia. She and Charles lived in a Jacksonville home located at 711 West Church Street. Although no information about their house survives, their purchase two years after their marriage of a new icebox, a luxury to say the least, speaks to their economic stability. Jerenia and Charles made an even more important addition to their household with the birth of their daughter, Valentine. Later they added a baby boy, Charles Jr., to their family.[40]

Unfortunately, domestic happiness lasted for Mrs. Dial only a short time, as negative circumstances quickly changed her course forever. In late 1910 Charles grew ill. Only speculation can convey the passion and concern with which Jerenia would have cared for him. Yet, by November he had passed away. The black community mourned the loss of Charles Dial and supported Jerenia and her family through the tragedy. Even though her occupation accustomed her to deal with death, the loss of her husband would have been difficult to bear. Jerenia soon found courage under these challenging circumstances and proceeded with life and the responsibilities of motherhood. She continued as well to afford the community with needed health-care services.[41]

Few details of Jerenia's life in the years immediately following her husband's death have come down to us. An obituary referred to her as "a graduate of South Carolin[a] State College in Orangeburg, S.C.," but the records of its predecessor institution, the Colored Normal Agricultural Industrial and Mechanical College of South Carolina, have not substantiated her studies there during the period. More certainly, by 1914 she headed the McLeod Hospital and Training School for Nurses at Mary McLeod Bethune's Daytona Normal and Industrial School in Daytona. Given that institution's beginnings in 1911 or 1912, perhaps Bethune had drawn Dial to the campus to foster the new facility intended to serve not only the school but also the broader community.[42]

In any event, Jerenia resurfaced in Jacksonville during 1915, when on August 30 of that year she married Leon S. Reid in that city. Little documentation on their union has survived. The city directory does not list them as residents, and reports on their activities have yet to be uncovered. Local black newspapers of the era have been lost, and white newspapers, such as the *Jacksonville Evening Metropolis,* that carried black community news stand silent save for a single unverified account that notes her service at an unspecified time at a hospital in Tuskegee, Alabama. Sadly, her marriage to Leon Reid also ended after a short time. He enlisted in the U.S. Army for service during World War I. His assignment took him to France, where he served as a private first class with the 369th Infantry. He never returned home. A casualty of war, Reid died on November 15, 1918, in an automobile accident that crushed his skull. As with many soldiers, authorities could not identify his body, so he rested in an unmarked grave in the French military cemetery Commune Viller Alsac. His wife meanwhile knew only that he was missing. After the war, military officials discovered their error and had the body exhumed and relocated to Meuse-Argonne in France. For the second time in her life, Jerenia had lost her husband. Once again, however, she did not permit her personal circumstances to prevent her from sustaining herself and providing for her family and community.[43]

Again, a curtain obscures Jerenia's activities for several years. By Leon's death in 1918, she had reached thirty-nine years of age and had worked in the nursing field for sixteen years. Assuming that during this prolonged period she had continued to practice her profession, she would have honed her skills to the levels associated with a mature and experienced practitioner. When Jerenia finally reappears in the 1920 Jacksonville city directory, the publication properly listed her as a registered nurse.[44]

Jerenia Reid's status as a veteran professional and a desire to advance in her career most likely drew her in the early 1920s to play an active role in the National Association of Colored Graduate Nurses (NACGN). Since the organization had been in operation since 1908 and Jerenia had been a nurse since 1903, she could have joined in its early years. Martha M. Franklin, a graduate nurse, originally headed the organization. A product of the Philadelphia Women's Hospital, she was the only black woman in her class. Interested in the working conditions that black women faced, she gathered data on the issue. Her findings propelled her to call a meeting to discuss the problems black women encountered. Fifty-two graduate nurses attended the New York City session in 1908, and NACGN resulted. Its purpose was "to advance the standards and best interests of trained nurses, to break down the discriminatory practices facing Negroes in schools of nursing, in jobs, and in nursing organizations; and to develop leadership among Negro nurses." In later years, the group developed an organized program and launched regional associations.[45]

The organization proved important to black nurses such as Jerenia Reid because it brought them together as a group to fight for their rights. It also gave them a voice. In most southern states African American women could not join the state nurses association, by whatever name it was called. Unfortunately, a requirement for joining the American Nurses Association (ANA) stipulated that nurses had to be members of the association of the state within which they practiced. The National League of Nursing Education (NLNE) also denied admission to blacks. African American nurses thus had no organization other than the NACGN to speak for them or to defend them against discrimination. They also did not enjoy the same professional opportunities as white women. Generally, black nurses could work only in black hospitals or in the segregated unit dedicated for blacks in public institutions. Unfortunately, not many opportunities in private duty existed for them. NACGN accordingly worked diligently to create opportunities for black women and helped them to maintain their dignity and respect within the profession.[46]

Jerenia's involvement with the NACGN may have dated to 1915, the year when the nurses of Jacksonville established a local chapter. Thanks to the Brewster Nursing School at the Boylan Institute, the city by then could count many black nurses, quite a change from when Jerenia had pioneered in the profession there. The importance of organizing, as the grip of Jim Crow racial discrimination tightened over the years, would have appeared evident to the women who united in 1915. Jacksonville's black nurses thereafter actively participated in NACGN and represented well the organization's work.[47]

As illustrated by a series of events that occurred a decade later, by that time, Jerenia had come to play a leading role in the NACGN. Importantly, in August 1925 the city hosted the annual NACGN meeting at Jerenia's home. The gathering represented a typical session. Before the group considered business matters, its members joined in prayer and the singing of a hymn. Next on the agenda came the reading of the previous year's minutes, followed by presentations by health-care officials on issues facing the black community. On August 8 Jerenia personally conducted a memorial service dedicated to the nurses who had died during the preceding year. In so doing she demonstrated her appreciation for the selfless women who spent their lives serving the community. At that year's meeting, the NACGN recognized Jerenia's hard work by electing her national recording secretary.[48]

Jerenia Reid's professional opportunities expanded considerably about the time that she received her position with the NACGN and may have resulted directly from contacts gained thereby. In 1926 she accepted an appointment as superintendent at Pine Ridge Hospital in West Palm Beach, Florida. Most likely she heard of the position from NACGN President Petra Pinn, who had worked as Pine Ridge superintendent from 1916 until 1926. The facility was the first and only black hospital in five conjoined South Florida counties. It had opened on April 15, 1916, with money raised by black residents, who continued to support the facility in line with their modest means. The permanent staff members consisted of three black doctors and two dentists, assisted by white doctors who had expertise in areas the permanent staff lacked. Although the presence of the hospital represented progress for the black community, its contribution to the welfare of African Americans was limited because of its inadequacies.[49]

The relocation presented Jerenia with significant challenges. Pine Ridge lacked necessary equipment, and its operating room lacked adequate ventilation. The premises did not have a darkroom, so x-rays were developed in a makeshift facility under the stairwell. The lack of a standard elevator forced staff members and patients to pull themselves up to the second floor in a dumb waiter, a device used to send goods from one floor to another. Although the hospital could not have been considered a prestigious institution, without question it provided a solid leadership opportunity for Jerenia.⁵⁰

Just as mutual involvement in NACGN most likely brought Jerenia and Petra Pinn together, so too did the organization bring Jerenia into contact with many others. Travel broadened and deepened her network of colleagues and friends, as her position in NACGN took her outside of Florida on an annual basis. To cite an example, the first national meeting she attended as recording secretary took place in 1926 in Philadelphia. The gathering stood out in Jerenia's career because active members reelected her as recording secretary. She defeated her opponent forty-seven votes to five.⁵¹

Reid's NACGN tenure of office substantially outlasted her tenure at Pine Ridge, although her service at West Palm Beach clearly enhanced her status. In the following year, 1927, Jerenia attended the NACGN annual meeting at the Tuskegee Institute in Alabama. Still acting as recording secretary, she now represented the community of Greensboro, North Carolina, rather than West Palm Beach. In the intervening year, she had accepted the superintendency at L. Richardson Memorial Hospital. There, she took charge of the hospital's nursing staff and nurse training program. All the work she had accomplished since her graduation from the Freedmen's Hospital's nurse training program now permitted her to perform at a level required by responsibilities of this magnitude.⁵²

Understandably, Jerenia gladly informed NACGN colleagues of her new position. A report of the session synopsized her comments as follows: "[There is] a magnificent new hospital gifted by the Richardson family and other donors for the hospitalization of Negroes in Greensboro, N.C. known as the L. Richardson Mem. Hospital of which she was appointed superintendent. She also spoke of the splendid equipment, the training school and the friendly relationship existing between the two races in N.C." In addition, the entry noted, the hospital housed leaders in the fields of surgery, obstetrics, pediatrics, orthopedics, and neurology. Jerenia fully embraced the work and the rewards that the opportunity presented.⁵³

In 1928, Jerenia attended the annual meeting in New Orleans. Although members elected her for another term, she declined the office of recording secretary. The minutes declared, "[She] resigned because she had an extremely busy year before her and felt she could no longer serve." This signified the end of Jerenia's tenure as a member of the NACGN executive board and her leadership role in an organization that fought for the rights of black nurses. She had

Figure 28. Wake Robin Golf Club members, c. 1940, including Jerenia Reid (second from right). (Courtesy of Wake Robin Golf Club.)

dedicated her life to serving others, and her NACGN activities had allowed her to perform that duty in politics as well as nursing.[54]

Jerenia's withdrawal from the NACGN executive board most definitely did not signify the end of her career. She continued to act as a member of the organization and also to work in her profession. By 1928, she held the position of superintendent of the People's Hospital in St. Louis, Missouri. Available records do not show when she retired from nursing, but by 1936 she resided in Washington, D.C., where she served as head ward nurse at her alma mater, the Freedmen's Hospital. In the next year she became one of the founding members of the Wake Robin Golf Club, an all-black female club that played a leading role in desegregating the city's public golf courses. In later years, the club furthered the movement that caused the Professional Golfers Association (PGA) to accept black golfers and assisted organizations such as the United Golfers Association (UGA) to put on tournaments specifically for black golfers. Jerenia thus found a variety of ways to contribute to the progress of the black community.[55]

Jerenia remained in Washington, D.C., after 1938. She continued to work for the Freedmen's Hospital into the 1950s and also participated actively in the congregation of St. Mary's Episcopal Church. She died on February 2, 1962, at the age of eighty-two. Reflecting her position within her profession and her service to the African American and medical communities of the District of Columbia, the *Washington Post* featured her obituary the following Sunday. It listed her survivors as a daughter, Mrs. Valentine D. Waddill, of Washington, and a son, Dr. Charles A. Dial, of St. Louis, Missouri.[56]

It is clear that Jerenia Valentine Dial Reid, an African American pioneer in the nursing field, illustrated with her life and career the contributions that African American women have made to health care in Florida and in the United States as a whole. The fact that her life's work uplifted the race cannot be denied. Jerenia lived a life full of achievements, saving in the process the lives of countless others. She made progress in the hostile and stifling climate of the early twentieth-century South, a climate not conducive to the intellectual and economic growth of its black citizens, and she carried with pride her distinction as the first black registered nurse in Florida. Jerenia used her position as a member of the elite to serve the black community in meritorious ways. Her hard work and dedication propelled her to the top of her class and allowed her to give to black communities in several states as a nurse, a teacher, an administrator, and an organizational and community activist.

Notes

1. Mary Elizabeth Carnegie, *The Path We Tread: Blacks in Nursing, 1854–1984* (Philadelphia, 1986), 1, 5–9, 17–19; Darlene Clark Hine, *Black Women in White: Racial Conflict and Cooperation in the Nursing Profession, 1890–1950* (Indianapolis, 1989), 1–6.

2. Carnegie, *Path We Tread*, 1, 5–9, 17–19; Hine, *Black Women in White*, 1–6. On Mary E. Mahoney, see Mary Ella Chayer, "Mary Eliza Mahoney," *American Journal of Nursing* 54 (April 1954): 429–31; Helen S. Miller, *Mary Eliza Mahoney, 1845–1926: America's First Black Professional Nurse: A Historical Perspective* (Atlanta, 1986); Althea T. Davis, *Early Black American Leaders in Nursing: Architects for Integration and Equality* (Boston, 1999), 25–60; Susan Muaddi Darraj, *Mary Eliza Mahoney and the Legacy of African American Nurses* (New York, 2005).

3. Carnegie, *Path We Tread*, 17–20; Hine, *Black Women in White*, 9–10.

4. Hine, *Black Women in White*, 7–9.

5. Carnegie, *Path We Tread*, 20–23; Hine, *Black Women in White*, 8–9, 26–29; Jacqueline M. Moore, *Leading the Race: The Transformation of the Black Elite in the Nation's Capital, 1880–1920* (Charlottesville, Va., 1999), 140–47; Cynthia Neverdon-Morton, *Afro-American Women of the South and the Advancement of the Race, 1895–1925* (Knoxville, Tenn., 1989), 12–14, 30–31.

6. Nathan Mayo, comp., *The Seventh Census of the State of Florida, 1945* (Tallahassee, 1945), 83; *Boston Daily Advertiser*, March 11, 1868, quoted in Canter Brown Jr., *Ossian Bingley Hart: Florida's Loyalist Reconstruction Governor* (Baton Rouge, 1997), 25; idem, *Florida's Black Public Officials, 1867–1924* (Tuscaloosa, 1998), 42, 54; Abel A. Bartley, *Keeping the Faith: Race, Politics, and Social Development in Jacksonville, Florida, 1940–1970* (Westport, Conn., 1965), 29; T. Frederick Davis, *History of Jacksonville, Florida, and Vicinity, 1513–1924* (St. Augustine, 1925; reprint ed., Jacksonville, 1990), 149–231.

7. Patricia L. Kenney, "LaVilla, Florida, 1866–1887: Reconstruction Dreams and the Formation of a Black Community," in *The African American Heritage of Florida*, ed. David R. Colburn and Jane L. Landers (Gainesville, 1995), 185–206; James Weldon Johnson, *Along This Way: The Autobiography of James Weldon Johnson* (New York, 1933), 56; Larry Eugene Rivers and Canter Brown Jr., "'The Art of Gathering a Crowd': Florida's Pat Chappelle and the Origins of Black-Owned Vaudeville," *Journal of African American History* 92 (Spring 2007): 169–90; Bartley, *Keeping the Faith*, 11–12.

8. *New York Freemen*, August 18, 1883; Kenney, "LaVilla," 188–90; 1880 U.S. Decennial Census, Duval County, Florida (population schedule); Bartley, *Keeping the Faith*, 11–12.

9. *Jacksonville Florida Weekly Times*, October 18, 1888; Brown, *Florida's Black Public Officials*, 133–34; Alachua County Deed Records, Book H, 80, Alachua County Courthouse, Gainesville; *New York Globe*, August 18, 1883, April 5, 1884; *Jacksonville Florida Times-Union*, January 20, 1884, September 10, 1886.

10. 1880 U.S. Decennial Census, Duval County, Florida (population schedule); 1885 Florida State Census, Duval County (population schedule); Alachua County Marriage License Records, Book 3, p. 71, Alachua County Courthouse, Gainesville.

11. Brown, *Florida's Black Public Officials*, 133–34; *New York Globe*, April 5, 1884; *Jacksonville Florida Times-Union*, January 20, 1884, and September 10, 1886; Bartley, *Keeping the Faith*, 13.

12. *Jacksonville Florida Weekly Times*, October 18, 1888; Brown, *Florida's Black Public Officials*, 133–34; Alachua County Deed Records, Book H, 80.

13. Daniel Smith Lamb, comp., *Howard University Medical Department, Washington, D.C.: A Historical, Biographical and Statistical Souvenir* (Washington, D.C., 1900; reprint ed., Freeport, N.Y., 1971), 162; *Washington (D.C.) People's Advocate*, October 20, 1883; *New York Freeman*, June 27, 1885. For more on Florida's pioneer black physicians, see Jonathan Hutchins, "William J. Gunn and the Beginnings of the Practice of Medicine by African Americans in Florida," in *Go Sound the Trumpet! Selections in Florida's African American History*, ed. David H. Jackson Jr. and Canter Brown Jr. (Tampa, 2005), 121–35; Canter Brown Jr., "Dr. James Alpheus Butler: An African American Pioneer of Miami Medicine," *Tequesta: The Journal of the Historical Association of Southern Florida* 66 (2006): 49–81.

14. Larry Eugene Rivers and Canter Brown Jr., "A Monument to the Progress of the Race: The Intellectual and Political Origins of the Florida Agricultural and Mechanical University, 1865–1887," *Florida Historical Quarterly* 85 (Summer 2006): 5–8; *Jacksonville Florida Times-Union*, June 9, 1891.

15. *Jacksonville Florida Times-Union*, June 9, 1891.

16. Johnson, *Along This Way*, 90–92; 1880 U.S. Decennial Census, Duval County, Florida (population schedule); Charlton W. Tebeau and William Marina, *A History of Florida*, 3rd ed. (Coral Gables, 1999), 273–74.

17. Tebeau and Marina, *History of Florida*, 273–74; *Jacksonville Florida Weekly Times*, October 18, 1888; Johnson, *Along This Way*, 90–92.

18. *Jacksonville Florida Times-Union*, March 13, 1895.

19. 1900 and 1920 U.S. Decennial Censuses, Duval County, Florida (population schedules); *Jacksonville City Directory, 1901* (Jacksonville, 1901), 424; *Jacksonville City Directory, 1902*, 491; Duval County Marriage Records, Book 5, p. 155, Duval County Courthouse, Jacksonville; *Washington* (D.C.) *Colored American*, May 9, 1903.

20. Thomas J. Ward Jr., *Black Physicians in the Jim Crow South* (Fayetteville, Ark., 2003), 3–6; Wilbur H. Watson, *Against the Odds: Blacks in the Profession of Medicine in the United States* (New Brunswick, N.J., 1999), 22–23.

21. *Report of the Freedmen's Hospital to the Secretary of the Interior, 1900* (Washington D.C., 1900), 5–6.

22. Howard University, *The Catalogue of Officers and Students from March 1900 to March 1901* (Washington, D.C., 1902), 20–22; *Report of the Freedmen's Hospital to the Secretary of the Interior, 1900*, 8–9.

23. Howard University, *Catalogue of Officers and Students*, 20–21; *Report of the Freedmen's Hospital to the Secretary of the Interior, 1900*, 8–9.

24. Howard University, *Catalogue of Officers and Students*, 20–21; *Report of the Freedmen's Hospital to the Secretary of the Interior, 1900*, 8–9; Adah Belle Thoms, *Pathfinders: A History of the Progress of Colored Graduate Nurses* (New York, 1929), 37–38.

25. Howard University, *Catalogue of Officers and Students*, 20–21; *Report of the Freedmen's Hospital to the Secretary of the Interior, 1900*, 8–9.

26. Howard University, *Catalogue of Officers and Students*, 20–21; *Report of the Freedmen's Hospital to the Secretary of the Interior, 1900*, 8–9.

27. Howard University, *Catalogue of Officers and Students*, 20–21; *Report of the Freedmen's Hospital to the Secretary of the Interior, 1900*, 8–9; *Washington* (D.C.) *Colored American*, May 9, 1903; Thoms, *Pathfinders*, 37–38; *Washington* (D.C.) *Bee*, May 2, 1903.

28. Moore, *Leading the Race*, 133, 140–41; Willard B. Gatewood, *Aristocrats of Color: The Black Elite, 1880–1920* (Indianapolis, 1990), 39–68.

29. *Washington* (D.C.) *Bee*, May 2, 1903; *Washington* (D.C.) *Colored American*, May 9, 1903; Neverdon-Morton, *Afro-American Women of the South*, 6–7.

30. James B. Crooks, *Jacksonville after the Fire, 1901–1919* (Jacksonville, Fla., 1991), 50–52; Bartley, *Keeping the Faith*, 14–15.

31. Crooks, *Jacksonville after the Fire*, 50–52; Bartley, *Keeping the Faith*, 14–15.

32. Crooks, *Jacksonville after the Fire*, 50–52; Bartley, *Keeping the Faith*, 14–15.

33. *Jacksonville Evening Metropolis*, July 27 and December 10, 1903.

34. Ibid., February 8 and December 30, 1904.

35. Ibid.

36. Ibid., April 8 and October 3, 1901, September 30, 1902, June 12, 1903, and December 5, 1904.

37. Moore, *Leading the Race*, 38–40; Gatewood, *Aristocrats of Color*, 190–92.

38. Personal interview with Canter Brown Jr. by the author, October 18, 2005, notes in possession of the author; Canter Brown Jr., *Henry Bradley Plant: The Nineteenth*

Century "King of Florida" (Tampa, 1999), 2–19. On A. Philip Randolph, see Paula F. Pfeffer, *A. Philip Randolph, Pioneer of the Civil Rights Movement* (Baton Rouge, 1990).

39. *Jacksonville Evening Metropolis*, December 13, 1906; Duval County Marriage Records, Book 10, p. 426; *Jacksonville City Directory, 1905*, 608.

40. *Jacksonville Evening Metropolis*, December 13, 1906, and April 7 1908; *Jacksonville City Directory, 1908*, 276; *Jacksonville City Directory, 1909*, 323; *Jacksonville City Directory, 1910*, 360; 1910 U.S. Decennial Census, Duval County, Florida (population schedule).

41. *Jacksonville Evening Metropolis*, April 7, 1908, and November 11, 1910; *Jacksonville City Directory, 1908*, 276; *Jacksonville City Directory, 1909*, 323; *Jacksonville City Directory, 1910*, 360.

42. *Washington Post*, February 4, 1962; personal communication with Ashley L. Till, archivist, South Carolina State University Archives, March 12, 2009 (notes in possession of the author); *Daytona City Directory 1914* (Daytona, 1914), 59, 125; Jacob U. Gordon, *Black Leadership for Social Change* (Westport, Conn., 2000), 138.

43. Duval County Marriage Records, Book 23, 113; *Washington Post*, February 4, 1962; *List of Mothers and Widows of American Soldiers, Sailors, and Marines Entitled to Make a Pilgrimage to War Cemeteries in Europe* (Washington, D.C., 1930), 158; Report of Disinterment and Reburial, December 27, 1922, Leon S. Reid file, Records of the Office of the Quartermaster General, Cemeterial Division, National Archives (hereafter, Reid file).

44. *Jacksonville City Directory 1920* (Jacksonville, 1920), 983.

45. Mabel Keaton Staupers, *No Time for Prejudice: A Story of the Integration of Negroes in Nursing in the United States* (New York, 1961), 5–19; Carnegie, *Path We Tread*, 92–94; National Association of Colored Graduate Nurses Records, NACGN Collection, 1–3, Schomburg Center for Research in Black Culture, New York Public Library, New York (hereafter, NACGNR).

46. Staupers, *No Time for Prejudice*, 15; Davis, *Early Black American Leaders in Nursing*, 75; NACGNR, 1–3.

47. *Jacksonville Evening Metropolis*, October 24, 1915.

48. NACGN meeting minutes, August 1925, NACGNR (hereafter NACGN minutes).

49. *Palm Beach Post*, March 1, 1999, and October 10, 2000; Thoms, *Pathfinders*, 222; *Indianapolis Freeman*, February 27, 1918; *New York Tribune*, February 29, 1924; 1920 U.S. Decennial Census, Palm Beach County, Florida (population schedule); NACGN minutes, 1926.

50. *Palm Beach Post*, March 1, 1999, and October 10, 2000; Thoms, *Pathfinders*, 222; *Indianapolis Freeman*, February 27, 1918; *New York Tribune*, February 29, 1924; 1920 U.S. Decennial Census, Palm Beach County, Florida (population schedule); NACGN minutes, 1926.

51. NACGN minutes, 1926.

52. NACGN minutes, 1927; *Greensboro* (N.C.) *News*, May 10, 1927; *Journal of the National Medical Association* 61 (May 1969): 205–28.

53. NACGN minutes, 1927; *Greensboro* (N.C.) *News*, May 10, 1927; *Journal of the National Medical Association* ibid.

54. Thoms, *Pathfinders*, 224–25; NACGN minutes, 1928.

55. Personal Interview with Ethel Williams by Eleanor DesVenex-Senet, Moorland Spingarn oral historian, December 12–13, 2005. The Wake Robin Golf Club Collection (available at Moorland Spingarn Research Center and Archives); Jerenia Reid, letter to the Cemeterial Division of the War Department, July 29, 1929, Reid file; 1930 U.S. Decennial Census, St. Louis, Missouri (population schedule); Thoms, *Pathfinders*, 224–25; *Birmingham News*, August 17, 1930; *Washington Post*, February 4, 1962; *Washington* (D.C.) *Afro-American*, June 12, 1937.

56. *Washington Post*, February 4, 1962.

Contributors

CANTER BROWN JR. received his undergraduate, law, and doctoral degrees from Florida State University. He additionally studied southern history at the University of Florida under the aegis of the distinguished historian and editor Sam Proctor. His many publications include the award-winning volumes *Florida's Peace River Frontier* (Orlando, 1991) and *Ossian Bingley Hart, Florida's Loyalist Reconstruction Governor* (Baton Rouge, 1997). Formerly professor of history at Florida A&M University, he presently serves as special assistant and counsel to the president and as professor of history at Fort Valley State University.

Brown and Larry Rivers jointly have written *Laborers in the Vineyard of the Lord: The Beginnings of the AME Church in Florida, 1865–1895* (Gainesville, 2001) and *For a Great and Grand Purpose: The Beginnings of the AMEZ Church in Florida, 1864–1905* (Gainesville, 2004). With Professor Richard Mathews of the University of Tampa, they coedited a revised edition of John Willis Menard's *Lays in Summer Lands* (Tampa, 2002).

JAMES M. DENHAM is author of *"A Rogue's Paradise": Crime and Punishment in Antebellum Florida, 1821–1861* (Tuscaloosa, 1997). He coedited with Canter Brown Jr. *Cracker Times and Pioneer Lives: The Florida Reminiscences of George Gillett Keen and Sarah Pamela Williams* (Columbia, 2000) and, with Keith L. Huneycutt, *Echoes from a Distant Frontier: The Brown Sisters' Correspondence from Antebellum Florida* (Columbia, 2004). He serves as professor of history and director of the Center for Florida History at Florida Southern College, Lakeland.

DAWN J. HERD-CLARK, in addition to her published essays and encyclopedia entries, is preparing for publication "Dorchester Academy: The American Missionary Association in Liberty County, Georgia, 1867–1950." She is assistant professor of history at Fort Valley State University.

DAVID H. JACKSON JR., author of publications including *A Chief Lieutenant of the Tuskegee Machine: Charles Banks of Mississippi* (Gainesville, 2002) and *Booker T. Washington and the Struggle against White Supremacy: The Southern Educational Tours, 1908-1912* (New York, 2008), also coedited with Canter Brown Jr. *Go Sound the Trumpet! Selections in Florida's African American History* (Tampa, 2005). He serves as professor of history and chair of the Department of History, Political Science/Public Administration, Geography, and African American Studies at Florida A&M University, Tallahassee.

ARVA MOORE PARKS has authored, among other works, *Miami: The Magic City* (Miami, 1991; rev. ed., 2008) and *The Forgotten Frontier: Florida through the Lens of Ralph Middleton Munroe* (Miami, 1977; rev. ed., Miami, 2004). An independent historian, she has served by presidential appointment on the Federal Advisory Council on Historic Preservation, chaired the Florida Endowment for the Humanities, and been honored by induction into the Florida Women's Hall of Fame.

TRACY J. REVELS is author of, among other publications, *Watery Eden: A History of Wakulla Springs* (Tallahassee, 2002) and the award-winning *Grander in Her Daughters: Florida's Women during the Civil War* (Columbia, 2004). She serves as professor and chair of the Department of History at Wofford College, Spartanburg, South Carolina.

LARRY EUGENE RIVERS has authored, among other works, the award-winning *Slavery in Florida: Territorial Days to Emancipation* (Gainesville, 2000). For a quarter century he served at Florida A&M University in numerous capacities, ending his tenure there as dean of the College of Arts and Sciences and distinguished university professor of history. In March 2006 he became eighth president of Fort Valley State University.

TERRANCE D. SMITH has published in the *National Association for Student Affairs Professionals Journal* and holds the position of president of the National Association for Student Affairs Professionals. Smith has taught in the Fort Valley State University Department of Business Administration and Economics and presently serves as FVSU vice president for student affairs.

ESTHER SPENCER holds a bachelor's degree in English from the University of Michigan and a master's degree in applied social sciences from Florida A&M University. Her thesis topic addresses origins of black female health-care professionals in Florida, 1880–1930.

CONSUELO E. STEBBINS translated and edited Fermín Valdés Domínguez's *Tragedy in Havana, November 27, 1871* (Gainesville, 2000) and authored *City of Intrigue, Nest of Revolution: A Documentary History of Key West in the Nineteenth Century* (Gainesville, 2007). She serves as associate professor in the Department of Modern Languages and Literatures and as vice president for internationalization at the University of Central Florida, Orlando.

FRED R. VAN HARTESVELDT is author of *The Boer War: Historiography and Annotated Bibliography* (Westport, Conn., 2005) and *Battles of the British Expeditionary Forces, 1914–1915: Historiography and Annotated Bibliography* (Westport, Conn., 2000). Professor of history and chair of the Department of History, Geography, Political Science, and Criminal Justice at Fort Valley State University, van Hartesveldt also serves as editor of the *Journal of the Georgia Association of Historians*.

CAROLYN WILLIAMS is widely recognized for her expertise in Florida and women's history and is author of, among other works, *Historic Photos of Jacksonville* (Nashville, Tenn., 2007). She serves as associate professor in the Department of History, director of the Gender Studies Program, and codirector of the Bette J. Soldwedel Gender Research Center at the University of North Florida, Jacksonville.

DARIA WILLIS holds bachelor's and master's degrees from Florida A&M University and is a student in the history doctoral program at Florida State University. She has published in the *A.M.E. Church Review* and is writing her dissertation on the life and works of Adella Hunt Logan.

SALLY J. ZEPEDA has published widely in the field of instructional supervision, including *The Principal as Instructional Leader: A Handbook for Supervisors*, 2nd ed.(Larchmont, N.Y., 2007) and *Instructional Supervision: Applying Tools and Concepts*, 2nd ed. (Larchmont, N.Y., 2007). She serves as professor and graduate coordinator in the Department of Lifelong Education, Administration, and Policy, Educational Administration and Policy Program, University of Georgia, Athens.

Index

Abraham Lincoln's Birthday, 272
Adair, A. P., 229
Adamson, Blossom, 194
Africa, 128, 134–35, 140. *See also* Congo; Liberia
African Americans, 36–37, 64–81, 92–94, 96, 106–8, 122–43, 151–66, 171–87, 192–208, 236–56, 263–82, 287–306. *See also* slaves and slavery
African Free School No. 2 (N.Y.C.), 65,
African International Association, 131
African Methodist Episcopal (AME) Church, 67–69, 73–80, 127–28, 134, 139, 200, 239
African Methodist Episcopal Zion (AMEZ) Church, 176–77, 200
Afro-American Industrial and Benefit Association. *See* Afro-American Life Insurance Co.
Afro-American Life Insurance Co., 244–45, 259
Afro-American Women's Association (Jacksonville, Fla.), 77–80, 247
Agriculture and agricultural experimentation, 3, 16, 34–35, 43–45, 48–49, 51–52, 57, 126, 133, 154, 175, 178–80, 182, 184, 186, 207, 267, 270, 274–75, 281, 290
Akerman, Joe A., Jr., 13
Alabama, 44, 49, 152–66, 266, 289, 294, 301, 304. *See also named places*
Alayeto, Carlotta Cenarro de, 109
Albany, Ga., 155, 205, 266
Albany Normal School. *See* Albany State University
Albany State University (Ga.), 266

Alexander, Adele Logan, 154
Alexander, Will W., 207
Allen, George, 65
Allen, Walter, 194
Allen Normal and Industrial School (Thomasville, Ga.), 210, 276–77
Allen University (Columbia, S.C.), 130
Allenhurst, Ga., 270
All the Days of My Life (book), 86
Alpizar y Poyo, Raoul, 112
Amelia Island, Fla., 237
American Baptist Home Mission Society, 130
American Baptist Missionary Union, 137–43
American Baptist Missionary Union, The (annual report), 139
American Bible Society, 128
American Canoe Association, 88
American Church Institute, 186
American Missionary, The (journal), 269
American Missionary Association, 128, 133, 155, 173, 240, 264, 266–70, 276, 281–82
American Nurses Association (ANA), 302
American Party, 30
American Red Cross. *See* Red Cross
Amherst College, 126
Anderson, Caroline Still Wiley, 128–29, 138
Anderson, Dan, 93
Anderson, Katherine, 93
Andrew Rankin Memorial Chapel (Washington, D.C.), 297
Andrews, Eliza Frances, 153

Andrews, Samuel Simeon, 153
Angola Fund (Dorchester Academy), 274
Anna Madgigine Jai Kingsley (book), xi
Anthony, Susan B., 161, 260
Antwerp, Belgium, 142
Arizona, 208
Armistice Day, 272
Armstrong, Samuel C., 157
Arnell, Ellis G., 185
Arthur, Chester A., 12, 135
Artrell, Victoria, 136
Artrell, William H., 135–36
Arts and artistic creativity, 64, 270–71
Asbury Methodist Episcopal Church (Savannah, Ga.), 278
Ashton, Lucy V., 296
Ashville, N.C., 79
Associated Charities (Jacksonville, Fla.), 248
Athletics. *See* Sports and sportsmanship
Atlanta, Ga.: and Selena Sloan Butler, 192–93, 197–201, 204–208, 211; mentioned, 138, 184, 279
Atlanta Baptist College. *See* Morehouse College
Atlanta Baptist Female Seminary. *See* Spelman College
Atlanta Constitution (newspaper), 194, 211
Atlanta Georgian (newspaper), 194
Atlanta Journal (newspaper), 194
Atlanta Life Insurance Co., 200
Atlanta Neighborhood Union, 193, 205, 214
Atlanta Riot (1906), 194–95
Atlanta Savings Bank, 211
Atlanta University. *See* Clark Atlanta University
Atlantic City, N.J., 186
Attire. *See* Clothing and fashion
Augusta, Alexander T., 294
Augusta, Ga., 164
Austin, Texas, 30
Averill, Clementine, 54
Avery Institute, 276

Babcock, Maltbie Davenport, 282
Bahama Islands and Bahamians, 92–93, 105–106
Baker, James, 271
Baker, Mrs. E. B., 206
Baker, Nettie E. L., 80
Baltimore, Md., 134
Banana Point, Congo, 137–38, 142
Banza Manteka, Congo, 137
Baptist Church, 14, 44, 46, 49, 51, 126, 130, 134–37, 142–43, 197, 241–42, 273, 278, 280. *See also* named churches
Baptist Foreign Mission Convention, 134
Baptist General Association of Western States and Territories, 137
Baptist Missionary Magazine, 139, 143
Barclay, Harry, 35
Barnes, Altamese, 81
Barr, Alice, 87, 100
Barr, Amelia Huddleston, 86–88, 100
Barr, Andrew, 87
Barr, Lilly, 87, 100
Barr, Mary. *See* Munroe, Mary Barr
Barr, Robert, 86
Bartow, Fla., 48, 216, 218, 220–21
Bartow Courier-Informant (newspaper), 220
Bass, W. A., 155
Bass Academy, 155
Bates College, 130
Batista, Fulgencio, 118
Battle Creek, Mich., 166
Bay View House (Coconut Grove, Fla.), 89
Bayard, Fla., 243
"Be Strong" (poem), 282
Beach High School (Ga.), 277
Beaufort, S.C., 221
Beauty contests, 278
Beecher, Charles, 131
Beecher, Henry Ward, 87
Beck, Nellie, 220–21
Belén Observatory, 114
Belgarnie, Florence, 203
Belgian Congo. *See* Congo

Belgium, 131, 142
Bell, Jefferson, 100
Belliny, D. S. D., 136
Bender, Shelby, 58
Beneficencia Cubana (Key West, Fla.), 108
Bennett, Charles, 255–56
Benton, Elizabeth. *See* Moore, Elizabeth Benton
Benton, Fannie Moore, 264
Benton, George R., 264
Bereavement, 5–6, 31, 166, 241. *See also* widowhood
Berlin Conference (1885), 135
Berrien County, Mich., 57
Betancourt, Antonio, 118
Betancourt, Arsenio, 118
Betancourt, Carmelina, 118
Betancourt, María Manas de, 109
Bethel AME Church (Tallahassee, Fla.), 67–69
Bethel Institutional Baptist Church (Jacksonville, Fla.), 126, 128, 132, 135, 137, 141, 242, 244, 247
Bethel Missionary Baptist Church (Tallahassee, Fla.), 74
Bethune, Mary McLeod, 250, 254, 301
Bibb County, Ga., 185
Bibb County Board of Public Welfare, 185
Biddle University. *See* Johnson C. Smith University
Big Bethel AME Church (Atlanta), 200, 212
Bigelow, Alexander G., 8–9
Bigelow, Anna Hayden Porter, 4, 8–9
Biographical Sketch of Honorable Ossian B. Hart (pamphlet), 19
Birds. *See* wildlife and wildlife preservation
Birney, Alice McLelland, 206
Bisbee, Horatio, 12
Biscayne Bay, 89–90
Biscayne Bay Yacht Club, 91
Black, Hugo, 255
Blackman, Lucy, 98
Black Side, The (book), 198
Bloomers, 54
Bloomingdale, Fla., 51, 58
Blount, Lydia Oregon Hendry, 45–48
Bloxham, William D., 37–38, 219, 222
Boarding and boarding houses, 6–8, 32, 174, 218–19, 222
Boating and sailing, 88, 90
Bok, Edward, 95
Bolengi, Congo, 14
Boone, Marion, 271
Boris, Joseph J., 212
Boston, Mass., 87, 137, 245, 288
Boule, The, 200
Boylan Industrial Home for Girls (Jacksonville, Fla.), 77, 299, 303
Braden Plantation, 12
Bradenton, Fla., 12
Bradley, Guy, 95–96
Brandon, Albert Jordan, 50
Brandon, Fla., 43, 46, 49–58
Brandon, James, 51, 53–54
Brandon, John LeRoy, 50, 56–57
Brandon, John William, 49–53
Brandon, Lovic Pierce, 50
Brandon, Mark, 55
Brandon, Mark Zachariah, 50, 54
Brandon, Martha Brown Carson, 49
Brandon, Sadie Ellen, 50
Brandon, Victoria Martha Seward Varn. *See* Sherrill, Victoria Martha Seward Varn Brandon
Brevard, Mary Call, 27, 29–30
Brevard, Theodore Washington, 30
Brewer, Fisk P., 173
Brewser, Georgia A., 299
Brewster Hospital (Jacksonville, Fla.), 299
Brewster Nursing School (Jacksonville, Fla.), 299, 303
Brick Junior College (N.C.), 275
Brickell, William, 89
Brooklyn, N.Y., 133–34
Brooklyn Improvement Club (Jacksonville, Fla.), 247

Brooks, Abbie M., 35
Brooks County, Ga., 195
Brooksville, Fla., 49
Broward, Napoleon Bonaparte, 38, 223–26
Brown, A. E., 228
Brown, Pauline, 220
Brown, Tobias, 220
Browne, Jefferson B., 110
Brownlee, Fred, 267, 276
Bruce, Blanche K., 264
Brunswick, Ga., 276, 278
Bryan, Nathan P., 224, 227
Bryan, Nathaniel C., 16
Bryan, William J., 224–25
Bryant, Mrs. Peter James, 206
Bryant, Mrs. S. C. J., 205
Buchanan, Mich., 57
Buffalo, N.Y., 79
Bullock County, Ala., 156
Bureau of Freedmen, Refugees, and Abandoned Lands. *See* Freedmen's Bureau
Burns, Hayden, 256
Burnt Country (Ga.), 153
Burroughs, Nannie Helen, 253
Busy Bee Club (Dorchester Academy), 273
Butler, Henry Rutherford, 198–201, 208, 211–12
Butler, Henry Rutherford, Jr., 199, 205–206, 208
Butler, James Alpheus, 259
Butler, Maggie Lewis, 81
Butler, Selena Mae Sloan: as community activist and organizer, 201–8, 213; death of, 208; early life and education of, 192–97; marriage and family of, 198–200, 212; as teacher 197–98; as women's suffrage advocate, 201
Butler, Slater & Co., 198–99
Butler County, Ala., 156
Buttrick, Wallace, 178
Bywater, Tanqueray & Co., 138

Caballeros de Martí, 118
Cady, George L., 269
California, 87, 208
Call, Ellen. *See* Long, Ellen Call
Call, Mary. *See* Brevard, Mary Call
Call, Mary Kirkman, 26–27
Call, Richard Keith, 26–28, 30–31, 38
Caloosahatchee River, Fla., 88
Calvary Baptist Church (Ga.), 273
Campbell, Abner, 2, 5
Campbell, Arthur E., 300
Campbell, Catharine Smith. *See* Hart, Catharine Smith Campbell
Campbell, Charles G., 12
Campbell, Charlotte ("Lottie"), 2–4, 6, 8, 11, 17–18, 20
Campbell, Deborah Conger, 2, 5–6, 10–12
Campbell, Emma F. R., 2–4, 6, 8, 11, 17–20
Cancer, 296
Canova, Paul Bartolo, 125
Carey, Alice D., 184
Carnegie, Andrew, 93
Carnegie, Lucy, 93
Carnegie, Mrs. Thomas. *See* Carnegie, Lucy
Carnegie philanthropy, 180
Carolina, Estey. *See* Fleming, Estey Carolina
Caroline M. Martin Fund, 269, 284–85
Carrasco, Antonio Díaz, 108, 110–11
Carrasco, María L., 109
Carroll, Charles, 202
Carroll County, Miss., 44
Carrollton, Miss., 44
Carrollton Baptist Church, 44
Carson, Kit, 87
Carter, Edward Randolph, 198
Carter, Richard, 155
Carver, George Washington, 166
Casa del Pobre, Mercedes. *See* Mercedes Hospital
Castillo, Loynaz del, 111

Catholic Cemetery (Key West, Fla.), 118
Catlow, Patty Munroe, 94
Cattle, 12–13, 49–51, 57, 216, 219
Catts, Sidney J., 247
Cecily (slave), 48–49
Cedar Key, Fla., 290–91
Centennial Exposition, 9, 33–34
Central of Georgia Railway, 178
Central Park Junior College, 276–77
Central South Conference (Congregationalist Church), 164
Céspedes, Manuel, 117
Chamberlain, Ella C., 220, 248–49
Chambers v. Florida, 255
Chandler, Henry Wilkins, 130
Chandler, Zachary, 106
Chapel Hill, N.C., 173
Chapman, Margaret, 34
Chapman, Mollie, 238
Chappelle, Patrick H., 290
Charleston, S.C., 269
Charlotte, N.C., 174, 176
Charlotte Graded School (Charlotte, N.C.), 174
Chattanooga, Tenn., 48
Chautauqua Circle of Atlanta, 193, 201
Chautauqua Movement, 201
Chicago, Ill., 34, 165, 176, 254, 289
Chicago World's Fair (1893), 220
Child custody, 30
Children and child care, 4, 6, 8–10, 27–29, 45–50, 87, 93, 96, 123–25, 140, 158, 164, 183–86, 202, 208, 216–21, 237–39, 264–66, 291–93, 300–301. *See also* Kindergartens
Christian Aid Hall (Jacksonville, Fla.), 78
Christian Endeavor Society (Dorchester Academy), 273
Christian Recorder (AME newspaper), 76, 78, 139
Christian Union, 87
Christiance, DeForest, 100
Christmas, 11, 16, 46–47, 94, 179, 182–83, 219, 272–73

Cigar industry, 105, 107, 113–14
Citrus, 3, 6, 16, 53, 57, 219
City Federation of Women's Clubs (Jacksonville, Fla.), 247–48, 251
Civil Rights movement, 254–56
Civil War, 5, 31–32, 48–49, 125–26, 152–53
Clara White Mission (Jacksonville, Fla.), 254
Clark, Frank, 249
Clark Atlanta University, 155, 163–64, 173–74, 205, 267
Clayton, Bruce L., xi
Cleveland, E., 278
Cleveland, Grover, 16
Clothing and fashion, 54, 141, 268–70, 223–24
Club Number 7 (Dorchester Academy), 273
Clubs and organizations. *See fraternal organizations; sororal organizations; women's clubs and organizations*
Clyde Steamship Line, 228
Cocoanut Grove, Fla. *See* Coconut Grove, Fla.
Coconut Grove, Fla., 89–101
Coconut Grove Audubon Society, 96–98
Coconut Grove Rangers, 96–98
Cohen, Etta Dzialynski, 224, 226
Cohen, Jacob R., 216, 222
Cohen, Louis E., 224, 226
Cohen, Mary. *See* Dzialynski, Mary Cohen
Coleman Manufacturing Co., 176
Coles, David J., 20
Collins, Thomas, 276
Colorado, 162. *See also named places*
Colored American (newspaper), 297
Colored American Magazine, 160, 201
Colored Citizens' Protective League (Jacksonville, Fla.), 251
Colored Memorial High School (Brunswick, Ga.), 276–77

Index 319

Colored Methodist Episcopal (CME) Church, 74
Colored Normal, Agricultural Industrial and Mechanical College of South Carolina, 301
Colored Old Folks Home (Jacksonville, Fla.), 247
Colored Orphans' and Industrial Association (Jacksonville, Fla.), 77
Colored State Teachers Association (Fla.), 74–75, 78
Columbia University, 266
Columbus, Ga., 266, 294
Commercial Hotel (Gainesville, Fla.), 222
Commission on Interracial Cooperation (CIC), 206–207
Commune Viller Alsac cemetery, 301
Community development, 43, 50–57, 218
Conchs, 105, 107
Confederate pension, 57
Confederate States Army, 4, 30–31, 35, 125–26, 153
Confederate States of America, 4, 8, 25, 30, 32, 123, 125, 237
Conger, Obadiah, 2
Congo, 135–43
Congo Free State. *See* Congo
Congo River, 136–38, 142
Congregation Ahaveth Chesed (Jacksonville, Fla.), 229–30
Congregation B'nai B'rith Jacob (Savannah), 216
Congregation Schaarai Zedek (Tampa), 220
Congregational Sunday School conventions, 273
Congregationalist Church, 164, 264, 266, 269, 271, 273, 278, 281
Connecticut, 6, 19, 135. *See also named places*
Conwell, Russell H., 141, 143
Cookman Institute (Jacksonville, Fla.), 241
Cooper, Charles, 237

Cooper, Knight, Adair, Cooper & Osborne (law firm), 229
Corbet, Gertrude Dzialynski: as attorney, 222, 229; death of, 230; early career of, 221–23; early life and education of, 215–21; as Internal Revenue Service appointee, 227–28; marriage of, 228–29; political involvements of, 223–29; suffrage and other causes advocated by, 228–30
Corbet, John Archibald ("Jack"), 228–229
Cosmetology, 241
Cotton Centennial and Industrial Exposition, 34
Cotton Valley, Ala., 266
Cotton Valley School (Macon Co., Ala.), 266
Council of National Defense, 251
Courtenay, S. E., 156
Courtland County, N.Y., 65
Crackers and cracker culture, 52, 218–19, 246
Crawford, J.T.G., 226
Credit unions and credit union movement, 230, 281
Creek Indians, 26
Crisis, The (journal), 162
Cromwell, John W., 265
Crooks, James, 247
Cross Roads Baptist Church (Ga.), 273
Crown Prince of Palabala, 140
Cuba and Cubans, 50, 104–111, 113–18, 216. *See also named places*
Cuban Liberating Army, 107
Culp, Daniel Wallace, 65, 155–57, 241
Cumberland County, N.C., 198
Cunard Line, 138
Curry, Lula, 271
Curry, William N., 271
Curtis, Austin M., 294, 296
Custer, George Armstrong, 87
Cuyler High School (Savannah, Ga.), 276, 281
Cuyler Opportunity School (Ga.), 276

Cypress Slash Congregational Church (Ga.), 271

Dade County, Fla., 92, 96
Dade County Federation of Women's Clubs, 96
Daniel Hand Educational Fund for Colored People, 269
Darnes, Alexander H., 129, 292, 294
Dartmouth College, 129
Darwin, Charles Robert, 202
Daughters of the Confederacy, 223
Davidson, Olivia A. *See* Washington, Olivia A. Davidson
Davis, Benjamin J., Jr., 211
Davis, Jefferson, 45
Davison, John W., 177
Day, Anna, 65, 76
Day, Peter H., 65
Day, Mary E. C. *See* Smith, Mary E. C. Day
Day Memorial Church (Ga.), 273
Daytona, Fla., 301
Daytona Normal and Industrial School, 301
De Lono, Angel, 107
Dean, James, 107
Decroix, F. W., 94
Deering, William, 98
DeFoor, Allison, xiii
Degrasse, Isaiah, 65
DeKalb County, Ga., 185
Del Monico Restaurant (Key West, Fla.), 111
DeLand, Fla., 240
Deland, Margaret, 35
Democratic National Committee, 226, 229
Democratic Party, 8, 16, 30, 34, 71, 107, 194, 219, 222–29, 242, 249, 252–54
Denmark, 184
Dial, Charles A., 300–301
Dial, Charles A., Jr., 301, 305
Dial, Jerenia Valentine. *See* Jerenia Valentine Dial Reid
Dial, Valentine. *See* Waddill, Valentine Dial
Dickison, John J., 31
Dickson, Amanda America, 152
Dinnis, Paul, 51, 58
Disease, 3, 27, 137, 139, 198, 289, 297. *See* health and health care. *See also named illnesses and diseases*
District of Columbia. *See* Washington, D.C.
Dittmer, John, 195, 205
Divinity High School. *See* Edward Waters College
Dix, Effie, 78
Dixie Hospital Training School (Va.), 289
Domestic responsibilities, 3, 6, 30, 45–46, 48, 56, 93–94, 158, 164–65, 174–75, 199–200, 218–19, 282, 300–301
Doherty, Herbert J., 35
Dolores Mayg Society, 109–12, 116
Donelson, Andrew Jackson, 26
Dorchester, Mass., 267
Dorchester Academy (Liberty Co., Ga.), 263–64, 266–82
Dorchester Academy Alumni Association, 279
Dorchester Athletic Association, 278
Dorchester Federal Credit Union, 281
Dorchester Parent-Teacher Association, 279–80
Dorsey, Allison, 192, 210
Douglas, Marjory Stoneman, 86, 94–95, 100
Douglas Co., Ga., 276
Douglas Hospital (Kansas City, Mo.), 296
Douglass, Frederick, 195, 264
Dover, Fla., 58
Downing, George T., 65
Drummond, Jane, 237
Du Bois, William E. B., 152, 162, 264
Dunbar, Paul L., 271
Duncan, E. B., 68

Dunham, Elizabeth, 58
Durant, Fla., 58
Durrance, Francis M., 47
DuVal, Nancy, 27
DuVal, William Pope, 27
Duval County, Fla., 73–74, 76, 249, 292
Duval County Law Enforcement Committee, 229
Duval County League of Women Voters, 229
Dzialynski, Bertha Zadek, 217–20, 222–24, 230
Dzialynski, Etta. *See* Cohen, Etta Dzialynski
Dzialynski, Fannie. *See* Greenfield, Fannie Dzialynski
Dzialynski, George I. P., 220
Dzialynski, Gertrude. *See* Corbet, Gertrude Dzialynski
Dzialynski, Jennie. *See* Hezog, Jennie Dzialynski
Dzialynski, Mary Cohen, 216, 218, 221–22, 226
Dzialynski, Morris, 219, 221, 224, 230
Dzialynski, Philip, 216, 218–21, 230
Dzialynski, Ruth Hope. *See* Leon, Ruth Hope Dzialynski
Dzialynski House (Ft. Meade, Fla.), 219

Eartha M. White Nursing Home (Jacksonville, Fla.), 256
East London Institute for Home and Foreign Missions, 136–38
East Florida Seminary. *See* University of Florida
Easter, 272
Eaton, John H., 26
Ebeneezer, Ga., 277
Ebersole, Sarah C., 296
Economic downturns. *See* Great Depression; Panic of 1873; Panic of 1893
Edison, Thomas, 95
Education, 2, 27–28, 32, 46, 126–30, 154–55, 157, 173–74, 177–87, 196–97, 217–21, 240–42, 266–82, 292–97. *See*

also kindergartens; Sabbath schools; teachers and teaching
Edward Waters College, 75–76, 78–79, 277
Elgin Watch Company, 52
Elizarde, Leopoldina, 109
Elks, Benevolent and Protective Order of the, 200
Elmira, N.Y., 29
Emancipation Proclamation, 197
Encyclopaedia Britannica, 276
England. *See* Great Britain. *See also named places*
English, Adam, 237
English, Clara. *See* White, Clara English
Enterprise, Fla., 240
Environment and environmental protection, 37, 98–99. *See also* wildlife and wildlife preservation
Episcopal Church, 186, 221, 237, 305
Episcopal Parish of Brunswick (Ga.), 278
Equatorsville, Congo, 137
Escalante, María, 109
Estey Seminary Course, 134
Eulonia, Ga., 277
Eureka Multigraphing Service, 227–28
Everglades, Fla., 94–97
Everglades National Park, 97
Evergreen Cemetery (Jacksonville, Fla.), 19
Executive Order 8802, 255
Extraordinary Lives (book), xii

Fahey, David M., 136
Fair Haven Infirmary (Atlanta), 211
Fair Oaks Plantation, 12
Fairbanks, Rebecca P., 269
Fairchild, David, 94
Farm Credit Board, 180, 186
Farmer's Cooperative Marketing Association (Dorchester Academy), 275
Farming. *See* agriculture and agricultural experimentation
Fayetteville, N.C., 198

Federal Emergency Relief Administration (FERA), 114
Fernández, Angelica, 109
Fernández, Ignacia, 109
Fessenden Academy (Martin, Fla.), 266
Fifteenth Amendment, 160, 243
First Congregational Church (Atlanta), 200, 212
First Congregational Church (Savannah), 273, 278–79
First Methodist Church (Brandon, Fla.), 51
First South Carolina Infantry, 125
Fishing, 46, 48, 89, 93
Fisk University, 158, 264–66
Flagler, Henry, 37, 43, 94–95, 97
Flagler, Mrs. Henry, 97
Flamingo Feather, The (novel), 90
Fleetwood, Sarah I., 296
Fleming, Augustina, 124
Fleming, Augustina Cortes, 124
Fleming, Chloe. *See* Hawkins, Chloe Fleming
Fleming, Estey Carolina, 140, 142
Fleming, Francis P., 107, 125, 127
Fleming, Frederick A., 126
Fleming, George Claudius, 123–24, 129
Fleming, Lewis, 123–25
Fleming, Louise Cecilia ("Lulu"): and African mission work, 133–40, 142–43; death of, 143; early life and education of, 122–32; early teaching career of, 132–33; higher education of, 133, 140–42
Fleming, Louis Isador Jr., 124, 126–27
Fleming, Lulu C. (niece of Louise Cecilia Fleming), 138
Fleming, Maggie, 132
Fleming, Margaret Seton, 124, 126–27, 132
Fleming, Scipio, 124
Fleming, William A., 124, 133, 135, 138
Fleming's Island, Fla., 123
Flemming, David, 125
Fletcher, Duncan U., 226

Florida: 1920s boom era in, 100, 114; antebellum race relations in, 46, 123–25; Civil Rights movement in, 254–55; as a "female frontier," 35; first black registered nurse from, 287–306; as frontier region, 3, 13–15, 43–48, 95; Great Depression in, 114–19, 253; Jim Crow era dawns in, 75, 106–107, 245–47; and political life during Redemption period, 219; poll tax imposed in, 242–43, 252; Progressive Era in, 95–100, 223–28; and Reconstruction era, 5–8, 32, 48–51, 67–71, 126–28; Redemption and Gilded Age in, 8–19, 32–38, 51–57, 71–76, 89–95, 105–6; secession and Civil War in, 5, 31–32, 48–49, 125–26; and southern peninsular explorations in 1880s, 88; women's suffrage activities in, 220, 229, 248–52; and World War I, 112. *See also named places*
Florida (newspaper), 113
Florida A&M College. *See* Florida A&M University
Florida A&M University, xiii–xiv, 75, 197–98, 206
Florida Annual, Impartial and Unsectional (book), 89
Florida Audubon Society, 95–99
Florida Baptist Academy (Jacksonville, Fla.), 241–42, 258
Florida Breezes, Or, Florida Old and New (novel), 28, 35–36
Florida Central and Peninsula Railroad, 54
Florida Congress of Colored Parents and Teachers, 206
Florida East Coast Railroad, 97, 108
Florida Equal Franchise League, 249
Florida Federation of Women's Clubs, 96–98
Florida Keys, 97
Florida Law Reporting Association, 224
Florida Memorial College, 258
Florida Railroad, 290

Florida State Fair, 10
Florida State League of Women Voters, 229
Florida State Normal and Industrial School. *See* Florida A&M University
Florida State University, xiv–xv, 28, 167
Florida supreme court, 7, 10–12, 222
Florida Templar (newspaper), 136
Florida Woman Suffrage Association, 260
Florida Women's Hall of Fame, 312
Fogarty, Joseph N., 110
Folio Club, 99
Foote, Julia, 77
Forestry, 35, 96
Forrester, Cyrus, 123
Fort Brooke, Fla., 4, 45
Fort Dallas, Fla. *See* Miami, Fla.
Fort Davis, Ala., 266
Fort Fraser, Fla., 45–46, 48
Fort Huachuca, Ariz., 208
Fort Lauderdale, Fla., 43
Fort Marion, Fla., 34
Fort Meade, Fla.: and Gertrude Dzialynski Corbet, 216–20; mentioned, 47–48, 53, 229; and Victoria Seward Varn Brandon Sherrill, 43, 49–51; and voting under Nineteenth Amendment, 229
Fort Myers, Fla., 88
Fort Pierce, Fla., 3, 17
Fort Valley, Ga., 177–87, 205
Fort Valley High and Industrial School. *See* Fort Valley State University
Fort Valley Message (newspaper), 186
Fort Valley State University, xiii–xv, 172, 177–87
Fortune, T. Thomas, 138–39, 239, 291
Foster, Charles H., 12
Fourteenth Amendment, 243
France, 184, 301
Francis, Mary Ann. *See* Valentine, Mary Ann Francis
Franklin, Md., 27–28
Franklin, Martha M., 302

Fraternal organizations, 200–201. *See also* Elks; Knights of Pythias; Masons and Masonic orders
Frazier, S. F., 277, 279
Freedman's Bank, 72
Freedmen's Bureau, 7, 70, 155, 240
Freedmen's Grove Presbyterian Church (Ga.), 278
Freedmen's Hospital (Washington, D.C.), 294–97, 305
Freedmen's Hospital Training School for Nurses, 296–97
Freemasonry. *See* fraternal organizations; Masons and Masonic orders; sororal organizations
Freezes, 16, 18, 53–54, 218. *See also* Great Freeze of 1895
Friendship Baptist Church (Atlanta), 197, 200, 210, 280
Frisbie, Louise K., 48
Frontier environment, 3, 13–15, 35, 43–48, 67, 87–89, 95, 216–18
Frow, Mrs. Joseph, 92
Fuller, Jane Gay, 6

Gadsden County, Fla., 67, 237
Gainesville, Fla.: and Gertrude Dzialynski Corbet, 217–18, 222; mentioned, 129–30, 290–91
Galveston, Texas, 86
Gamble, Cora. *See* Long, Cora Gamble
Gammon, Samuel F., 226
Gano Parent-Teacher Association (Ft. Valley, Ga.), 183
Garnet, Henry Highland, 65
Gate City Free Kindergarten Association, 205, 213
Gato, Eduardo H., 109–112
Gato, Fernando, 112
Gato, María Marques de, 112
Gato, Mercedes, 109, 111
General Education Fund, 178
Genovar, Bartolo, 243
George Washington's Birthday, 90, 272
Georgia: antebellum race relations in,

152; Civil War in, 153; constitutionally mandated segregated schools in, 267; and the Great Depression, 181, 270, 274–75; and Jim Crow racial discrimination in, 172, 177, 179–80, 193–96, 267; mentioned, 44, 67, 130, 171, 174, 176, 206, 215, 252, 294; state capitol of, 208. *See also named places*
Georgia and South Carolina Congregational Church Conference, 273
Georgia Commission on Interracial Cooperation (CIC), 193, 206–7
Georgia Congregational Church Conference, 273
Georgia Federation of Colored Women's Clubs, 184–86, 193, 204–5
Georgia Medical Society for Colored Physicians, 211
Georgia Parent-Teacher Association, 206
Georgia State College of Agriculture, 267
Georgia State Fair, 275
Georgia State Industrial College, 279
Georgia Women of Achievement, 208
Germany, 184
Geter, Rhina G., 239
Gibbs, Jonathan Clarkson, 129
Gibson, R. A., 16
Gibson, Thelma Anderson, 93
Giddings, Paula, 199
Gifford, Edith, 96–97
Gifford, John, 96
Giles, Harriet, 197
Girlhood, 2, 27–28, 44–48, 65–67, 86–87, 106, 124–32, 152–55, 173–74, 193–97, 217–21, 237–41, 264–66, 289–94
Glasgow, Scotland, 86
Glogowski, Bertha Brown, 220
Glogowski, Herman, 220
Godwin, Carmen, 245, 251–53, 257
Golf and golfing, 305
Gonzalez, Annie Maloney, 107
Gonzalez, Antonio, 107
Good English Week (Dorchester Academy), 274

Good Templars, International Order of, 128, 130, 133, 136
Gordon, Ga., 153
Gordon, Nora Antonia, 138–39
Governor Milton (steamer), 125
Grace Baptist Church (Philadelphia, Pa.), 141
Grace Hospital (Philadelphia, Pa.), 143
Grant, Ulysses S., 9
Gray Ladies Corps, 193, 208
Great Britain, 135, 184, 203. *See also named places*
Great Depression, 114, 181, 184, 253–54, 275
Great Fire of 1901 (Jacksonville, Fla.), 79, 244–45, 247, 298–99
Great Freeze of 1895, 18, 43, 221
Great Migration, 246, 259, 270
Green, Mary Frances, 77
Green Cove Springs, Fla., 123, 240
Greenberg, Mark I., 218
Greenfield, Fannie Dzialynski, 219–21
Greenfield, Myer, 219, 221
Greensboro, N.C., 304
Greensville, Ala., 156
Greenwood, Janette Thomas, 176
Grimké, Charlotte Forten, 73–74, 130
Grimké, Francis James, 130
Griots, xii
Grito de Yara, 110, 114
Grove, The (home), 26–31, 33, 35, 37–38
Groveland, Ga., 270
Groveton, Ga., 194
Guinness, Fanny E., 136–38
Guinness, H. Grattan, 136–38
Gunn, William J., 129
Gutsens, Antonio, 106–107, 113, 116
Gutsens, Luis, 113
Gutsens, María Valdés ("Mamá") de: early life of, 104–6; death of, 118–20; marriage of, 106–107; and Mercedes Hospital, 108–18

Haden, Mrs. Florence, 94
Haiti, 65, 128

Hall, Jacquelyn Dowd, 207
Hall, W. A., 142
Halloween, 272
Hambright, Tom, 120
Hampton, Effie Carrie Mitchell, 130
Hampton, William Wade, 222–23
Hampton Institute, 157
Hancock County, Ga., 152–54, 174
Harmon, Henry S., 129
Harper Brothers, 92
Harper's Bazar, 93
Harper's Young People, 87
Harris, Cicero Richard, 177
Harris, Meriah Elizabeth Goin, 176
Harrison, Charles E., 53
Harrison, Mary Magdalene Cooper, 237–38
Harrison, Robert, 237
Hart, Catharine Smith Campbell: and the Civil War and early Reconstruction eras, 4–7; decline and death of, 17–20; early life of, 1–2; early widowhood of, 8–11; as Florida's First Lady, 7–8; with Henderson family at Tallahassee, 11–12; as Kissimmee pioneer, 12–17; married life of during antebellum era, 2–4
Hart, Eli, 291
Hart, Isaiah, 2, 5, 124
Hart, Mary Ellen. *See* Stribling, Mary Ellen Hart
Hart, Mrs. O. B. *See* Hart, Catharine Smith Campbell
Hart, Oscar, 8
Hart, Ossian Bingley, 1–8, 11, 261
Hart, Virginia ("Jennie") Crews. *See* Wells, Virginia ("Jennie") Crews Hart
Hart and Valentine (builders), 291
Hart Memorial Library (Kissimmee, Fla.), 13
Harvard University, 87
Harvard University Medical School, 198, 208
Havana, Cuba, 105, 113
Hawkins, Betsy, 126

Hawkins, Chloe Fleming, 124–26, 129
Hawkins, Clem, 126
Hawkins, Emma M., 140–41
Hawkins, Thomas, 126
Hawks, Esther Hill, 126
Hayes, J. O., 137
Hayes, Roland, 274
Hayes and Fleming Foreign Mission Society, 137
Health and health care, 3–4, 14–15, 17–18, 28, 86, 107–19, 132, 140–43, 157, 182–83, 221–22, 274, 282. *See also* medical education and practice; nurses and nursing. *See also named illnesses and diseases*
Hearst, Phoebe, 206
Hebrew Collegiate Institute (Savannah, Ga.), 216
Henderson, John A., 4, 8, 11–12, 16, 19
Henderson, Flora A. *See* Waldo, Flora A. Henderson
Henderson, Mary Turman,
Hendry, Frances S. Varn, 46, 50
Hendry, George Washington, 50
Henry Rutherford Butler Elementary School (formerly Yonge Street School, Atlanta, Ga.), 205–6, 208
Hermitage, The (Nashville, Tenn.), 26, 34, 37
Hermitage Ball, 37
Hernández, Palmenia, 109
Hernando County, Fla., 49
Herndon, Alonzo, 200, 211, 213
Herzog, Jennie Dzialynki, 219
Herzog, Louis, 219
Hetherington, Alma, 18
Hibernia (plantation and tourist hotel), 123, 126, 131, 135, 141
Hickman, Amy, 124
Hickok, Wild Bill, 87
High Street Baptist Church (Baltimore, Md.), 134
Highlands City, Fla., 45
Hill, Holly Bowen, 47
Hills, J. Seth, 299

Hillsborough County, Fla., 49, 51–53, 58
Hinesville, Ga., 277
Hinesville Telephone Co., 278
History and historical preservation, 99
History of the University of North Carolina (book), 173
Holidays, 271–72, 282. *See also named holidays*
Hollinger, Edwin K., 37
Hollinger, Eleanora Kirkland ("Nonie") Long, 28, 32, 37–38
Holloway, E. F., 72
Holmes, Norman A., 279
Holy Communion Church (New York), 89
Home Missionary Society (Mass.), 276
Homestead, Fla., 97
Hooker, Cuthbert Lanier. *See* Rockner, Cuthbert Lanier Hooker
Hooker, John I., 50
Hoover, Herbert, 208, 253
Hope, John, 205, 211, 279
Hope, Lugenia Burns, 192, 205, 213
Horne, Frank, 180
Horne, Lena, 180
Hornsby, Alton, 210
Hospitals, 107–19, 126, 182–83, 299, 301–4. *See also named hospitals*
Hotel Ponce de Leon, 37
Houghton, Mifflin and Company, 36
Housekeeper's Club, 92–94, 96, 98–99
Houston, Fla., 67
Houston, Sam, 26
Houston County, Ga., 177
Howard, David T., 211
Howard University, 264, 297
Howard University Law Department, 130
Howard University Medical Department, 128–29, 137, 292, 294
Howe, Julia Ward, 34
Howell, Clark, 194
Hubert, B. F., 279
Huddleston, Amelia. *See* Barr, Amelia Huddleston

Hull House (Chicago, Ill.), 254
Hunt, Adele J., 174
Hunt, Adella. *See* Logan, Adella Hunt
Hunt, Charles, 38
Hunt, Dorothy, 174
Hunt, Florence Johnson: as clubwoman and advocate of Progressive-era causes, 176–77, 184–86; contributions and service at Ft. Valley, Ga., 177–86; death of, 186–87; early life and education of, 171–74; marriage and family of, 174; as professional partner to her husband, 174–75, 179–83, 186; as temperance advocate, 175–76
Hunt, Hal, 174
Hunt, Henry Alexander, 152, 154
Hunt, Henry Alexander, Jr., 154, 171–72, 174–75, 177–82, 184–86
Hunt, Mariah, 152
Hunt, Reinette Gamble Long, 38
Hunt, Susan, 152
Hunt Memorial Library (FVSU), 187
Hunting, 44–46, 48, 53, 95, 195
Huntington philanthropy, 180
Hunton, Addie Waits, 184, 205
Hunton, William A., 211
Hurricanes, 3, 18, 112, 268

Illinois, 51, 130. *See also named places*
Illnesses. *See* health and health care
Independent Temperance Society (Jacksonville, Fla.), 128
Indiana, 9, 20. *See also named places*
Indian River, Fla., 3, 89
Indian war. *See* Seminole Wars
Influenza, 268, 289
Ingraham, James, 94, 96–97
Institute for Colored Youth (Philadelphia, Pa.), 128–30
Insurance, 10, 200, 244–45
Internal Revenue Service, 227–28
International Association of the Congo, 135
Irebu, Congo, 142–43
Italy, 184
Izaguirre, Mrs. Antonio, 109

J. H. Blodgett Improvement Club (Jacksonville, Fla.), 247
Jabour, Anya, xiii
Jack, James W., 203
Jackson, Alice, 108
Jackson, Andrew, 26, 38
Jackson, Ga., 174
Jackson, Wilmetta, 187
Jackson County, Fla., 67
Jacksonville, Fla.: and Gertrude Dzialynski Corbet, 222, 226–30; and Louise Cecilia Fleming, 125–32, 135–37; and Catharine Smith Campbell Hart, 1, 5–12, 17, 19–20; mentioned, 34, 107, 124, 219; and Jerenia Valentine Dial Reid, 289–94, 297–303; and Mary E. C. Day Smith, 73–81; and Eartha Mary Magdalene White, 236–48, 251–56
Jacksonville Board of Health, 300
Jacksonville Business and Professional Woman's Club, 229
Jacksonville Daily American (newspaper), 239
Jacksonville Evening Metropolis (newspaper), 298, 300–301
Jacksonville Evening-Telegram (newspaper), 76
Jacksonville Florida Times-Union (newspaper), 99, 109, 229, 294
Jacksonville Florida Times-Union and Citizen (newspaper), 19
Jacksonville Graded School. *See* Stanton Institute
Jacksonville Journal (newspaper), 230
Jacksonville Republican (newspaper), 131
Jacksonville Woman's Club, 248
Jacquith, Elizabeth, 270
James, Arthur Curtis, 98
Jeanes, Anna T., 177–78, 180
Jefferson County, Fla., 67
Jenkins, J. R., 277, 282
Jennings, May Mann, 97, 229, 247–48
Jennings, William Sherman, 95, 97, 247
Jerusalem Baptist Church (Ga.), 273

Jewish culture and religion: 215–16, 218–20, 228–30, 288
Jim Crow and Jim Crow era, 75, 106, 113, 165, 172, 175–77, 187, 193–94, 242–43, 245–46, 253, 255, 288, 302–303. *See also* race relations
John G. Riley House (Tallahassee, Fla.), 81
Johns, Paul, 278
Johnson, Clay, 13
Johnson, Columbus, 173
Johnson, Edward Austin, 173–74, 176
Johnson, Eliza A., 173
Johnson, Florence. *See* Hunt, Florence Johnson
Johnson, Helen Dillet, 242
Johnson, James, 240
Johnson, James Weldon, 127, 129, 240–42, 244–46, 290
Johnson, Joan Marie, xii
Johnson, John Rosemond, 241–42
Johnson, Solomon C., 277, 284
Johnson, Thomas, 173
Johnson C. Smith University, 174, 176
Jones, Charley, 194
Jones, Marcella, 271
Jones, Maxine D., 250
Jordan, Ida Mae, 183
Jordan, Jacob, 133
Jordan, James Lloyd, 241
Journalism and journalists, 16, 54–57, 88, 111, 115–17, 130, 136, 138–39, 220, 279, 284. *See also* writing and writers
Jubilee Singers, 265
Juvenile courts, 162

Kansas City, Mo., 296
Kebo, Fla. *See* Coconut Grove, Fla.
Kebo's Odd Fellows Hall (Coconut Grove, Fla.), 93
Kehoe, Minnie E., 224
Kellogg, J. H., 166
Kelsay, Rufus B., 133–34
Kenney, John, 212
Kentucky, 15

Key West, Fla.: and María Valdés de Gutsens, 104–120; and Catharine Smith Campbell Hart, 3–4, 14; mentioned, 33–34, 88–90
Key West Citizen (newspaper), 115, 118
Killingray, David, 134
Kindergartens, 2, 199, 205, 213–14. *See also* children and child care
Kingsley, Anna Madgigine Jai, 124
Kinglsey, Zephaniah, 124
Kinlaw Rosenwald School (St. Mary's, Ga.), 281
Kirkland House (home), 100
Kirkman, Mary. *See* Call, Mary Kirkman
Kissimmee, Fla., and Catharine Smith Campbell Hart, 12–20
Kissimmee Leader (newspaper), 16
Kissimmee Presbyterian Church, 14, 16–17, 19
Kissimmee River, Fla., 13, 45, 88
Kissimmee Valley Gazette (newspaper), 16
Kite-Powell, Rodney, 58
Knapp, J. G., 52–53
Knights of Pythias, 200, 212, 269, 284
Know-Nothing Party. *See* American Party
Ku Klux Klan, 173, 252

L. Richardson Memorial Hospital (Greensboro, N.C.), 304
Labor unions, 300
Lafayette, Marquis de, 34
La Fe, Esperanza, 109
LaGrange, Ga., 205
Lake Chautauqua, N.Y., 201
Lake City, Fla., 67, 126
Lake Monroe, Fla., 131
Lake Worth, Fla., 89
Lakeland, Fla., 45
Lakeland Highlands, Fla., 45
Lambert, Mrs., 279
Lancaster, Joseph B., 4
Lane Bryant Award for Volunteer Service, 256
Laney, Lucy Craft, 164

Lanier, Cuthbert. *See* Cuthbert Lanier Hooker Rockner
Lanza, Gutiérrez, 114
Latinos and Latino experience, 104–20
Laurel Grove (plantation), 124
Laurel Grove, Fla. *See* Orange Park, Fla.
LaVilla, Fla., 6, 79, 131, 290–92
Lawrence Scientific School, 87
Lays In Summer Lands (book), 131
Layton, Julia, 163
League of American Wheelmen, 88
League of Democratic Women (Duval Co., Fla.), 249
League of Women Voters, 249, 251, 255. *See also* Florida State League of Women Voters
Ledbetter, Anna, 276
Ledbetter, C. S., 278
Lee, J. R. E., 206
Lee, Joseph E., 128, 130, 136
Legal education and practice, 222, 229, 254–55
Lemon City, Fla., 89
L'Engle, Edward M., 8, 10
Leon, Ruth Hope Dzialynski, 223
Leon County, Fla., 67, 69, 72
Leonard Medical School, 137
Leopold II (king of Belgium), 131, 135, 142
Leopoldville, Congo, 137, 143
Lerner, Gerda, 204
Leslie, Kent Anderson, 152
Levy County, Fla., 290
Lewis, Abraham Lincoln, 244–45, 259
Lewis, Amos E., 226
Lewis, David Levering, 152
Lewis, H. H., 227
Liberia, 137
Liberty County, Ga., 266–68, 274–75, 280–82
Liberty County Teacher's Institute, 281
Liberty County Training School, 267
Library of Congress, 101
"Lift Every Voice and Sing" ("Negro National Anthem"), 290
Lightbourne, Annie, 76

Limona, Fla., 51–56
Limona Park Association, 52
Lincoln, Abraham, 130–31, 272
Lincoln Academy (Tallahassee, Fla.), 70–73
Lincoln Fund Drive (Dorchester Academy), 272
Lincoln Memorial Church (Washington, D.C.), 264–65
Lincoln's Birthday, 272
Lincoln University, 129–30, 198, 292
Lindenmeyer, Kriste, xii–xiii
Lindsey, Benjamin Barr, 162
Linsley, Charles, 57
Lithia, Fla., 58
Live Oak, Fla., 277
Lives Full of Struggle and Triumph (book), xi
Livingstone, David, 136
Livingstone Inland Mission, 136
Lloyd, Betsy, 279
Locklear, Mrs. J. M., 194
Logan, Adella Hunt: as advocate for women's causes, 159–66; death of, 166–67; early life and education of, 151–55; early teaching career of, 155; marriage and family life of, 157–58; mentioned, 174, 178; service of at Tuskegee Institute, 155–58
Logan, Rayford, 193
Logan, Warren (father), 157–58, 166
Logan, Warren (son), 158
London, England, 135, 138
Long, Cora Gamble, 33
Long, Eleanora Kirkman ("Nonie"). *See* Hollinger, Eleanora Kirkman ("Nonie") Long
Long, Ellen Call: early life and education of, 25–28; marriage and early family life of, 28–30; separation of, 30; and the Civil War and Reconstruction eras, 31–33; and participation in public affairs, 33–35; as writer and novelist, 35–36; increased financial problems of, 36–38; death of, 38

Long, Ellen Douglas, 28–29
Long, Hugh, 28–29
Long, Maria Louisa, 28–29
Long, Medicus A., 28, 30
Long, Reinette Gamble. *See* Hunt, Reinette Gamble Long
Long, Richard Call, 28, 31–33, 37
Lono, Angel de, 107
Los Angeles, Calif., 208
Louise Maloney Hospital (Key West, Fla.), 108
Louisiana. *See* New Orleans
Louisville, Ky., 15
Lukunga, Congo, 137
Lynching and lynchings, 193–95, 246, 250–51, 270. *See also* racial violence

Mabbette, I. M., 13, 15
Macfarlane, Frances, 43
Macon, Ga., 158, 184–85, 205
Macon (Ga.) Junior Chamber of Commerce, 185
Macon County, Ala., 266
Macon Telegraph (newspaper), 184–85
Madam Hall Beauty School, 241
Madison, Fla., 67
Madison, Wis., 52
Madison County, Ala., 49
Madison County, Fla., 67
Magbee, Julia, 220
Magnolia, Fla., 123
Magnolia Springs, Fla., 299
Mahoney, Mary Eliza, 288
Maine (battleship), 111
Malaria, 178, 268, 289
Majors, Monroe A., 198
Mallory, Stephen, 224–25
Maloney, Annie. *See* Gonzalez, Annie Maloney
Maloney Hospital (Key West, Fla.), 108
Maloney, John B., 108
Mañas, María, 112
Manatee River, Fla., 12
Mandarin, Fla., 35, 131–32
Mango, Fla., 51, 58

March on Washington (1941), 255
March on Washington (1963), 255
Marietta, Ga., 204
Marine Hospital (Key West, Fla.), 108, 117
Marion County, Fla., 130, 237, 240, 266
Marriage and marital relations, 2, 5, 28–30, 48–50, 57, 74, 87–89, 106–107, 157–58, 174–75, 199–201, 228, 299–302
Martha Reid Chapter, UDC, 228–29
Martin, Fla., 266
Martinez, Carmelina, 107
Martinez, María, 107
Masonic Grand Lodge of Georgia, 269
Mary E. Smith Club (Jacksonville, Fla.), 247
Maryland, 27, 134. *See also named places*
Masons and Masonic orders, 118, 177, 200, 211, 269, 284, 291–94. *See also* Knights of Pythias
Massachusetts, 12, 135, 137, 267, 269, 288. *See also named places*
Matheson, William, 98
Mathis, Sallye B., 243
Matthews, Victoria, 79
Maxwell, Miss P., 274
Mayflower Hotel (Jacksonville, Fla.), 293
Mayg, Dolores, 108–9, 111. *See also* Dolores Mayg Society
Mayport, Fla., 125
McCleary, Margaret, 246–47
McCook, Edward M., 32
McFarlane, Flora, 90, 95
McGill, Simuel S., 254–55
McKay, Donald B., 54
McKinley, William, 161
McLeod Hospital and Training School for Nurses (Daytona, Fla.), 301
McTier, Annette, 271
Meacham, Robert, 67–68
Medical education and practice, 128–30, 134, 137–38, 140–41, 198–99, 208, 211, 292, 294–95

Meharry Medical College, 198
Memphis, Tenn., 197
Menard, Elizabeth, 131
Menard, John Willis, 130–31
Mendieta, Carlos, 114
Menocal, Mario G., 114
Mercedes Hospital (Key West, Fla.), 105–119
Methodist Church, 14, 51, 200, 241, 271, 280
Metropolitan Tabernacle (London, Eng.), 135
Meuse-Argonne cemetery, 301
Miami (steamer), 111
Miami, Fla., 43, 85, 89, 91, 93, 95, 97, 108, 226, 258. *See also* Coconut Grove, Fla.
Miami Audubon Society, 97
Miami Herald (newspaper), 96, 99, 101
Miami Metropolis (newspaper), 92, 228
Miami Woman's Club, 97
Michigan, 57, 166. *See also named places*
Middle Florida, 67
Middle Georgia, 153–54
Midway, Ga., 263
Midway Congregational Church (Liberty Co., Ga.), 271, 273
Midway Presbyterian Church (Liberty Co., Ga.), 273
Midwives, 288
Miller, William, 31
Milton, John, 125
Milton, L. R., 228
Ministry, 77–78
Minnesota, 98. *See also named places*
Missionary Ridge, Battle of, 48
Missionary training programs, 134–35
Missions and missionaries, 67–81, 127–28, 134–43
Mississippi, 44–45, 49. *See also named places*
Mississippi Women, xiv
Mississippi Women's History Project, xiv
Missouri, 296, 305
Missouri Press Association, 203

Mitchell, Effie Carrie. *See* Mitchell-Hampton, Effie Carrie
Mitchell, Henry L., 53, 219
Mitchell, Joseph David, 298–99
Mitchell, Reuben S., 130
Mitchell, Susie M., 130
Mitchell-Hampton, Effie Carrie, 130
Mitchell Street School (Atlanta), 174
Mite Missionary Society (Jacksonville, Fla.),
Monroe, Mrs. A. Leight, 97
Monroe, Charlotte, 271
Monroe County, Fla., 107, 116–17
Monroe County Public Library, 120
Montgomery, Ala., 156, 266
Monticello, Fla., 67
Moody, Thomas, 142
Moore, Elizabeth, 264
Moore, Elizabeth Benton: early life and education of, 263–66; and Congregationalist Church and American Missionary Association, 264–66; early career of as educator, 266; death of, 282; as principal at Dorchester Academy, Ga., 266–82
Moore, Ella Sheppard, 264–66
Moore, Fannie. *See* Benton, Fannie Moore
Moore, George Washington, 264–66
Moore, Mrs. E. B., 279
Moore, Mrs. T. V., 97
Moore, Rice, 264
Moore, Sadie, 271
Morehouse, Miss, 79
Morehouse College, 205, 279
"The Morning Toilet" (article), 165
Morris Brown University, 276
Morrison, Eleanor, 271
Morrison, Wilhelmina, 271
Morristown, N.J., 6, 8, 11, 17, 19
Morristown Jerseyman (newspaper), 19
Mortality rates, 157, 164, 289, 297–98
Moseley, Julia, 51–52, 58
Moss, Joseph R., 126
Mount Vernon Ladies Association, 37

Mt. Olive Cemetery (Jacksonville, Fla.), 80
Mt. Sinai Church (Liberty County, Ga.), 271
Mt. Zion, Ga., 152–53
Mt. Zion AME Church (Jacksonville, Fla.), 77–80, 241
Mt. Zion Baptist Church (Waycross, Ga.), 280
Mt. Zion Cemetery (Philadelphia, Penn.), 143
Mukimbungu, Congo, 137
Mukimvika, Congo, 137
Mulberry School for Colored Children (New York City), 65
Munroe, C. K. *See* Munroe, Kirk
Munroe, Jesse, 95
Munroe, Kirk, 85–101
Munroe, Mabel Stearns, 101
Munroe, Mary Barr: as backer of women's organizations, 92–93, 96–97; as community benefactor and hostess, 93–95; death of, 100–101; early life of, 85–87; as environmental and wildlife activist, 95–99; and historical preservation, 99–100; marriage and early married life of, 88–89; relocation of to Coconut Grove, Fla., 89–92
Munroe, Mrs. Kirk. *See* Munroe, Mary Barr
Munroe, Patty. *See* Catlow, Patty Munroe
Munroe, Ralph, 89, 94–95
Munroe, Susan. *See* Stowe, Susan Munroe
Murdock, J. N., 137, 139
Murray, Margaret. *See* Washington, Margaret Murray
Music and musical training, 51, 64, 68, 77, 181–82, 241, 265, 271–72, 274, 290, 303
Myrtle, Melvina, 96. *See also* Munroe, Mary Barr

Nashville, Tenn., 26, 28, 30, 203, 264–65
Nassau, Bahamas, 105

Nassau County, Fla., 237
Nation, Carrie, 226
National American Woman Suffrage Association (NAWSA), 161, 260
National Association for the Advancement of Colored People (NAACP), 162, 186, 246, 252, 254–55, 290
National Association Notes (NACW journal), 163
National Association of Afro-American Women, 193
National Association of Colored Graduate Nurses (NACGN), 302–5
National Association of Colored Women (NACW), 79, 162–63, 165, 176, 193, 204–205, 253
National Audubon Society, 95
National Baptist Foreign Mission Convention, 137
National Buyers Association, 281, 286
National Chautauqua Movement, 201
National Congress of Colored Parents and Teachers (NCCPT), 206
National Conservation Congress, 98
National Conservatory of Music, 241
National Council of Women, 163
National Forestry Association, 35
National Freedman's Savings and Trust Company. *See* Freedman's Bank
National Health Week, 274
National League of Nursing Education (NLNE), 302
National League of Republican Colored Women, 253
National Medical Association, 211
National Negro Business League, 245–46, 281
National Parent-Teacher Association, 206
National Republican Committee, 279
Negro a Beast, or, In the Image of God, The (book), 202
Nelson, Alice Dunbar, 251
New Albany, Ind., 9, 20
New Deal, 114, 185, 254–55

New England Baptist Missionary Convention, 135
New England Hospital for Women and Children, 288
New Hampshire, 54. *See also named places*
New Haven, Conn., 135
New Hope, Fla. *See* Brandon, Fla.
New Hope Church (Brandon, Fla.), 51–53, 56
New Jersey, 2, 5–6, 8, 11, 134. *See also named places*
New Orleans, La., 28, 30, 34, 105, 197, 223, 304
New Scotland, Conn., 19
New South, 197, 259
"New women," xii
New Women of the New South (book), 161
New York (city), 18, 65–68, 73, 76, 79, 87–90, 105, 220, 228, 241, 266, 281, 288, 291
New York (state), 29, 65, 79, 88, 133, 184, 201. *See also named places*
New York Canoe Club, 88
New York Central College, 65
New York Colored Orphan Asylum, 76
New York Freeman (newspaper), 138–39
New York Globe (newspaper), 291
New York Infirmary (N.Y.C.), 288
New York Sun (newspaper), 87–88
Newark, N.J., 2, 11–12
Newbold, Mrs. Benjamin, 92
Newport (schooner), 89–90
Newton Theological Seminary, 135
Nineteenth Amendment, 229, 249, 252
Nineteenth Street Baptist Church (Washington, D.C.), 176
Nixon, Richard, 256
Noble, C. S., 54
Noel, H. T., 198
Norris, Mattie, 204
Norris, Mrs. L. B., 204
North Carolina, 44, 79, 130, 134, 136,

Index 333

143, 173–76, 198, 275, 304. *See also* named places
North Carolina Colored Women's Christian Temperance Union, 176, 181
Northern, W. J., 155
Noted Negro Women (book), 198
Nurses and nursing, 287–89, 287–89, 295–306. *See also* Gray Ladies Corps

Oak Grove Congregational Church (Liberty Co., Ga.), 271
Oakland School (Jacksonville, Fla.), 73, 76, 80
Oberlin, Ohio, 264
Oberlin College, 128, 264
Ocala, Fla., 130, 237, 266
Ocean Street Presbyterian Church (Jacksonville, Fla.), 19
Odd Fellows, International Order of, 200
Okefenokee Swamp, 88
Ohio, 43, 155, 264. *See also named places*
Oklawaha River, Fla., 240
Old City Cemetery (Jacksonville, Fla.), 256
Old Midway Church (Liberty Co., Ga.), 266
Olive Cemetery (Philadelphia), 143
Omega Psi Phi, 200
Only One Florida (book), 52–53
Orange Park, Fla., 125, 131
Orangeburg, S.C., 301
Orchard Pond Plantation, 28, 30
Order of Carlos Manuel de Céspedes, 113–15
Order of the Eastern Star, 193
Oriental American Opera Company, 241–42
Orlando, Fla., 12, 77, 101, 216, 220
Osceola County, Fla., 16, 18
Owen, Ruth Bryan, 100
Owens, George W., 279
Owsley, Frank L., xii

Pacho, Mrs., 109
Packard, Sophia, 197

Page, James, 67
Palabala, Congo, 137–40, 142
Palacios, Lucy, 108
Palatka, Fla., 125, 240
Palm Beach, Fla., 89
Palmer, Solomon, 156
Palmer Theater (N.Y.C.), 241
Panic of 1873, 72
Panic of 1893, 18, 221
Paradise Key, Fla., 96–97
Paradise Plantation, 5
Parent-teacher associations, 183, 193, 206, 279–80
Paris Universal Exposition, 34
Parrish, Maxfield, 100
Pastors' College, 135
Patria (orphanage), 114
Patrollers, 153
Payne, Buckner, 203
Payne, Daniel A., 67, 73, 239
Peabody, George Foster, 178, 180
Peace River, Fla., 45–46, 49
Peach County, Ga., 177, 182, 187
Peacock, Charles, 89
Peacock, Isabella, 89, 92
Peacock, Mrs. C. J., 92
Pearce, Charles H., 67–68, 70, 127
Pearce, William H., 46
Peas Creek Baptist Church, 46, 49
Pelican Island, Fla., 96
Pennsylvania, 100, 198. *See also named places*
Pensacola, Fla., 224–26
Pensions, 57
People's Advocate (newspaper), 292
People's Hospital (St. Louis), 305
Perez, Blanca Ferriol de, 109
Pérez, Theodore, 109
Perkins, Daniel W., 255
Perrine, Lebarron, 99
Perry, Edward A., 35, 219
Perry, J. Clyde, 278
Perry, Mrs. Richard, 277
Perry, Richard, 277
Peterson, Carla L., 65

Philadelphia, Pa., 5, 9, 124, 127–30, 134, 138, 141–43, 290, 304
Phonography, 223
Phosphate, 54, 221
Phyllis Wheatley Branch, YWCA, 193, 207
Piedia, Manuel, 111
Pinchot, Gifford, 99
Pineneedles (girls' club), 93
Pine Ridge Hospital (West Palm Beach, Fla.), 303–304
Pinn, Petra, 303
Pinnell, Louise Rebecca, 222, 229
Pitman shorthand, 223
Pittsburgh, Pa., 100
P. K. Yonge Library of Florida History, 20
"Plain folk," xii, 218
Plant, Henry Bradley, 12, 16, 53, 300
Plant City, Fla., 53
Plessy v. Ferguson, 243, 267
Plumes and plume hunting, 95. *See also* wildlife and wildlife preservation
Plymouth Congregational Church (Ga.), 278
Poland, 216
Politics and political activity, 95, 97, 107, 133, 215, 223–29, 243, 248–53. *See also* Women's rights. *See also named political parties*
Polk County, Fla., 45, 48, 54, 216, 219, 221
Poll tax, 242–43, 252
Pomegranate Hall (home), 152
Pompey (freed slave), 123
Porter, Anna Hayden. *See* Bigelow, Anna Hayden Porter
Porter, Henrietta Curtis, 201
Porter, Joseph Yates, 108
Porter, Louisa Brown, 4, 8
Porter, Mary Brown, 4, 8
Powers, Pennie, 72
Pratt, E. E., 52
Presbyterian Church, 2–3, 5, 14, 16–17, 19, 134, 200, 273, 278

Prince George County, Va., 26
Prince Hall Masons, 200
Princeton Theological Seminary, 129
Proctor, Hugh H., 211
Progressive era and movement, 172–73, 184, 194, 215, 259
Prohibition, 225–26, 229. *See also* Temperance
Providence Conference Institute, 6
Provident Hospital School of Nursing (Chicago), 289
Psyche (sailing vessel), 88
Public School Society (N.Y.C.), 65
Pullman porters, 300
Punta Rassa, Fla., 88
Puterbaugh, Travis, 58

Quaker philanthropy, 177
Quarles, Frank, 197
Quarterman, J. E., 277, 279
Quincy, Fla., 237
Quincy, Mass., 269
Quitman, Ga., 195

Race relations, 16, 32, 36, 48–49, 93–94, 106–7, 123–24, 152–55, 160–63, 172, 179–80, 193–96, 247–48, 289–90, 304. *See also* Jim Crow and Jim Crow era
Race Relationship Week (Dorchester Academy), 274
Racial violence, 194–95, 246, 270. *See also* lynching and lynchings; Seminole Wars; violence
Railroads, 16, 18, 37, 43–44, 52–55, 57, 95, 178, 219, 241, 290, 300. *See also names of specific railroads*
Rakestraw, E. W., 278
Raleigh, N.C., 130, 134, 140, 142, 173, 176
Ramírez, Concepción, 109–110
Randall, Gusster, 300
Randolph, A. Philip, 246, 255, 262, 300
Ranktow, J. A., 279
Ray, Charles B., 66
Reason, Charles L., 65, 67, 76

Reconstruction era, 7, 68, 70, 134, 151, 176, 193, 219, 251, 264, 290
Recreation, 133, 253. *See also* sports and sportsmanship. *See also named sports*
Redemption era, 70, 160, 202, 289
Red Cross, 208, 253
Reed, George, 194
Reed, Harrison, 36
Reform schools, 184
Reid, Jerenia Valentine Dial: death of, 305–6; early life and education of, 287–97; first marriage of, 299–301; as golfer, 305; second marriage of, 301–2; and National Association of Colored Graduate Nurses, 302–5; nursing career of, 297–99, 303–5
Reid, Leon S., 301–302
Religion. *See named denominations*
Republican National Committee, 253
Republican National Convention, 133
Republican Party, 7, 12, 19, 34, 70, 106–7, 161, 227, 251–53, 279, 291
Reyes, María, 114
Rhode Island, 6
Richardson, A. St. George, 78
Richardson, Clement, 212
Richardson, Joe M., 64, 67
Richardson Memorial Hospital (Greensboro, N.C.), 304
Ricketts, J. E., 137
Ridgeway, Charles, 66
Ridgeway Prize, 66
Riley, James Whitcomb, 94
Riley House (Tallahassee), 81
Ritter, Alicia Scott, 120
Roberts, George, 89–90
Roberts, Kitty Frow, 89–90
Robbins, Sarah Stuart, 35
Rockefeller, John D., Sr., 197
Rockefeller, Mrs. John D., 196–97
Rockefeller philanthropy, 180, 196–97, 289
Rockner, Cuthbert Lanier Hooker, 43, 50–51, 53–54, 218
Rockner, Julius C., 50–51, 218

Rockner, Mrs. C. M. *See* Rockner, Cuthbert Lanier Hooker
Rodríguez, Caridad, 109
Rodríguez, Salina, 58, 118
Rogers, Henry, 153
Rolo, Juan Pérez, 105, 112
Roman Catholic Church, 118, 200
Rome, Ga., 194
Roosevelt, Eleanor, 254
Roosevelt, Franklin Delano, 171–72, 186, 253–55
Roosevelt, Theodore, 19, 98
Roseada (boat), 13
Rosenwald Fund, 180, 184, 267, 281
Ross, George Eugene, 243
Ross, J. Gardner, 135, 137
Roth, Darlene, 199
Rouse, Jacqueline Anne, 171, 192, 205, 213
Royal Palm Park, Fla., 97, 99
Rubber trade, 142
Rueda, Felicia Rodriguez de, 109
Rueda, Pedro, 112
Ruth Chapter, Order of the Eastern Star, 193

Sabbath schools, 67–68, 74, 78, 241, 273
Sailing. *See* Boating and sailing
Salinero, Fred, 120
Salisbury, N.C., 198
Salmond, John A., xi
San Antonio, Texas, 30
San Carlos Institute (Key West, Fla.), 111
Sanders, D. J., 174
Sandhill, Ga., 277
Sanderson, John P., 8, 10
Sanford, Fla., 131
Sanford, Henry S., 131, 135
Sañudo, Regla, 112
Sarah's Court, 77
Savannah, Ga., 67, 205, 216, 218, 220, 253, 263, 269, 273–74
Savannah Tribune (newspaper), 269, 279–80, 284
Sayre, Nathan, 152
Schafer, Daniel L., xi–xii, 123

Scholes, Theophilus E. S., 137
Schooling. *See* education
Science and scientific interests, 34
Scientific racism, 202
Scotland, 86–87, 228
Scott, Anne Firor, xi
Scott, John R., Jr., 136
Scrububs (home), 90, 93–94, 96, 100–101
Scruggs, Lawson A., 143
Secades, Manuel, 111
Secession and secessionism, 5, 30–31,
Seffner, Fla., 51, 58
Selden Institute, 276–77
Seminary West of the Suwannee, 28
Seminole Indians, 27, 86, 92, 217
Seminole Wars: first, 26; second, 3, 45; third, 46–47
Semi-Tropical, The (magazine), 36
Semple, John B., 100
"Separate but equal," 243, 267
Servo Club (Quincy, Mass.), 269
Seventh Florida Infantry, Company E, 48
Seward, Ellen. *See* Varn, Ellen Seward
Seward, Jim, 44, 46–47
Seward, Mary. *See* Varn, Mary Seward
Seward, Sarah, 44
Seward, Victoria Martha. *See* Sherrill, Victoria Martha Seward Varn Brandon
Seward, Zachariah, 44, 49
Seward, Zachariah Jr., 49
Seward Lake, Fla., 45, 48
Shackleford, Thomas M., 221
Shaw University, 130, 134–35, 137, 140–42
Sheats, William Nichols, 222
Sheffield, Ceasar, 194
Sheppard, Ella. *See* Moore, Ella Sheppard
Sheppard, Simon, 265
Sherman, William Tecumseh, 153
Sherrill, Charles Clark, 57
Sherrill, Victoria Martha Seward Varn Brandon: and Civil War, 48–49; death of, 57–58; early life and education of, 42–48; first marriage of, 48; second marriage of, 49–53; third marriage of; 57; as widowed community developer, 53–57
Shine, R. A., 72
Sigma Gamma Rho, 193
Sigma Pi Phi, 200
Silk Farming in Florida (book), 35
Silone-Yates, Josephine, 163
Silver Springs, Fla., 237, 240
Singleton, Mary, 243
Six Mile Creek, Fla., 48
Sixth Avenue Baptist Church (Brooklyn, N.Y.), 134
Slater, Thomas Heathe, 198
Slaves and slavery, 5, 44, 46–49, 122–25, 152–53, 237, 288
Sleeping-car porters, 300. *See also* railroads
Sleeping sickness, 143
Sloan, Selena Mae. *See* Butler, Selena Mae Sloan
Sloan, William, 196
Smallpox, 297
Smalls, W. C., 299
Smith, A. W., 299
Smith, Abby H. Campbell, 2–3, 9–10, 13–15, 17
Smith, Charles, 74
Smith, Ed, 14
Smith, Hoke, 194
Smith, Isaac P., 13
Smith, J. McCune, 65
Smith, James, 72
Smith, James R. W., 15
Smith, Katie, 9–10
Smith, Lizzie, 14
Smith, Lydia, 72
Smith, Mary E. C. Day: brief return to New York City in 1893 by, 76; early life and education of, 64–67; last years and death of, 78–81; marriage of, 74; ministerial career of, 77–78; as missionary and teacher at Tallahassee,

Smith, Mary E. C. Day, *cont.* 67–73; and relocation to Jacksonville, 73–81; at Edward Waters College, 75–76, 78–80
Smithwick and West (law firm), 224
Snelson, Floyd, 267
Snodgrass, Dena E., 20
Sociedad Dolores Mayg, 112
Society for the Promotion of Education among Colored Children, 66
Socrum, Fla., 46
Solid South, 253
Sororal organizations, 193, 200
Sorrow, Timmy, 20
South Carolina, 44, 67, 127, 221, 237, 301. *See also named places*
South Carolina AME Conference, 69
South Carolina State College, 301
South Eastern Convention of Congregational Churches, 273
South Florida Bulldogs, 48
South Florida Railroad, 12, 16, 53
Southern Express Co., 300
Southern Federation of Colored Women's Clubs, 204
Southern Ladies, New Women (book), xii
Southern Loyalists Convention, 5
Spanish-American War (1898), 106–7, 243
Spann, Joe, 58
Sparta, Ga., 152–55, 158
Spelman, Lucy Henry, 196
Spelman College, 138, 141, 196–97, 208, 289
Spelman Messenger (magazine), 202
Spelman Seminary. *See* Spelman College
Spencer, Herbert, 202
Spingarn Medal, 171, 186
Sports and sportsmanship, 37, 195, 276–78. *See also named sports*
Spruill, Marjorie Julian. *See* Wheeler, Marjorie Spruill
Spurgeon, Charles Haddon, 135
St. Augustine, Fla., 34, 37, 133, 243, 276, 292

St. James CME Church (Tallahassee, Fla.), 67
St. James Hotel (Jacksonville, Fla.), 239–40
St. John's Baptist Church (Ga.), 278
St. Johns County, Fla., 126, 133
St. Johns River, Fla., 35, 88–89, 123–26, 131, 136, 240, 289, 292, 298
St. Louis, Mo., 305
St. Marks, Fla., 38
St. Mary's, Ga., 281
St. Mary's Episcopal Church (Washington, D.C.), 305
St. Nicholas, Fla., 136
St. Paul, Minn., 98
Stanley, Henry M., 136
Stanton Institute (Jacksonville, Fla.), 127–28, 131–33, 136, 240–44, 292–93
State Federation of Colored Women (Fla.), 248
Staten Island, N.Y., 89
Statesboro High and Industrial School, 266–77
Steamboats and steamboating, 240
Stearns, Mabel. *See* Munroe, Mabel Stearns
Stephen, Henry M., 140, 142
Stewart, William G., 36
Still, Caroline. *See* Anderson, Caroline Still Wiley
Still, Mary, 127–29, 131, 137, 241
Still, William, 124–25, 127, 133, 135, 138–39
Stillman, W. J., 123–24
Stock Island, Fla., 118
Stock market crash (1929), 268, 270. *See also* Great Depression
Stockton, Guy Henry, 237–38
Stockton, John N. C., 237
Stockton, Julia Telfair, 237
Stockton, Mary. *See* Young, Mary Stockton
Stockton, Telfair, 237
Stockton, William, 31
Stockton, William Tennent, 237

Stoiber, Louis, 269
Stoiber, Mrs. Louis, 269
Stone Mountain, Ga., 252
Stowe, Charles, 88, 91
Stowe, Harriet Beecher, 35, 88, 131–32
Stowe, Susan Munroe, 88
Stranahan, Ivy, 43
Straughan, Dulcie, 160
Stribling, Mary Ellen Hart, 4–6, 11
Stribling, Thomas E., 11
Stockton, Guy Henry, 237
Suffrage movement, 160–64, 201, 220, 229, 248–52
Summerlin, Jacob, 216
Summerlin Institute (Bartow, Fla.), 218
Sumner, F. A., 275
Sumner, William Graham, 202
Sumter County, Fla., 11
Supreme Court of Florida. *See* Florida supreme court
Suwannee River, Fla., 88
Sweat, Brother, 280
Swimming, 276–77
Switzerland, 184

Taft, William Howard, 99
Taliaferro, James P., 226
Talladega College, 270, 275
Tallahassee, Fla.: and Selena Sloan Butler, 197–98, 206; and Gertrude Dzialynski Corbet, 222–24; and Catharine Smith Campbell Hart, 3, 11–12, 16; and Ellen Call Long, 26–38; mentioned, 219, 228; and Mary E. C. Day Smith, 67–73
Tallahassee Girl, A (novel), 32
Tallahassee Land and Improvement Company, 37
Tallahassee Weekly Floridian (newspaper), 37
Tallahassee Weekly True Democrat (newspaper), 38
Tampa, Fla.: as center for women's activities and causes, 219–20, 248–49; and Gertrude Dzialynski Corbet, 216, 219–21; and Catharine Smith Campbell Hart, 4–5, 12; mentioned, 43, 53–54, 105, 107, 129; and Victoria Seward Varn Brandon Sherrill, 45, 49
Tampa Business College and Literary Institute, 218, 221
Tampa Daily Times (newspaper), 220
Tampa Journal (newspaper), 56, 220
Tampa Morning News (newspaper), 220
Tampa Morning Tribune (newspaper), 77–78
Tampa Sunland Tribune (newspaper), 15
Tampa Tribune (newspaper), 53–55, 220–21
Tampian, The (magazine), 220
Tanzler, Hans, 256
Tarpon Springs, Fla., 114
Taylor, Anna K., 300
Taylor, Charles D., 300
Taylor, Mary, 220
Taylor's Creek Methodist Church (Ga.), 280
Tea-totaling. *See* temperance
Teachers and teaching, 67–80, 126–28, 133–34, 139, 155–57, 174, 180, 197–98, 223, 243–44, 264, 266, 294. *See also* education; Sabbath schools
Teachers' institutes, 156–57
Tebeau, Charlton, 114
Temperance, 3, 128, 131, 136. *See also* Good Templars, International Order of; Prohibition
Temple, the. *See* Grace Baptist Church (Philadelphia, Pa.)
Temple Cemetery (Jacksonville, Fla.), 230
Ten Years War (Cuba), 104, 110
Tennessee, 26, 28, 48, 264–65. *See also* named places
Tennis, 37, 217, 276–77
Terrell, Mary Church, 163, 165, 176, 199
Texas, 30, 32–33, 86. *See also* named places
Thanksgiving, 181, 272, 277
Thirteenth Amendment, 243
Thirty-Fourth Regiment, USCT, 237

Thomas, William R., 217
Thomas County, Ga., 193, 195
Thomasville, Ga., 193, 195–96, 210
Thompson, John H., 294
Thompson, Panchita N. Valentine, 291–93, 300
Thompson, Maurice, 32
Thomson, William Henry, 90
Torbert, J. H., 177
Torriente, Cosme de la, 114
Trammell, Park, 227–28
Triumph Lodge, IOGT, 128
Tropic Magazine, The, 99
Tropical Hotel (Kissimmee, Fla.), 14, 16
Tuberculosis, 166, 241, 289
Tucker, Thomas DeS., 75
Turner, Henry McNeal, 200
Tuskegee, Ala., 155–61, 164, 166, 289, 301
Tuskegee Normal and Industrial Institute. *See* Tuskegee University
Tuskegee University, 155–58, 160, 164, 166, 177–78, 246, 266, 289, 304
Tuskegee Woman's Club, 158–60
Tuttle, Julia, 43, 94
Twentieth Century Negro Literature (book), 157
Typhoid fever, 178, 225, 289, 296–98

Uncle Tom's Cabin (novel), 88, 131, 271
Underground Railroad, 124
Union army, 125, 237, 290
Union Benevolent Association (Jacksonville, Fla.), 247
Union Brotherhood Society, 281
Union Springs, Ala., 156
Unionism, 5
United Daughters of the Confederacy, 228–29
United Golfers Association (UGA), 305
United States Army, 45, 294, 301. *See also* Union army
United States Department of Agriculture, 267
United States District Court, Middle District of Florida, 12

United States District Court, Northern District of Florida, 226
United States House of Representatives, 12, 19, 130, 249
United States Internal Revenue Service, 227–28
United States Navy, 50
United States Senate, 7, 195, 224–26
United States Supreme Court, 243, 255, 267
University of Florida, 217, 223
University of North Carolina, 173
University of Pennsylvania, 129
University System of Georgia, 172
Usher's Temple CME Church (Ft. Valley, Ga.), 177

Valdés, Francisca, 106
Valdés, María. *See* Gutsens, María Valdés ("Mamá") de
Valdés, Raphael, 106
Valdés, Rodríguez, 118
Valdez, Maximo, 118
Valdosta, Ga., 194
Valentine, Jerenia. *See* Reid, Jerenia Valentine Dial
Valentine, Mary Ann Francis, 290–91, 294
Valentine, Panchita N. *See* Thompson, Panchita N. Valentine
Valentine, Sarah, 291
Valentine, Tillman, 290–94
Valentine, William, 291
Valentine's Day, 272
Valrico, Fla., 51, 54–55, 58
Van Hartesveldt, Fred R.,
Vannevar, Lucie, 220
Varn, Annie, 48
Varn, Ellen Seward, 46
Varn, Frances S. *See* Hendry, Frances S. Varn
Varn, Frederick N., 50
Varn, Josiah, 48
Varn, Mary Seward, 50
Varn, Victoria Martha Seward. *See*

Sherill, Victoria Martha Seward Varn Brandon
Varn, William, 48
Varn, William B., 46, 50
Vaudeville, 290
Victorian ideals, 165, 199, 201–202, 204
Violence: antebellum Florida, 39n4; Congo, 142–43; opposing black female suffrage, 252–53; racial, in the South, 193–95, 246–47, 251, 252; Seminole Wars, 46; vigilante, 4, 285n17. *See also* racial violence; lynching and lynchings
Virginia, 26, 157, 289. *See also named places*
Vorhees Institute, 276–77
Vunda, Congo, 140

Waddill, Valentine Dial, 301, 305
Wake County, N.C., 173
Wake Robin Golf Club (Washington, D.C.), 305
Wakulla (novel), 89
Waldo, Flora A. Henderson, 4, 6, 8–9, 11–12, 16–19
Waldo, George E., 18–19
Waldron, J. Milton, 244
Walker, David, 11
Walker, George,
Walker, Robert, 140
Wall & Wall (law firm), 221
Walls, Josiah T., 129
Walthourville, Ga., 270
War Camp Community Services (Savannah, Ga.), 253
War of 1895 (Cuba), 106
Ward, Samuel R., 65
Ward, Thomas M. D., 77
Warfield, William A., 296
Washington, Booker T., 155–57, 160, 164–66, 178, 195–96, 204, 246, 250–51, 265–66, 271
Washington, D.C., 128, 176, 180, 238, 251, 264–65, 288, 294–97, 305
Washington, Margaret Murray, 158–61, 199, 204

Washington, Olivia A. Davidson, 155–56, 163
Washington General Hospital and Asylum Training School for Nurses (Washington, D.C.), 288
Washington School (Raleigh, N.C.), 173–74
Washington's Birthday, 90, 272
Waters, James C., 128, 130
Waycross, Ga., 277
Wayman, Alexander W., 127
Way's Station, Ga., 277
Weatherford, Doris, 43, 58
Webster Street Baptist Church (New Haven, Conn.), 135
Wells, George M., 8
Wells, Virginia ("Jennie") Crew Hart, 8, 10
Wells-Barnett, Ida B., 199
Wesley, Charles, 205
Wesleyan College (Macon, Ga.), 185
West, Thomas F., 224
West Palm Beach, Fla., 303–4
West Tampa, 43
Wheat Street Baptist Church (Atlanta, Ga.), 206
Wheeler, Marjorie Spruill, 161, 219
Whig Party, 3, 28
White, Bertha, 238
White, Clara English, 236–41, 247
White, Deborah G., 159
White, Eartha Mary Magdalene: and Civil Rights Movement, 254–56; and Clara White Mission, 254; as community activist, 245–48; death of, 256 death of, 256; and death of fiancé, 241; early employment of, 244–45; early life and education of, 236–43; as political activist, 248–53; and teaching, 243–44; during World War I and World War II, 253
White, George, 238, 272
White, Lafayette, 237–38
White, Philip, 66
White caps and whitecappings, 270, 285n17

Index 341

White House Conference on Child Health and Protection (1929), 208
Whitted, J. A., 143
Widowhood, 1, 8–20, 30, 37–38, 48–49, 53–58, 74–80, 116, 186–87, 208, 229–30, 301–6
Wilder Park (Jacksonville, Fla.), 247
Wildlife and wildlife preservation, 86, 95–99. *See also* environment and environmental protection
Williams, Fannie B., 199
Williams, I. D., 277
Williams, Mrs. I. D., 277
Williams, Robert, 271
Williams, Winnie, 196
Williams Singers, 274
Willis, Daria, 167
Williston, D. A., 281
Willoughby, Hugh, 94
Wilson, Mrs. George F., 279
Wilson, Woodrow, 227, 253
Windsor Hotel (Jacksonville, Fla.), 10
Winter Park, Fla., 77
Wisconsin, 52, 87
Wisconsin State Journal (newspaper), 52
Woman's Baptist Foreign Missionary Society, 137, 142
Woman's Club of Jacksonville, 247
Women of Distinction (book), 139, 143
Women's American Baptist Foreign Missionaries Society, 134
Women's Christian Temperance Union (WCTU), 16, 176, 181
Women's clubs and organizations, 92–94, 96–97, 108–12, 158–66, 175–77, 184–86, 199, 203–8, 228–30, 246–48, 302–5
Women's Club Movement, 86, 192
Women's Democratic League of Duval County (Fla.), 227
Women's exchanges, 34
Women's Hospital (Philadelphia, Pa.), 302
Women's Medical College (Philadelphia, Pa.), 128, 137–38, 141–42
Women's Missionary Society, 73–74
Women's rights, 34, 215, 220, 248. *See also* suffrage movement
Women's suffrage. *See also* suffrage movement
Woodlawn Park (cemetery, Fla.), 100–101
Woodmen of the World, 200
"Working women," 1–2
Works Progress Administration (WPA), 117, 185, 254
World War I, 100, 112, 180, 183, 228, 247–48, 251, 253, 259, 301
World War II, 42, 208, 253
World's Columbia Exposition, 34
Wright, John C., 275
Writing and writers, 2, 6, 18–19, 28, 35–36, 86–90, 92–95, 99–100, 157, 160–65, 178–80, 202, 217, 239, 280. *See also* journalism and journalists
Wyoming, 160

Yale University, 173
Yates, Josephine, 165
Ybor City, Fla., 107
Yellow fever, 4, 9, 18, 74, 86, 105, 132, 240, 293, 297
Yom Kippur, 219
Yonge Street School. *See* Henry Rutherford Butler Elementary School (Atlanta)
Yonge Street Parent-Teacher Association (Atlanta), 206–7
Young, John Freeman, 237
Young, Mary Stockton, 237
Young Men's Christian Association (YMCA), 211
Young Women's Christian Association (YWCA), 184, 193, 206–7, 247

Zion Sunday School Convention (Ga.), 273

www.ingramcontent.com/pod-product-compliance
Lightning Source LLC
Chambersburg PA
CBHW020941230426
43666CB00005B/118